D1253639

No Wood, No Kingdom

THE EARLY MODERN AMERICAS

Peter C. Mancall, Series Editor

Volumes in the series explore neglected aspects of early
modern history in the western hemisphere. Interdisciplinary
in character, and with a special emphasis on the Atlantic World
from 1450 to 1850, the series is published in partnership with the
USC-Huntington Early Modern Studies Institute.

No Wood, No Kingdom

Political Ecology in the English Atlantic

Keith Pluymers

PENN

UNIVERSITY OF PENNSYLVANIA PRESS

PHILADELPHIA

Copyright © 2021 University of Pennsylvania Press

All rights reserved.
Except for brief quotations used for purposes of review or scholarly citation,
none of this book may be reproduced in any form by any means
without written permission from the publisher.

Published by
University of Pennsylvania Press
Philadelphia, Pennsylvania 19104-4112
www.upenn.edu/pennpress

Printed in the United States of America on acid-free paper
10 9 8 7 6 5 4 3 2 1

Library of Congress Cataloging-in-Publication Data
Names: Pluymers, Keith, author.
Title: No wood, no kingdom : political ecology in the English Atlantic /
Keith Pluymers.
Other titles: Early modern Americas.
Description: Philadelphia : University of Pennsylvania Press, [2021] |
Series: The early modern Americas | Includes bibliographical references and index.
Identifiers: LCCN 2020040730 | ISBN 9780812253078 (hardcover)
Subjects: LCSH: Forest policy—England—History—16th century. | Forest policy—England—
History—17th century. | Political ecology—Great Britain—History. | Forests and forestry—
Political aspects—England—History. | Forests and forestry—Political aspects—Ireland—
History. | Forests and forestry—Political aspects—Atlantic Ocean Region—History. |
Scarcity. | Great Britain—Colonies—America—History.
Classification: LCC SD601 .P58 2021 | DDC 333.750941—dc23
LC record available at https://lccn.loc.gov/2020040730

CONTENTS

Note on Spelling and Dates   vii

Introduction. A Wooden World   1

Chapter 1. Scarcity, Conflict, and Regulation
in England's Royal Forests   14

Chapter 2. Creating Scarcity in Ireland's Woods   59

Chapter 3. The Political Ecology of Woods in Virginia   108

Chapter 4. Conservation and Commercialization in Bermuda   131

Chapter 5. Deforestation and Preservation in Early Barbados   167

Chapter 6. Toward an Atlantic or Imperial Political Ecology?   193

Archives Consulted   239

Notes   241

Index   297

Acknowledgments   303

NOTE ON SPELLING AND DATES

Throughout this work, I have modernized spelling in manuscript sources except where doing so would impede meaning or significantly alter the tone and character of a quotation. Prior to 1752, England and its colonies used the Julian calendar in which the new year began on 25 March. I have adopted dual dating, listing the Julian/Old Style year and the Gregorian/New Style year together for dates falling between 1 January and 24 March (i.e., 17 February 1606/1607).

INTRODUCTION

A Wooden World

In early modern Europe, wood scarcity was a consistent concern across all levels of society. Royal officials, artisans, and common people expressed their fears in laws, petitions, and pamphlets describing the severity of the problem, speculating on its origins, and proposing solutions to it.

In 1611, the agricultural writer Arthur Standish worried that England faced just such a crisis. "There is not," he warned, "Timber left in this kingdom at this instant only to repair the buildings thereof another age, much less to build withal." "Want of wood" threatened more than construction. According to Standish, deforestation led to dearth—undermining tillage and leading desperate people to burn straw for fuel instead of feeding their cattle. Moreover, he cautioned, scarcity sparked "discontents and mutinies among the common sort" like the Midland Rising of 1607, a popular revolt that began as an anti-enclosure riot in Northamptonshire before spreading to Leicestershire and Warwickshire over six weeks of rebellion. Standish saw wood shortages as a threat to England's material, social, economic, and political order. As he succinctly put it, "No wood, no Kingdom."[1]

Standish's claim that wood scarcity posed a problem for political order attracted royal attention, which Standish used to more aggressively promote his proposed solutions. Two years after warning of the dire consequences of deforestation, he published an updated version of his tract, which bore an endorsement from King James I praising Standish for setting forth projects "for the increasing of woods, the decay whereof in this realm is universally complained of." Standish described the royal approbation in grander terms. In his rendering, James recognized that Standish's tract promised a method "for repairing the ruin of this kingdom, for the good of every particular person, the public good of the commonwealth, and the preserving and maintaining of the same for all posterity."[2]

Standish offered wide-ranging proposals to stave off this bleak outcome. In 1611, he claimed that landowners should replant their hedges with trees for timber, fuel, and fruit; they should raise animals in shaded pastures covered with newly grown trees; and they should experiment with new agricultural techniques like intercropping oats and rye with developing trees. He railed against pigeons, rooks, crows, and sparrows as a scourge on agricultural productivity and urged landowners to build elaborate houses to keep fowl surrounded by dense woods as part of a broader plan to "destroy all kind of Vermin, especially the feathered kind." Throughout the text, he defended his recommendations against objections about cost, theft, and the presence of alternatives to wood.[3]

By 1613, he had adopted an even more aggressive posture. Attempts to preserve England's woods, Standish claimed, had failed. "It is generally conceived," he warned, "that within a very few years, there will be little or no wood left for any use." Laws passed to preserve woods, which, as Standish noted, dated back to the middle of the sixteenth century and which James I had "earnestly" championed, failed to deter greedy subjects seeking profits or the desperate poor forced to break hedges for fuel. The only solution was "a general plantation" that would drive the price of wood so low "as the poor would rather choose to buy than steal it."[4] Scarcity unleashed "discontents and mutinies" that threatened the commonwealth; abundance would usher in social harmony.[5]

Standish was optimistic that a timber plantation following his recommendations would usher in a sustainable system that could supply England's needs indefinitely. Iron and glass manufacturing, he wrote, caused "the greatest decay of wood." Nonetheless, planting hedges with trees and using their lops and tops would provide a regular supply of charcoal without felling mature timber trees. Standish claimed that iron and glass manufacturing were extremely destructive and potentially unnecessary (foreign iron was "better iron and better cheap than the English iron"). Nonetheless, he argued that his plan could supply even these questionable enterprises in perpetuity.[6] Standish conceived of England's shrinking woods as a problem of management that could be solved by reformed practices, not as an issue of natural limits.[7]

Writers representing the Virginia Company of London interpreted the problem of wood scarcity very differently. In 1609, London alderman and Virginia Company deputy treasurer Robert Johnson worried that "continual cutting [in England] . . . [was] such a sickness and wasting consumption, as all the physick [medical knowledge and practice] in England cannot cure." Wood shortages, in this account, were a terminal illness. In 1610, the Council of

Virginia reiterated this complaint in another pamphlet promoting the North American colony. "Our mills of Iron and excess of building," the council members wrote, "have already turned our greatest woods into pasture and champion within these few years; neither the scattered Forests of England nor the diminished Groves of Ireland will supply the defect of our Navy."[8] Unlike Standish, they argued that English woods alone could not sustain ironmaking, construction, and naval shipbuilding. The solutions to scarcity were to be found across the sea, not in replanted hedges.

Standish, Johnson, and the authors of the Virginia Company pamphlet all agreed that England faced a potentially catastrophic wood shortage, even if they disagreed on the details. Other writers in the 1610s and 1620s, however, questioned the very existence and severity of this scarcity. In 1615, Sir Dudley Digges, the politician, diplomat, and member of the Virginia Company, wrote a pamphlet in defense of the East India Company (EIC) and foreign trade. Taking the opposite stance of his Virginia Company colleagues, he claimed that laments about declining forest resources and proposals to preserve English woods were disingenuous. Inciting fears of wood shortage, Digges suggested, was little more than a ploy by "beggars" to preserve their common rights or a means for landowners to extract profits by cramming poor cottagers and vagrants onto otherwise unprofitable land. Despite his role in the Virginia Company, Digges blasted their calls to move timber-intensive industries across the Atlantic, claiming that Virginia promoters relied on the rhetoric of scarcity because it was a colony with which "men know not what to do withall." In 1621, the merchant and writer Thomas Mun echoed Digges's contempt for those who worried about wood shortages. "Would men have us," he wondered, "keep our woods and goodly trees to look upon? . . . Do they not know that trees do live and grow and being great, they have a time to die and rot, if opportunity make no better use of them?"[9] Standish worried about the welfare of the poor and the consequences for public order. Digges and Mun denounced anxieties about wood scarcity as hollow rhetoric deployed by aesthetes, the parasitic poor and the feckless landlords who profited from them, and desperate colonial promoters seeking to justify their poor investment.

Wood scarcity was a consistent concern in early modern Europe, but, as the writings of Standish, Virginia Company pamphleteers, and East India Company backers demonstrate, there was no consensus on the nature, severity, and scope of, or the solutions to, wood shortages. Part of their disagreement surely stemmed from their particular interests. Standish hoped to promote his project. The Virginia advocates wanted to justify their colony. The East India Company defenders sought to head off any new regulations that might impede their ability to build ships wherever they pleased. Yet, beneath these interests lay deeper issues with early modern English conceptions of wood scarcity and a struggle to define exactly what the problem was and how to solve it. Did England suffer from wood scarcity? What activities constituted waste, and which were necessary uses of a natural resource? Should woods serve common people, the state, manufacturers, or merchants? Did issues of dearth result from poor management or were English people bumping against natural limits? Should English people seek to relieve pressure on their woods by trade with other Europeans or by exploiting colonial sources (and, if so, which ones)? How should trade and colonies fit into English political economy?[10] *No Wood, No Kingdom* explores how contemporaries attempted to understand the problem of scarcity and how those conflicting understandings shaped responses in England and abroad.

*   *   *

Only rarely does scarcity mean absolute and complete absence. Nor is it always an issue of supply and demand. In most cases, scarcity emerges at the intersection of the material world and human systems of use, distribution, and value. It can reflect current issues of circulation: practical problems, such as the inability to move something due to impassable paths; abstract distributional issues like hoarding or inequality; or a mixture of material, social, and political conditions. Determining exactly which of these or what combination is responsible is difficult and perhaps impossible.[11] Friction between conflicting ethical ideas and practices—What people or things have moral standing? What are they owed and by whom?—can produce talk of scarcity. And what one group calls a natural accident, another may call an artificial punishment. Moreover, notions of scarcity depend on individual and societal understandings of time and the obligation to future generations. How much of a valuable good was available in the past? Should some be left over for subsequent uses? How much and for how long? In short, scarcity is political; it requires questions about power within a society.

To understand scarcity, then, we must interrogate the historically specific political conditions surrounding scarcity claims. I show that investigating wood in the early modern period is a question of political ecology—ideas and practices governing the definition and use of natural resources—not just a matter of counting trees. It requires understanding how early modern people understood both their material and their social worlds. Which trees or wooded landscapes became defined as resources? Should they be measured and, if so, how? Who controlled them? Who had access to them? Did the definition of wooden resources represent a change from an actual or an imagined past?[12] These questions were part of broader debates about knowledge of the physical environment and human attempts to control the natural world. Historians of early modern natural philosophy have shown that contemporaries fought over how to classify and use new plants.[13] They debated the roles and responsibilities of experts in public works and private enterprises.[14] Natural philosophy and commercial enterprises were frequently intermingled.[15] Defining landscapes and their inhabitants created and erased communities, institutions, and ways of knowing, and it foreclosed some futures for those people and places while advancing others.[16]

I use the concept of political ecology to capture these aspects of the relationships among people, trees, and landscapes. Political ecology encompasses a wide range of theoretical, disciplinary, and definitional perspectives, but at its core is the notion that systems of power in human societies shape and are shaped by physical environments.[17] Immense, complicated, and often contentious questions about trade, domestic policies, settlement abroad, and the planting of colonies swirled around sixteenth- and seventeenth-century England and through its colonies and trade networks. Concerns about resources and the physical environment were key parts of those questions. Royal counselors, projectors, and myriad early modern government functionaries created policies and proposals that, at their most ambitious, sought to knit together resources from around the world. In doing so, they imagined new powers and responsibilities for subjects and the state at home and they considered the creation of colonies abroad. Others offered imperial and extractive visions. Some sought to create local self-sufficiency. Treating these competing ideas and practices as efforts at political ecology shows that Standish, East India Company supporters, and Virginia Company proponents were not simply confused or self-interested; they had competing political ecologies. Recognizing this demands that we take early modern environmental thinking seriously, just as historians have done for early modern political economy.[18]

*   *   *

Wood scarcity became a critical issue for early modern people because the early modern world was a wooden one. Wood was crucial to the survival of the poor and to the security of the state. It built and fueled commercial enterprises, ranging from cottage industries to manufacturing projects aimed at international markets. Wood served as a construction material and fuel for

domestic and commercial uses. Wooden furniture, utensils, and other household goods adorned homes, ranging from castles to cottages. Wooded lands
sheltered game and served as the sites of elite pastimes. Those lands provided
common pastures for pigs, cows, and other animals. Wood was ubiquitous
and served a wide range of uses. But it was precisely its ubiquity and its range
of uses that bred conflicts over woods and contributed to anxieties about
impending scarcity.[19]

Wood was an essential part of early modern life, and that made substitution difficult. Standish warned that without wood there would be no fuel
to heat homes; shortages of all timber, brick, tile, lime, lead, and glass for
building; no ships for trade or defense; no fuel to brew beer or poles to grow
the hops in it; no bark to tan leather; no bridges over rivers; and no pales to
enclose land. Even as coal became a critical fuel source in London, questions
remained about its broader viability. According to Standish, it was uncertain "how long [coal] may endure [and] it is apparent coal-mines do decay
too fast in most countries." Even if more reliable supplies could be found,
"they are not to be got without the use of much wood."[20] Seeking alternative
construction materials or fuel to wood offered limited relief because the processes to produce those alternatives required wooden fuel, tools, or construction materials.

The interconnected nature of wood use in early modern England meant
that attempts to emphasize one use threatened to undermine other uses.
Attempts to regulate wood, such as the laws surrounding royal forests in
England, demonstrate how the tools available to the early modern state
struggled to provide for a range of different uses. In the early modern period,
the word *forest* carried multiple meanings. It sometimes denoted a large
wooded area. The word also referred to an area subject to a specific body of
laws. John Manwood's *A Treatise of the Lawes of the Forest* (1598) described
English forests as a combination of the physical environment, human use,
and a unique legal system. Royal recreation, according to Manwood, was the
crucial element tying together diverse landscapes, animals, and laws. Some
areas might have trees, but other areas would be "fruitful pastures for [game
animals'] continual feed."[21]

This definition privileged a particular arrangement of plants that favored
one use while precluding others. The purpose of trees, shrubs, bushes, and
plants was to provide deer, boar, and other hunted animals "places of secrecy
to rest in." Manwood wrote that these spaces, which he called "coverts,"
should be "thick." The goal of providing shelter for game animals required
dense undergrowth. Without these spaces to provide shelter, even a wooded

area was not a forest. As Manwood put it: "To destroy the coverts of the forest is to destroy the forest itself."[22]

Destroying a forest, however, was not as simple as felling the trees. Manwood distinguished between acts that removed shelter for game temporarily but allowed for regeneration and those that sought to permanently convert the land to tillage or pasture. To do this, he attempted to explicate the differences between "waste" and "destruction" in a forest. "Waste," according to Manwood, was a temporary state. "A man may fell the woods of a covert," he wrote, "and destroy the covert for the time, and yet preserve the woods, so that the same may in time come to be a covert of the forest again." In contrast, to "destroy the woods of a covert of the forest is to waste the same, that they will never come to be a covert anymore." The intermingling of "waste" and "destroy" throughout Manwood's definitions of each term conveyed the conceptual blurriness in the exercise. A temporary destruction was a waste and a permanent waste was a destruction.[23] In every effort to distinguish between them lay different senses of the past and visions for the future.

In addition, competing definitions of scarcity and abundance emerged from the erosion of the multiple-use norm that had governed medieval forestry. Manwood, drawing on this tradition, asserted that royal hunting was the foundation for royal forests, but he sought to render a definition flexible enough to allow for other uses. Hunting provided the legal status and defined the regulations in forests, but Manwood claimed that, despite the emphasis on shelter for game in undergrowth, the Forest Laws were the only barrier protecting large trees and timber. He offered the standard warning that cutting down "great woods and timber trees" threatened the navy but offered no clear explanation for how laws focused on protecting habitats for game animals could serve the highly specific needs of shipbuilders.[24] With limited pressure, there was little need to clarify.

Other users became increasingly assertive in the sixteenth and seventeenth centuries. Increasing trade called for more vessels, and, particularly after the 1588 victory over the Spanish Armada, ships were central in rhetoric, strategy, and practice of war. Early modern English shipwrights made specific demands on woods. Tall trunks of trees allowed to mature over decades provided straight boards. "Compass timber," curved pieces selected with great care from limbs with a suitable bend, required ship carpenters to hunt for ideal angles on living trees and that other forest users leave limbs intact. Shipwrights made dozens of different parts from these broad categories of timber. Different parts also might require different types of wood: A keel should be made of elm, the keelson laying atop it, oak. An anonymous 1620 treatise suggested that planks in the bilge be cut from beech or elm, "which lasteth best under water or where it is always wet."[25] Shipwrights needed specific shapes, sizes, and types of wood to build a ship's skeleton, to fill it in with planks, and to fasten boards together.

The Forest Laws offered general restrictions on cutting trees without a permit, but, because the laws were designed, primarily, to protect hunting, they contained provisions that might threaten the specific needs of shipwrights. Building a ship required trees that would provide each of the pieces, including curved limbs used as elbows, in proportion to the overall size of the ship, which for larger vessels meant trees of significant age and size that had not, as a result of natural factors or human action, grown into shapes ill-suited to shipbuilding. Yet the Forest Laws permitted forest officers to cut branches and limbs as "browse wood" for deer to feed on and offered license for landholders in the forest to take wood for construction, maintenance, and fuel with the permission of forest officers.[26] Combining only these two uses required clear communication and coordination among forest officers, shipwrights, and landowners—cooperation that frequently broke down in the sixteenth and seventeenth centuries. Add in calls for common pasture rights from both wealthy and poor forest dwellers, demands for fuel from iron makers and other manufacturers, and attempts to establish commercial timbering and the lines of conflict become clear.

In addition to conflicts among users, seasonality and transportation created limits to the exploitation of woods. Early modern people understood that pruning trees during warm months risked exposing the plants to disease and they offered advice on the best times of year and phases of the moon to transplant, trim, or dress trees to ensure that the sap would be appropriately "quiet" or "stirring" to prevent disease and promote healing. Failing to follow these guidelines risked killing the tree. Felling trees for timber was also a seasonal activity. The natural philosopher John Evelyn advised his readers not to fell oaks for timber before November. "Premature cutting down of trees before the sap is perfectly at rest will be to your exceeding prejudice," he warned, "by reason of the worm, which will certainly breed in the timber which is felled before that period."[27] Consistent access to timber or fuel throughout the year required advanced planning and the ability to store materials where damp and pests would not damage them.

Likewise, transportation also shaped patterns of use and exploitation for early modern woods. Hauling large trees or even charcoal over muddy, rutted roads was difficult and time-consuming. As a result, early modern

English people either waited for the roads to dry or sought out trees growing near rivers to access easier water transportation.[28] To an early modern merchant, shipwright, or iron manufacturer, high costs of overland transportation often ruled out any activities in an area with abundant trees but far from any river.[29] The economic geography of exploitable wood constantly shifted not only in response to prices for boards, staves, masts, charcoal, and iron but also because of yearly and seasonal variations in carriage costs due to the condition of roads and the availability of labor.

*   *   *

Rethinking the meaning of English wood scarcity forces us to reassess why English people sailed across the sea to colonize, what they found when they arrived, and how those colonies fit into different early modern English political ecologies. Generations of economic and environmental historians have described European colonization of North America as a "windfall" that released Europeans from the constraints of limited natural resources. In these accounts, Old World scarcity defined New World abundance and helped drive Europeans across the Atlantic.[30] But this easy trajectory, in which colonial abundance cures European shortfalls becomes problematic when examining England's early modern expansion. One historian has noted that, before 1800, North American timber exports to Britain were "trivial." Though North American colonies were essential for Europe to be able to evade hard natural limits, the colonies did not begin to supply significant quantities of timber to Britain until the nineteenth century.[31] This does not mean that wood scarcity played no role in English expansion. Instead, it requires that we look to early modern politics and perceptions to see how competing claims about depleted domestic forests and abundant colonial woods sought to forge or sever connections among places, people, and trees.[32]

Doing so creates a more nuanced picture of English expansion in the early modern period. The historian Abigail Swingen has argued that English imperial projects across the Atlantic during the second half of the seventeenth century were "not a foregone conclusion."[33] The same uncertainty, I argue, also characterized earlier projects in the 1500s and early 1600s, and the fraught political ecology of wood can help to explain why. To understand the relationship between scarcity and expansion, I examine promotional rhetoric and pamphlets, domestic and colonial projects, and the attempts to regulate and govern woods in England and colonial settlements around the Atlantic basin in Ireland, Virginia, Bermuda, Barbados, and, to a lesser degree, New England. Historians have come to see each of these places as part of an Atlantic World created in the early modern period through the movement of people and goods and through the linkages these interactions created.[34] In the earliest years of settlement, however, how or if different places fit together was uncertain and contentious. Was scarcity a purely domestic concern, as Arthur Standish suggested? Should England acquire colonies that would exist to provide flows of timber and forest-derived naval stores to the metropole, as the Virginia Company intimated?[35] Did English, Irish, or Virginian woods fit into the political ecology of the emerging "company-state" of the East India Company or a vision of empire in which territorial expansion existed to serve trading companies?[36] Were colonial woods replacements for Baltic trade or the India of the contemporary English imagination?[37] Might woods in the colonies serve other colonies rather than England at all? In their efforts to answer these questions, contemporaries experimented with different models and imagined or attempted different policies and connections. In short, these were issues of political ecology. English expansion and the commercial exploitation of nonhuman nature was never inevitable or assured, even after the first attempts at trade and settlement.[38]

Rather than a seamless narrative of scarcity spurring colonial expansion, this is a story of fits and starts, of experiments often ending in failure, and of confusion and conflict. Attempts to define, measure, and manage woods in England and in potential colonies took place within the context of deep uncertainties and limited access to information that in practice might mean older initial impressions defined thinking in one place even as newer understandings, grounded in different experiences, shaped distinctive political ecologies in another location. Contemporaries often acted as though their actions occurred in isolation while nonetheless seeking commercial and material connections around the Atlantic basin. *No Wood, No Kingdom* is thus organized to reflect these chronologically overlapping and geographically and conceptually diverse characteristics. I begin in England with sixteenth-century anxieties about wood scarcity and efforts to reform and manage domestic wood supplies before turning to late sixteenth- and early seventeenth-century promotional plans for Ireland and Virginia. England, Ireland, and Virginia operate as a triptych, illustrating the efforts to solve domestic scarcity in this early period. These places were connected in some contemporary political ecologies but have distinct histories, occupying at times overlapping chronologies. Each tells its own story, but, taken together, they reveal the multiple perspectives that shaped and frustrated efforts to forge a coherent imperial political ecology that might link them together. From there, I turn to seventeenth-century Bermuda and Barbados, places that developed important transatlantic connections based on trees but for different uses: as drugs, dyes, or materials for luxury goods. Even if they were never imagined as solutions to English scarcity, these islands nonetheless reflected, if only partially and incompletely, contemporary English political ecologies and wood-management techniques. Again, in Bermuda and Barbados, early modern English political ecologies were refracted through local experience and environment. Concerns about wood scarcity and efforts at preservation in Bermuda and Barbados demonstrate that many of the same issues that obsessed Arthur Standish quickly reemerged across the Atlantic. I conclude with an examination of the political ecology of wood in England and its colonies in the 1660s to show how early modern English ideas about scarcity and natural resource preservation had changed and had remained constant over the past century in the light of experiences both domestic and abroad.

Histories of early modern European expansion have often emphasized the networks forged through the movement of people and things. In contrast, *No Wood, No Kingdom* balances stories of connection with the close analysis of specific places. English colonial expansion saw groups of (mostly) men weave together webs of empire (to adapt the phrase of the historian Alison Games) through trade, travel, and colonization ventures to the east as well as across the Atlantic. Their experiments with different models of trade and settlement had a profound effect on the shape of places in the Atlantic and beyond.[39] At the same time, the particularities of these places mattered. Adaptation to diverse, specific local environments created distinctive colonial societies, a process that entailed continuously learning and reclassifying the environment as well as an effort to understand and anticipate long-distance market patterns and trends.[40] Close, place-based studies of English royal forests, Ireland, Virginia, Bermuda, and Barbados give a sense of the diverse environments in the Atlantic basin, albeit a necessarily incomplete one, and of the various political ecologies that sought to exploit each place or to connect them. This approach demonstrates how English attempts to define, reshape, and exploit the woods of each place fit competing and often contradictory needs and desires.

Situating analysis in places rather than following mobile people or objects reveals the often fleeting and nearly always contested nature of linkages, a fragmented geography of uncertainty and not yet an interconnected world.

At the same time, it poses narrative challenges, refusing to yield a single, linear, chronological story. Instead, plans for and realities of Atlantic or imperial integration ebb and flow through the chapters. Some moments recur multiple times in distinctive forms, reflecting the unique conditions and chronologies of each particular place. I ask readers to allow themselves to become embedded in the details and perspectives of these places and the distinctive aspects of early modern English political ecologies of wood that emerge from them.

The efforts to understand and use trees and woodlands across each of these places depended on different visions for how, or if, they should fit together and what other connections might be possible. Efforts to manage and reform English royal forests often reflected ideals of local self-sufficiency that largely ignored contemporaneous calls for trade or colonization to address English needs. Over the course of the sixteenth and seventeenth centuries, the Crown periodically but inconsistently explored these options in Ireland and Virginia. Rather than produce a coherent imperial political ecology in which colonial woods in Ireland or Virginia would serve English ends, English policies at home and in Ireland and Virginia created space for competition among enterprises in all three places. Moreover, as scattered references to unrealized ironworks in Newfoundland indicate, competition could always expand to new sites.[41] Promoters for and colonists in Ireland and Virginia often attempted to address imperial demands that the colonies redress purported English scarcities, but there were the considerable difficulties realizing this vision. In addition, colonists also pursued alternative strategies to satisfy their own political and economic ends that might lead to conflict with plans from Westminster.

Wood scarcity was not solely an English problem. Emerging fears of wood scarcity in Ireland created problems for planters in Munster but also reverberated back to English fears. In Bermuda, where colonists developed a successful trade in luxury woods with England, they found that intensive commercial agriculture created fears of wood scarcity on the islands. Bermudians attempted to rectify these issues with an aggressive program of woodland regulation. Meanwhile, Barbados saw a dramatic transformation in its landscape and, by the later seventeenth century, had become a key node in networks of timber exchange with English colonies in the greater Caribbean and in New England. Deforestation and dependence on woods elsewhere in the Caribbean and Atlantic were not inevitable and represented a shift from the earliest patterns of woodland management on the island. Through these examples, I demonstrate that colonies were never just exporters of raw materials unconcerned with local resources. Colonists also worried about wood scarcity and sought to address it through regulation and by forging connections beyond investors and provisioners in England.

From the middle of the sixteenth century to the moment when waves of war, rebellion, and revolution coursed through England, Ireland, and Scotland and out across the Atlantic, members of royal governments, projectors, investors, and colonists had sought to transform woods.[42] Uncertainty and conflicting visions had characterized these efforts from their inception, and, after decades of experience, uncertainty and conflict remained.

CHAPTER 1

Scarcity, Conflict, and Regulation
in England's Royal Forests

"Former times," according to Arthur Standish, had "left a precedent and plenty" of rich woods. In Standish's narrative, this bounty of natural resources grew from careful and deliberate management. Those past eras knew "how to plant, preserve, and maintain the blessings of God." Abundant woods were a consequence of sustainable actions and deliberate decisions that considered subsequent generations. In turn, the ailments that faced "this our destroying age" were symptoms of a shift in attitudes and practices that led most English people to pursue the "profit present, but few or none at all [to] regard the posterity or future times."[1]

Unlike contemporaries who blamed population increase for pressure on natural resources and myriad other ills, Standish treated deforestation as a problem of policy and practice. Healthy and reliable yields of firewood, acorns and other animal forage, and timber resulted from an expansive sense of both monarchy and commonwealth that explicitly included future generations.[2] Although James I offered only a tepid endorsement for Standish's work, he and his government gave specific directions on managing royal forests, launched commissions to investigate woodlands and prevent their destruction, and endorsed inventions and techniques to save trees that looked toward posterity but also focused on the present.

James's actions are part of a broader history of royal concern with forestry in the fifteenth through seventeenth centuries. Tudor and early Stuart monarchs' activities fell into three major categories—describing and surveying woodlands, regulating royal forests and other woods, and supporting projects to reduce deforestation or to restore forests—that were designed, often explicitly, to manage these resources for purportedly common interests and to ensure the welfare of future generations. Nonetheless, each of these activities produced conflicts at numerous levels. Different branches of royal forest bureaucracy fought against each other; members of the nobility protested against the state and plotted against each other. Owners of and workers on manufacturing projects battled forest officials dedicated to hunting, while small tenants and agrarian estate-holders protected embattled common rights. In short, myriad conflicting visions defined English attitudes toward woodlands in the sixteenth and seventeenth centuries.[3] At the heart of these struggles lay different political ecologies. Locals dependent on forest commons and ship carpenters seeking timber for the navy might both use the language of commonwealth—the ubiquitous, powerful, and contested conception of political community organized around the common good that defined much early modern English thinking—but they disputed who was included therein and whose interests should come first.[4] At the heart of these disputes were different visions for local economies and societies, which had implications for trade and colonization.

Previous accounts that stress the destruction of wooded land miss out on these conflicts and paper over more complex early modern English attitudes toward woodlands. Monarchs like James and Charles I did not simply treat royal forests as a source of extra-Parliamentary revenue, and viewing them in this way ignores the prevalence of early modern conservation rhetoric.[5] Surveyors and officials frequently framed policies and actions that facilitated the sale or commercial exploitation of forests as an antidote to wasted woods. Contemporaries on opposite sides of disputes over forest policies and grants invoked posterity and decried spoil. Crown officials were not precocious environmentalists. They adopted these policies to address fears that wood scarcity would deplete royal revenues or harm naval defense. For at least some early modern thinkers, alleviating scarcity and improving Crown finances were complementary.[6]

Rather than being a battle against exploitative royalty, most disputes over forest management stemmed from changes to how the Crown and members of the nobility managed royal forests and wooded lands on their estates (which were not subject to the same laws as royal forests). Royal forests in England trace their lineage to the aftermath of the Norman Conquest and the policies of mapping and granting lands under William the Conqueror. In popular memory and in many historical narratives, royal forests emerged from efforts to set aside land and protect landscapes for hunting, though recent work has argued that concerns with timber, fuel, and other woodland products emerged much earlier. By the thirteenth century, regulations aimed at preserving trees reinforced forests' role as sources of timber and fuel. Henry VIII began the shift to a new system of forest management with a series of bureaucratic changes in forest administration, part of a broader program of reform that one historian has described as a "revolution" in government. Beginning in 1511, Tudor monarchs created new positions, which would answer directly to the exchequer, to survey and regulate royal forests. Rather than replacing the preexisting constables, wood wardens, and distinct courts that operated under the medieval Forest Laws, the exchequer officers operated in tandem with them.[7] These new officers, alongside independent commissions appointed by the exchequer, periodically surveyed forest lands counting trees, listing access rights and conditions, and chronicling abuses. Parliament also assumed a new role; it passed acts under Henry VIII and Elizabeth I prohibiting tree felling near coastlines or navigable rivers to preserve these sites for naval carpenters, setting out and modifying rules to protect growing trees in coppices, and regulating industrial uses of wood, particularly ironworks.[8] James intensified these trends, sending out surveyors and commissioners to evaluate royal forests while simultaneously allowing substantial manufacturing works. These policies culminated in Charles I's revival, in the 1630s, of the Forest Laws, the largely unenforced code championed by authors like John Manwood, which governed tree felling, resource gathering, land sales, enclosure, and hunting, a policy that produced significant discontent, including uprisings in Dean and other western forests.[9]

Forests stand at the center of my account because debates in England about scarcity and attempted solutions to it focused on lands potentially or actually under Crown control despite calls from reformers like Standish for a widespread program of replanting, drawing in the gentry and nobility and including hedges as well as woods. As a practical matter, the wood sources Standish mentioned did play an important role as resources, but most of Standish's contemporaries focused on royal forests to define the problem and explore solutions. The number and geographic extent of these forests in early modern England was a complex question that bedeviled Tudor and Stuart governments (and continues to challenge historians and geographers). Sixteenth- and seventeenth-century governments drew on the work of a new group of professional "improvers" conducting surveys and reexamining local history and geography to reform government and increase revenue. As those governments conducted these assessments, anxieties about scarcity frequently emerged. Royal efforts to combat wood scarcity thus focused on lands over which the Crown had (or might acquire) control and about which it had some information. Similar to other state-sponsored efforts, such as the draining of the English Fens in the 1600s, defining and combating wood scarcity was a state project, albeit one that saw contests over the ideal relationship between royal control and regulated private management.[10]

This does not mean that there were no problems accessing wood beyond forests. According to one estimate, in 1550 there were approximately 900,000 hectares of woodland in England, which, using a generous estimate for yield, would provide about 2.7 million cubic meters of wood, or about one cubic meter per person per year. Even with the addition of trees standing outside woodlands and hedges, this still left English people with one of the lowest levels of wood-fuel availability in early modern northern Europe, without factoring in competing industrial uses. Those uses could consume significant quantities of fuel. For example, a glazier in London might burn 2,000 wagonloads of wood annually, with brewers burning as much as 20,000 wagonloads. Wood consumption for ironmaking, the most commonly attributed cause in early modern scarcity discourses, is more difficult to estimate, but, according to historian Michael Williams, peak consumption was 8,771 to 7,516 hectares of wood annually—"hardly enough to cause the crisis that was so often said to be imminent."[11]

There is an important distinction between the potential material scarcities or lack thereof in historians' estimates and contemporary understandings of scarcity. In contemporary discourses, the problem of scarcity was most often understood as a threat to the monarchy and the state, particularly after the victory over the Spanish Armada in 1588 saw rumors of foiled plots and future schemes to destroy forests in support of a Spanish invasion.[12] The struggles of surveyors, commissions to investigate royal revenue, and other Crown officials defined scarcity; war and political strife in early modern Europe made it a pressing issue. Wood-scarcity fears, although purportedly grounded in material conditions, were always entangled with the ideas, concerns, and ambitions of those articulating them—they were a product of political ecology.

The ambiguous relationship between the conditions of the physical environment and contemporary perceptions of it is essential to understanding efforts to reform forest management and land use in England and to discussions of wood resources abroad. England was not a wholly deforested land, even as pressure in particular areas or between competing user groups might seriously stress supplies, and, as a result, England was more than the material background for an expanding resource frontier. Anxieties about woods ebbed and flowed in response to specific actions—a new survey, trade policy, or plans for naval expansion—even if those anxieties consistently resurfaced. Rather than a permanent push to locate and exploit new resources, scarcity fears provided moments of demand that might quickly disappear. Moreover, reformers promised that new resources might be found at home in old forests as well as across the seas.

∗   ∗   ∗

Actions taken under Elizabeth I laid the foundation for early modern English ideas about domestic wood supply, scarcity, and the reforms needed to combat it. Although colonial promoters increasingly pushed the queen to look to Ireland and North America for wood, at the same time Elizabeth's government took measures to identify and reform domestic wood supplies. Elizabeth reiterated and expanded statutes, previously passed during Henry VIII's reign, to prevent felling of trees near water and she launched new surveys of royal forests, parks, and chases while also revisiting the sale of lands that had been disafforested (the process of removing land from the specific legal protections of the Forest Laws, enabling it to be sold and converted to agricultural use or pasture) by previous monarchs. This resulted in a mixed policy toward forests. At times, she sold wood rights or disafforested land, but her government also aggressively investigated titles and engaged in lawsuits to bring former forests and leased lands back to the Crown.[13] Although contemporaries continued to complain about scarcity, Elizabeth's government sent out surveyors and passed regulations to more efficiently manage royal forests and preserve trees outside the forests. These actions became the bases for James's and Charles's more intensive plans for England's woods and forests. They also revealed limitations to reform, stemming from surveyors' difficulties consistently measuring and defining forest resources and the disputes that erupted when untangling conflicting claims of common rights and privileges.

Legislation dealing with English woods and forests was narrow, focusing on particular uses and places, rather than on an effort at widespread reform. In the first year of Elizabeth's reign, Parliament passed an act prohibiting the conversion of trees into charcoal to fuel ironworks. The act, however, only preserved certain types and species of trees—oak, beech, or ash with trunks measuring one square foot at ground level lying within fourteen miles of the sea or any navigable river.[14] These conditions made it clear that the act addressed commercially viable timber—defined by size and proximity to water transportation. Moreover, it provided an exception for ironworks in Sussex, the Weald of Kent, and three parishes of Surrey, areas with abundant ironworks that produced weapons for the state.

Parliamentary attempts to regulate iron production before and during Elizabeth's reign were often locally specific or were targeted measures to protect London's fuel supply. In 1552, during Edward VI's reign, the House of Commons debated two bills, one prohibiting "iron mills" in Horsham, Sussex, and one in the entire county. These bills established a trend that persisted after Elizabeth took the throne. Injunctions against mills brought before the Commons in 1563 targeted specific places. The major focus of the Commons regarding ironworks from 1552 until 1581 was an attempt to prohibit ironworks along the Thames and around London, but in 1581, after nearly three decades of debate, the members still could not agree on whether the ban should extend eight or eighteen miles from the city. A bill eventually passed in 1584-1585 barring new iron mills in Kent, Surrey, and Sussex but exempting existing manufacturers.[15] Unlike the 1558 act, these bills sought to preserve stores of firewood for London and its suburbs, part of a broader effort to secure London's domestic and industrial fuel supply. Ultimately, London would come to depend largely on coal imported from elsewhere in England with dramatic environmental, political, and economic consequences.[16] Despite the metropolis's economic and political centrality, it remains important to distinguish between local issues in London and pervasive conditions throughout the country.

Elizabeth's government recognized this and began several ambitious projects to survey forests, chases, and parks, as well as woods that had been previously disafforested and placed in private hands. The goal of these surveys was to provide a comprehensive view of wooden resources across all of England. The most notable of these projects were two major surveys by Roger Taverner and his son John. Roger began his service as surveyor for the Court of Augmentations sometime in the 1540s, then became deputy surveyor of the woods south of the Trent under the exchequer, a profession after which his son John followed in 1572.[17] Their surveys of woods in England from the 1560s through the 1590s, along with similar works by other contemporary surveyors, offer a glimpse at the Elizabethan state's view of woods. The Taverners attempted to answer questions of access and use while also providing a record of the physical state of the trees in each area. In doing so, their work, along with other sixteenth-century surveys of woods, provided a vision for English forests, one that blended social, legal, economic, and environmental characteristics together.

The view revealed in sixteenth-century surveys was limited to particular species or types of trees, leaving a blurry image of actual use patterns in royal forests. Surveyors provided numerical counts in either trees or acres for oaks, beeches, or "timber"—a general term used to refer to trees that were of appropriate size, straightness, and maturity to produce boards. They often made notes of coppices—stands of trees, usually oak, ash or beech, that would be felled and allowed to regenerate from the stumps, with enclosures to protect the growing shoots, that were crucial sources of fuel.[18] At times, the surveys could offer rich details. Taverner's "Book of Survey" recorded that the eight acres and two rods of Medman Coppice in Fremantle Park, Southampton contained "about 3 Acres of 7 years growth much bitten with Beasts the residue of 14 years growth." The description offered a glimpse into management practices—portions of the coppice were felled at different intervals, producing trees at different stages of regrowth—and of their failure to protect tender trees from animals' teeth.[19]

The utility of such descriptions becomes difficult to discern when the survey is considered as a whole. To the right of the descriptions for the forests and parks listed throughout the survey, lay numbers of acres and rods. At the bottom or to the right of these numbers lay the total number of acres in the forest or park. In this total, coppices "bitten with Beasts" blended together with notes on underwoods of different ages to the eighty-one acres and two rods present in Fremantle Park. To compute the quantity of underwoods, trees or coppices classified as healthy, ready for harvest, or any value other than total acreage required separate calculations extracted from descriptions of coppices, walks, and other smaller units within forests and parks.

Undertaking such calculations posed its own problems. Smaller units within forests and parks could vary significantly in size, as well as quality. The forest of Eastbeare in Southampton was divided into "The West Walk," containing 200 acres, and "The East Walk," containing 36 acres. Within the East Walk, "Foxgrove corner lying in the East part of a ground call'd the Kings Pound" was "sett with Oaks both Timber and firewood of middle growth containing 20 acres." Another parcel, called "Kingswood lying on the North Part of a ground there call'd Plant ground," was "very thin set with Old Oaks, and in manner no Timber containing, 6 acres." Another "Kingswood" located on the West Walk contained 190 acres "set with Oake Timber and Firewood of ancient growth."[20] The significant differences in size make it difficult to isolate quantities of land with any particular characteristics, even where there are relatively precise descriptions. Were there areas equivalent to the East Walk's Kingswood inside the boundaries of the West Walk's Kingswood or were all 190 acres uniform? The form of Taverner's survey left it impossible to know.

In addition to these issues, the emphasis on timber and coppices in the survey failed to acknowledge the crucial role that other trees played in early modern forestry. In a 1585 report on the privileges of foresters in Shotover and

Stowood in Oxfordshire, John Taverner outlined the process by which the foresters were to receive firewood. First, they were to draw on windfalls and deadwood lying on the ground. If there was not sufficient wood there, the foresters might cut branches—a set of processes called "lopping," "cropping," "topping," or "pollarding," terms that refer to distinctive actions but which were sometimes used interchangeably or inconsistently in the early modern period—from thorns, hazels, maples, poplars, and sallows/willows. If done correctly, pollarding would also allow for regeneration from the standing trunk of usually six to ten feet in height.[21] Other species were left uncounted. But notes and orders requiring forest officers to take their firewood from these species indicate their importance. To keep foresters and forest residents and neighbors with common rights from the counted timber, the woods needed to also contain enough thorns, hazels, maples, poplars, ashes, and willows to supply other uses. Diverse forests acted to preserve commercially and militarily valuable trees by providing fuel, fodder, and building materials, but surveyors only mentioned these trees obliquely and did not provide anything like the concrete rules for management and use that applied to beeches, oaks, timber, and coppices.

Functional concerns drove early modern wood surveyors' practice. They looked for and counted trees that fit with specific uses. Counting "timber" trees, as many surveyors did, defined the organisms as the product they yielded, but it is only the most obvious example. Shipbuilders had extremely specific requirements for trees that were to serve as construction material for ships. They required trees of particular size and shapes. Shipwrights struggled most to locate compass timber and elbows—curved trunks and bent limbs that formed crucial supports for straight timbers in ships. Moreover, ship timber needed to be of the highest quality because excessive knots or rot could produce disastrous structural weaknesses. Shipwrights produced invoices outlining the types and quantities of trees they needed for each ship.[22]

A series of documents to measure the woods at "Canke" (Cannock) in Staffordshire from the end of 1588 in the papers of Elizabeth I's Lord Treasurer William Cecil capture the ways in which function and intended use colored attempts to measure woods. An unnamed author offered a relatively optimistic description of the land. It was a "great and wide ground set with much great timber which hath been cropped for the making of iron." Nonetheless, the ground contained four "stately" manors, "many stately and goodly oak," and another area called the Timber Copse "which was never cropped and there is a great quantity of good, young, and fair timber." The areas that had been "cropped," or subject to some type of pruning or more dramatic cutting, were well fenced to prevent animals from consuming trees in a vulnerable state. Some coppices were only two to three years from being ready to cut to serve as fuel for the ironworks again, while many others "beareth young oak, birch, and other woods grown and containeth a great quantity of ground." The anonymous author claimed to have great faith in this information because the queen's surveyor "hath surveyed and measured" the area and "there hath been four substantial Juries in those four manors charged upon their oaths to find the value truly."[23] For this writer, Cannock provided fuel for ironworks and offered several trees useful for timber.

John Taverner offered a strikingly different assessment. In his letter to Cecil, Taverner lamented that the forest only contained two to three timber trees per acre, "old oaks heretofore in manner all lopped and shredded for the maintenance of the Ironworks there so that there now remaineth in effect but the bodies of the said trees." "The truth is," he added, the lopping and shredding had so harmed the trees that within the next ten to twelve years "most of them will neither be good timber nor good firewood." Worse still, the land lay too far from any navigable river to be useful for any of the queen's unspecified "works." The best solution, Taverner concluded, was to convert the woods to iron, because otherwise it held little use or value. Felling the woods to support ironmaking risked popular protest because "there are very many of the Inhabitants thereabout that could be well contented that it should never be employed that way." In the end, Taverner left it to Cecil to decide which uses of the woods he deemed most efficient and which would avoid conflict with local people.[24]

These conflicting assessments about the quality and quantity of Cannock's woods reveal several major issues in early modern wood surveys. Experts were increasingly essential to early modern English projects, but defining expertise, or claiming it, was always fraught.[25] For administrators like Cecil, these conflicting reports made management difficult. One observer might claim that lopped trees were still "great" and could serve as timber, while another might complain that regular limb removal had ruined them. Taverner implied that converting the trees to iron was a move of last resort to be used only on woods that had lost their value as timber through chronic waste and mismanagement. His anonymous counterpart suggested great value in woods that could continuously regenerate and serve ironworks. Both reports urged Cecil to support exploitation for ironworks but for very different reasons. Ironworks could be either a profitable option to continue drawing on a vibrant and regenerating woodland or a final attempt to salvage some profit from human-induced decay.

Perhaps most problematic for contemporary administrators, the observers' differing visions of economic utility led them to report different numbers of trees—two to three per acre against a "great quantity." Numbers, however, mattered. The remainder of the documents describing Cannock were attempts to quantify and delineate the costs and profits in operating an ironworks with a blast furnace and a hammer forge, relatively new technologies for manufacturing iron that created opportunities for increased production and allowed for the use of different ores but that required greater amounts of wood that had been converted into charcoal. The accounts differed on details and a note between them questioned whether the author of the first account "doth understand . . . what belongeth to an ironwork." Disputes over the costs and value of iron production were crucial to determine whether producing iron would yield greater revenue than simply selling off the wood. After allegedly proving that point, the writer of one account nonetheless attempted to hedge, noting that the works could consume wood at the rate he outlined for the next twenty years without touching any of the coppices or timber trees and instead subsisting on deadwood, windfalls, and occasional felling of trees that had been damaged through cropping.[26] The competing surveyors focused on questions about ironworks, leaving local inhabitants' claims to common rights or longstanding custom, at best, as a matter for Cecil's lordly discretion.

The surveyors' disregard for common rights in Cannock reflected a wider indifference or hostility to custom in surveys of forests and woods. Beginning in the 1550s, the Elizabethan government began making inquiries about customs and rights in the Forest of Dean in Gloucestershire. Commissioners collected testimony and searched for records about the rights of forest officers, landholders, and tenants, looking to compile a list of customary rights that captured rights based on specific localities, positions, and grants to individuals. They inquired about past transgressions, ranging from damaging enclosures for the queen's horses to exceeding the rights to take pigs during pannage—a customary season when tenants and freeholders with common rights could let their pigs feed on acorns or beechnuts in the forest. In 1569, Roger Taverner compiled a substantial list of offenses against the Forest Laws taken from local forest officials that recorded large and small offenses ranging from collecting firewood from downed limbs without permission to felling timber trees.[27]

The goal of these initial inquiries later became clear. In 1586, the Crown took several prominent local landholders to court, claiming they had quietly encroached on royal forest lands. A summary of the trial in the court of the exchequer over a plot of land called the "Prior's Mine" in Gloucestershire reported that the case turned on issues of measurement. The Crown argued that although the landowners had valid titles from Henry VIII, they had nonetheless taken land without permission. The landholders' argument turned on different standards for measurement under the Forest Laws: "The Forest acre is measured at 21 foot long to the perch and therefore containeth in it more ground than a common statute acre doth." Their grants, they claimed, were issued in Forest acres, not common statute acres. The Crown attempted to rebut this argument with a litany of surveys, reports on commissioners' perambulations of the boundaries of multiple grants, and a call to show written proof of rent payments, but, according to the irritated reporter, the judge offered excessive time to the defense and cut the queen's representative short. When the Crown attorneys offered written reports directly to the jury, the jurors refused to hear the evidence with "vehement note of affection [and] partiality by them borne to the defendant."[28]

The Crown launched other cases designed to regain control over wooded lands and royal forests in Gloucestershire at the same time. Beginning in 1572, Elizabeth and Henry Berkeley, Lord Berkeley, fought a protracted legal battle about Kingswood Forest, that continued into the first decades of the seventeenth century. As in the case for the Prior's Mine, the Crown launched its proceedings by claiming that Roger Taverner had discovered that Berkeley had a defective title. The suits against Berkeley were part of a much broader campaign in the area to reassert royal control over forests and to retake lands that had been previously granted from them.[29]

In Kingswood, the Crown used surveys as critical tools for setting out royal forest policy, a trend that began under Elizabeth and continued after James VI/I became king after her death. John Norden, author of a popular contemporary tract on surveying and James's royal surveyor at the beginning of the seventeenth century, wrote that Lord Berkeley and his codefendant Lady Newton were "very clever for that they can show grants and considerations [from the Crown] for long time of lands and woods in Kingswood, not mentioning where it should lie nor how much it should be." As a result, Norden wrote, they "carry away above 1,300 acres of soil, wood, coal, and all other profits" without the state being able to determine the legal status, the physical extent, or the geographical location of the land from which they took it. Norden (roughly) quantified the land and resources Berkeley and Newton had taken, but the remainder of Norden's report shows that issues of law and customary rights muddied attempts at precise measurement. The king, claimed Norden, had "a rich portion of herbage for his deer," but, since the deer had died or fled, it was unclear whether the king could still use Forest Laws grounded in royal hunting rights to lay claim to trees there.[30]

Norden noted that the situation was not merely confined to Kingswood. Indeed, "such abuses are in most of his Majesty's forests, chases, and wastes." Despite Roger and John Taverner's extensive surveys in the sixteenth century and his own work at the beginning of the seventeenth, Norden still feared that the Crown officials were struggling to define and protect royal lands from private interests. Surveyors could identify these issues, but they struggled to ensure that the "king's sparing for love of posterity" overcame "subjects' spoiling for present luchre [profit]."[31]

Norden's invocation of posterity set assessment and categorization of trees and woodlands and detailed inquiries into titles, deeds, and customs into a contest that spanned generations. Such a rhetorical maneuver was by no means uncommon. Concerns about wood scarcity in the early modern period frequently turned into questions about obligation toward the future.[32] In this case, Norden's concerns for the health and security of subsequent generations expressed a political ecology with profound consequences for the present and memories of the past. To protect the future, he claimed, required the reimposition of direct royal control in the present and reformed management grounded in surveyors' skilled assessments. Customary rights and practices, which contemporaries sought to trace to time immemorial and to ground in intimate, multigenerational engagement with the landscape, instead became myopic, selfish, and shortsighted acts of destruction.[33] Local communities, like the jurors and judge who had rowdily rejected the Crown's arguments in a 1586 Gloucestershire trial, were not, according to Norden, defending valid and valuable local traditions; they were imperiling the future.

Stark divisions between a profligate present and a livable future or between a benevolent monarchy and self-interested localities were politically useful for surveyors like Norden, but they radically oversimplified the situation on the ground.[34] The ecologist and historical landscape consultant David Lovelace's analysis of a 1576 royal record of 200 wood sales at Bringewood Chase, which lies along the boundary of Herefordshire and Shropshire, found that the lands produced approximately 870 tons annually, mostly, though not exclusively, of firewood. Lovelace estimates that such yields would require 21–30 percent of the available land at Bringewood, hardly evidence for the ruinous consequences of local customs.[35] Contemporary accounts from Kingswood demonstrate that commoners and members of the gentry might make common cause against each other as the Crown pursued its own, separate interests. As Berkeley and Elizabeth fought over the boundaries and title of Kingswood, Berkeley simultaneously skirmished with his neighbors over poaching, broken enclosures, and common rights of pasture for animals; those skirmishes frequently wound up in the court of the Star Chamber.[36] The disputes could turn violent. In one particularly notable display, one of Berkeley's woodwards, individuals tasked with monitoring forests and woods and administering regulations in them, reported that Thomas Throckmorton, a member of a distinguished Gloucestershire family who served as sheriff and Justice of the Peace (JP), and a band of armed men "came with monstrous threatening words most furiously to my hedge" intending to force entry into the land to graze their sheep on freshly planted corn. Throckmorton and his band denounced the enclosures as illegal usurpations of common lands. Despite the woodward's urging, the intruders opened a gap in the hedge and began driving their sheep into the breech. Only after the woodward killed two to three of the ovine intruders did the men begin "to speak more reasonabler." Other incidents did not resolve themselves so quickly. In 1601, Berkeley's park keepers engaged in a pitched battle with intruders clothed in full armor, bearing "long forest bills, welch hooks, long staves, guns, swords, and daggers," again seeking to forcefully establish common rights. In the melee, one of Berkeley's keepers killed one of the heavily armed poachers, leading to yet another court battle over the legality of both the enclosures and the killing.[37]

These struggles formed along complex lines that reflected both personal and local allegiances and social and economic position. It was not simply a conflict between the queen and nobility or poor commoners and greedy landlords. Berkeley made it clear in a complaint to the queen that he believed these violent and destructive incidents occurred because royal inquisitions had made his title insecure. But his own correspondence and notes on the dispute undermine this simplistic analysis. In a 1584 petition to the Star Chamber, Berkeley acknowledged that his troubles began before Elizabeth questioned his title, noting that a court of the Welsh Marches had declared that there was a year-round right to common on land Berkeley claimed as his own. The battle erupted over common rights, but Berkeley's chief opponent Sir Thomas Throckmorton was a member of Gloucestershire's elite, who, as the dispute was ongoing, nonetheless married into the Berkeley family. Edward and Thomas Trotman, who Berkeley separately complained had organized servants into an armed band to break enclosures, were not as prominent as Throckmorton, but they nonetheless hailed from a well-established Gloucestershire family prosperous enough to contribute to a fund to defend against the Armada and to serve as churchwardens in the early seventeenth century.[38] The Crown and individual members of the gentry, nobility, middling sort, and poor all had distinct positions regarding Kingswood. Elizabeth, in a pattern that James would follow, sought to establish royal control over the forest, including its coal and timber. Berkeley sought to defend forest land he had used as an enclosed game preserve against the Crown's title challenges and enclosure breaking as well as illicit animal pasturing by his neighbors in the gentry and middling sort by invoking traditional protections associated with hunting. Throckmorton and the Trotmans sought access to common pastures to feed their sheep—animals generally not allowed access to common land.

Against Throckmorton, Berkeley cast himself as the champion of ordered enclosures, a protector of game, and a victim of illegal commoning. His lawsuits portrayed him as a defender of traditional elite uses of royal forests, parks, and chases. Letters from the earls of Warwick and Leicester, who had competing claims to parts of Kingswood, portrayed Berkeley as an avaricious waster of woods. The earls complained that upon their recovery of the land in the 1570s, Berkeley had sent out workmen to fell and sell as many trees as possible, stripping the forest's most valuable assets before ceding possession. In 1584, twelve years after Warwick and Leicester's complaint, Elizabeth issued a new injunction, attempting to prohibit Berkeley from felling trees in Kingswood.[39] The Crown had looked to surveys to provide order and clarity over the natural and legal landscape, but, in Kingswood, inquisitions had instead set off a power struggle between members of the nobility and the gentry in which all parties claimed that their opponents had damaged the land, trees, and animals.

The wave of surveys and lawsuits from Elizabeth's government attempted to assert control across England, but most surveyors and officials still sought to address shortage in locally specific ways to protect particular species and types of trees. They saw woodlands through the lens of legal rights and economic value and took action to assert royal rights and to ensure that woods would serve the Crown as sources of revenue or raw materials. This vision, however, had its limitations. Contemporary assessments of Cannock offered different assessments of its trees that turned not just their physical state but also their proximity to transportation: Distance was a key factor in determining whether a tree was great timber or mere firewood. Similarly, sixteenth-century surveyors and Crown administrators struggled to understand the value trees would hold over time, leading to uncertainties about whether trees should be harvested immediately or whether they might have future value. These factors created an indeterminacy in surveys. The number of trees counted in a forest depended on a surveyor's understanding of shifting values in multiple markets for different types of timber as well as for fuel. Attempting to clarify legal title and rights likewise produced friction. Tenants, freeholders, and even cottagers might side with the local gentry against the Crown to protect their own common rights. In other cases, legal ambiguities unearthed by inquiries into titles could provoke disputes between elites where felling trees, breaking enclosures, and grazing animals were tactics for struggle.

In seeking to define rights and trees in particular ways, surveyors knew they courted controversy. Norden opened his *Surveyor's Dialogue* (1607) with an extended debate between a farmer and a surveyor about the value of the profession. Norden's farmer began the conversation by claiming that he had heard many bad things about surveyors, adding that he too found the profession "both evil and unprofitable." Over the course of their discourse, the farmer accuses surveyors of stealing long-held rights, twining the cords round the commonwealth "whereby poor men are drawn into servitude and slavery," and arguing that both the nobility and tenants should absolutely refuse to let a surveyor see their lands. Norden's fictitious surveyor eventually won over his interlocutor with arguments that surveyors were fair and neutral arbiters whose efforts would undermine falsehood, whether it came from above or below.[40] The struggles set off by surveys of royal forests show that disputes beyond the page were less easily solved.

Rather than persuading local tenants and landholders that surveyors' assessments served the side of truth, Elizabethan surveyors saw the cascading physical confrontations, lawsuits, and petitions that their inquiries produced. They responded with radical solutions that sought to reimagine the relationship between the state and its woods. In 1585, John Taverner wrote to Cecil and Sir Walter Mildmay warning that enclosing royal forests, chases, and parks "doth yearly consume more than half as much good timber" as naval requisitions and repairs to buildings and bridges. Using fines against forest officials, tenants, and commoners was ineffective, he lamented, and did nothing to curb this waste since forest officers claimed they were performing their assigned duties. Simply maintaining the status quo was not an option. Instead, Taverner urged them to evaluate all the queen's forests, chases, and parks. The best should be fenced well and rigorously maintained using good timber; middling lands would receive a ditch or quickset hedge. The rest to be "disposed of as your honors shall think good."[41] Taverner argued that the costs, in timber alone, to vigorously maintain all the queen's forests, chases, and parks were simply too high. Tough choices needed to be made. The issue was not merely enforcing existing laws but rather developing new guidelines to aggressively manage valuable forests through enclosures and determining which woodlands were sufficiently good to warrant this new investment.

This logic first emerged under Elizabeth but came to dominate after James I took the throne. In 1604, James set out conditions for the sale of Crown lands, including forests. He prohibited his commissioners from selling any lands adjacent to forests, parks, or chases and from granting any wood or timber rights to forests near frequently used royal houses. He ordered his agents to sell only houses and lands not reserved for his "necessary use" that required significant costs to repair or maintain. Even then, the lands were only to be sold if they were either "so removed from our access as very rarely we are like to have use of them or else so much wasted or decayed as without expense of good sums of money the same can not be repaired" or if they had been leased at such a long term that neither James nor his heirs were likely to gain unfettered access to them.[42] The conditions for sale make it clear that James viewed the sale of Crown holdings as a way to improve efficiency and eliminate wasteful spending by ensuring that the Crown would only main-tain lands the king used and which did not require excessive investments to maintain at the quality James desired. James's directive ensured that he would be able to hunt wherever he pleased, but it acknowledged that he could not use every property that he owned.

His government took the same approach when outlining conditions for the keepers of royal forests in 1609. The first five requirements sought to update forestry practices and prevent corruption, prohibiting forest-ers from selling the wood that came with their position, requiring them to draw their entitlements only from the outskirts of the forest, banning the topping of trees, and reiterating exclusive royal right to oaks and bans on allowing grazing cattle within coppices. Subsequent conditions pushed for greater efficiency in the management of Crown resources. The Crown was only to be responsible for lodges where the king regularly visited. Keepers were to maintain their own lodges and were expressly prohibited from using great timber to do so. Repairs to "lawns and enclosed grounds" were to cease unless those grounds were absolutely necessary to feed the king's deer. For-esters were to save coppice gates after the fences were removed and reuse them for subsequent enclosures.[43]

James and his advisers emphasized efficiency and thrift but saw those principles as compatible with pleasure and beauty as well as with revenue and the production of usable wood products. In doing so, he sought to apply new and improved methods to long-standing concerns about aesthetics, rec-reation, and enjoyment.[44] Early in his reign, James drafted a note declaring his love of hunting and threatening to vigorously revive the Forest Laws if subjects did not desist from harming his game. He likewise issued directives to fence in certain areas for deer and gave orders to preserve trees as shelter and food for game.[45] James's correspondence and directives to the Earl of Huntingdon, who served as ranger of Leicester Forest, show that James had a careful eye for the state of his forests while he hunted. In 1613, James complained to Huntingdon that deer in Leicester Forest were in decline and two years later gave order for forest lands to be enclosed to protect them. In addition, James issued directives over the next decade prohibiting the holders of neighboring estates from killing deer that strayed onto their field or even from chasing them off. Even as James considered selling parts of Leicester Forest, he was adamant that particular areas remain forested and enclosed and ordered cattle and hogs barred from particular areas, in which, as Huntingdon wrote, "his Majesty took notice breeds the greatest deer." James even sought to protect the animals from frights by curtailing gunshots.[46]

Norden explicitly appealed to James's aesthetic sense when describing wood sales in Alice Holt Forest in Hampshire. In his report, Norden noted that the navy had previously felled trees within Alice Holt, suggesting its importance for shipbuilding, and he justified the 379 trees he felled and sold by claiming that they were merely "dotardes"—trees having lost their upper branches and in a state of decay. Nonetheless, Norden also qualified this statement by noting that the eighty-five trees he took from the forest proper were from "confines and skirts of the same where (I trust) his majesty shall find no defacings." He added, "The beauty of the forest [is] yet maintained to his majesty's no worse contentment . . . than the fairest forest or chase in the kingdom."[47] A 1609 report on wood sales from William Glover, surveyor of Norfolk and Suffolk, used similar language. Glover crowed that he had exceeded the set prices offered for timber. In doing so, he wrote, "I have not only respected the beauty and future time for necessary use of tenants, but also the loss to his Majesty and Successors for to sell the young timber for small value which in time will be much more worth then treble the value of now."[48] Norden and Glover were both involved in a larger effort to extract revenue from several royal forests by selling dead and decaying trees.[49] Nonetheless, aesthetic concerns mattered. Norden and Glover attempted to balance profit with beauty and a concern for future supply. Like James's program for selling royal estates, Norden's sales of dead and decaying trees were an attempt to enhance revenue by reducing waste, not by razing land entirely.

These concerns with beauty reflected the complex goals of early modern forestry. Surveyors produced quantitative assessments and cartographic representations of royal forests and made recommendations to increase revenue and reduce waste. At the same time, they acknowledged the importance of characteristics that could not be accounted for in their ledger books. Yet neither drew a complete distinction between practical and aesthetic concerns. Norden and Glover implied that "beauty" encompassed use for both elite recreation and the provision of common resources. Focusing on commercial production privileged the tree species counted in surveys at the expense of the trees, shrubs, and other plants not worthy of quantification. Both acknowledged that forests felled for commercial timber were displeasing to the royal eye, but Glover pushed even further by connecting aesthetics, the provision of resources for the poor, and a concern with posterity. Preserving a diverse landscape that contained many different types of tree species at different ages was, he suggested, beautiful, but it also ensured a landscape that would continue to produce commercial timber for the future and common resources for the poor. Their comments suggest that the most beautiful forests harmoniously balanced practical, social, and aesthetic concerns.[50]

Surveyors, however, struggled to achieve that ideal. Later that year, Norden conducted a detailed quantitative survey of trees in Alice Holt and the New Forest that illustrated the interplay between the push for clearly defined surveys and aesthetic concerns. Norden drew tables for each forest and offered numbers of dead or decaying trees and timber trees sold, their price, the number of timber trees standing and the number of decaying trees remaining. The survey appears designed to offer the king and his councilors the ability to calculate present and future revenue streams based on wood sales. Nonetheless, the appearance of wooded land played a part in his calculations. In a marginal note, Norden argued that Langley Wood, in New Forest, was a "little waste piece of ground" which ought to be clear-cut and sold. He justified this claim by noting that the trees there "stand merely out of all view of the main forest and would daily more and more rot and decay."[51] Norden sought to cull sparingly trees that were contiguous with a "main forest" to preserve a wooded aesthetic that he perceived as fair or beautiful, but there was no reason to spare rotting trees outside of that view.

Beauty, however, was not the only reason to fell or spare rotting or decaying trees. Norden argued that price also mattered in forestry decisions. He noted that more decaying trees could be sold in Alice Holt, but that they would not fetch the same prices as did trees from the previous sale. Norden attempted to justify the sale at a poorer rate, saying, "The places would be fuller incoppiced if more trees were taken that are unapt for timber."[52] Norden saw the potential for commercial and regenerative forestry that served future generations through regular felling and sales of decayed trees, but he worried that Crown officials would view lower sale prices as evidence of mal-feasance or corruption.

This kind of thinking stemmed from the system of valuation for woods. The Crown granted wood at a fixed rate for a specified number of acres or a measure of wood often for a longer term when valuing woods in grants and any decline in the value of wood was likely to provoke accusations of undervaluing Crown assets.[53] The administrative math of Jacobean forestry, aptly demonstrated in a 1611 commission to investigate the Forest of Dean, required clear and consistent values for land, trees, and pricing to facilitate long-term management. To make the equation work required an adminis-trative fiction that undermined geographic and ecological distinctions. The commission asked the deponents to assume that each acre in the forest con-tained an equal number and distribution of trees. The deponents were then to answer what proportion of the forest would be felled if 30,000 cords of wood were felled yearly for a ten-year period. Finally, they were asked to speculate whether "that wood will grow again in the same place and what course is best to be held to provide for the increase of the said wood in time to come," thus enabling a new cycle of sales and felling.[54]

Surveyors like Norden and commissioners had plans to create a system of forest management that would provide steady supplies of wood and yield tidy profits to James and his successors, but pricing and profitability proved persistent problems in implementation. Historian Philip Pettit has chroni-cled the spectacular failures of James's attempts to price woods in the 1610s and 1620s in which individual "farmers" purchased the right to sell wood on the Crown's behalf but failed to generate a fraction of the promised return. The farmers fled with charges of fraud hot on their heels, having failed to deliver any profits to the king.[55] Norden's proposal to better manage Alice Holt recognized a version of this issue. Norden believed that active forest management through felling decaying trees would lead to a healthier and more profitable woodland, but he hesitated to act on this belief out of fear of the lower returns generated from selling bigger quantities of decayed wood. Instead, he simply listed the number of decayed trees remaining, noting only that their value would continue to decline over time.

Contemporaries recognized the problems with this approach to measure-ment and valuation. In a different survey investigating coppices in the New Forest, Norden pointed out the problem with assuming consistency across an entire woodland, even a managed one. He wrote that North Wood coppice contained "several growths and the acres much differing in value." In a line drawing attached to the report, Norden illustrated this problem, showing a portion of densely forested land set against a portion clearly less forested. The current lease, however, took rent at a fixed rate across the entire coppice. Norden attempted to correct for this by assigning lower value to the majority of the coppice (forty-two acres) and charging a higher rate for the fourteen acres deemed most valuable, then calculating the total rent based on the sum at each value. Despite this acknowledgment, Norden hoped that variable quality might be eliminated over time by careful management. He sought to attach a condition to any lease of the coppice requiring "acorns and nuts to be cast for better increase of trees and underwoods" in "vacant places."[56]

English forestry struggled with multiple, sometimes contradictory values—not neglect. Foresters were to protect royal hunting and notions of beauty. They were tasked with balancing these concerns against present profits and future stocks. All of these requirements embodied an idea of conservation and, as the 1611 commission sent to the Forest of Dean makes clear, some contained an embryonic idea of sustainability, where royal forests would yield James and his successors consistent revenue in perpetuity by virtue of sound measurement, sensible grants, and rigorously enforced programs for regeneration.[57] James's government had responded aggressively to scarcity fears with a program for domestic renewal.

Efforts to address scarcity fears by reimagining English forests could come with significant social costs. In two letters attached to his surveys of the New Forest and Alice Holt, Norden outlined two somewhat contradictory but equally radical plans for the king's woods. These echoed some of the anxieties from Taverner and Elizabethan surveyors but imagined transformative changes that would sweep away the entire regime of English royal forestry. First, Norden called for the outright abolition of all royal forests, chases, parks, and wastes and their conversion to tillage. Maintaining these lands entailed, he claimed, an intolerable cost in money and timber. Worse still, these lands were "the very nurseries of idleness, loathsome beggary, perfidiousness and mere disobedience to God's and the laws of the kingdom." Norden noted that many people would object, but he wrote most of them off as "ignorant to the knowledge of God." Norden did not mention timber, except to claim that converting royal forests would save wood spent on fencing and maintaining lodges. He did not address in any way the persistent concerns about defense through shipbuilding or the development of domestic manufacturing that had shaped law and policy since Henry VIII's reign. The only impact worth serious consideration was the harm to the king's game, an issue he left to James's discretion because "he that wisheth not his Majesty's full contentment in every of his princely recreations is not only not a good subject but merely void of all civil understanding."[58]

Unlike his simultaneous proposal to turn all forests, chases, parks, and wastes to tillage, Norden's second plan explicitly addressed purported wood scarcity. But this plan also involved a radical departure from tradition. Norden again claimed that the status quo of English forestry was utterly untenable: Woodwards were corrupt and incompetent and their poor management destroyed more wood than they saved. He accused them of consistently digging up coppice fences before the trees had grown strong enough, leaving the regenerating shoots exposed to the destructive jaws of cattle and deer. It was better, Norden wrote, to lease coppices "under provident conditions" and entrust their care to the leaseholder's desire for profit rather than forest officers' sense of duty. In addition to abolishing traditional forest positions, Norden sought to enact a set of tree-farming schemes that would ensure that the woods produced the trees most necessary for royal purposes. Norden urged James to order forests to be cleared, tilled, and sowed with acorns, ash keys (seeds), and beech mast and either fenced in or planted with thorny bushes to protect the shoots from browsing animals, a program that bore striking similarities to proposals for silviculture in seventeenth-century Japan.[59] Ideally, the land would be enclosed and all common rights removed—hardly a problem, argued Norden, since commons decreased profit, produced sloth, and forced farmers to follow outdated customs. Norden acknowledged that his plan was radical, but he claimed that significant reforms "put in due execution shall breed great hope that future ages shall as well taste of our care."[60] Norden's work as a surveyor made him aware of the delicate balance among royal profit, custom, royal recreation, and less definable concerns like beauty, but his recommendations argued for a radical departure.

Other advisers expressed similar concerns, without endorsing Norden's most radical proposals. In 1612, Sir Henry Slingsby, a member of Parliament and chief forester for Knaresborough in Yorkshire, lamented the decay of "springs of wood" in royal forests. The farmers—grantees holding rights in the forest—"utterly destroy the spring to make more benefit of the herbage" for grazing their animals. Their desire to maximize the value of their grant imperiled future generations by preventing wood from regenerating. Forest officers and surveyors only exacerbated these incentives toward destruction through annual redefinitions of which trees belonged to the farmer and which to the Crown. Like Norden, at least in his second proposal, Slingsby saw privatization as the solution to mismanagement and bad incentives. Granting the lands out to private individuals, while reserving timber for the king would ensure more wood for "future times." Royal commissions, Slingsby claimed, consistently underpriced wood "for fear of a glut by so great a fall." In doing so, they deprived the king of revenue while doing nothing to prevent spoil. Instead, he argued, the combination of prices set by the timber market and long-term, secure leases pushed owners to fell responsibly, lest they drive down the price of their trees by flooding the market.[61]

While Norden and Slingsby urged James to undertake policies to derive greater profit from his royal forests, the king also supported projects that, if they succeeded, might undermine the value of royal woods by reducing the need for charcoal in manufacturing. In 1610, James had granted a patent to Slingsby and three other men to manufacture iron and glass using mineral coal for twenty-one years explicitly for "sparing wood and charcoal." He also granted a patent to Simon Sturtevant, who published a treatise on metallurgy in 1612 explaining his method for producing iron from turf and coal. James made a similar grant in 1620 to Sir Giles Mompesson, the projector who had simultaneously secured a grant from James to extract £100,000 in profit from royal forests without any spoliation, which ended disastrously in a lawsuit alleging that Mompesson had failed to pay the king and had destroyed £10,000 worth of trees.[62] James, as well as at least two projectors who appealed to him, simultaneously pursued projects that depended on the judicious management of woods as a profitable resource and projects that would enable resource substitution in manufacturing and metallurgy, undermining the value of charcoal. The seemingly contradictory endeavors suggest that, despite James's plans for a systematic, organized forest policy, he was prone to supporting any project that promised to alleviate scarcity, even if it contradicted other royal plans.

Nonetheless, the consistent emphasis on profitability and efficiency and the distrust of traditional forest officials point toward the coalescence of trends begun under Henry VIII and Elizabeth into a new political ecology of wood under James. It challenged custom and claims to traditional rights, asserted the salutary power of a profit motive, and questioned the ability of state officials to manage forests efficiently. The proposed transformations were radical. Scarcity had become the justification for a sharp break with the past. These plans promised to eliminate scarcity through domestic reform, reducing or eliminating the need for woods abroad. In practice, resistance to attacks on custom and existing rights often fueled further claims about scarcity.

The most detailed presentation of this view came in *An Olde Thrift Newly Revived* (1612) written by "R. C." in response to his experiences as a surveyor in the sales of royal woods and coppices undertaken at James's behest.[63] During the course of his surveying duties, R. C. claimed he "found lamentable scarcity, and exceeding abuses (which I fear to be universally as well over the Realm, as in the said particular places)." For R. C., correcting the abuses that led to wood scarcity "will prove most profitable to you [the 'Nobility, Gentry, and Yeomanry of Great Britain'] and your posterity for ever."[64] R. C. promised a perpetual and profitable supply of woods in England, but to attain it would require dramatic shifts in the purpose and management of and rights to woods.

Through a contrived discourse among a surveyor, woodward (a forest officer tasked with caring for a portion of a forest and documenting violations of the Forest Laws), landowner, and small tenant, R. C. laid out a vision for reformed forestry and widespread replanting that rehearsed the radical suggestions from Norden and Slingsby and fully imagined their social and political consequences. He addressed issues of bureaucratic and regulatory reform; the nature and uses of different types of trees; conflicts over commons, rents, and lease conditions; and sources of knowledge and methods for measuring and assessing individual trees and entire forests.[65] Like many of his contemporaries, R. C. sought to replace the often nebulous and inscrutable tangle of local custom and tradition with a system of management based on consistent and quantitative surveys and fueled by the pursuit of profits. Yet the dialogic form of *An Olde Thrift Newly Revived* enabled R. C. to engage with the consequences of these reforms. In doing so, he hinted at unease with his own vision.[66]

Multiple characters call attention to the social consequences of reform. The woodward, the embodiment of an ignorant, grasping, small-minded forest officer railed against by reformers, attempted to defend the old laws and practices. Cutting browse wood maintains poor forest officers. Enclosures threaten to reduce the poorest commoners to "extreme penury and famine."[67] Jenings, a tenant farmer, proves an even more dogged opponent, despite an initial declaration that the surveyor's complex discourses on trees were "beyond my capacity or profit." He argues that whatever benefits might come from planting trees would accrue to landlords, not farmers, and leaving those who did the planting destitute "so that we have nothing but our labours for our hire." Echoing the woodward, he claimed that enclosing woodland commons left copyholders (tenants holding land according to the customs of the manor rather than holding it without such restrictions as freeholders), farmers, and cottagers owing "a racked rent for that which they were wont to have gratis among their other grounds."[68]

Beyond their concern with the welfare of the poor, the surveyor's interlocutors warn him that his sweeping vision of forestry reform is unlikely to be profitable. The woodward notes that new plans for massive new plantations, "while a most excellent course . . . the charge thereof will somewhat dismay men from entering thereinto."[69] Jenings also objects to the surveyor's calls for farmers to plant trees and tend them like hops, claiming "young trees grow up and prosper well without such pains and charge, and that only by the natural nourishment and fruitfulness of the ground or climate." Peregrine, another interlocutor and a holder of several copyholds from the king, complains that planting hedges according to the surveyor's plans "seemeth an infinite labour and charge" not worth undertaking without large returns. Jenings, characteristically, offered a blunter assessment: "I believe your treble profit will be eat up, scarce to make you a single saver."[70] Profit served as a substantial motivation under James and in the radical reforms championed by Norden, R. C., and other champions of surveying; without it, the justification for such extensive projects became unclear.

Throughout the work, the surveyor attempts to smuggle these novelties in under the guise of revived tradition, vacillating in the passage providing the work's title between celebrating "the excellency and great commodity of this new kind of industry" and downplaying it by calling it "rather an old thrift newly revived." But the substance of the surveyor's proposals belied this framing. He decries the current enforcement of the Forest Laws and statutes passed under Henry VIII and Elizabeth I and hints that existing laws may not be sufficient to preserve the woods "if the heady and headlong clamour of the vulgar sort be not . . . moderated in the balance of equity." He calls for massive replanting of hedges for fuel and the creation of large stands of timber for shipbuilding and construction. The process of creating these new plantations required measures to plow and enhance existing soil as well as significant inputs of labor pruning, weeding, and otherwise tending the trees like they were agricultural crops. They likewise envisioned a new social and economic structure built on wages and contracts, not on convoluted thickets of customs, commons, and overlapping rights.[71]

Even with these demands, R. C. hinted that wood scarcity might be a thornier problem because of the relatively long timescales on which trees grow and their uneven distribution around the country. Both the surveyor and the copyholder Peregrine discuss scarcity as a problem at the intersection of present decisions and future conditions. Peregrine initially welcomes the surveyor's discourse "considering how forward every man is in these days to fell down Timber, and grub up Copies [coppices], & none endeavors to

plant any, whereby in time must needs follow a general waste of all." Peregrine describes "general" scarcity as a situation that will necessarily occur but
that has not yet gripped all of England. The surveyor worries that few tenants
and landlords will plant trees out of fear that they will not see profits in their
lifetimes. In his letter to the reader, R. C. worried about "present scarcity" but
framed it as a concern about future conditions. "If Coal should fail (as it is
too apparent it beginneth to grow dear and scarce, and in many places there
is none to be had)," he warned, "how then should we do for this material of
fuel?"[72] Future problems do not always ensure present profits; thus the surveyor assures readers that planting trees "will in short time make a plentiful
harvest yielding returns beyond corn or hops.[73]

Despite these assurances, tensions between profit and value derived from
utility remain. In contrast to the custom in Crown surveys and in the management of woods on private estates, R. C. looked beyond oaks in his description
of England's wooden wealth.[74] Alders grew rapidly in moist soil, quickly producing boughs, prompting even the recalcitrant Jenings to exclaim, "These
kinds of trees grow a pace without any great labor or charge, and the profit
thereof for fuel is very great." Birch were "very profitable and serveth well to
make charcoal, and also for Turners to make bowls, dishes, and other necessary things for the house." Poplars made excellent pipes. Beech "beareth Mast
very profitable for fatting of Swine." Walnuts provided timber that is "large,
smooth, pleasant, and serveth to many good uses for joiners," but they also
bore nuts that are "very excellent good for many griefs and diseases."[75] Different trees yielded different products, including fuel; construction material;
food for people or animals; medicines; and materials for plumbing, storage,
and household goods. And each had its own preferred soil type, moisture,
and temperature.[76] R. C.'s loving descriptions of diverse trees and their myriad uses sat uneasily with his emphasis on profitability.

R. C.'s program to address scarcity revealed tensions from multiple
angles. Small tenants, commoners, forest officers, and even elites within
forest communities objected to measures that curtailed customary practices and common rights with clear hints at the explosive potential of the
conflict. Landholders and commercial interests demanded profits to enact
the radical reforms the surveyor envisioned, and, as the dialogue intimated,
such actions were unlikely without the promise of relatively quick returns. In
R. C.'s dialogue, the surveyor largely triumphed; in attempts to put his ideas
into practice, the results were far more mixed.

Contemporaneous conflicts over wood and mining rights in the Forest of Dean saw the tensions to which R. C. had hinted erupt into lawsuits

and violence. In 1610, James granted the right to William Herbert, Earl of Pembroke, to fell trees and create charcoal to establish an ironworks in the Forest of Dean. Pembroke claimed that he planned to establish blast furnaces, forges, bloomeries, and "iron mills," indicating that his works would use both the direct and indirect processes to manufacture different types of iron. James's grant ended royal prohibitions against ironworks in Dean but also ignited several controversies that ultimately halted Pembroke's endeavor. Contemporary observers denigrated protests against Pembroke's ironworks as "riots." Other documents from Dean show the complex politics at play. First, the major source of trouble came from the free miners, who asserted their customary right as men born in the Forest of Dean to dig and sell ore in accordance with their own system of regulation and payments to the king. Other opponents accused Pembroke of illegally felling trees, a charge he vigorously denied. Pembroke accused William Hall, who had previously been cited for illegally erecting an ironworks, and Edward Wheeler, also known as Edward Partridge, of cutting timber, digging ore, and manufacturing charcoal to be shipped to Ireland "intending to hinder his Majesty to make any benefit or profit of his said woods" all on the basis of the common rights, particularly estovers, or the right to cut wood for fuel and to maintain or construct buildings and fences.[77]

In response to these disputes, the Crown began curtailing common mining and wood rights in Dean. One case against Dean's free miners stripped their right to freely mine and sell ore; instead, the exchequer court allowed them to mine out of charity and mandated that the king's ironworks and the Earl of Pembroke had right of first refusal. A petition "from many thousands the poor inhabitants of the Forest of Dean" addressed to Pembroke from this period made it clear that much contemporary anxiety and conflict stemmed from concern about lost common rights and uncertainty about woodlands. The petitioners worried that granting licenses to erect ironworks would create more coppiced lands where they could no longer pasture animals, threatening the livelihoods of long-standing residents. Uncertainty about the physical environment lay at the heart of their complaint. The petitioners asserted that neither they nor Pembroke, in his role as royal forester, knew how many trees were in the Forest or how quickly cut trees regenerated, or, if woodlands, once felled, would return to their previous state. As a result, they asked Pembroke to appoint a commission of "indifferent gentlemen not interested in ironworks" to answer these questions and to determine how much wood the Crown could give away without sacrificing the commoners' rights.[78] James's advisers sought to develop a calculation to produce consistent revenue through wood sales; the petitioners demanded that they modify the equation.

In the face of these bitter conflicts, James's government largely backed down. Crown attorneys and officers sought to clarify the extent of common rights through the courts but were unwilling to persist with controversial grants of wood rights. Throughout the 1610s and early 1620s, James repeatedly issued grants to build ironworks in Dean, only to rescind them whenever controversy or allegations of wasted woods surfaced. A 1613 order to halt all felling in Dean made the Crown's rationale clear: Felling amid disorder and controversy "tend to the utter devastation and spoil of the said Forest."[79] Competing users marshaled the rhetoric of scarcity to support their visions for royal forests and Crown woods. The result was a sense of uncertainty about the quantity and quality of resources or the impact that ironworks or wood sales to serve the Crown would have on them. James had begun his reign with plans to reform forestry practices and the management of Crown lands that would preserve aestheticized landscapes for royal recreation, generate increased revenue, encourage domestic iron production, and leave a healthy store of woods for future generations. In practice, efforts for reform failed to produce this harmonious vision and instead laid bare conflicting political ecologies: These conflicting political ecologies could not be rectified through a surveyor's ledgers and measurements alone. Rather than eliminating scarcity, reform had produced new anxieties about it.

Charles I's accession to the throne following his father's death prompted a wave of new plans to address scarcity and solve the problems that remained from James's reign. The first proposals submitted urged Charles to not abandon woods or sell them off to be managed by private hands but to improve state-sponsored forestry practices. An early proposal urged the king to redouble the efforts of surveyors to mark trees in every forest that were fit for naval service and to strictly enforce prohibitions against unauthorized felling, the system of wood management that had been in place since Henry VIII's reign. Two tracts from 1625 and 1627 urged Charles to sow acorns, as Lord Burleigh had allegedly done at Cranborne Walk in Windsor Forest. The authors saw prohibitions to protect current woodlands as ineffective, but they argued that regeneration, not privatization would alleviate destruction and scarcity. Moreover, replanting forests would be cost neutral or even would generate profit since wood sales to thin the stand of trees would easily offset or even surpass the cost of labor to plow and plant. Richard Daye, who submitted two separate proposals on the subject, cast replanting as an uncontroversial endeavor. Without replanting, he warned, "it is thought this kingdom will run it very shortly, and that the other ages shall have cause to speak hardly of this age, and of the state of government that hath suffered the matter to run on so far into inconvenience." Fortunately, solutions were relatively simple. Bishops and churchwardens, he argued, should be forced to replant trees in "decayed woods," a labor that would protect churches from strong winds and ensure a ready supply of construction materials for their upkeep. The timber for the navy and the king were merely a fortunate by-product.[80]

Proposals to reform forestry continued through the 1630s and show that the fundamental problems associated with competing uses remained unsolved. A letter writer complained that foresters continually pollarded trees in Hainault Forest in Essex. By taking branches for firewood, they ruined "the straightest and handsomest trees as any eye could behold and could have been within short time fit for the use for his Majesty's Navy."[81] Hainault lay close to navigable waterways and to London. For this reason, its trees were useful for both shipbuilding and to supply firewood to the capital and its suburbs. Pollarding provided a renewable supply of firewood, but it rendered trees unfit for use in shipbuilding. The question facing Charles's government was how to manage the conflict and whose interests should be prioritized. In answering throughout the kingdom, his government chose strategies to maximize timber for shipbuilding and profit from leases while enacting regulations to ensure a steady supply of timber over traditional practices and rights to common resources.

Unlike his forbears' administrations, Charles's government appeared determined to complete implementation of reforms to forestry and the management of royal lands even when these measures provoked controversy by threatening customary uses or by attacking forest officials. He sent commissions out to investigate the privileges accorded to foresters with the express goal of eliminating waste.[82] In many cases, commissions and surveys were the precedent to substantial sale of wood rights or disafforestation—removing royal protections and law from the land that allowed it to be sold and converted to agriculture. These policies affected people across the social spectrum. In the final years of James's reign, surveyors had investigated the customs and woods of Leicester Forest. Upon the disafforestation and sale of Leicester Forest, the Earl of Huntingdon enumerated the privileges he was losing while also noting that upholding the Forest Laws to prevent poaching and to preserve the deer had reduced the value of his neighboring lands substantially.[83] These measures put the health and financial security of an increasingly centralized, monarchical state above local, particularistic interests, whether poor commoners seeking fuel and fodder for subsistence or nobles and gentry defending customary revenues.

In the Forest of Dean, Charles's government adopted a slightly different strategy, seeking to improve Crown revenue while simultaneously drawing on the forest for naval supplies and using it as a site of iron production. To do so, it used selective leases and sales of rights to woods alongside vigorous legal enforcement on violations of the terms of previous grants and illicit felling. This pattern of entangled grants and suits simultaneously created additional opportunities for raising revenue through fines after the initial grant and it enabled the Crown to pursue strategies to curtail waste and manage use in lands it no longer directly managed. In 1628, Charles's attorney general brought a case against Sir John Wintour (also Winter), Benedict Hall, and other inhabitants. The suit alleged that Wintour, Hall, and other residents of Dean took wood from the forest without right. In particular, the attorney general alleged that Wintour and Hall had packed Dean with poor cottagers who had no right to use common lands or take wood from the forest for fuel or for repair to their homes. The attorney general argued that tenants and landholders in Dean were unable to show any valid title for their rights and insisted on a strict interpretation of existing grants. This meant that either forest officers or the Speech Court tasked with hearing cases involving Forest Laws were to supervise and administer the right of "houseboot"—felling wood to build or maintain a house. Moreover, "no ancient tenement [can be] enlarged, but maintained in the former and ancient bigness and extent." Fireboot—the right to gather fuel in the forest—was to be confined only to dead and downed trees and violators were to be taken before the Speech Court. Finally, any new cottagers given leases after the grant were not entitled to any common rights whatsoever. If the inhabitants wanted these rights, the attorney general noted that the king was willing to disafforest and sell land that would include those rights, but that they would not be taken for free. Wintour and Hall protested that the king's officers sought to impose ridiculous conditions, but the barons of the exchequer ruled in the king's favor.[84]

At one telling moment, the attorney general offered a candid statement justifying the suit against the forest inhabitants. He acknowledged that royal actions "have hindered the said complainants from using their said commons and freedoms in the said Forest," but he explained that large grants to supply ironworks provided "better profit" than traditional use patterns. The king hoped "that the same profit may be always maintained and continued," but securing a regular revenue from the forest required changes in policy, notably the rigorous maintenance of enclosed coppices to ensure that felled trees would regenerate. The attorney general stated that the complainants deserved their "just common," but they were only due the rights explicitly allotted in grants.[85] Charles's government had designed a formula for predictable, continuous supplies of wood in perpetuity, but profit, rather than the maintenance of paternalistic social harmony, was the goal. New cottagers, bigger houses, or expanded animal grazing, practices that had been tolerated for many years, simply did not work in the new equation.

Wintour and Hall appeared to quickly adapt to the new circumstances and purchased the right to fell 4,000 cords of wood for £10,000 the same year. The conditions attached to the contract also fulfilled Charles's vision for Dean. Wintour and Hall were to consult with the king's surveyors Robert and Andrew Treswell to determine which trees might be felled and which were required for the navy.[86] In 1631, violent protests erupted against Charles's attempts to sell and enclose parts of the Forest of Dean. Groups of forest inhabitants attacked newly enclosed lands that had been sold off in the 1620s, tearing down fences and breaking hedges. Some protesters may have been the poorest cottagers and tenants deprived of their commons, but Charles's government also suspected that Hall had played a part and issued a bill of complaint against him.[87] Charles and his advisers had devised a new formula to ensure steady revenues for the king, ship timber for the navy, and resources for posterity, but many of Dean's residents were unwilling to be written out of the equation.

Charles's government had pushed its forestry reforms and challenges to customs and commons further than had Elizabeth's or James's, but anxieties about scarcity remained. In 1633, the surveyor John Broughton reported on the state of Dean. As in previous surveys, Broughton offered a quantitative assessment of the number of trees and of their utility for shipping or ironworks. Broughton expressed some anxiety about the store of trees closest to the royal ironworks and proposed that foresters begin completely uprooting decayed or dying trees to maximize the yield of timber rather than leaving a stump. Like Norden and Slingsby, however, Broughton doubted the efficacy of small reformations in forestry practice. Forests, he wrote, should be managed for the king's "profit and honor and for the public good." The traditional system of regulation by royal officials was failing to do that. Private ownership would prove more efficient because any "private man" operating an ironworks could make substantial profits (£6,600 per year) for "a long time and perhaps forever." To do so required private owners to adopt reformed forestry practices; with these incentives, however, they "would never entertain a thought of selling the Forest wood" but "would enclose and incoppice the ground of the Forest to breed wood and timber."[88] Unlike Norden, who saw disafforestation and the sale of woods and commons as a way to increase agricultural land, Broughton's proposal sought to preserve woods. He saw the sale of royal forests, with appropriate conditions to ensure timber for the navy, as a way of circumventing corrupt and inefficient bureaucracy and allowing compelling economic incentives to ensure a steady, renewable supply of wood in perpetuity.

Charles's government did not immediately accept Broughton's proposal; instead, in July 1634, it organized an eyre, an eight-day meeting of an itinerant court in which forest officers presented indictments and allegations and in which trials were held for violations of the Forest Laws in Dean. The Dean eyre was the second held under Charles, following the 1632 proceedings for Windsor and Bagshot. One historian has noted that the 1634 eyre captured the "inconsistencies" in Charles's forest policies and their role in a program of extra-parliamentary taxation, but that the proceedings gestured toward a plan for conservation.[89] Rather than antagonistic forces, however, the enforcement efforts in 1634 reveal that, for Charles and his officers, maximizing royal revenue and ensuring supplies of woods for posterity were complementary goals.

The proceedings continued and escalated the legal and regulatory actions taken in Dean under James and Charles that sought simultaneously to exploit woods for profit and to ensure their long-term viability. The court reopened earlier controversies over ironworks in Dean with presentments resulting in fines against several prominent individuals, including Richard Challoner, who had benefited from earlier controversies over waste and theft in Dean's ironworks. The most notable was the series of presentments against Sir Basil Brooke and George Mynne, who were operating ironworks ostensibly using wood granted to the Earl of Pembroke. In his notes, Sir John Finch, the king's attorney for the eyre, outlined a two-pronged series of allegations against Brooke and Mynne. First, they had exceeded the quantities of wood permitted in their patent through both outright illegal felling and the manipulation of measurements to deceive forest officers. Finch alleged that they had used cords of wood longer than the length permitted in their grant and, in addition, had schemed to produce "half" cords, three of which equaled two full cords. Second, there were "abuses in taking" trees. Brooke and Mynne, Finch alleged, had felled trees on hillsides, "destroying the shelter of great timber trees" by removing windbreaks and the root systems securing the soil. This created conditions for erosion: "When winter came the wind having power upon them blew down a great number of goodly timber trees, a thousand in one night, many of them marked for the king, and those they took as windfalls." Beyond promoting erosion to make preserved trees available for their use, Finch claimed that they had felled "springs," newly growing oaks and beech and, in doing so, threatened not only the present but the future. The Crown's case identified incidents beginning as early as 1608 with specific presentments addressing decades of actions and implying that the illegal behavior of grantees, not Crown grants, was responsible for any shortages or destruction in the forest. Ultimately, the jury found Brooke and Mynne guilty of illegally cutting 178,200 cords of wood and the judge fined them about £58,000, an act of mercy since the Forest Laws specified a penalty twelve times the value of the felled wood. The results of the case swayed Sir John Wintour to abandon a not-guilty plea and to accept some of the charges presented against him with a fine of £20,230.[90]

Beyond the charges against prominent individuals and the owners and operators of ironworks, the eyre continued to challenge the rights of the poor dwelling in Dean. Fines of £5 were routinely assessed against individuals who erected cottages in the woods. Most of those presented and fined were identified as laborers, with other listed professions including colliers, woodcutters, widows, and spinsters. For the poorest men and women earning roughly nine and four pence per day, respectively, for unskilled labor, these fines would have almost certainly been unpayable. Presentments for offenses against "vert," or underwoods, reflected efforts to eliminate unpermitted small uses of wood for fuel or for maintaining dwellings. Here, too, the penalties could be staggering, as in the case of the laborer Edward Baddam of Blakeney, who was presented for felling the top branches of a beech, totaling two loads of wood worth two pence and received a fine of 20 shillings, 120 times the stated value of the branches and which might have required nearly a month of wages to pay off.[91]

The fines leveled against prominent subjects operating ironworks and poor cottagers served distinct but complementary purposes. The Crown's cases against Brooke, Mynne, Challoner, and Wintour emphasized narrow and specific interpretations for any royal grant or sale and made it clear that Charles and his government did not see the sale of woods and their conservation efforts as contradictory actions. As Finch put it, "Being a forest the grant of woods gives no power to cut them unless there be special words for the purpose." Monarchs could sell forest land to raise revenue without sacrificing wood supplies through precise, narrow legal language and courts willing to take a similar approach to earlier grants.[92] Finch's claim was in keeping with the efforts under James and Charles that, at least ostensibly, showed concern for posterity. Ensuring sufficient wood supplies for those large, lucrative grants required increased regulation on poorer forest residents' small acts of felling for construction and fuel gathering and limits on the population of the

forest poor through crackdowns on unpermitted cottage building. To produce wood for the present and the future entailed vigorous oversight of the
gentry and left those without the means to pay Crown rents with little access.

Charles's next grant put this model into practice. Shortly after the eyre,
he sold wood rights in the Forest of Dean to Sir John Wintour. Wintour paid
£8,000 up front and was to pay £4,000 per year for the thirty-year term of the
lease. In return, he was to have the right to cut down and convert to charcoal
every tree in the forest not "marked for timber" or reserved for the navy,
except for 12,500 cords of wood assigned to the Earl of Pembroke. This contract even allowed Wintour to trim branches—the "shredding" much decried
in earlier surveys—"if by so doing the timber be not impaired" and as long
as naval officials had not marked particular curved limbs as compass timber.
Within a year, Wintour had turned to Benedict Hall for a loan, promising to
pay him back £4,500 in iron produced from Dean's woods. From 1636 until
the outbreak of the Civil War in England, the Crown investigated allegations
of spoil and pursued charges against Wintour and other prominent figures
in Dean based on well-worn complaints about wood rights, the use of forests as common pastures for animals, and disputes over whether felled trees
constituted "timber."[93] Neither intensified surveillance and enforcement of
regulations nor shifting management into the hands of a "private man" had
alleviated worries about scarcity and allegations of destruction in Dean.

Dean had emerged as a critical site for shipbuilding and iron production
by the beginning of the seventeenth century, but disputes in the forests of
Shotover and Stow in Oxfordshire show that similar patterns also occurred
in different locations with far less importance to new woodland industries.
John Taverner had first surveyed the forests in the 1580s. In 1615, surveyor
Matthew Baker and the shipbuilder and naval administrator Phineas Pett
wrote to the Privy Council with information from an updated survey of Shotover and Stow. Baker and Pett wrote that they had marked 800 trees across
the two forests and "Barnewood" (Bernwood Forest), but that the timber lay
some distance from water. The trees were good but worth felling only "if the
good his Majesty shall receive by the quality of the provisions to be had from
thence, will easily countervail the charge of carriage."[94] James's government
had taken responsibility to balance the value of trees in the forests against the
costs to access and transport them. Charles's government, seeking revenue
from the forests but unwilling to assume the risks themselves, instead offered
a 51-year lease of Shotover and Stow, reserving for the crown 4,000 trees to be
marked by naval officers for immediate use and 10,000, 50-year-old trees to
serve as ship timber at a future date.[95]

Richard Hore and Richard Parne, preservators for Shotover and Stow, wrote to Charles, protesting the decision. The contract, they argued, both undervalued and overvalued the trees in the wood. There were 8,000 valuable trees worthy for current use, double the number reserved in the lease. Hore and Parne worried, however, that the forest did not contain enough young trees likely to become timber to meet the demand in fifty years. They warned that the contract, designed to supply current and future needs, would do neither. Moreover, by only reserving a few trees for ship timber, Hore and Parne claimed that the contract missed the purpose of a forest: "If other trees (wherein the profit and beauty of the Forests do chiefly consist) become passed from his Majesty to be felled (besides the great loss of so much excellent Shiptimber) there will be no pannage left either for the Kings game or the relief of the poor borderers' cattle; Nay, in our Judgments there cannot remain so much as the face of a Forest." Charles's plan sought to ensure a consistent supply of timber for the navy over multiple generations while increasing royal revenue through wood sales. Hore and Parne objected that it failed to accomplish these goals, but they also offered a contrasting vision for the purpose of woods. Beauty and profit stemmed from provision of pannage and pasture for royal deer and commoners' cattle. Their notion of the forest was paternalistic. It was a place dedicated to recreation that reinforced social distinctions, but it also offered sustenance to society's most vulnerable.[96] Hore and Parne's complaint made explicit the conflicting visions underlying bureaucratic squabbles or quibbles over quantitative assessment. This was a fight over political ecology, over who should have access to forests and who they should be managed to serve.

Rather than compromise, as his father's government had done, Charles's government bore down harder to implement its vision. It rejected Hore and Parne's complaints. In 1630, the Privy Council wrote a letter chastising Oxfordshire JPs for failing to fell trees, an order they reissued a year later. In the meantime, Charles had granted the right to the controversial Archbishop William Laud to set workers to take wood from Shotover and Stow to build St. John's College at Oxford. He backed the privilege with a ban on felling or collecting any wood unless it served the college, supported the effort to make the Thames navigable, or had been marked to supply the navy. In 1631, both the officers of the navy and the Privy Council issued warrants authorizing surveyor William Willoughby to fell 800 trees for shipbuilding and lop, top, and strip bark from them to be sold to enhance the king's revenue.[97] These actions, rather than being signs of short-term exploitation, emerged from a clearly stated concern for the future and reflected the arguments from several promoters for how best to combat scarcity.

The people of Shotover and Stow reacted strongly to these efforts to exploit the forests. Sir Timothy Tirrell, bailiff for Shotover, seized the lops, tops, and bark from Willoughby, threatening the surveyor and his workers with imprisonment. In doing so, the naval officers alleged, Tirrell had disobeyed explicit, written orders from the Lords of the Admiralty. Phineas Pett reported that "the abuse [in Shotover and Stow] is unspeakable." Pett reported that two "squire knees"—curved pieces of timber crucial for early modern shipbuilding and difficult to locate—had been cut up for firewood. All these spoils, according to Pett, were done under the color of providing browse for deer and cattle. When Pett challenged Tirrell, the bailiff replied, "How should the keepers live having but 26s 8d a year, and that unpaid these 10 years, yet those places (as I am informed) sold at £100 a piece?"[98] Resistance to the new policies came not just from poor commoners but also from agents of local government.

These new and controversial efforts to shift forest management at Shotover and Stow were a response to alterations in the economic geography of wood in England. Since 1615, when Pett had noted that Shotover and Stow lay some distance from the water and questioned whether carriage costs would make it worthwhile to fell the wood, the navy's perception of the forests had changed. A 1632 report on several forests and their fitness for shipbuilding claimed that Shotover and Stow were "the only place for supply of his Majesty's service both in regard of the excellent quality and soundness of the timber as also for convieniency of land and water carriage to his Majesty's Timber yards."[99] So long as the woods were not economically exploitable, traditional uses and rights proceeded unabated. Charles's government made it clear, however, that common rights and foresters' privileges held no value as authorities sought to exploit woods efficiently and with an eye toward both present and future profits and use.

A 1638 report captures this thought. Opponents claimed, according to the report, that the navy's woodcutters had spoiled more trees than their contract allowed. The authors replied that only 260 trees had been felled. Moreover, the authors claimed, the inhabitants only complained about shipbuilding because "the aforesaid timber being converted to other uses as pipestaves, barrel boards, and other to turner's ware may yield somewhat more." But focus on profits "hath bene the only cause of Scarcity of serviceable long timber for the use of his Majesty's Navy and for building and repairing of Merchant ships and other vessels built in this kingdom." Even if, they continued, timber sold as pipe staves might raise three times the value, supplying the navy should take precedence.[100] Profit, widely distributed and with benefit to both the state and private actors, had become a key rhetorical strategy for forestry reformers since James's reign. Here, in contrast, the argument was that state interests, particularly military ones, outweighed *all* other claims.

In the Forests of Dean, Shotover, and Stow, Charles's vision for a new, efficient policy that would preserve wood and supply regular revenue came into multiple conflicts. Old forest officials railed against the loss of their privileges. Long-standing landholders in the forests or at their edges protested loss of commons and threats to their ability to improve their rents by allowing cottagers and other small tenants to settle on marginal lands. Many of the poor protested against the newly detailed examinations of grants and leases that threatened hard-won rights to pasture their animals and collect wood in the forests. These conflicts provide crucial context to understand Charles's revival of the Forest Laws in the 1630s. Historians have perceived the revival as a desperate act in search of revenue or a moment when Charles's government decayed into near parody. But placing this action within the context of the long history of conflicting visions about the best uses and management practices for royal forests, demands a more nuanced perspective. The records of the Swainmote Courts convened to hear cases under the Forest Laws from the New Forest show that enforcement frequently targeted forest officials. Crown surveyors Robert and Andrew Treswell received a staggering £2,000 fine for allegedly felling 1,500 oaks and beeches.[101]

Almost from the beginning of his reign, Charles had distrusted forest officials. His feelings were not new developments. R. C.'s ignorant and avaricious woodward captured criticisms of forest officials as ignorant, inefficient, and wasteful that had been building since the sixteenth century. Many surveyors and projectors had urged monarchs to curtail the power of forest officials by removing the officers, fining them, or selling lands to private individuals to allow economic incentives to preserve woods without interference from corrupt individuals. Revived Forest Laws provided another way for Charles to undertake his broader program to achieve profitable and renewable forestry that would alleviate scarcity. Charles's motivations were hardly new, but, unlike Elizabeth or James, he was willing to stand by controversial measures even as they alienated allies.

English monarchs from Elizabeth through Charles regularly took actions to measure and protect royal forests, parks, and chases in response to complaints about wood scarcity. These policies were more than just reactions and, particularly under James and Charles, often set out long-term visions of steady, consistent yields without loss of woodlands. Parliament passed laws to curtail purported wastes. The exchequer sent out surveyors and commissions to collect information on the state of the woods and to investigate abuses. At the same time, records from these efforts make it clear that Elizabeth, James, and Charles and their governments sought to alter the practices and personnel of English forestry. Rather than cynical or incompetent attempts to extract short-term profits to shore up creaky royal finances, their policies represented a different vision for royal forests as a state-sponsored means to improve revenue and secure needed supplies for military endeavors in the present and the future.

Reports from surveyors, schemes from projectors, and policies from monarchs and members of the Privy Council frequently argued that taking woods out of royal control and granting them to private individuals would enable private efforts at preservation and reforestation. Motivated by extensive opportunities for profits in ironworks, barrel and pipe-stave production, and timber sales for construction, they argued, private individuals would steward their trees much more carefully than the overlapping and often corrupt and incompetent forest officials. Timber for the navy could be secured through regulations, reserving particular trees from private exploitation. The complex system of laws, rights, and privileges overseen by overlapping groups of forest officials, according to their argument, was bloated and inefficient. It destroyed royal revenue. Worse still, it wasted the woods while doing so. Foresters' privileges and practices, even without corruption, were seen as incompatible with efficient management for timber and shipbuilding. Overreach and abuses made the situation even worse. The push to reform forestry through expropriation of royal and common resources and the distrust of the bureaucracy that had hitherto managed Crown woods translated into legal action: Foresters were frequent targets for prosecution under the revived Forest Laws—the very code that created their positions and defined their privileges. The revival of the Forest Laws was an attempt to secure more revenue for Charles without recourse to a hostile Parliament, but it also represented an attempt to redefine the goals for and management of natural resources.

From the outset, many people challenged these new policies. People with common rights to royal forests, ranging from the poorest cottagers to the gentry and nobility, protested against having their rights curtailed. At the heart of their challenges lay a different vision for the purpose and form of woods. Managing forests as timber farms to feed ironworks and shipyards required enclosures and restrictions on grazing animals. It necessitated bans on older practices like pollarding and shredding that provided fuel and some building materials. It rendered many traditional rights and activities the enemies of the forest rather than an essential part of it. Even James sometimes rejected this logic by promoting hunting at the expense of timbering enterprises and through his concern for beauty, as reflected in surveyors' reports outlining their care to preserve the aesthetics of a forest even as they sold off trees.

A profit calculation based on particular wood prices lay at the heart of many of the challenges to older forestry practices and policies. Surveyors or Crown officials tasked with deciding whether to sell or maintain royal forests, parks, and chases had to justify their decision by comparing the potential profits from disafforestation and sale against the maintenance costs to retain royal control. Likewise, surveyors took the sale prices for timber into account when determining whether and what quantities of decaying and healthy trees should be cut at any given time. It is clear from many of the most optimistic accounts both for improving royal revenue and for the profit-driven preservation that would follow disafforestation that surveyors, projectors, and members of the government assumed high and growing wood prices, driven upward by scarcity.

Economic realities confounded these royal visions. Crown profits from wood sales were paltry and extracting those meager profits required the government to use a costly bureaucracy that could easily consume 25-50 percent of the returns from royal forests. Moreover, forest land with woods regularly rented below the customary rate for agricultural land. Put simply, estimates based on growing scarcity underlay many plans to manage royal forests and woodlands, and these estimates did not pencil out.[102]

* * *

Efforts to reform domestic forestry under Elizabeth, James, and Charles had sparked complex debates about scarcity, conservation, property, and profit. For almost a century, from the mid-1500s until the end of Charles's reign in 1649, the Crown and Parliament largely sought to address scarcity concerns through efforts at domestic reform. At the same time, colonial promoters often seized on moments of concern about scarcity or, when controversies erupted over woods, suggested that abundant woods abroad could serve as a solution to England's problems. However, domestic reformers rarely took notice of these promotional efforts to a significant degree because advocates for colonies did not address critical local concerns, the complex politics of English forestry, or the significant financial difficulties forest projects encountered. The earliest colonial proposals were simultaneously attuned to opportunities created by domestic-scarcity fears and detached from the struggles to define and address problems of scarcity that had taken place. As a result, many proponents of English expansion in the sixteenth and early seventeenth centuries engaged in two acts of ecological imagination: to redefine English woods and forests and to describe potential colonies. Doing so carried risks as promotional rhetoric and domestic realities grew apart. Nonetheless, colonial promoters hoped that by defining landscapes of scarcity and abundance they could show the necessity for a colonial political ecology.[103]

Comments on the utility of colonial woods began in Ireland as early as the 1580s, when promoters and government officials debated the best course of action in the wake of the Desmond Rebellion of 1579–1583. This occurred nearly simultaneously with the Elizabethan government's increasingly aggressive actions to regain control over royal lands and to survey forests. Plans to make Irish woods useful for the Elizabethan state shared some characteristics with new policies in England—as in English royal forests, actions in Ireland sought to strengthen royal rule—but they also reflected uniquely Irish concerns—namely, that attempts to control woods in Ireland were entangled with English complaints about Irish cultural degeneracy and rebellious tendencies.[104] Moreover, they demonstrated only passing familiarity with the surveys, court cases, and other actions to reform domestic forestry, largely treating England's wooded landscapes as an unchanging backdrop.

In the proposals that emerged in the 1580s to use Ireland's woods, colonial promoters argued that deforesting Ireland would simultaneously pacify the rebellious people and buoy Crown finances. The endeavor would remove a landscape thought to harbor rebels while providing loyal English men who, "being furnished with shot and other convenient munition, may not only defend their works: but also be employed upon occasions for your Majesty's other services." Such a radical change to the Irish landscape was feasible because the woods needed to supply the navy were, according to promoters, "greatly decayed in England."[105] Military concerns motivated many English observers to recommend deforestation, but the discourse of English wood scarcity was necessary to justify it financially in a way that plans to increase agriculture did not require.

The shift in the rhetoric describing Irish woods created tension in reformers' plans for Ireland and for promises that colonial expansion could provide a long-term solution for England. If Ireland's woods were cut down all at once, where would the timber come from to repair and replace the new English fleet? If these woods were preserved as a permanent source of timber for the English navy, would that imperil the political order sought in Ireland? After the defeat of the Spanish Armada in 1588, these issues only became more difficult. The threat of Spanish invasion made the need to secure Ireland even more pressing, but the need to maintain a strong navy demanded reliable stores of wood.

These tensions are best displayed in the poet Edmund Spenser's *View of the Present State of Ireland*, which was composed and circulated during the 1590s but not printed until 1633. At the beginning of the text, which takes the form of a dialogue between two fictional characters, one of Spenser's interlocutors claims that Ireland is "adorned with goodly woods, fit for building of houses and ships, so commodiously, as that if some princes in the world had them, they would soon hope to be lords of all the seas." Yet, for the remainder of his text, Spenser's characters denounced Irish woods as a source of Irish cultural degeneracy and a haven for criminals. Spenser's animosity toward woodlands was so strident that it almost overwhelmed his earlier claim about their utility for the navy. He compared the disordered state of Ireland to early medieval England. At that time, according to Spenser, England was "greatly infected" with criminals and outlaws who thrived in thick woodlands. Spenser's historical argument implied that the absence of dense woods in England was a triumph of law and civilization, not a fact to be lamented.[106] In casting deforestation as a marker of progress, Spenser raised troubling questions for his own earlier assertion that Irish woods would provide enough shipping to rule the seas. The specter of English wood shortages gave an economic and political imperative to maintain Irish woodlands, but preserving Irish woodlands also threatened to imperil the most radical plans to transform the Irish landscape.

Not all colonial promoters relied on the assumptions about English scarcity that characterized plans in Ireland. Writing around the same time, the prominent colonial promoter Richard Hakluyt offered perhaps the most subtle discussion of the close connections among natural limits, scarcity, and colonial expansion. At the same time as plantation promoters argued that the English state needed to plant in Ireland, in part to assuage dangerous wood shortages, Hakluyt summoned the rhetoric of decay and scarcity to launch his argument for colonial expansion in North America. Unlike the roughly contemporary works from Ireland, however, Hakluyt avoided claims that England's economic woes stemmed from natural shortages. Hakluyt had been sent to Paris in 1583 to investigate Spanish and French colonial efforts and to report back to the Elizabethan government. The result, his 1584 "Discourse of Western Planting," was composed as a secret report, intended as a policy paper for Elizabethan ministers, rather than as an appeal to a wider audience. Nonetheless, Hakluyt opened his account with a discussion of the decline in England's fortunes that echoed the rhetoric found in more public forums. Foreign trade, claimed Hakluyt, had grown "decayed." In England, "multitudes of loiterers and idle vagabonds" plagued the country despite "all the statutes that hitherto can be devised, and the sharp execution of the same in punishing idle lazy persons." Despite his grim prognosis, Hakluyt asserted that the problems facing England stemmed from economic rather than environmental factors. Tariffs had slowed English exports and undermined industry at home; however, if the population could be put to work, then England would achieve unprecedented riches. Hakluyt argued that England could sustain increased population. "The honor and strength of a prince," he wrote, "consisteth in the multitude of the people." So long as they "know how to live and how to maintain their wives and children," England could support more people and even produce an agricultural surplus.[107]

Hakluyt's exposition of the commodities available in North America and the environment that produced them was a direct response to his economic narrative. North America "from Florida northward to 67 degrees (and not yet in any Christian prince's actual possession)" was, according to Hakluyt, "answerable in climate to Barbary, Egypt, Syria, Persia, Turkey, Greece, all the Islands of the Levant Sea, Italy, Spain, Portingale [Portugal], France, Flanders, high Almanye [parts of modern Germany], Denmark, Estland [Eastland], Poland, and Muscovy."[108] His list of climate types corresponded almost entirely to the list of places where English trade had decayed because of religious hostility, tariffs, or war, a pattern that followed the still-prominent early modern understanding that climate followed latitude and a tradition of conflating economic opportunities and climate that persisted into the eighteenth century.[109] Hakluyt's description of the North American climate in terms of commodities offered a compelling argument in favor of English expansion to overcome the destructive trade policies of continental, Baltic, and Mediterranean polities.

At times, Hakluyt also seemed to suggest that the purported decay of shipbuilding and naval stores manufacturing in England might stem from scarcity as well as from trade policy. He contended that the recent English claim on Newfoundland would provide England's naval and commercial fleets with "tar, rosen, masts, and cordage . . . all which commodities cannot choose but wonderfully invite our men to the building of great shipping." This boon in supplies, Hakluyt remarked, would lure able English shipwrights back from Denmark, where they had been driven "for want of employment at home."[110] He offered no further elaboration on the reasons for English shipwrights' underemployment, but his argument for Newfoundland's value, part of a wider but unsuccessful effort to promote a colony there, hinted at the absence or cost of domestic naval stores. This implicit nod toward scarcity suggested that the decay of at least one English industry stemmed from a dearth of resources rather than from the onerous demands of European and Mediterranean potentates or religious persecution.

By the time Hakluyt published the first edition of his compilation of travel narratives, *Principall Navigations*, in 1589, wood shortages made a small but explicit appearance in one of the texts it contained: Thomas Harriot's *Brief and True Report*. Harriot noted that iron might profitably be produced in "Virginia" (the present-day coast of North Carolina) because of the "want of wood and dearness thereof in England."[111] Though Harriot's brief comment was the only mention of wood shortage in Hakluyt's collection of texts on Virginia, it explicitly introduced the fear of resource shortages as a justification for expansion. Hakluyt's writings made recourse to the language of decay and redemption but cast shortages as the result of political and economic actions, not the natural fertility of England. As such, his writing stands out for its relatively nuanced political ecology and for his capacity to put natural limits, trade policy, and improvement into conversation. Few contemporaries would follow this approach.

In contrast, promotional writing to justify the settlements along the James River in Virginia at the beginning of the seventeenth century made consistent arguments about acute shortages of natural resources and largely ignored the trade policies that Hakluyt had emphasized. Moreover, the publication of these tracts coincided with James's early efforts to rationalize royal landholdings and reform domestic forestry practices. In doing so, Virginia Company promoters set their enterprise in direct competition with contemporary efforts to discover new stores of resources in England through surveying and reformed forest management. In his 1609 tract, *A Good Speed to Virginia*, Robert Gray used a pastoral metaphor to explain the need for English expansion overseas: "For we see the husbandman deal with his grounds when they are overcharged with cattle, he removes them from one ground to another, and so he provideth well both for his cattle and for his ground." According to Gray, England had a fixed productive capacity. Once the population increased beyond a breaking point, "hereupon comes oppression, and diverse kinds of wrongs, mutinies, sedition, commotion, & rebellion, scarcity, dearth, poverty, and sundry sorts of calamities, which either breed the conversion, or eviction, of cities and commonwealths." To avoid these impending upheavals, colonization was essential.[112] Unlike Hakluyt, however, Gray argued that England's population was bumping against natural limits. To "provide well" for English subjects and the natural world required population reduction through migration to colonies, not reforms in policies or practices.

Gray's *Good Speed* argued that England's increased population had threatened the commonwealth and had pressed England's natural resources to the limit. There was neither enough land to support the population without destructive enclosure nor enough grain to feed them. Other writers promoting Virginia specifically described catastrophic wood shortages to make their cases. A 1610 pamphlet from the Council for Virginia lamented, "Our mils of Iron, and excess of building, have already turned our greatest woods into pasture and champion, within these few years; neither the scattered Forests of England, nor the diminished Groves of Ireland, will supply the defect of our Navy." Another worried that "continual cutting [in England] . . . [was] such a sickness and wasting consumption, as all the physick in England cannot cure."[113] Timber shortage was crucial to the construction of landscape in Virginia. In 1612, the notable settler and writer John Smith began his description of "things which are natural" with trees. Oak and walnut, according to Smith, dominated Virginia's woodlands. These trees were "so tall and straight, that they will bear two foot and a half square of good timber for 20 yards long."[114] Smith's description of Virginia's oaks corresponded exactly to "standards," the tall, straight trees most desirable for shipbuilding and those counted in surveys of royal forests.[115]

The Virginia Company promoters' appeal to wood shortages was a canny political maneuver. Hakluyt's early writings and Harriot's *Brief and True Report* predated the 1588 defeat of the Armada. In the aftermath of that battle and England's improbable victory, naval power became even more important for the English state. Moreover, after James I became king following Elizabeth I's death, he took a personal interest in the active management of royal forests, a maneuver that the politically connected leaders of the Virginia Company would have noticed.[116] Casting Virginia as the solution to a domestic problem that had become part of James's royal agenda offered a powerful justification for the colonial enterprise that transcended the profit-driven nature of the Virginia Company. At the same time, the Virginia Company's proposals tacitly assumed that James's efforts to reform domestic English forestry would fail.

Early writers in Virginia persisted in arguing for shortages, despite experiencing firsthand the difficulties of producing economically viable timber in Virginia. Writing after the so-called Massacre of 1622, Edward Waterhouse claimed, "The Iron, which hath so wasted our English Woods, (that it self in short time must decay with them) is to be had in Virginia (where wasting of Woods is an ease and benefit to the Planter)." Like promoters of Irish plantations in the 1580s, Waterhouse used purported wood shortages in England to justify deforestation in support of English settlers and at the expense of the Native populations. John Smith, whose 1624 *General History* suggested familiarity with arguments from Sir Dudley Digges and other East India Company defenders, nonetheless persisted in citing wood shortage as an economic incentive to plant colonies. Smith knew the risks that came with the failure to be economically viable. In a later text, he recalled how the stores of timber, wainscot, and other woodland commodities sent back from Virginia in the earliest days of settlement had failed "to answer the Merchants' expectations with profit," without which "they would leave us there as banished men."[117] Smith and other promoters used the rhetoric of wood scarcity to cast Virginia as the only viable option for timber, but their words did not sway merchants who could acquire woodland products closer to home.

The shifting notions of scarcity in descriptions and promotional pamphlets reveal that England's Atlantic colonies fit awkwardly into English political ecologies of wood. Colonial promoters' timing suggests that they responded to attempts to survey woods or reform forest bureaucracy and practices, but the challenges and difficulties that domestic projects faced went unmentioned. In pamphlet literature designed to attract skilled colonists, that is unsurprising, but the efforts to profit from colonial woods suggest that promotional rhetoric had taken root in many investors' and governors' minds. Many attempts to exploit colonial trees failed because of the difficulty understanding the unique characteristics of woods and trees outside England; struggles finding markets; the absence of labor both skilled and general; and competition from domestic, colonial, and European enterprises. Others never got off the ground due to lack of interest and investment. For many early modern English observers, Digges's quip about Virginia being a land "men know not what to do withall" must have seemed an accurate assessment of many early colonial projects.[118] Nonetheless, just as some domestic reformers had promised both profits and preservation by transferring royal woods to private control despite evidence to the contrary, colonial promoters similarly held out hope that profits would, eventually, arrive.

Contrary to colonial promoters' claims about scarcity, the history of domestic forestry in the late sixteenth and early seventeenth centuries demonstrates that England was not a completely deforested land. Nor had English leaders given up on the ability of English woods to meet domestic needs. Policies from Tudor and Stuart monarchs sought to create a forestry system that would provide for present and future needs while yielding consistent profits. Political conflict and the failure of wood prices to meet anticipated levels left many wooded lands unexploited. Colonial promoters had claimed that the lack of wood in England necessitated timbering and manufacturing projects in Ireland and across the Atlantic. In reality, projects to exploit colonial woods had to compete against ongoing domestic enterprises, rather than simply taking over activities halted by scarcity.

CHAPTER 2

Creating Scarcity in Ireland's Woods

In 1611, Lord Deputy Arthur Chichester, the king's chief representative and head of the quasi-autonomous English government in Ireland, warned the English Privy Council, the monarch's chief advisers who also exercised significant control over Irish affairs from Whitehall, about the state of Ireland's woods. The Privy Council, wrote Chichester, was concerned about the "rarity and decay" of timber in England and had urged the royal government in Dublin to "have the king's woods preserved here for the building and repairing of his Majesty's ships and royal navy." Unfortunately, Chichester replied, "there are no woods of his Majesty's left here."[1]

As we saw at the end of Chapter 1, with the notable exception of Richard Hakluyt, most colonial promoters writing since the 1580s had sought to establish an imperial political ecology based on a simple premise: England suffered from wood scarcity and colonies stocked with abundant woods provided a solution. The Privy Council's request to Chichester served as an early test for that claim. His response represented a failure. Less than three decades after promotional promises about Ireland's arboreal abundance, at a moment of intensified concern about scarcity in England, following James's efforts to survey, sell, and reform royal lands, and as the competing colonial enterprise in Virginia championed its own supplies of woods, the leader of the Dublin government lamented that the king had no woods in Ireland. Rather than offering a solution to scarcity anxieties in England, Chichester's response suggests that, to some contemporaries, Ireland had become yet another problem.

To ascribe this moment of scarcity to deforestation or to the disjuncture between metropolitan plans and on-the-ground realities, however, minimizes its complexity. According to Chichester, the issue was not simply a lack of trees. He lamented that it was true that colonists had cut down the "best and fairest timber" to sell "in parts beyond the seas" despite his repeated public proclamations against their actions. But other parts of the letter suggest the continued presence of usable woods. Chichester informed the Privy Council that, despite the lack of royally owned timber, the state could still "purchase such woods and woodlands by exchanges or some other good means."[2] There were enough serviceable trees in Ireland, despite the actions of colonists, to serve the Crown, but those trees were in the hands of private individuals not the state. The actions of the Dublin and London governments had created scarcity in a kingdom still stocked with trees.

As Chichester's letter to the Privy Council suggests, concerns about wood scarcity in Ireland were often the result of paper deforestations. Scarcity was conjured in struggles over legal title and access to woods or in efforts from London and Dublin governments to locate supplies they controlled rather than the actual mass clearance of trees, but there were changes in the Irish landscape that reflected the political ecologies of planters. Relying on claims from the London and Dublin governments, historians have tended to argue that planters, the English and Scottish individuals who acquired land in Ireland made available through the mass seizure and redistribution of land known as plantations, engaged in significant woodland destruction. Either planters engaged in "asset stripping" fueled by their ravenous desire for instant profit or, only marginally better, they saw Irish woods as an "opportunity cost" that detracted from their more valuable rentable land, quickly leading to deforestation.[3] The estate papers of large landholders offer a contrasting view, revealing planters' often obsessive concern with guarding wood rights against competitors and purportedly destructive tenants.[4] As both perspectives indicate, there were real changes in the seventeenth-century Irish landscape, and understanding them requires disentangling the London and Dublin governments' critiques over use and ownership from the landholders' efforts at estate management. It requires distinguishing their contrasting political ecologies.

Woodland management on the estates of Richard Boyle, Earl of Cork and the largest landholder in seventeenth-century Ireland, offers an example of how planters adopted strategies to manage woods for consistent yields as well as present profits. Boyle and other planters developed an alternative political ecology from that of the London or Dublin governments. Theirs was not simply instrumental or parochial. Instead, they sought to build commercial connections from Ireland's woods to English and Continental markets and to manage woods to serve these enterprises. Boyle and his estate managers worried about scarcity and destruction, too, but their concerns reflected a different political ecology than that put forth in complaints about waste coming from London or Dublin. These competing political ecologies are essential to understanding the discourse of scarcity in Ireland and beyond and the shifts in Ireland's wooded landscape in the late sixteenth and early seventeenth centuries.

*　　*　　*

Chichester's inability to meet the Privy Council's demand for Irish woods to address English scarcity began in the aftermath of a revolt by Irish nobility angry at their diminished power and at the increasing interference from England in the sixteenth century known as the Second Desmond Rebellion. According to the poet and Irish colonial official Edmund Spenser, hunger and famine more than military victory ended the conflict in 1583. "Out of every corner of the woods and glens they came creeping forth upon their hands," he wrote, "for their legs could not bear them; they looked Anatomies [of] death, they spake like ghosts, crying out of their graves." The famine was so brutal that the Irish "did eat of the carrions, happy where they could find them, yea, and one another soon after, in so much as the very carcasses they spared not to scrape out of their graves." Military conflict in Munster, one of Ireland's four provinces, had spilled over into an ecological war, and "a most populous and plentiful country [was] suddenly left void of man or beast."[5] In the wake of this destruction, politicians, soldiers, and intellectuals weighed in on Munster's future. Their solutions ranged from relatively conservative calls for exemplary punishments of a few rebel leaders and a return to the status quo to radical plans to seize vast tracts of land and remake the landscape and the people. In the end, the Elizabethan state favored a radical solution that had been hinted at and attempted on a smaller scale throughout the sixteenth century—plantations.[6]

The Munster Plantation was a project of unprecedented scale and bureaucratic complexity in Ireland, comparable to the seizure and redistribution of church lands in England by Henry VIII, known as the Dissolution of the Monasteries. The goal of the policy was to remake Ireland into an orderly and profitable kingdom through the seizure of vast swaths of land from rebels and the replacement of the existing population by planting English settlers who would blossom into productive subjects and whose example would lead the Irish to reform their rebellious ways. To accomplish this goal, however, the governments in London and Dublin faced profound technical challenges. English officials lacked knowledge about land in Munster. They were uncertain how to value it and what exactly was there. As a result, they undertook a series of mapping projects and surveys to determine the extent and value of the land available to English planters and to determine the tax revenue due to the Crown from the newly planted lands. Like roughly contemporary projects to survey English royal forests, these documents represented efforts to "see" land in ways that would maximize its potential to increase royal revenue.[7] Many of the same problems that plagued surveys in England carried over into Ireland—quantitative data was inconsistent, definitions of resources or landforms were imprecise, and local people often resisted divulging information that they feared might harm them—but lower quantities of already existing records; the disorderly aftermath of war; and the barriers of religious, cultural, and linguistic difference made the task even more difficult. Architects of the plantations hoped for a clearly presented landscape, but the resulting maps and surveys reveal blind spots and blurred vision that would go on to shape the grants of seized land that followed.

Throughout the sixteenth century, English writers railed against perceived Irish land use and connected the state of the Irish landscape to the state of Irish politics. The Irish, according to these writers, refused to farm, preferring to keep large herds of cattle. Irish pastoralism, they complained, enabled disorder and rebellion by allowing warlike chiefs and criminal "horseboys" to dominate the countryside. Sixteenth-century English writers used invective about the Irish landscape to impugn the Old English—largely Catholic descendants of the twelfth-century Anglo-Norman conquest—as well as any English planters who failed to turn Ireland to tillage. According to these writers, anything short of the radical transformation of the Irish landscape signaled that English settlers had "degenerated" to the level of the Irish.[8]

Proponents of the Munster Plantation claimed that the project would lead to cultural reformation, military security, and profits for the Crown and planters, but attitudes toward Irish woods as repositories of barbarism complicated these goals. John Derricke's *The Image of Irelande with a Discovery of Woodkarne* (1581) embodied this animosity. The "woodkarne" or "woodkern" of the title "affirm their dissolute life and inordinate living better to pertain unto infidels and heathen than for those which in any respect profess the name of Christ." They possessed "wild shamrock manners" and were like "the Devil" and "the Wolf." An image of a defeated rebel consorting with wolves surrounded by trees ensured that readers connected these perfidious individuals with the landscape included in their title (Figure 1).[9] Yet supporters of plantations vacillated between condemnations of a disordered, woody landscape and calls for the Crown and planters to put Ireland's woods to use for the state.[10] These two perspectives on Irish woods pushed in different directions. If wooded landscapes were necessarily shelters for rogues and rebels,

Figure 1: A defeated Irish rebel consorts with wolves in the woods. John Der-ricke, *The Image of Irelande with a Discoverie of Woodkarne* (London, 1581), plate 11, Centre for Research Studies, Special Collections (De.3.76), University of Edinburgh Library. Image courtesy of University of Edinburgh Library, Cre-ative Commons License.

then deforestation was essential to good order. If Irish timber was an essential resource for an English state facing scarcity, then English planters and the Dublin government would need to preserve them while finding other ways to control rebellious subjects. The systems of measuring, valuing, and distributing lands for plantations reflected attempts to balance these impulses.

In the articles that plantation commissioners developed to govern the plantation over the course of the 1580s, ideas about improvement through agriculture trumped calls to use Irish woods for the state. Only one of the sixteen articles propounded to govern the Munster Plantation addressed evaluating the physical environment, requiring that land be valued "according to the goodness of the soil" and taxed by the acre.[11] The instructions, however, offered no method to assess "goodness," a problem that contemporaries immediately perceived. In a marginal notation on one edition of this document, Geoffrey Fenton, secretary to the Lord Deputy of Ireland, questioned whether land measured and taxed included "wood, bog, and other barren ground."[12] In June 1586, roughly six months after the draft articles were written, Sir Valentine Browne, one of the commissioners for the plantation and a planter himself, added two amendments to the articles. His first required that planters "replenished" wasteland and used it to maintain protestant clergy to serve the English planters and convert the Irish. Immediately thereafter, he created an exemption for planters holding lands in any of the mountain ranges in Kerry, arguing that those wilds were unimprovable.[13] Fenton's marginal comments and Browne's amendments reveal a system that emphasized conversion of so-called wastes to tillage but offered generous tax exemptions from a system of valuation that would encourage that transformation. Moreover, the instructions avoided any discussion of woods or bogs as state resources, a departure from an initial order to locate woods fit for timber near navigable rivers, the type of woodlands regularly preserved in contemporary English statutes.[14]

The final version of the document, produced in June 1586, codified these patterns for evaluating the landscape.[15] Land was to be valued by county without any distinctions based on the "goodness" of soil. Bogs, woods, and wastes were to be treated as tax-exempt commons, but they, nonetheless, were granted as part of planters' seignories. Planters were only responsible for the tax burden of these lands if they admitted to improving them, though they would be taxed at a lower rate. The only reference to woods was an allowance for the undertakers of 12,000-acre seignories to impark 600 acres for deer, for breeding horses, or as a free warren, with smaller undertakers allowed to enclose a proportionate amount of their granted lands.[16] The articles for the undertakers treated woodlands either as a wasteland or as a space for planters to engage in elite pastimes. The Elizabethan government failed to reserve any woodlands for the Crown or the navy while simultaneously creating an ambiguous system of taxation and measurement that offered half-hearted incentives for improvement.

Two maps from 1586 captured the uncertainties about Irish land reflected in the articles governing the plantation. The "Plot of the attainted lands" (Figure 2) cast Munster as a blank space, divided by red lines representing the boundaries of lands available for plantation. Large rivers and six castles, representing Kinsale, Cork, Youghal, Dungarvan, Waterford, and Limerick, provided the only acknowledgment of physical or built environments.[17] The "Plot for a Parishe in Ireland" (Figure 3), a schematic drawing for the layout of a model seignory in Munster, exemplified the plantation authorities' emphasis on universal solutions rather than on responses to specific local conditions. The image of the model parish was organized on a square grid set against a white background, intimating its ability to be placed down anywhere and widely reproduced across the planted lands. Unlike the articles, this system of division assumed a landscape without bogs, woods, marshes, or other landforms considered waste. Its only nod to the variations within

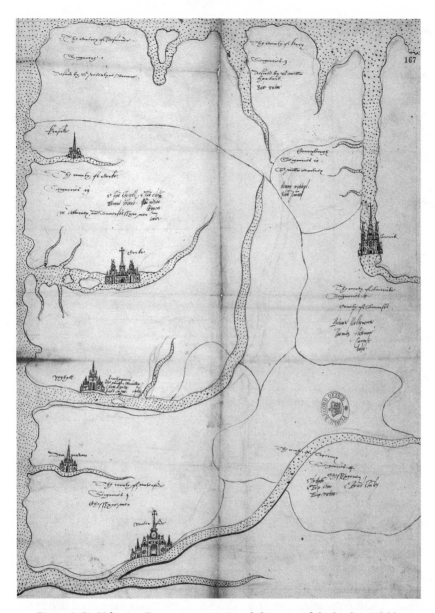

Figure 2: Sir Valentine Browne commissioned this map of the lands available for plantation in Munster. The mapmaker focused on waterways and urban settlements, leaving the remainder of the landscape as blank space. "Ireland: Munster," 17 June 1586, Maps and Plans Extracted from the State Papers (MPF) 1/273, National Archives (UK). Image reproduced by permission of the National Archives (UK).

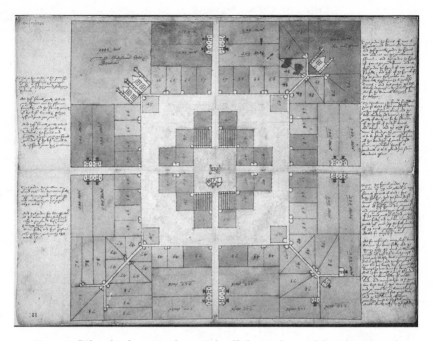

Figure 3: "The plot for a Parishe in Ireland" depicted a model settlement and
arrangement for lands granted in Munster. The marginal text offered further
instructions and clarifications on the image, noting the locations for buildings
and providing a key to the color scheme. "The platte fro a parishe in Irlande,"
January 1585/1586, MPF 1/305, National Archives (UK). Image reproduced by
permission of the National Archives (UK).

actual landscapes was the reluctant admission that the mill should be located
"as the commodity of water will serve." All the land in the parish was divided
into cornfield and common pasture.[18]

Other documents from the same period reinforce the plot's emphasis
on reproducible settlement patterns and a lack of concern for provisions for
woods. The authorship of the plot is uncertain, but its original placement in
the State Papers indicates that it may have accompanied a set of orders sent
to Sir Valentine Browne by Elizabeth I's advisers William Cecil, Christopher
Hatton, and Francis Walsingham. This set of orders for Munster dated at the
same time as the letter offered further instructions on settling parishes. Like
the plot, the instructions offered a universal vision of a settlement that could
be reproduced throughout the province. Some land was to be reserved from
each parish for the queen, but the instructions specified that it was to "consist only of tithe corn." The instructions elaborated on some of the categories

mentioned in the plot, providing a breakdown of the professions of settlers, but these too point to an emphasis on agriculture. There were to be farmers, gardeners, people skilled in growing hops, a tailor, and a shoemaker. The only professions suggesting some interaction with wood were a carpenter and a smith, though the smith was to be there "for shoeing [animals] and ploughstaffs."[19] At no point did either the plot or its accompanying instructions outline the regulation of common resources. In their grants and plans, plantation authorities focused on ways to create an agricultural society but did not make efforts to secure resources for the state or to suggest regulations to provide woods as common resources to support their model communities.

Instead, a sample form of a land grant demonstrates that the plantation granted nearly absolute control over all natural resources to individual undertakers. Undertakers held "land, tenements, meadows, pastures, wastes, heaths, moors, bogs, woods, underwoods, waters, watercourses, fishings, mines, quarries, profits, commodities, and hereditaments." The list recognized diverse landforms, including pastoral and nonagricultural lands like woods and bogs as something separate from waste. It also looked beyond a landed economy by granting aquatic and mineral rights. It did not, however, leave anything for the state.[20]

Other documents from 1587 show that plantation authorities and planters remained focused on arable land as the sole measure of value. A survey of Walter Ralegh's seignory only concerned itself with "countable" land—not bog, heath, or waste.[21] A series of twenty-seven certificates recording the transfer of land between undertakers followed a similar pattern. Only six certificates gave any detail about land other than the presence of a castle or the number of plowlands contained therein. Four of these six made brief references to wood, with two noting the presence of a "great wood." The other two recorded fishing rights and the presence of a park with a water mill.[22] The references to woods in some of the certificates indicated that at least some individual planters and state authorities were beginning to recognize woods, particularly large ones, as potential resources. Nonetheless, the lack of detail beyond the number of plowlands or the presence of a castle in most certificates suggests that the focus of many planters and plantation authorities remained focused on land as an abstract commodity.[23]

Maps from 1587 show that English surveyors provided more detailed representations of the Irish landscape. Arthur Robins, one of the four surveyors appointed to survey and map the area to be planted, depicted escheated lands in County Limerick (Figure 4). Robins attempted to situate the lands available for plantation, marked with a red line, within the social and physical

Figure 4: Arthur Robins's map of County Limerick displayed much more detailed local and natural knowledge than previous representations by including the presence of wooded land and mountainous terrain. "The Plotte of the greatt Countey of Lymbrik," 1587, MPF 1/97, National Archives (UK). Image reproduced by permission of the National Archives (UK).

geography of the county, depicting rivers, hills, and wooded lands. He clustered trees in particular areas, suggesting the broader geography of woodlands in the county.[24] One of the most detailed maps from the period, a hand-colored plat of the manor and lands of Tralee, County Kerry (Figure 5), struggled to capture the complexity of the Irish landscape. It depicted the legal distinctions within the recently escheated lands, showing the fragmentary nature of settlements even within a single manor and attempted to capture natural features. It marked wooded areas with images of trees, bogs with dotted clusters and a label, and hilly or mountainous land with images of

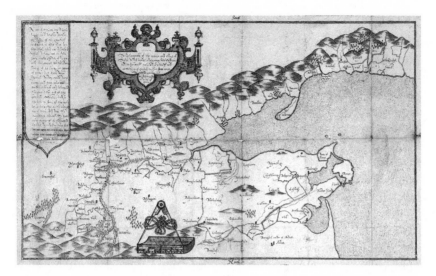

Figure 5: This map was also likely produced as a part of the survey of plantation lands. The text in the upper left describes the image and land measurement. A tear obscures the name of the maker. Map of the manor and abbey of Tralee, County Kerry, September 1587, MPF 1/309, National Archives (UK). Image reproduced by permission of the National Archives (UK).

mountains. It used textual markers to identify waste against larger settlement holdings. Yet both maps admitted the difficulties in coping with the Irish landscape. The dense but indistinct scattering of trees and hills in Robins's map frustrated his precise red borders. The boundaries of escheated lands might be clear, but the state struggled to see inside those lines. Even when mapmakers took a closer look, as in the survey of Tralee, they were unable to create a clear picture. The maker of that map noted that more waste and bog occurred throughout the lands than he had labeled or depicted. Even without this omission, woods blurred boundaries, sometimes appearing within granted land and sometimes adorning land clearly labeled as "waste."[25] Despite these struggles, mapmakers at least attempted to wrestle with the complexities of the Irish landscape.

In contrast, the plantation administration plodded forward, championing tillage and disciplined animal husbandry. In 1589, the Elizabethan government sent a survey of twelve questions to undertakers to gauge the progress of the plantations; the questions focused on crop yields, the number of cattle, and the number of settlers. The answers ranged from relatively detailed descriptions of the estates to chronicles of ignorance and disappointment about the land, people, and even legal title of their holdings.[26] The system of taxation and land valuation contained in the articles governing plantations colored the responses to the survey and left the plantation authorities and the Elizabethan state unable to see how planters used their lands. Land grants, the articles, and plantation administrators had strongly encouraged improvement and tillage, but they imposed increased taxes on settlers who had improved land. As a result, planters needed to strike a balance in their replies between providing evidence that they had made an effort at fulfilling the conditions attached to their grant and disclosing improvements that might substantially increase their tax duties. Between the incentives for evasive responses and questions focused on quantities of settlers, cattle, and crops, the Irish governors had only an obscured, partial view of the newly planted landscape.

The 1589 surveys, even with their limitations, offered at least a rough view of the contours of plantation agriculture in Munster, but woods fell entirely outside their bureaucratic gaze. The 1587 certificates previously had hinted at the potential to develop Munster's woods as a resource, and images like Robins's map showed that wood was an essential part of the Irish landscape and implied that it should not be ignored when assessing planted lands. Elizabethan plantation authorities, however, remained focused on agriculture and pastoralism. They measured success or failure in quantities of settlers, grain, and cattle. If the authors of the surveys were familiar with the contemporaneous efforts to gather information on and more effectively manage English forests, the questions they sent to Munster planters bore no evidence of the connections between Irish woods and English needs championed by earlier plantation promoters.

In contrast, individual planters collected much more detailed information about their seignories that recognized the potential to exploit a diverse range of natural resources. The disjuncture between private and government knowledge can be seen clearly in John White's 1598 estate map of Mogeely, County Cork (Figure 6). White, the artist who painted the images of Carolina Algonquians that appeared in the 1590 edition of Thomas Harriot's famous *Briefe and True Report*, created an estate map in 1598 for Sir Walter Ralegh that showed how Ralegh had categorized lands according to use on the estate. White depicted the castle and settlement at Mogeely as well as surrounding settlements along the River Bride. The map showed a well-wooded landscape with heavy concentrations of trees at "Mogile Wood," "Kilcorane," "the Wood Close," and along the banks of the Bride. Fences with visible gates surrounded named lands from the eastern edge of Bromfield and the Lime Field to the western edge of the Lower Road Close and the New Close and from

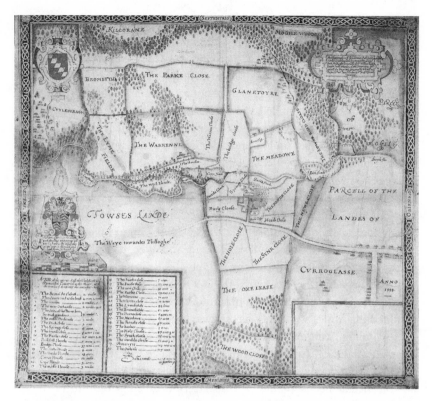

Figure 6: This estate map of Mogeely, County Cork, showed land use and division. Vague writing in a contemporary hand listing tenant names near images of cottages suggests that the map served a pragmatic function as well as an aesthetic one. John White (attributed), "A topographical lineament of all such enclosed lands as are holden by Henrye Pyne, Esquire, from the Right Honourable Sir Walter Raley, Knight," 1598, Lismore Castle Papers, MS 22,068, National Library of Ireland. Image reproduced by permission of the National Library of Ireland.

the northern edge of the Park Close to the Tallow Road. Labels on the map show a landscape divided, organized, and enclosed according to different economic and social needs. The map showed an agricultural system focused on mixed husbandry (the barley field, heath, and meadow) as well as elite sport and diet (the park and warren).[27]

Leases for the same area show that White's map was, in many ways, a fiction. Rivers, marshes, and woods that served as boundaries in leases for Curraglass and Lisnabreen are absent from the map. Several leases for Lisnabreen and Curraglass mention a creek dividing the two settlements, a natural feature

that is absent amid White's linear, planned cluster of houses. Edward Lochland's provision for Henry Morris to build a mill and watercourse also demonstrates the presence of water in and around the settlement, acting as a natural
barrier and a resource. Woods served as boundaries in Lee's and Morris's
leases, suggesting that Curraglass was not as distinct from the surrounding
woods as White's map implied. On the western side of Mogeely Castle, a lease
between Guy Toose and Henry Pyne recorded a plot of marshland adjacent to
Mogeely.[28] White's map sought to render woods as a resource clearly demar-
cated from other uses. Nonetheless, it managed to show systems of management for a diverse array of landscapes, including woods. The state only saw
white space or scattered trees: individual landowners had a much richer view.

Yet even with access to more detailed information about Irish land,
woods continued to pose a problem for sixteenth-century planters. Thomas
Harriot, who took up some of Ralegh's lands in Munster after returning from
North America, struggled with the same issues defining good and bad land
that had plagued the state. Harriot's 1589 map of Munster (Figure 7) drew
on Robins's survey and the land descriptions reported to commissioners. It
provided the names and locations of several settlements in the area as well as
the location of rivers and woodlands. The map showed a landscape with considerable stands of woods surrounding the settlements at the confluence of
the Blackwater and Bride: Mogeely, Lisfinny, Tallow, and Kilmacow. The keen
naturalistic and ethnographic interests Harriot had shown for the landscape
and peoples surrounding Roanoke did not appear in this map. Instead, a cap-
tion in the upper left noted, "There is much barren and very bad grounds"
and warned that to "divide the same exactly from the good ground [was] a
matter very intricate to be performed and scant worth the travail." Harriot
visually and textually effaced the cultivation history of the area. Moreover,
his text undermined the official definition and division of the Irish landscape
that underpinned the valuation and taxation of granted lands.[29] Instead, both
his image and his text claimed that the Irish landscape was too complex to
divide land into good and bad.

Harriot seemed to worry that Munster's landscape resisted easy division between waste and cultivation, but the makers of other records had a
clearer vision. A written survey of the lands at the former Blackfriars abbey
at Molana showed a long history of use and the presence of the infrastructure
for agriculture, light manufacturing, and urban settlements. The map labeled
"waste grounds and commons" belonging to Molana and "part of the lands
of the abbey of Molana" on the near shore at Templemichael, but it gave no
further verbal or visual information on these lands. The survey, in contrast,

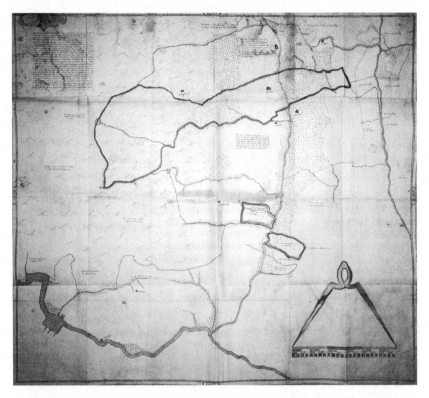

Figure 7: The interplay between the text and visual representations in this map detailing lands in Counties Cork and Waterford captures the difficulties representing the Irish landscape. Thomas Harriot (attributed), "The description of Mogeley Shahan Lissinien Tullough Kilbeg [. . .]," 28 August 1589, Dartmouth Collection of Maps of Ireland, P/49(29), National Maritime Museum. © National Maritime Museum, Greenwich, London.

provided rich detail on the lands affiliated with the abbey and their use. The abbey itself was ruined, but nonetheless contained two damaged but functional weirs and the remnants of a garden and an orchard, a common feature of late medieval monastic lands in Ireland. The abbey also held lands and rectories throughout the surrounding countryside that the survey described in detail. Templemichael had twelve acres of arable land, six acres of pasture, and a weir. Other assets included a ruined mill, one town with eight cottages, two waste towns, and two wasted monasteries. The survey recorded the quantities and values of arable land for each. The list of duties due to the monastery, included in a later copy of the survey, suggested that the divisions between arable and pasture maintained preexisting limits, noting that Templemichael could return enough corn to begin repairs on the ruined church "if the said lands are tilled and manured (as in times past they have been)."[30] The survey for Molana gestured toward a return to past productivity and gradual improvement to existing structures, not to the radical transformation of blank space.

The survey and other estate records from the first decades of the Munster Plantation make it clear that many planters valued woods. The survey reported that multiple towns had wood and underwood that yielded a yearly rent. It also listed a value for furze and turf—alternatives to wood fuel—assigned to another town.[31] Ralegh took several steps to prevent exploitation of his woods. His leases provided only limited rights to timber, and he hired a woodward to enforce these limitations. Tenants were allowed to cut timber in the wood at Lisfinny for the purposes of building their houses. Ralegh explicitly exempted "great timber" from another lease and retained his rights to the woods at the Shane Wood and Ballyduff, granting the tenant access to coppices, indicating that he had adopted a system of woodland conservation and regeneration as early as the 1580s. Between 1602 and 1611, Richard Boyle, who purchased Ralegh's seignories and eventually became the Earl of Cork, began acquiring substantial woodland rights along with lands around Ballynatray, Kilmacow, Kill St. Nicholas, Mogeely, and Cappoquin. Like Ralegh, Boyle's grants and leases show that he carefully regulated woodland access and rights for his tenants.[32] The state largely ignored the presence of woods in Ireland, and several planters expressed distaste at the quantities of "bad" lands they possessed. In contrast, Ralegh and Boyle took steps to manage and preserve the woods on their newly granted lands.

The Dublin government and planters like Ralegh and Boyle simply saw Irish woods differently. The state, when it perceived Irish woods at all, had treated them mainly as wastes that reduced the taxable value of granted lands or nuisances that blurred clear lines of demarcation on maps. Planters, in contrast, sought to mirror English techniques for estate management and treated Irish woods as resources to be husbanded and exploited as sources of profit.[33] This difference created the conditions for the London and Dublin governments' worries about wood shortages at the beginning of the seventeenth century once they finally took up earlier proposals to seek solutions for English scarcity in Irish woods.

The London and Dublin governments' new concern with Irish woods emerged directly from contemporary events in England. Beginning in 1604 when James I attempted to rationalize Crown forest holdings and reform forestry practice, the wave of surveyors and commissioners sent to collect information necessary to enact this program returned reports that stoked new fears that England's forests were in dire shape.[34] These reports drove further efforts at domestic reform, but the Privy Council also looked to Ireland to find other, hopefully better maintained sources of wood.

The newfound desire for preservation marked a shift in government policy toward Irish woods. In 1601, as the Nine Years' War, the revolt led by Hugh O'Neill, Earl of Tyrone, which marked the bloody and ignominious end of the Munster Plantation, raged in Ireland, the Privy Council ordered George Carew, Lord President of Munster, to investigate Henry Pyne at the behest of Sir Walter Ralegh. According to an informant, Pyne had defrauded Ralegh and other business partners who had jointly invested in a plan to convert woods on their estates to pipe and barrel staves and to sell those abroad. Pipe and barrel staves were the raw materials for the containers carrying commercial products around Europe and would become profitable trade goods, but, despite the potential profits, Ralegh objected to Pyne's actions. He alleged that his woods had been so spoiled by the successful enterprise that his losses reached into thousands of pounds. In 1593, in a note to Ralegh describing the scale of the business, Pyne claimed to have shipped 350,000 pipe staves from Munster to Seville, the Canary Islands, Middleborough, London, and Bristol. The Privy Council focused on the allegation of fraud; the heavy felling of trees went unmentioned outside the role of woods in providing possible reparations to Ralegh. Yet, in 1583, as the plantation was being planned, several tracts of wood near Mogeely had been marked as "lands as have timber trees fit for building of ships to be reserved."[35] In his response to the charges, Pyne never addressed the allegations that he spoiled the woods. Instead, he informed the Privy Council that they had been given bad information, detailed his actions to defend Mogeely Castle against the Irish rebels, and solicited a letter from Lord Deputy Charles Blount, Baron Mountjoy attesting to Pyne's good character. The Privy Council accepted this defense and judged that Pyne "hath honestly discharged himself of all such matters whereof he was accused."[36]

Pyne had previously been accused of spoiling woods in the same area and evaded consequences even more easily. In 1593, the Irish landowner Patrick Condon claimed that Pyne had illegally felled trees on his Munster lands. The judges who adjudicated the case ruled that Pyne had done nothing wrong. He had felled trees, but they were not part of the lands granted in the plantation. Moreover, Pyne was able to produce a lease from Condon that the court accepted as justification for cutting.[37] As in the later allegations from Ralegh, the issue was not spoiling woods—it was about permission, title, and properly distributing the profits thereof. Boards cut from Irish trees were being shipped to several European ports instead of buttressing the wooden walls of the English navy or merchant ships, but Irish judges and the Privy Council seemed unconcerned with upholding the political ecology put forth by plantation promoters in the 1580s.

James's push to measure England's royal forests and manage them to produce ship timber for the navy and profits for the Crown prompted the Privy Council to look again at Munster's woods as a state resource. But when the Privy Council began to do so, the members found that their previous inattention had created difficulties supplying trees to the state. In 1608, Robert Cecil, Earl of Salisbury and James I's secretary of state, sent over a servant, Philip Cottingham, to investigate available ship timber in Ireland, take a sample of the woods, and provide a list of trees to be reserved for the navy. He received warning from Ireland that Cottingham would struggle to complete his task. Lord Deputy Arthur Chichester worried that all the best timber near rivers and coasts had been wasted. Without these trees, he lamented, the navy would have difficulty building ships.[38] Chichester informed Cecil that Ireland could not supply the trees the Privy Council requested and claimed that deforestation was responsible.

Other government officials, however, disagreed on both the severity and the causes of issues procuring timber. Geoffrey Fenton, who had helped author the regulations and grants for planters in Munster, warned that if the king sought woods to which he held title he would find little on offer, but Fenton did not share Chichester's anxiety about the destruction of trees. Instead, he treated scarcity mainly as a problem of ownership. According to Fenton, the king did not have rights to most of Munster's woods and would need to take his supply from the "pretended proprietors." This was not to be a serious problem: "I am of mind that the matter will not be stuck at nor any opposition made since the cutting down of the woods will greatly secure the Country and yet bring no damage to the owners who take no benefit by them other than to look upon them."[39] Just as he and his colleagues had done in the 1580s, Fenton assumed that woodlands were a nuisance to be destroyed in the course of bringing civilization to Ireland.

Fenton's claims rested on several difficult-to-reconcile assumptions. The Crown, he conceded, did not hold absolute title to trees in Irish woods as it did in England's royal forests, but he claimed that these legal niceties were unnecessary in Ireland. Irish woods were worthless, except as sources of diversion and aesthetic pleasure. And Fenton clearly implied that security, order, and service to the state should outweigh such uses and that, in most cases, planters would eagerly accept nominal sums to clear their land of woody nuisances to productive agriculture. At the same time, Fenton failed to recognize that Crown interest in Irish timber conveyed value to the woods and suggested that a market existed for Irish trees. Finally, Fenton's description of Irish woods implied that they should be felled completely, and the land permanently converted to agriculture. They were to provide a single, large infusion of timber into the navy's shipyards. This contrasted with the goals of James's reforms to the management of royal forests in England, which sought to create a consistent source of profit and resources.

As Cottingham moved from Dublin to Munster, he discovered the flaws in Fenton's optimistic predictions. Upon Cottingham's arrival in Munster, Boyle and Pyne immediately grabbed hold of him. Pyne recounted in a letter to Cecil how he took Cottingham on a tour of Munster's woods all while arguing that the only realistic choice for quality, low transportation costs, and safe harbors for lading ships were woods that Boyle and Pyne held in partnership. Boyle and Pyne convinced Cottingham that they held the only reliable, cheap, and accessible source of timber in Ireland and immediately set him to work procuring a sample for shipment back to England, providing workmen and charging the Crown for all the costs.[40]

Pyne and Boyle had cornered the market and were eager to lock the Crown into a contract that would allow them to sell wood to the king. Pyne had been exporting pipe staves on Dutch vessels since the 1590s, always skirting the boundaries of legality and surviving investigations from the Privy Council. He knew the land, the merchants, and the market. He and Boyle had plans to ensure that the ships carrying their timber would be Dutch vessels long enough to keep carriage rates down. Other Irish officials, such as the Lord Deputy Sir Arthur Chichester and the Vice Treasurer of Munster Thomas Young, sought to direct the king to other areas, some of which might contain valuable timber, but, as Cottingham reported, none of those locations lay close enough to the sea. Even in those remote areas, the king would need to act swiftly before "some prying and pragmatical heads do . . . forestall the market and engross the woods into their own hands." Their proposals simply could not match those of Pyne and Boyle. Cottingham complained that Pyne "hath sold out all the best timber" but saw no other choice and set to work with Boyle's laborers to assemble a shipment for England.[41]

Fenton had predicted that planters would eagerly part with their trees at cheap rates. Instead, Cottingham encountered a sophisticated commercial enterprise that sought to dictate terms to the state and avaricious Englishmen who responded to the Crown's interest by snapping up any alternative sources of timber. The architects of the Munster Plantation considered woods to be little more than a nuisance, which English settlement would wipe away. As a result, despite calls to identify woods for ship timber in the 1580s, the plantation failed to measure or count woodlands in its grants or to regulate them in the conditions for undertakers. Instead, plantation authorities offered woods to planters with no restrictions. Dutch, Spanish, and other European merchants, however, saw acres upon acres of staves, the raw materials for building the barrels, pipes, and other containers that were essential for early modern European commercial expansion. The English state had failed to look for woodlands, and, when it found them, they were all in private hands.

Chichester responded to the struggles finding wood in Munster with a plan to reform the management of Irish woods. He pleaded with the Privy Council to provide a skilled surveyor to compile an inventory of woods in Ireland and asked for authority to reserve timber trees for naval service from private lands. As members of the English and Irish governments began to plan for a second plantation in Ulster in 1610, they took a more active interest in woods. Royal officers, representatives of the City of London guilds who were to start a plantation, and members of the Irish government went through several rounds of debate over who would own woods and how they should be used. This time, in part at Chichester's urging, the state took care to look out for woods. Nonetheless, the results were similar. The Londoners won possession of woods near Derry and Coleraine on the condition that they be used solely to build the plantation and "not to be converted to merchandise." One year later, Chichester again complained that the king had no woods in all of Ireland and that the only available option was to trade concessions for wood rights with large landholders or to prohibit wood sales except to the king at "reasonable rates."[42] Despite Chichester's pleading, plantation authorities had not changed the policies that had allowed Boyle and Pyne to bully Cottingham into their enterprise in Munster; they merely reproduced it in Ulster.

Chichester's pleas for changes to plantation policy in Ulster reflected shifts in his thinking about the causes of wood scarcity. In 1608, Chichester had worried that the actual destruction of trees threatened the navy's supply, but by 1611 he focused more on use rights and land grants. Chichester had not abandoned his concerns with preserving Irish trees, but his actions suggest that he felt the government would struggle to protect trees on lands it did not control. His pleas to learn from the Munster Plantation and set aside royal forests in Ulster had fallen on deaf ears. Yet again, the issue facing royal access to Irish woods was political scarcity created by overly generous land grants and a lack of foresight by plantation authorities.[43]

Despite years of warnings that the booming international pipe-stave trade and permissive grants of wood rights to planters threatened royal and naval access, the London and Dublin governments only took steps to regulate forestry practices in Ireland in 1611—after plantation authorities refused to set aside woods for the state in Ulster. In January, the Privy Council wrote to Chichester urging him to study "how timber may be maintained and preserved in other places where it is for the good of the State." With this new mandate, Chichester and the Dublin government took actions to preserve woodlands three years after Chichester had first voiced his concerns about the state of Munster's woods. Royal woodwards marked trees throughout Cork and Waterford to be reserved for the king's shipping. The Dublin government also proposed a law to the Irish Parliament banning the removal of bark from standing oak trees and calling for the preservation of timber. The Privy Council and the Dublin government focused their conservation efforts on oak trees deemed useful for the navy. Other actions taken the same year suggest that they were willing to tolerate potentially damaging timber enterprises. Propositions to increase the King's revenue in Ireland suggested taxing ironworks and pipe staves, indicating their willingness to allow actions they believed threatened Irish woods so long as those actions enhanced royal coffers. This kind of thinking became practice when marking trees: Boyle's woods were exempt from royal supervision since he agreed to provide the Crown a portion of any woods he felled.[44]

The exceptions to preservation measures were an effort to achieve compromise between plantation promoters and members of the Dublin government who saw Ireland's woods as a state resource and those, like Fenton, who regarded it merely as a nuisance to be exploited for profit, but they only provided a brief respite from fears of scarcity. In 1615, "E. S.," the author of a survey of Ireland, advocated that planters "ought to be restrained, and if they have offended, against any former proviso to the contrary to be punished, for they have destroyed a mast of good timber for shipping and in the end will consume all the good timber upon South coast." He went on to call for an outright ban on pipe staves, "for no other but ship timber will make pipe staves."[45] The Dublin government had attempted to balance the imperative to preserve ship timber for the navy against the profits to be reaped from pipe staves, but, four years later, a surveyor warned that balance could not be achieved.

The government appeared to heed this warning, but yet again exceptions ensured that the most powerful planters could continue to exploit Ireland's woods. In 1615, they attempted to ban the export of pipe staves. The Irish member of Parliament (MP) and planter John Jephson wrote to Boyle that he was "most undone by this new restraint of pipe staves." In the light of the new restrictions, he informed Boyle that he would "leave now troubling you any farther" over woods. Jephson's fears appear to have been unfounded. He and Boyle entered into a partnership to access woods and sell pipe staves that continued through 1618. Both Boyle and Jephson continued to export pipe staves in such large numbers that, in 1619, a merchant refused to purchase any of the boards from Boyle, claiming, "He was cloyed with that commodity from Sir John Jephson."[46]

Boyle and Jephson were not the only planters to evade the new regulations. In April 1615, the Privy Council wrote to Chichester complaining that English planters and foreigners alike were exporting the best ship timber in direct violation of the ban on exporting pipe staves and called for a complete ban on timber exports. By September, however, the council sent him another letter, ordering him to allow any merchants trading to the East Indies to move timber from Ireland to England for building ships or casks to enable their voyages.[47] For prominent individuals like Boyle and Jephson or important entities like the East India Company, regulations on Irish woods were nuisances to be circumvented, not catastrophic threats to their enterprises. These exceptions were not merely preferential treatment for the powerful; the exception for the East India Company suggested that Irish woods should provide the ligneous sinews for the expanding company-state as well as for England's wooden walls.[48]

Commissioners sent out in 1622 to investigate the state of the Irish plantations reiterated similar complaints to those of Chichester, E. S., and the Privy Council about the destruction of Irish woods. One report lamented that making pipe staves and operating ironworks had created great waste in Munster's woods, listing it as one of the primary defects of that plantation. But, just as earlier analysis had done, the report immediately noted that the waste stemmed not merely from exploitative industries but also from issues of access that left nothing for the state. Another certificate focusing exclusively on the state of the woods, noted great waste but blamed pipe staves and tanneries. It proposed a ban on stripping bark from trees (to be used in the tanning process) and a ban on felling any tree classified as timber within ten miles of a river or coastline, a law that paralleled an Elizabethan act in force in England.[49]

Yet again, a commission had argued for the strategic importance of Ireland's woods and sought to enact rules to protect them. Just as before, however, there were exceptions. In a letter to the commissioners, the Privy Council informed them that Calcott Chambers of Shillelagh, County Wicklow, had petitioned for relief from any ban on exporting pipe staves to foreign merchants. Chambers, the Privy Council noted in its letter, had done "good service . . . in those parts, being formerly rude and uninhabited." Moreover, Chambers had promised that he had faithfully preserved ship timber for the Crown while cutting wood on his land. For that he deserved "all lawful favor and encouragement." Nonetheless, the council noted that James "hath so often declared his pleasure for preserving of the woods and timber within his dominions from that lavish and excessive waste, as formerly hath been used" and requested that the commissioners personally investigate Chambers to ensure that he was indeed following instructions to mark and preserve ship timber. If the council found him to be honest, it was to immediately grant the request in his petition and permit him to resume his exports. Chichester had forcefully argued, again, for a ban on exporting pipe staves. And again, the Privy Council had undermined his action.[50] The 1622 reports showed the state taking a much more active view of woods in Ireland. But when that view produced allegations of widespread waste, the Privy Council resisted or undermined attempts from Dublin to assert tighter state control over Irish woods. Instead, repeated exemptions for favored planters and the East India Company permitted self-regulation.

Nearly four decades after the planning for the Munster Plantation had begun, the relationship between political order and the preservation of woods remained conflicted. In 1624, economic downturn, harvest failure, and rumor of rebellion prompted English and Irish authorities to consider means to strengthen and defend the plantations.[51] In response to these conditions, the Privy Council of Ireland, still led by Chichester, wrote to the king asking him to modify the conditions for the Londonderry plantation. In it, they advocated for the construction of two to three ironworks. There are "great store of small timber trees in the Barony of Clanconkeine and Killetra and other small woods in great abundance more than the Country hath use of, and the timber not portable but in cloven ware, which is forbidden under the word of merchandising." This proposal circumvented the prohibition against converting the woods to merchandise included in the original plantation conditions, offered as a concession to Chichester's pleas for the state to directly hold and control woods in Ulster, as well as the more recent bans on exporting pipe staves (which were classified as "cloven ware"). The emphasis on "small woods" implicitly sought to exclude great timber sought by the navy, but, in doing so, it introduced a new opportunity for planters or officials to take a broad interpretation of legal limits on the use of the woods in Ulster. The Privy Council adopted this measure because "it will be a means to people and civilize those waste and obscure Countries." Without opening the woods to ironmakers, "we see not how those parts will be reformed."[52] This clarifying incident demonstrates that, for many governors, fears of the woodkern and rebellious Irish sheltering in the woods had never left. In the face of economic downturn and anxieties about revolt, the Irish government was willing to modify its previous attempts to curtail felling woods to induce more migration from England and to prop up its plans to civilize through plantation.

Despite more than a decade of actions to protect Irish woods and restrict pipe-stave exports and the exemptions that followed and despite a recent commission launched to assess the state of the plantations, the Dublin government had not developed the bureaucracy or enforcement structures to survey and regulate Ireland's woods. In 1626, two of Richard Boyle's partners in several ironworks petitioned Charles I for the right to exploit a newly discovered iron mine and made a proposal to protect ship timber. Henry Wright and Richard Blacknall warned that Irish ship timber was in danger of becoming scarce, just as ship timber purportedly was in England. The issue, they wrote, was inadequate supervision. In the eighteen years since Cottingham had been sent over to mark Munster's trees and reserve the best for the state, there had not been another survey. In their absence, Wright and Blacknall were "confident that if the said Cottingham and Povey accounts were perused it would be found that a great quantity of that timber hath been converted to many private men's use."[53]

Wright and Blacknall outlined a plan to preserve Ireland's best ship timber. Their solution called for annual surveying, marking trees to give public notice that they were reserved for the Crown, improved record keeping, and the creation of new laws to punish those who felled trees illicitly. Their system, however, only worked with regular supervision and updates. Without these measures, "it will be to as little purpose to cause these trees to be marked."[54] Wright and Blacknall treated the problem of Ireland's supply of ship timber as a bureaucratic and legal exercise. Their plan lacked the strategies for replanting or regeneration that some English forestry reformers proposed. It did, however, reveal problems in gathering basic information, which hampered the Irish government's efforts to manage woods. No one in Dublin or London knew how many trees in Ireland were fit for ship timber and they had no way to assess how that number changed over time.

These issues had not been resolved when the specter of wood scarcity in England again pushed the Irish government toward conservation. In 1629, after two years of disafforestations in England aimed at rationalizing state forestry and securing an extra-Parliamentary revenue source for the king, the Privy Council issued a sweeping ban on timber exports. "Ship timber and pipe staves and more particularly knee timber is grown very scarce," their proclamation warned, and therefore customs officers and other officials in every port in England and Ireland were to prohibit their export without royal permission.[55] Anxieties about ship timber were a long-standing worry. In contrast, Irish government officials and commissioners sent to investigate the plantations had frequently claimed that pipe staves were a threat to ship timber. By 1629, they had become a commodity worthy of preservation.

As with earlier export restrictions, exemptions followed. In 1631, the Privy Council granted requests from merchants asking for the right to export pipe staves from Ireland to Spain and other European destinations. The merchants claimed that the pipe staves had been purchased prior to the export ban. One lamented that the boards "do lie rotting upon his hands and in a short time will be unserviceable." The Privy Council ordered Customs officers to ensure that the staves were old, to collect the duties due on them, and to permit their export.[56] The exemptions seem a sensible way to avoid waste of already felled trees; however, allowing their export to the Continent sits oddly with the Privy Council's earlier assertion that pipe staves had grown scarce in England and Ireland.

The greatest challenge to planter hegemony and the periodic state anxieties about wood scarcity it prompted came from Lord Deputy Thomas Wentworth, Earl of Strafford. Strafford was a controversial figure in the seventeenth century and continues to generate debates among historians. During his term as Lord Deputy, Strafford sought to assert royal authority over Protestant planters, to ensure peace and political obedience, and to enhance the royal revenue. His actions generated considerable opposition in Ireland, which contributed to his attainder and execution in 1641.[57] Wood played a small but notable role in Strafford's policies in Ireland. Unlike previous governors, Strafford attempted to rigorously enforce rules and regulations for Ireland's woods. In doing so, Strafford reopened earlier disputes and undid compromises and settlements where the state had ceded its authority to planters.

In 1635, the court of the Star Chamber heard a case against the London companies that had been granted lands in the Ulster Plantation. The state had amassed a prodigious list of complaints against the Londoners, including the allegation that the planters, led by Tristram Beresford, had destroyed "a forest 20 miles long and 19 broad full of goodly trees fit for shipping." According to the allegations, this action had been expressly prohibited by article 7 of the plantation conditions, which prohibited the planters from "mak[ing] merchandise of the timber." The Crown's counsel argued that the damage amounted to £30,000 and urged £20,000 a fine against the London companies and £5,000 against Beresford.[58] This condition had been an object of controversy in 1610. Chichester had called for the Crown to retain some of the woods in the plantation area as royal lands, and the prohibition against making "merchandise" from them was an attempt at compromise that would allow the planters to take possession of the woods while preserving ship timber for the Crown. The allegations levied against the Londoners suggest that the compromise had failed.

Beginning in 1638, Strafford turned his attention to Richard Boyle.[59] Strafford's attacks on Boyle's right to woods reopened old disputes over the ownership and preservation of woods in Munster. One of the major contested sites was Ballydorgan, a plowland located along the Cork–Waterford border between Tallow and Fermoy. These woods and others, referred to by contemporaries as "Condon's Country," were part of the lands that had been seized from members of the Condon family after the Desmond Rebellion of 1579–1583.[60] Boyle had gained access to these woods in 1608 and used them to supply pipe staves to a Dutch merchant.[61] Title and access rights to these woods had been a source of contention since they were first granted in the late sixteenth century as members of the Condon family, Henry Pyne, and Boyle all fought for their control.[62] In 1638, the disputes over Boyle's behavior on these lands wound up before the council table in Dublin. Strafford took this opportunity to batter his rival. He threatened a host of punishments and issued an injunction prohibiting Boyle from access to the woods, "save only for necessary uses on the land." This case brought Boyle's woodland activities under even greater scrutiny as Strafford pressed the council to investigate whether Boyle had defrauded the government of naval stores from other woods.[63]

The next year, the Condons reappeared in the picture, offering a lease on woods but warning that Boyle would be liable for any "impeachment of waste," words Boyle took as an implicit threat of further action before the council table in Dublin. At the same time, the Lord Deputy dealt Boyle two blows in battles over woodland use. First, he decided that Boyle had wrongfully used woodlands belonging to the Bishop of Cork and Ross and ordered Boyle to pay rent for those woods. Second, he ruled that Boyle's tenants at Bandon had damaged the king's woods and that the king's naval stores should be cut from Boyle's woods, denying Boyle's petition that the stores should be taken from the bishop's land.[64] Since the beginning of the seventeenth century, Boyle had relied on exemptions from state supervision and regulation to produce and sell pipe staves. For decades, the London and Dublin governments had treated Boyle's economic successes as victories for the plantation enterprise. Strafford sought to disentangle Boyle's personal achievements from the Crown's goals in Ireland.[65]

The rigorous enforcement of rules and regulations governing woods under Strafford reflected both Strafford's personal ambitions and his conflicts and broader anxieties about England's wood supply. Strafford made his motivations and goals for governance in Ireland clear in a 1636 report to the king. "I found," he wrote, "a Crowne, A Church, and a People Spoiled. I could not imagine to redeem them from under the pressure with gracious smiles and gentle looks." "Sovereignty (be it spoke with reverence) was going down the hill," and this dire situation called for extreme measures. The "nature of man did so easily slide into the paths of uncontrolled liberty," he warned, "as it would not be brought back without Strength, not to be forced up the hill again, but by vigor and force."[66] He saw a crisis of order exemplified by planters' disregard for the Dublin government. Policing the use of woods was simply another way to shove Ireland's English planters uphill to obedience.

At the same time, Strafford's efforts to assert state control over Irish natural resources coincided with a moment of increasing anxiety about wood scarcity in England from Charles's government and shipwrights. In 1634, the diplomat Sir Thomas Roe had written to Strafford with an optimistic assessment of the plan to revive the Forest Laws. The plan, he predicted, "will for the present bring money and a cure of timber to posterity."[67] Charles's disafforestations and sales of royal forests and his attempts to revive the Forest Laws, however, had generated protests and riots. Anxieties about wood scarcity still remained. Ireland offered some relief from those issues. In 1637, the officers of the navy informed the lords of the admiralty that they had contracted with Andrew Burrell to transport "two hundred loads of square knee timber from the Kingdom of Ireland for the use of his Majesty's navy here, whereof we have special occasion at this time, it being a commodity very difficult to be had in any considerable quantity."[68] The next year, Strafford, who had been informed about the navy officers' deal with Burrell, began his inquisition into Boyle's woods.

*   *   *

Strafford's investigations into Ireland's woods and the allegations of reckless waste they produced followed the pattern that had begun under Chichester. Moments of anxiety about the state of English woods and royal forests prompted inquiries into whether Ireland could provide an alternative store of trees for the navy and the Crown. These efforts to integrate Irish woods into assessments of English resources produced new scarcity fears as the Dublin government found that it did not have title to the trees it sought. These tense moments reveal the multiple political ecologies at play in English plantation efforts in Ireland. Planters and some administrators imagined a reformed Irish landscape supporting royal-revenue-enhancing enterprises that attracted English artisans and tenants. In this vision, planters' profits and the Crown's programs to reform Ireland were compatible, needing only self-administered regulations to ensure emergency supplies of timber for the navy. In contrast, Chichester and Strafford saw conflicts between plant-ers' and the Crown's interests in Ireland's woods. They sought to articulate a political ecology for Irish woods that emphasized their role meeting royal demands, even if doing so limited what was available to attract planters.

The conflict between competing political ecologies was essential to the perception that Ireland faced wood scarcity in the early seventeenth century, but, taking the perspective of the Dublin and London governments leaves planters' motivations and behavior opaque. Reports from commissions sent to investigate the plantations and complaints from Lord Deputies suggest that participants in colonial projects in Ireland attacked natural resources like a plague of locusts. In these sources, planters, particularly Boyle, appear as crafty opportunists or unscrupulous destroyers of resources, undermining attempts from Chichester or Strafford to protect Irish woods (even if English scarcity fears motivated their concern). Boyle's efforts to manage his estates demonstrate the need for a more nuanced portrait of planter political ecol-ogy. As historian David Edwards and archaeologist Colin Rynne put it, "Boyle was indeed crooked, and a land-grabber, but he was an asset-protector, not an asset-stripper." He developed a long-term vision for personal and familial success and took pragmatic steps to ensure the continuity of his wealth and power.[69] This vision included plans for Ireland's trees to serve local commu-nities and markets for commercial goods in England and on the European continent in both the present and the future.

Boyle's estate papers, which include the few surviving records of Sir Wal-ter Ralegh's estate management in Munster, offer rich evidence for a colonial approach toward woods that was simultaneously predatory and protective and that shared many attributes with contemporary efforts to manage woods as resources in England. At different times and different places in the plan-tation period, Ralegh, Boyle, and other English planters sought to exploit woodlands for short-term profits, while at other times and places planning for longer-term sustainability. From the outset of the Munster Plantation, Ralegh included restrictions on access and uses of woodlands. Boyle expanded on these regulations with rigorous constraints on woodland use, developed alternative fuel sources, and practiced coppicing to preserve long-term supplies of wood. Yet, contemporaries, including other Munster planters and Boyle's business partners, railed against him for destroying woods. Just as in England, where attempts to regulate woodlands for particular uses provoked bureaucratic scuffles, riots, and lawsuits in royal forests, conflicts in Munster drew from similar sources of contention. From 1602 through 1642, Boyle's woodland management policies evolved to encourage different types of landscapes that would provide sufficient resources for timber industries, deer parks, construction, and fuel. Despite these conscious attempts to regulate his estates for profit and self-sufficiency, Boyle's policies failed to deliver the desired results, sparking conflicts with tenants, estate agents, and other colonists.

Planters carried multiple understandings of the uses and value of woods across the sea to Ireland that reflected the diversity of ideas about woods in England. They felled wood to produce iron and pipe staves and sought oaks to build ships. Their tenants used bark to tan leather. With wattles made of saplings, they built weirs and enclosures. Elite landowners reserved woods to build deer parks and eyries. Birch trees could be uprooted and burned to fertilize fields. Common resources supplied households and towns.[70] As in England, efforts to manage multiple uses provoked conflicts. The forces that shaped English woods did not disappear when English people boarded boats but continued to shape woods in Ireland.

From the outset of the Munster Plantation, Ralegh and his agents sought to balance measures to improve the value of lands and the construction of infrastructure with efforts to preserve woods. Ralegh required several tenants to build English-style houses, repair castles, or enclose land as a condition of their tenancy. His lease of two weirs at Lismore to Roger Carew required Carew to "build a good large and sufficient sluice or flood gate in some convenient place of 12 foot broad" to transform the existing weirs along the model of English ones. He provided access rights to woods to support these endeavors.[71]

At the same time, Ralegh took several steps to prevent exploitation of his woods. His leases provided only limited rights to timber, and he hired a woodward to enforce these limitations. Tenants were allowed to cut timber in the wood at Lisfinny for the purposes of building their houses. Ralegh explicitly exempted "great timber" from another lease and retained his rights to the woods at the Shane Wood and Ballyduff, granting the tenant access to coppices, indicating that he had adopted a system of woodland conservation and regeneration as early as the 1580s. Ralegh's lease to Henry Dorrell for

Ballyghilly near Youghal exemplified the measured rights Ralegh granted. He allowed Dorrell to cut timber from woods near Youghal and provided him permission to build a mill and divert water to feed it, but he limited Dorrell's timbering and restricted the volume of water he might take to prevent injury to neighboring tenants.[72] Ralegh treated trees on his lands as a resource to be used carefully and monitored by specifically appointed wardens.

This attitude extended beyond the most elite planters like Ralegh, though many smaller landholders did not regulate their woods with Ralegh's rigor. Leases from his larger tenants, who also rented out portions of their land, also set regulations to govern wood use. William Floyer and Nicholas Myn prohibited their tenants from cutting their great woods but, like Ralegh, allowed access to wood and underwood.[73] Most of Ralegh's tenants allowed more latitude. Edward Lochland's seven leases for lands at Lisnabreen and Curraglass placed no restrictions on how his tenants could use the woods except that Lochland or his agents could access some of their lands to cut timber for himself. The lack of regulation did not condemn these forests to overexploitation, but it removed one check against it. Moreover, Lochland maintained rights to fell timber on many of these lands, leaving trees his tenants preserved vulnerable to Lochland's incursions. Another of Ralegh's tenants, Edmond Colthurst, also created a situation that threatened the long-term viability of a wood. Colthurst restricted access to timber at Lisfinny but allowed his tenant at Tallowbridge to pasture animals there.[74] Cattle eat the shoots of trees, hampering regeneration. Pasturing animals in woods was common in Highland Scotland, but landlords frequently specified the number of cattle allowed to pasture or only allowed them into the woods during winter.[75] Colthurst's lease did not limit the right to woodland pasture: He guarded his right to one generation of timber trees while simultaneously allowing behavior that threatened his continued access to the resource.

Ralegh's practices bore similarities to those in England, but they also shared similarities with indigenous methods for managing woods. Irish landowners who rented woodlands to new English planters recognized that woods were a potentially valuable resource. They selectively distributed rights for exploitation and set regulations for felling and use. In 1593, Conogher O'Callaghan granted the planter Thomas Norris nine plowlands of Cromore wood to supply an ironworks for seven years. O'Callaghan restricted the use of the woods solely to Norris, emphatically adding, "but only the said Sir Thomas." He further added that Norris was not to "spoil" any woods except those that had been explicitly marked out for him. O'Callaghan's lease restricted Norris to cut only a fixed area for a set period of time. Yet O'Callaghan's lease lacked many of the detailed regulations common to contemporary English and Scottish forest leases. O'Callaghan made no mention of coppicing. His description of the rights included in the land added both pasture and grass, suggesting that the land had previously been stocked and might continue to be used for woodland pasture.[76] Both English and Irish landlords had rules of forest management that sought to treat wood as a resource. They differed, however, in specificity and in restrictions on the use of woods for pastoralism. Munster never provided open, unregulated woods, but, at the onset of the plantation, it offered greater latitude than found in many parts of England.

In part, the lack of detailed woodland-management policies may reflect the small scale of extractive industries in the late sixteenth century. Two versions of a map dating from the 1590s or early 1600s showed Norris's ironworks at the edge of O'Callaghan's woods.[77] That both versions depicted Norris's ironworks was a sign that O'Callaghan did not let his leased land sit idle. The size of the ironworks and the land surrounding it was much smaller than O'Callaghan's holding, which the artist(s) showed well-stocked with trees. Although nine plowlands might contain roughly five-hundred acres of woodland, O'Callaghan had not leased all of his woods to Norris nor did he grant him a long lease to the woods. This strategy allowed O'Callaghan to

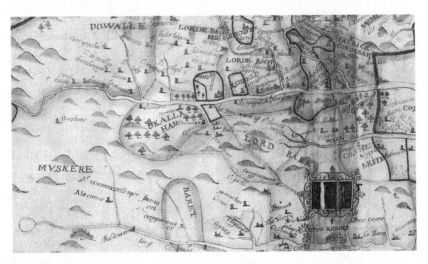

Figure 8: Detail showing Thomas Norris's ironworks. The map shows that O'Callaghan possessed a substantial amount of land, dotted with trees relative to Norris's two holdings. Francis Jobson, "The Province of Mounster [Munster]" (detail), c. 1595, Dartmouth Collection of Maps of Ireland, P/49(20), National Maritime Museum. © National Maritime Museum, Greenwich, London.

retain long-term control over his woods. Even if Norris clear-cut the plow-lands, they would return to O'Callaghan, who could allow them to regenerate.

By the 1590s, however, new planters were beginning to intensify their use of Munster's woods. Ralegh launched a partnership with Henry Pyne to produce pipe staves that took the first steps to link woods in Munster with markets in London, several Dutch ports, Seville, and the Spanish colony on the Canary Islands.[78] Munster's woods were no longer just features of the Irish landscape but were becoming increasingly integrated into broader mercantile networks. These new connections and the commercialization that accompanied them brought new pressures that would intensify over the course of the seventeenth century.

Individuals involved in commercial timbering in Ireland set regulations to support long-term use, not a rapid, singular wave of extraction. In 1610, Henry Becher (also, "Beecher"), Nicholas Blacknall, and John Shipward allocated woodlands across three plowlands with numerous restrictions. The lease reserved "the said woods underwoods, timber, and trees, standing, growing and being" on three plowlands (a unit of measurement in early modern Irish land records) south of the highway near Blacknall's home over the course of twenty-four years. Like O'Callaghan's leases, this document limited the area for felling; however, it also preserved "all and every young timber tree which shall be hereafter left unfelled for standalls and storons." Like Ralegh's earlier lease, this document provided clear evidence for a regeneration scheme, not just restrictions on access.[79] Commercial timber production created new pressures on Munster's woods. Some planters sought to adapt by introducing regulations that both limited cutting and required regeneration measures like those in English royal forests.

Upon acquiring Ralegh's lands, Boyle followed the general pattern of the 1580s and 1590s demonstrated by Ralegh and Norris, setting guidelines in leases to control access to and use of woods to which he held title while obtaining wood rights outside his estates to fuel manufacturing enterprises. Boyle changed his policies over time in response to perceived wood shortages, shifts in the markets for pipe staves and iron, and changing settlement dynamics, but the overall pattern remained similar. Between 1602 and 1641, Boyle's woodland management began to include stricter prohibitions on wood gathering, the integration of alternative fuels into leases, and the creation of coppices to regenerate wood. In tandem with this approach, he sought leases for woods that he could use to supply pipe-stave enterprises or to protect his own woods while supplying the growing demand of iron-works. Just as efforts to balance traditions of multiple use with intensified manufacturing produced conflicts in royal forests, Boyle's neighbors and tenants resisted efforts to provide resources for him in perpetuity that they believed came at their expense.

Between 1602 and 1611, Boyle began acquiring substantial woodland rights along with lands around Ballynatray, Kilmacow, Kill St. Nicholas, Mogeely, and Cappoquin.[80] In addition, he made deals with Conogher and Terlagh O'Callaghan for the right to cut timber in their woodlands, just as Norris had previously done. These leases carried specific conditions for the kind and quantity of wood to be cut. Both leases included a surcharge of £5 per oak or timber tree cut, in addition to the yearly rent, but granted "so many ash trees, witch elm trees, birch trees, or such like wood" at no additional cost. The terms of Boyle's lease emphasized "standards," mature oak trees that were lauded in contemporary English commentaries on woodlands. Conogher O'Callaghan had previously leased these woods to Sir Thomas Norris and explicitly granted him the right to use his trees to fuel an iron forge.[81] The leases from the O'Callaghans were explicitly commercial transactions. They treated sections of O'Callaghan's woods as commodities to be taken and used for commercial benefit.

In contrast, Boyle's early leases on his own lands limited rights to exploit woods. His 1607 lease for Ballyphilip, County Waterford, provided unambiguous guidance for woodland use. According to the document, Boyle reserved all woods and underwoods save "six small boatloads of wood to be exchanged yearly for sand to be used in mending the demised premises and lands and also mete and sufficient houseboot, hedgeboot, cartboot, fireboot, and plowboot."[82] Boyle's lease to Christmas Heward regulated woods on the land she was leasing and highlighted the diverse uses of timber as a part of a holding that also contained agricultural land. As in many leases, trees, branches, and twigs provided fuel and building supplies. Trees also served as barter to acquire sand, which could be used to dry boggy soil. These regulations strove to preserve a resource on an individual property, while allowing it to be used for necessary household purposes or to make improvements to the land. Boyle's 1606 extension of Ralegh's lease to Robert Carew for mills and weirs around Lismore added the right to take wood and timber to enclose the land, to repair houses, and to repair the weir and mills.[83] These different uses pointed to the value of diverse types of wood. Construction drew on the timber planks and trees, some of which might also have served as pipe staves. Repairing the weir required flexible branches to make wattles. Together these leases show that Boyle did not treat his woodlands as mere timber repositories but as diverse resources that could serve many different functions.

In these early leases, Boyle attempted to balance the need to attract tenants with generous terms against the desire to protect his woods. A 1605 lease to Thomas Fitz-John Gerald for several townlands near Tallow highlighted the difficulty of doing both. Boyle granted Fitz-John Gerald all the commodities growing in the woods but later reserved woods, underwoods, and timber except for what was sufficient to repair his house and hedges, fuel his fires, or maintain carts. Boyle noted that he had appointed a woodward to ensure that these conditions were followed. The conditions themselves remained unclear. A confused contemporary left the marginal query, "Whether those woods be not well reserved?"[84] Fitz-John Gerald took advantage of the ambiguities in Boyle's leases, granting the rights to cut timber for building new houses instead of confining wood cutting to maintenance purposes only.[85] Fitz-John Gerald's lease was exceptionally ambiguous, but the dense, potentially overlapping, and possibly contradictory sets of rights were characteristic of Boyle's earliest attempts to regulate woodlands. His 1615 lease to Mathew Harris for five plowlands granted woods at one point only to later reserve "all timber trees, woods, underwoods in and upon the premises" to Boyle.[86]

At the core of these leases was the belief that woods could be exploited without diminishing the resource. Nowhere was this clearer than in one of the earliest proposals to Boyle to establish an ironworks. Boyle began dealing in iron in 1604 shortly after receiving confirmation of his purchase of Ralegh's lands. In a request dated the day after that confirmation, William Greatrakes wrote to Boyle asking for access to woods to set up an ironworks. Greatrakes, whose brother John was already producing iron for Boyle, promised to leave Boyle's woods as he found them and reserve any trees fit for timber to Boyle.[87] William Greatrakes's appeal to Boyle suggested two goals for forest management. First, promising to leave the woods as he found them suggested that he would replace felled trees through coppicing or replanting. Second, reserving timber trees to Boyle promised to protect the most valuable part of the woodlands—salable timber—for Boyle's own use. In theory, this was a proposal for an ironworks that could operate over a long time span without exhausting its fuel supply or preventing other uses.

In practice, tensions quickly emerged between commercial products (pipe staves and iron) and other woodland uses. The attempt to balance profitable exploitation against resource preservation defined his actions until the cataclysmic 1641 Uprising. Boyle's first responses to complaints of woodland destruction simply attempted to ensure that those exploiting his resources did so efficiently. In 1606, Thomas Ball wrote to Boyle complaining that Henry Pyne, who had plagued Ralegh's timber activities in the 1590s, was an unreliable partner.[88] The next year, Pyne wrote to Boyle informing him that he was pressing his woodsmen to work through the winter in Mogeely to meet the growing demand for wood from iron forges and pipe stave merchants.[89] In 1608, Boyle's agent Henry Wright sought to slow Pyne's felling. Pyne's workmen cut the best timber and then converted it to planks or fuel for the furnaces, rather than working through other trees. In addition, Pyne's men wasted wood by leaving downed trees or cut planks deemed inferior to rot in the woods. According to Wright, Pyne had ordered his men to fell as many trees as possible and then to draw out the best to make planks. Wright ordered Pyne's woodcutters to cease working and set laborers to square already felled trees before any more were cut, fearing that the downed wood would rot before they could finish it.[90] Wright feared that Pyne was exploiting his rights to Boyle's woods by felling more timber than he could process and by taking tall, straight hardwood trees to produce pipe staves and cordwood fuel. His fear was that Pyne was both cutting trees that should have been reserved for other uses and inefficiently using those that were cut, a complaint that echoed landowners who had leased wood rights to Boyle.

As Boyle struggled to manage commercial enterprises, he began to restrict other uses to alleviate pressure on his woods. In 1611, Richard Boyle brought a suit against Thomas FitzGerald, another member of the powerful Munster family and one of Boyle's largest tenants, that ended up before Lord Deputy Chichester. The controversy purportedly stemmed from disputes between animal husbandry and woodland conservation. As Boyle complained,

> Divers poor people, amongst which some 40 of them or thereabouts did only build poor cabins near the wood side and live by brewing and baking and keeping of alehouses none of them paying above a noble a year and very many of them lesser rents, who committed such daily waste and spoil in your petitioner's woods, as it was lamentable to behold, and the said Thomas placed also very many Irish tenants in the very wood, who cut down [a] number of trees in the winter for their cattle to house on the tops of them and with keeping great herds of goats and otherwise almost destroyed the aforesaid woods.

By lodging this complaint, Boyle suggested that he was concerned with wood shortages; however, the substance of the complaint deflected blame from his own commercial timbering activities.[91] Boyle's distaste for poor tenants was palpable in the complaints and the action was likely designed to remove cottagers from the land, an action similar to those undertaken by nobility and gentry across England. Boyle, however, couched his complaint as a worry about destructive pastoralism and implicitly suggested that Fitz-Gerald's actions threatened degeneration to the worst Irish behavior. The Lord Deputy and Irish Privy Council sided with Boyle, condemning FitzGerald for wasting the woods and granting Boyle control over them.[92] Unlike in England, where commoners might appeal to English custom and tradition, Boyle could use stereotypes of Irish wastefulness and barbarism to attack woodland pastoralism.

By bringing Munster's woods to the attention of Chichester, Boyle helped to open questions about his own management of woods. The Bristol merchant William Kellet, with whom Boyle sought to establish a trade in iron, queried Boyle why a "Gentleman of your quality" would permit a tenant who cut down and spoiled woods to remain in his holding.[93] More pressing, Boyle had helped to draw Chichester's attention to Munster's woods. Chichester began in 1608 to voice his concerns to the Privy Council that Munster planters were destroying valuable state resources.[94] Nonetheless, Boyle continued to fill orders for pipe staves and to expand iron production by adding another works at Kilmacow and developing the infrastructure to support an ironworks at Cappoquin, County Waterford.[95] Rather than abandon the controversial Pyne, Boyle negotiated a new agreement with him for manufacturing pipe staves at Mogeely. When the Dublin government passed new restrictions aimed at protecting Munster's woods to serve the navy, Boyle simply negotiated an exemption.[96]

Boyle circumvented regulations from Dublin but intensified restrictions on woodland use on his own estates. In 1612, Boyle attempted to change the conditions for woodland access with Thomas Ball, his partner in several ironworks. Ball rejected these claims. Ball refused to reserve any timber trees or bark save those marked out prior to the agreement. In addition, he demanded that he be allowed to clear-cut "steep glens" without coppicing the trees there. He refused any restrictions on barking wood and Boyle's request that he enclose woodlands. Ball claimed that all Boyle's requests were impractical. Cattle, he argued, cannot feed on regenerating shoots in steep glens, so coppicing is unnecessary. He objected to the restriction on barking, claiming that bark "will not strip but in unsensible times for the felling of wood." He protested that colliers needed access to the steep glens without any restrictions or the cost of producing charcoal would exceed the cost of building scaffolding to access the trees. Enclosing timber to protect regenerating wood from animals might cost more than the coals manufactured from it would yield. Boyle lost the early rounds of this dispute. In a note summarizing the case, William Greatrakes and Nicholas Blacknall reported that Ball was held harmless for his activities in the woods. After this setback, Boyle continued to deal with Ball and, by the end of the year, Ball's account reported that he had felled more trees to feed the forges and manufacture pipe staves.[97]

In response to the failure to introduce conservation measures to his business partners, Boyle sought both to acquire wood rights to ease pressure on his own lands and to enact restrictions on access against tenants and some of his business partners. In 1613, Boyle and his Dutch pipe stave partner began paying tenants around Tallow to rent woodlands.[98] These leases near Tallow were a stopgap measure designed to shift the consequences of intensive pipe stave production out of Boyle's woods. In 1614, Boyle received several requests to cut woods as well as reports naming those who cut without permission. These letters complained that wood was difficult to get, in part because Boyle had created strict new regulations against felling trees. These actions limited woodland access to both small tenants and international merchants.[99] Boyle only granted carpenters the right to woods they had been felling without permission after his agent informed him that they had not been licensed to cut wood in six years. A report of timber cut near Cappoquin detailed why a stand containing fourteen trees was felled and outlined the uses for the wood.[100] Boyle's earliest grants demonstrated his concern with his rights as a landlord, but the grants following 1614 signaled his move toward the aggressive and active management of woods in response to more detailed information about their condition.

Boyle began including stricter prohibitions in his leases against using standing trees. Beginning in 1616, most of Boyle's leases restricted tenants to windfalls, roots, and "moots" for their firewood and building materials.[101] Confining tenants to downed trees and roots departed from previous grants that had permitted cutting trees with the permission of Boyle's woodward. The concentration of leases with these restrictions is unique in the surviving documents. Only five leases spread over a twenty-year span contained similar conditions.[102] Imposing these conditions in Lisfinny wood and other stands of trees near Tallow marked a unique attempt to preserve existing woodland by prohibiting felling.

Boyle's tenants and workmen claimed that they were following these restrictions. Nicholas Symonton, a tenant accused of unlicensed felling near Bandon, justified his action by claiming that he had taken only boughs from the tree. Moreover, the trees he surreptitiously pruned were "not worth felling, utterly uncut for any kind of timber or wood being unfit to clear."[103] Tenants were beginning to draw on fallen trees, saving growing wood for other purposes. Carpenters, joiners, and builders claimed they were using boughs and crooked trees in an attempt to distinguish the trees they needed for their trades from those Boyle sought to sell abroad as pipe staves. Symonton attempted to argue to Boyle that the diverse types of living trees in Munster's woods could sustain multiple uses. Some woods were "fit to clear" and could be regenerated in coppices. Others should be selectively cut for specific joints or boards. Still others should only have boughs felled. In contrast, Boyle sought to reserve all the best timber for himself, leaving his tenants to pick through rotten and wind-felled trees to serve their needs.

The move to harvest windfalls was also a response to perceived shortages and the failure of other restrictions. Boyle had a woodward at Lisfinny to regulate his trees but nonetheless added lease conditions between 1616 and 1627 to halt felling for household use. His 1637 lease to William Browning, which restricted Browning to downed trees and stumps, renewed a lease granted in 1625 that had only required Browning to confine his wood use to assigned trees.[104] These moves suggest that Boyle felt his own attempts to regulate felling through a woodward had failed. Forcing tenants to harvest downed and rotting timber represented a significant downgrade in the quality of wood. Nonetheless, William Cook pleaded with Boyle in 1615 to keep forty wind-felled trees from the ironworkers, arguing that they were necessary to serve the local population. In 1616, Cornelius Gaffny, a tenant from Tircullen, County Waterford, voiced a similar concern. He begged Boyle for wood to finish his mill. According to his request, Gaffny had already built the walls of the mill from timber purchased nearby but was unable to locate any more wood. "There is no manner of timber at all," he lamented, "but only firewood." Gaffny's requirements were modest. He sought only "some oaken saplings" to keep the wind and rain from spoiling his building.[105]

Boyle's push to restrict his tenants to windfalls stemmed from his desire to preserve woods for long-term use while continuing to produce iron and pipe staves. Boyle's actions paralleled developments in England, where the Crown's attempts to manage royal forests to produce profits and naval supplies led to controversial restrictions on common rights and attacks on commoning animals as well as pruning, lopping, topping, and other older forestry practices. Similarly, Boyle attempted to curtail behaviors that emerged out of customs on English commons to ensure that he would be able to achieve the maximum commercial value from his woods.

In England, efforts to curtail customary rights to take wood for construction and repair provoked resistance. Likewise, some of Boyle's tenants refused to obey his new wood-saving dictates. Boyle acquired lands and the right to hold a fair at Bandon in 1614 and immediately sought to bring similar woodland restrictions there. He appointed a woodward and had his agents order workmen out of the woods. Boyle's woodward, John Nobbes, informed Boyle that he had "been careful of your woods . . . and forbidden the workmen, yet they came on still." Unable to physically stop the influx, Nobbes promised to report the incursion at the next assize. Another tenant, Herbert Nichollas, provided Boyle with a list of men who cut his woods near Bandon without permission but noted that none of those accused seemed likely to stop. John Shipward disputed Boyle's right to the woods and dared Boyle to take the case to court. The miller Robert Sheate bluntly informed Boyle's agent that "he will cut and carry away in spite of you." On newly acquired land far from Boyle's major holdings, his writ held little sway. The failure of these requests drove Boyle to try buying out his opponent. At the end of 1614, he acquired Henry Becher's lands, using the purchase to neutralize one of the men who refused to cease cutting his woods. Nonetheless, complaints continued. The next year, Nathaniel Curteys lamented to Boyle that large numbers of Irish cottagers and cattle allowed to roam across boundaries threatened his woodlands. By 1618, these confrontations had become violent. Walter Cooke, Boyle's woodward for Clonakilty and Bandon, wrote that he had tried to preserve the trees but that a group of men "struck me on the head with a dagger, and sent me to the ground, and rising again cut me [across] the head." The previous woodward, wrote Cooke, had experienced similar treatment. An angry crowd "had broken his man's head" when he tried to prevent them from taking wood.[106]

In response to the resistance his restrictions faced and complaints from his merchant partners and Chichester, Boyle sought to reduce pressure on his woods. Around the same time as he tightened restrictions on felling trees, Boyle began granting rights to cut turf in his leases. The earliest turbary grants came in Clonakilty in 1615 and in Bandon in 1618. Both towns in west Cork had bogs that were used to provide fuel for tenants almost as soon as Boyle acquired them. Each of Boyle's surviving leases from Clonakilty granted turbary rights to his tenants and, when Boyle leased the bog that served Clonakilty, he required that his tenants have uninterrupted access to the bog to cut turf.[107] In 1619, Boyle finalized his purchase of Bandon and several surrounding townlands from Henry Becher.[108] From this date forward, Boyle rarely granted wood rights near Bandon. The only leases that granted access to woods were for larger holdings outside the town. For the town itself, turf was the only source of fuel granted between 1619 and 1635.[109] At Tallow, leases in 1620 and 1622 provided access to turf for fuel. The 1622 lease indicated that gathering turf at Tallow may have been more expansive than the surviving documentary evidence indicates because it granted "turf and turbary to be had and taken of the mountains where the rest of the tenants of Tallow shall dig or cut the same."[110] Boyle enumerated turbary rights in two areas where conflict over woods had been greatest: Tallow and Bandon. English and Irish inhabitants had likely used turf in these areas since their first arrival; the enumeration of turbary rights represented an effort to formalize the process and substitute a new source of energy.

In addition to substituting fuel sources, Boyle sought woodland leases from his neighbors where he would not need to consider fuel, timber for carpentry, or any other noncommercial uses. The longest lasting of these relationships was with the O'Callaghans with whom Boyle had negotiated wood rights earlier in the seventeenth century. On the lands Boyle held from the O'Callaghans, he had pursued pipe stave manufacturing and clear-cut woods. They seemed to approve of this behavior. After Boyle's first lease expired, they agreed to a new lease in 1618, authorizing Boyle and his agents to fell "so long and until the woods are wrought clear out."[111]

The O'Callaghans' relatively harmonious relationship with Boyle and transactions with English planters suggest that they used tightly regulated and selective wood leases to planters as a strategy to retain control over their land, secure profit, and preserve existing customs in a new political and economic context. In 1617, the O'Callaghans gave the timberman Christopher Colthurst liberty to cut as much timber as necessary to produce 30,000 pipe staves from two areas of woods "without disturbance or imposition." Colthurst, who made pipe staves for Boyle and other planters, agreed to deliver these woods at Youghal or Cork.[112] In 1618, Sir John Jephson wrote to Boyle inquiring about his relationship with the O'Callaghans. In the course of these letters, Jephson noted that he too enjoyed a lease from them to cut timber and also to supply his tenants with necessary wood for construction and fuel.[113] In 1640, the O'Callaghans "spared" Sir Philip Perceval enough land for a park, which Colthurst was to "square," though its final acreage was uncertain.[114] The content and conditions for the O'Callaghans' dissemination of woodland rights changed from 1593 to 1640—the first leases sought to ensure woodland pasture for O'Callaghan tenants, whereas the final grant to Perceval created a park to pursue noble pleasures like hunting and hawking—but the O'Callaghans remained firmly in control of their woodlands throughout. The only complaint to arise regarding the O'Callaghans' woods came in 1620 against

John McTeig Garrosse, alleging raids aimed at terrorizing woodcutters and taking pipe staves.[115]

Boyle negotiated leases with other Irish landholders that were similarly relatively harmonious. Beginning in 1613, Dermod McCarthy provided Boyle with a series of contracts to cut pipe staves from his woods. He offered Boyle similar terms, allowing Boyle's workmen liberty to access his woods to cut timber. McCarthy, however, specified how many pipe staves the cut timber should produce, rather than granting Boyle broad access to a parcel of woods and charging him for the number of oak trees felled. This difference from the O'Callaghans' leases led to periodic conflicts between Boyle and McCarthy. Granting a parcel of land, allowing clear-cutting, and charging per tree placed the burden of efficiency on English sawyers. McCarthy's grants for specific numbers of pipe staves offered no such guarantees. In 1615, McCarthy wrote to Boyle worrying that the sawyers were "very careless." McCarthy asked for greater oversight for the enterprise and the ability to mark trees—particularly those nearest to bodies of water and easiest to access—and ensure that workmen got as many pales and staves as possible from them. McCarthy disputed the way timber rights were being exercised but not the rights given. After his complaint that workmen were not harvesting his best timber efficiently, he engaged in several larger orders for pipe staves and no further complaints survive.[116]

Boyle also sought access to woods on the lands of other English colonists, which created far greater conflict than his negotiations with Irish landholders. In 1617, Allen Apsley, Boyle's father-in-law, who had served as a commissioner for victuals in Munster during the Nine Years' War and held posts as a naval administrator during the seventeenth century, wrote to Boyle complaining that Boyle's agent, Nicholas Blacknall, had violated the terms of their woodland agreement. According to Apsley, Blacknall cut beyond the confines of their agreement, destroying woods valued at £20 per year. He demanded that Boyle cease forcing him to fell all his trees.[117] Unfortunately for Apsley, Boyle capitalized on his father-in-law's debts in 1618 and 1619 as Boyle began to fear shortages in his own woods and pressured Apsley to surrender part of his woods to be felled for pipe staves.[118] In 1623, Apsley again attempted to halt Blacknall's activities in his woods. He complained that Blacknall's destructive felling had ruined his mineral and battery works. In 1623, Apsley alleged that Boyle's workmen had spoiled his woods in defiance of an order by the Lord Deputy and Privy Council of Ireland prohibiting them from doing so.[119]

At roughly the same time that Boyle came into conflict with Apsley, he encountered an even greater threat to his efforts to commercially exploit

Munster's woods. By 1617, the East India Company ironworkers at Dundaniel, near Bandon, had begun to exhaust their original store of wood and began looking for a new supply. Their search placed them in direct competition with Boyle, who, his enemies claimed, resorted to dirty tricks to fend them off. They accused the sheriff of Cork, who had partnered with Boyle in earlier woodcutting enterprises, of commanding the East India Company ironworkers to tear down their weirs in order to hamper their ironworks, claiming that they impeded salmon migrations, a tactic that Boyle would see Strafford use against him twenty years later.[120] Boyle's attempt to hobble the competing ironworks was an act of desperation. In 1618, his partner, Thomas Ball, complained that high transportation costs and growing fuel prices resulting from cutting restrictions had made the business untenable. Ball resigned his leases to Boyle, but they did not part amicably. Boyle accused him of absconding with the timber, ore, and other stocks from an ironworks and selling them to the East India Company. The case found its way before the Privy Council and the Star Chamber, which set up arbitration. The settlement, reached in October 1619, dealt Boyle a heavy blow. His opponents retained the disputed stocks, and the Star Chamber ordered Boyle to pay more than £1,000 in cash or sow iron in punitive damages.[121]

Boyle's efforts to recover from the disastrous settlement with Ball coincided with harvest crises and coin shortages that threw the Irish economy into disarray.[122] Competing ironworks in Ireland and the Forest of Dean and a proposed ironworks in Newfoundland began to limit the market for Boyle's iron. One of Boyle's Bristol clients refused to honor a contract with Boyle and invested in the Dean works instead. In addition, Boyle's conflict with Ball prompted him to export sow iron, a less-refined product, instead of the more valuable bar iron he had previously sold. Bristol merchants complained that there was no market for sows and pressed Boyle to resume selling bars.[123] Boyle did so, but English ironmongers complained that there were quality issues with Boyle's iron, threatening to refuse further purchases unless it improved.[124]

Boyle's attempts to reduce wood consumption may have contributed to these production issues. In 1622, Richard Blacknall provided instructions to Peter Baker to repair the mines at Ballyregan, which provided some of the supplies for Boyle's ironworks. Water had flooded the pits, but by sinking them deeper and building a waterwheel and pump in accordance with the plan included in the letter, the mine might again produce. Over the next year, Baker complained that he was unable to carry out this request due to lack of wood. He informed Boyle that he sought to use trees carefully and when possible to take only bark or limbs, but "the mineworks must be kept up and propped by timber."[125] According to his agent, Henry Wright, the stock of ore and wood that Ball took during his dispute with Boyle in 1620 had not been replaced three years later. Blacknall seconded Wright's complaint about stock shortages in 1623.[126] Boyle, however, appeared to ignore complaints about wood shortages at the mine.

Issues with Boyle's ironworks persisted throughout the 1620s and 1630s, but new production sites in Ireland and new commercial connections with merchants in London and on the European continent enabled the enterprise to persevere. By 1623, he had developed new relationships selling iron in Dublin and to Dutch merchants. He also partnered with Thomas Ridgeway, first Earl of Londonderry, to expand iron production into the north of Ireland and improve his relationships with the Dutch. In the 1630s, he began a contentious but ultimately successful agreement with London ironmongers and further enhanced his ironworks by partnering with the powerful international financier Philip Burlamachi.[127]

In the 1630s, other projects continued to draw on woodlands. In 1634, workers began felling timber to build the almshouse at Bandon. Boyle's construction venture displayed many of the hallmarks of his previous woodland activities. He sought to reduce pressure on and competition for standing trees. In this case, Boyle's agent, Augustine Atkins, attempted to purchase access to a turf bog to provide fuel for tenants. He also sought to protect his own trees by acquiring woods on lands he did not own. Another of Boyle's Bandon agents, William Wiseman, sent workers to fell trees on Donogh McCouger's plowlands. According to Wiseman, McCouger consented to the workers' harvesting his trees but then changed his mind and threatened to bring the case before Boyle to stop Wiseman.[128] In addition to cutting timber to build his almshouse, Boyle also had workers strip bark from trees near Bandon.[129]

Boyle's moves to scale back iron production appear to have corresponded with a decline in his previously stringent lease restrictions in the 1630s. After 1627, leases at Tallow began to provide inconsistent wood rights. Some offered no wood rights at all. Others continued to limit collection to fallen trees and roots. Still others allowed the tenant to fell wood for fuel and construction. One lease requiring the construction of an English house mandated that the tenants build a roof "of sawed timber and covered with slat." Many of the leases made no mention of woodlands as assets reserved to Boyle or granted to tenants.[130] In 1637, Boyle's leases at Tallow began to include more frequent references to turbary rights, along with the suggestion that other tenants at Tallow whose leases have not survived also had those rights.[131]

Even as he and his agents appear to have relaxed some restrictions on cutting and using trees, there are indications that Boyle and his estate managers attempted to enact a program to regenerate felled woodlands. Leases and letters from the 1620s and 1630s provide scattered references to coppicing in Cork and Waterford.[132] Between 1628 and 1636, Boyle's agent for lands in west Cork, Morgan Polden, prohibited his tenants from "doing any waste or spoil upon any the young timber trees," suggesting conscious plans to manage regrowth. These restrictions represented a departure from earlier leases that simply restricted felling.[133] Boyle and his agents had come to realize by the end of the 1620s that they needed to supplement restrictions on woodcutting and promoting turf as an alternative fuel with actions to regenerate felled trees. Before these trees could mature, political conflicts would create a crisis in Boyle's woods.

From his first land acquisitions in Munster until the 1630s, Boyle had used the regulation of his own woodlands and strategic purchases of wood rights from English and Irish neighbors to supply multiple ironworks and pipe stave manufacturing ventures that connected Munster with merchants and commercial networks in England and on the European continent. Boyle's actions prompted conflicts with tenants, neighbors, and commercial competitors, but he had evaded serious regulation from the Dublin or London governments. In 1638, however, Strafford's inquisition into Boyle's exploitation of Munster's natural resources threatened the system of regulation and exploitation that had supplied Boyle's pipe stave enterprises and ironworks since the beginning of the seventeenth century.

Strafford and the parties suing Boyle accused him of thoughtless destruction motivated by unchecked greed, but Boyle's correspondence with his Lismore estate agent John Walley shows that the motivations for Boyle's actions were far more complex. Walley warned Boyle that "preservation of your Lordship's woods [. . .] is one of the most necessary things to be looked unto." Walley's letter implied that those efforts had failed miserably as a result of incompetent execution of Boyle's conservation policies and excessive demand. Walley replaced Boyle's woodward at Lisfinny and informed Boyle that the coppices that were supposed to supply Boyle's forges at Mogeely, Araglin, and Cappoquin were insufficient. Felling those coppices to provide timber for one forge would leave the others without fuel because they were too small and had been raided by wood-hungry tenants. In the meantime, Walley and Adam Waring began searching for woods to purchase to make up for the shortage. They struggled to do so. The lord of Kilmallock in County Limerick refused to sell any wood besides green wood and windfalls, "all of it in such deep and narrow glens as little use can be made of it."[134] Boyle had long relied on purchased wood rights to supplement shortfalls in production and avoid despoiling woods on his own land, but conflict with Strafford and his neighbors increasingly foreclosed this option.

Over the next two years, legal and political trouble surrounding his use of woods threatened to halt production at Boyle's ironworks and provoked a stream of complaints about forestry practices on his lands. In 1639, his agents searched for wood around Munster, but their desperation led to continued problems with the Lord Deputy and Anglo-Irish lords who blocked his attempts to buy woodlands. After procuring some timber and felling coppices, Walley informed Boyle that he would run out of fuel well before he completed the 200 tons of bar iron he was tasked to produce that year and continued to issue forth a torrent of complaints about wasted woods.[135] The year 1640 brought no relief. Accusations of destruction flew in west Cork, and one correspondent informed Boyle that tenants simply ignored his orders to cease felling trees. Walley's anger with the woodward at Lisfinny grew: "For the waste of wood, Charles Pyne is the cause, that doth look to prevent it." Allegations of mismanagement and waste sought to explain the harsh reality: Boyle's agents could not find wood to keep up with the demands of their ironworks.[136]

Boyle was not alone in his struggle to find wood. In 1641, the Munster planter Sir Philip Perceval's agent informed him that, after months of searching, he still had not found a supply of timber. Woodworkers, the agent complained, refused to cut trees "because that they might lose their labor because they had been so often stopped and lost their labor."[137] The woodworkers' challenge and the refusal of Irish landowners to sell their timber made it increasingly difficult for large planters to satiate their demand for woods. The woodworkers feared that rapid exploitation threatened their livelihood and attempted to preserve trees they did not own by withholding their labor. Their action makes clear that English laborers were willing to challenge forestry practices they deemed exploitative, even when those practices took place in Irish woods.

The wood shortage that plagued Boyle from 1638 to 1641 emerged from the failure of Boyle's wood-management practices, not from their absence. From his first arrival in Ireland, Boyle had used a combination of leases for wood rights and his own woodlands to provide fuel, construction materials, and the supplies for his pipe stave and ironmaking ventures. On his own lands, Boyle enacted numerous measures to preserve woods, and those measures grew stricter in response to wood shortages in the 1610s and 1620s.

Boyle did not rely solely on prohibitions to preserve woods but deployed regeneration programs that contemporaries used to manage English forests. He also sought to ease the pressure on his own woodlands by promoting turf as a fuel where it was available. These policies failed to produce enough timber to meet the demand from Boyle's ironworks. In moments of political and economic crisis in 1619 and from 1638 to 1641, the flaws in Boyle's conservation and replanting strategies became apparent. Boyle sought to maintain the forests on lands he owned while also continuously profiting from pipe stave and iron production. His antagonistic relationships with his neighbors and with Lord Deputy Strafford threatened the precarious basis for his system.

*   *   *

Struggles with scarcity in Ireland always had wider implications. In promotional writing, Ireland's woods had been hailed as the solution to threats of scarcity in England, a promise that both James's Privy Council and Strafford took seriously. These plans and actions bound together English forests and Irish woods. Despite these ambitions, Ireland never served this vision as a strategic reserve of trees to patch and buttress England's wooden walls. The connections that did form reveal the multiple, competing frameworks into which the island's trees might fit. The East India Company looked to Ireland as an additional source for ships and iron, connecting woods in County Cork with ventures in the Indian Ocean. Boyle's iron and pipe stave enterprises forged links to Bristol, London, and immense Dutch commercial networks. Fears of scarcity, conflict over resources, and the effort to locate woods by the state or on estates had the potential to dramatically shift how and where Ireland fit.

Contemporaries were aware that Irish woods could serve multiple ends and understood that their use could shape the wider world. Arthur Chichester had consistently argued for regulations to prevent waste and for restraint in issuing land grants to ensure that the state retained unfettered access to Irish woods. His writing suggests that this accorded with his broader political philosophy, in which he viewed the plantations as a critical project for England's success and disdained actions he saw as shortsighted and motivated by greed. In 1605, he lamented that "few [English leaders in Ireland] love the service or like the country accounting it base and obscure in that it is not countenanced with greatness." In contrast, he did "verily believe that the king shall more strengthen and confirm his estate, better content his subjects, and leave a more honorable memory behind him in the reformation and making civil of Ireland than in regaining France." Five years later, he echoed those sentiments. Establishing order and prosperity in Ireland "will be a great happiness to all your dominions and memorable to all posterity."[138]

Chichester's ambitions for Ireland informed his concerns about Ireland's woods. He made it clear that, to him, success in the plantations was a long-term project that would continue to bear fruit for "all posterity." As he wrote in a letter to James I, "Great things move slowly."[139] To ensure that English government in Ireland would achieve these aims, Chichester had sought to set aside woods to serve as state resources and to ensure that government-appointed shipwrights and woodwards supervised cutting and preserved the best trees for the Crown and the navy. Chichester likely shared many of his contemporaries' anxieties about densely wooded lands, but, unlike Geoffrey Fenton, he sought to ensure that any transformation of the Irish landscape occurred deliberately and served the state first.

Chichester argued that England should look beyond its own shores for resources but wanted those explorations to end at Ireland's Atlantic coast, expressing skepticism about transatlantic colonial ventures. In 1605, he blasted those who preferred "finding out of Virginia, Guiana, and other remote and unknown countries and leave this of our own waste and desolate," calling their actions "absurd folly or willful ignorance." In a 1610 letter to James I, he again framed governance in Ireland against colonization across the Atlantic: "I had rather labor with my hands in the Plantation of Ulster, than dance or play in that of Virginia."[140] Chichester described the Virginia colony as a ridiculous game to be contrasted with the serious labor of Irish plantations. But his repeated swipes against Virginia suggest that he saw the new project, despite his dismissal of it, as a threat to his ambitions for Ireland if the Dublin government failed to curb planter greed and carefully manage natural resources.

A 1610 pamphlet from the Council for Virginia challenged Chichester's vision of Ireland's role in the English Atlantic. "A fit emblem that painted death," the pamphlet warned, stared across the English Channel. The Catholic leaders of France, Germany, and Spain had designs on England, but "so long as we are Lords of the narrow seas, death stands on the other shores, and only can look upon us: but if our wooden walls were ruinated, death would soon make a bridge to come over and devour our Nation." Trees were essential to England's security, but "our mils of iron, and excess of building, have already turned our greatest woods into pasture and champion, within these few years; neither the scattered Forests of England, nor the diminished Groves of Ireland, will supply the defect of our Navy."[141] For the Virginia

Company, the only salvation from the grim menace stalking England was Virginia's abundant woods.

This 1610 pamphlet's invocation of Irish scarcity stands out in seventeenth-century writing about Virginia. Promoters for colonial enterprises regularly invoked looming wood scarcity to justify their enterprises. Most of these tracts, however, focused on domestic shortages. This missive included Ireland. Two years after Chichester had first begun raising alarms to the Privy Council about destruction of ship timber in Munster and at roughly the same moment as the Privy Council began asking the Dublin government to report on royal woods in Ireland, the Virginia backers sought to exploit the reports of destruction in Ireland to promote their own enterprise.

The Privy Council had taken notice of anxieties coming out of Ireland, but it missed the sources of those conflicts. The problem in Ireland, according to the pamphlet, was deforestation and destruction, not ownership or management. Officials in the Irish government and the surveyor sent from England all remarked on issues of ownership, price, and access, even if they disagreed about the severity of these issues, but the pamphlet depicted issues with Irish timber as an absolute shortage of trees. This lack of nuance accorded with their explanation of Virginia's economic promise: "In Virginia there is nothing wanting, but only men's labors, to furnish both Prince, State, and merchant, without charge or difficulty."[142] Chichester had emphasized the need for careful management and slow, deliberate action to ensure that Ireland's riches served the Crown over generations. The council argued that Virginia's abundance was so great that regulation of any sort was unnecessary.

Both Chichester and these Virginia promoters argued that their colonies were essential for England. Chichester argued that the English and Irish governments needed to carefully manage Ireland's natural resources by reserving woods for the Crown and passing regulations to prevent planters from wasting trees on their own lands that might serve the navy. He worried that Virginia's luster would drive the best governors across the Atlantic, leaving Ireland to wallow with feckless administrators and self-interested planters. The council members for Virginia, anxious about the grim reports circulating that the first settlers along the James River had found only death, disease, and disorder, saw Ireland as competition. They sought to amplify anxieties about Irish wood scarcity to buttress the increasingly shaky case for their own colony.[143] Rather than a world of increasing connections, both saw colonies as antagonists, not colleagues in empire.

Many promoters of English expansion imagined a coherent collection of colonies that would serve the metropole. Chichester and, later, Strafford struggled to achieve this goal, but their efforts to make Irish woods serve the Crown's needs represented the most well-developed efforts to create this imperial political ecology anywhere in the seventeenth century. In contrast, most other ventures sought to take advantage of resources and to exploit competition among colonies, kingdoms, and empires to craft commodities for English or, in some cases, European markets.[144] Rather than flows of people and objects connecting colonies in an Atlantic World, fears of wood scarcity and competitive efforts to exploit woodlands created multiple, competing geographies built from the material world and ephemeral linkages.

CHAPTER 3

The Political Ecology of Woods in Virginia

Promotional writers described "Virginia," first at Roanoke in present-day North Carolina and then the settlements along the James River, as a place of fantastic abundance that defied the normal rules of European agriculture and climate. Their accounts of the wondrous diversity of plants and the welcoming climate suggested that colonists would find ease and abundance across the sea.[1] North America, in these accounts, was a cornucopia.[2] Amid this celebrated abundance, the first English colonists struggled with cold, hunger, and death. Disease and starvation ravaged them. Rather than yielding quick, easy profits to English investors, Virginia colonization produced tales of suffering and woe that Virginia Company officials sought to combat in print.[3]

The failures of the Virginia Company and its colonists to provide wealth and material goods invite us to reexamine how ideas about scarcity and abundance and the projects to exploit them created and failed to create transatlantic connections. Promoters of North American colonization since the 1580s had used claims about wood scarcity to advocate for their projects. Attempts to develop woodland industries in Virginia reveal the nexus of economic, political, and ecological conditions that impeded the development of the so-called merchantable commodities—plants, animals, minerals, or their by-products that could produce profits in transatlantic commercial markets—in the first half of the seventeenth century. The Virginia Company and its colonists attempted to establish trade in silk, iron, pitch, tar, and timber, all to no avail. Efforts to produce silk, pitch, and tar reveal the significant distinction between abundance as the presence of diverse types of plants and abundance as the presence of trees or plants at densities and quantities necessary to make them commercially viable for early modern English people. For the first decades of the English colony along the James River, Virginia offered the wrong kind of abundance, leading many colonists to treat Virginia's woods as nuisances to be cleared rather than as commercially viable resources to be preserved with measures like those used in England and Ireland. Ironworks brought early colonists closest to successfully commodifying Virginia's woods, but the extremely limited achievements of these projects belied claims about domestic scarcity and transatlantic exchange. Instead, they reflected the commercial dynamics of the domestic iron industry and intercolonial competition. Colonists, governors, and local leaders in Virginia; investors in England; and the leadership of the Virginia Company had rich, frequent debates about how to make their project fit into imperial or Atlantic networks. Promotional writers advanced a political ecology emphasizing scarcity at home and cornucopian abundance in Virginia. As the promised profits failed to materialize, colonists and supporters of projects began to experiment with diverse new political ecologies for the colony's woods, including efforts to succeed in the competition between colonial and domestic enterprises and pleas for royal patronage and legal protections for trade. Even as harsh experience suggested flaws in the promoters' vision, their sense of Virginian abundance remained powerful.

*　*　*

The area along the James River where the English first settled overlapped with a series of ecological borderlands where vegetation and terrain slowly transition. Moving from south to north, the longleaf pine became less prevalent and oak-hickory-pine forests became more common. Moving from east to west, the terrain became hillier and oak began to dominate forests. The river also carved out further division with the ebb and flow of its waters. Floodplains and patches of swampy land housed bottomland oaks, red maple, green ash, sweetgum, and American elm, as well as areas of bald cypress, pond cypress, and water tupelo. Variations in soil nutrients and flood patterns produced variations in vegetation. The blurry boundaries and subtle gradations among geology, hydrology, and climate supported a diverse range of plant and animal life.[4]

Long before the English arrived, Native peoples in the region had developed economic, political, and cultural practices to draw on the diverse plants and animals that surrounded them. Algonquian-speaking peoples from the James River to the Chesapeake Bay supported themselves with agriculture, hunting, fishing, and gathering that shifted according to seasonal availability. Their activities further contributed to the shape of the landscape. They used fire to clear fields for agriculture, fertilize land, and hunt deer. Periodic burning shaped the forests and vegetation, creating stands of successional pines and grasslands in abandoned fields. There were notes of discord within this relatively harmonious relationship. Some scholars have speculated that overhunting may have threatened the white-tailed deer population, though these claims are tenuous.[5]

This does not mean that Native peoples or the physical environment remained static. Beginning around 1300 CE, changes in social organization reordered political and religious landscapes in Tsenacommacah. In the sixteenth century, Wahunsenacawh (known in English sources as "Powhatan") asserted increasing power in the region and sought to create a distinctive Powhatan landscape. Other peoples sought to resist Wahunsenacawh's expansion or to negotiate independent but allied spaces under these shifting historical conditions. These shifts in cultural, political, and religious landscapes saw changes in the physical environment as well. Archaeological analysis of pollen and charcoal indicates a decline in oak and hickory and an increase in weedy species after 1200 CE, evidence for more cleared fields and disturbed woodlands. These data indicate that most clearances likely occurred in the sixteenth century, a period corresponding to increases in maize consumption.[6]

English colonists entered into landscapes constructed through deep interactions between people and places and in the course of changes as peoples and individuals struggled for power in the sixteenth and seventeenth centuries. English contemporaries acknowledged this—partially—noting the presence of cleared fields and repeating catalogs of merchantable commodities gathered during the failed attempt to plant a colony at Roanoke that reflected efforts to draw on Native knowledge and practices. The sites for early English settlement, particularly Jamestown and Elizabeth City, further reinforce that English colonists actively sought lands that Native people had already prepared for agriculture. Efforts to gain control over Native fields suggest a desire to quickly assimilate these places into forms of use that colonists perceived as productive and profitable. Creating English uses from the wooded lands beyond these fields, which promotional writers had claimed were repositories of rare and profitable commodities, proved difficult.[7]

The earliest plans to exploit Virginia's woods represented a search for a successful model. As archaeologist Audrey Horning writes, "Early modern entrepreneurs [were] willing to try almost any moneymaking scheme, no matter how outlandish they may appear in hindsight." Efforts to determine what projects could make money or how a scheme could become profitable show how colonists and the officers of the Virginia Company understood Virginia's woods and sought to fit them into different political ecologies.[8] At the core of these efforts to fit colonial woods into a profitable model lay questions about scarcity in English forests, royal support for projects essential to England's naval defense, and the role of labor in exploiting those things purported to be resources.

Some of the earliest attempts to exploit North American woods focused on silk and iron, projects that indicate how ideas about scarcity, abundance, and exotic rarity shaped English conceptions of Virginia woodlands. The first efforts to produce silk drew enthusiasm from the claims about the cornucopian abundance of Virginia's woods. James I was a strong proponent of sericulture and understood the need for mulberry trees for a silk-making industry, ordering the trees planted across England, including at his palace at Westminster. The planting and maturation of enough trees to support a vibrant industry, however, takes time. Virginia offered the opportunity to begin production immediately. The "strong and lusty soil" naturally produced silkworms and mulberry trees in great abundance. The climate was so warm that it "may cherish and feed millions of silkworms, and return us in a very short time, as great a plenty of silk as is vented into the whole world from all the parts of Italy." According to these arguments, nature was so fruitful that little skill was needed to succeed at sericulture. "Ladies, Gentlewomen and little children," one author claimed, "may be all employed with pleasure, in making Silk, comparable to that of Persia, Turkey, or any other." This confidence was not merely promotional rhetoric. In 1609, the only instructions the company offered Governor Thomas Gates were to set his men to labor "providing the worm" alongside their efforts to make wines, pitch, tar, sope ashes, steel, iron, and pipe staves. The company appeared equally optimistic toward silk grass, ordering Gates to send his laborers out to collect sufficient quantities of the plants to ship to England. The struggle for survival amid harsh weather led these enterprises to fizzle.[9]

Plans to make iron in Virginia drew on arguments about Roanoke and the area along the James River, arguing that wood scarcity in England made North American woods easy sources of profit.[10] English colonists sought to take advantage of Virginia's iron deposits shortly after arriving; unfortunately, though, little evidence of these efforts survives. Still, John Smith and William Strachey each wrote about Virginia's great potential for ironworks. According to Strachey, the East India Company purchased ore shipped from Virginia in 1609 and preferred it "before any other Iron of what Country soever."[11] The promotional character of both authors' work makes it difficult to assess the veracity of the company's evaluation, but even if the East India Company had viewed Virginia iron as favorably as Strachey claimed, it did not pursue more shipments and instead launched its ironworks and ship-building facility at Dundaniel Castle in County Cork in 1610.[12]

The Virginia Company had promised superior ore and cheap timber, but the East India Company had instead chosen to build ships and produce iron in Ireland. The same year that the East India Company set its ship-wrights and iron makers to work in Munster, promotional writers claimed that "neither the scattered Forests of England, nor the diminished Groves of Ireland, will supply the defect of our Navy" and that the only appropriate sites for ironworks lay across the Atlantic.[13] There were intense anxieties about wood scarcity in Ireland from 1608 to 1611, but these worries reflected issues of ownership, access, regulation, and cost more than absolute shortages.[14] By describing wood scarcities in Ireland and England as a problem for the navy, the Virginia promoters shifted their justification to push iron production across the Atlantic. After the failed partnership with the East India Company, Virginia investors hoped the Crown, acting to ensure the navy would be able to protect its kingdoms, would pass laws forcing ironworks to Virginia.

The Virginia promoters' argument placed the Crown at the center of its political ecology. In their conception, Virginia's woods were no longer a merchantable commodity whose value derived from trade. Instead, they were state resources essential to naval defense, an argument that Strachey would also use to promote pitch and tar production in Virginia in a dedicatory preface to the naval official and Irish planter Sir Allen Apsley.[15] England's colonies, they argued, should be organized and regulated to serve the Crown, not according to the desires of private actors. This argument implied that, in turn, the Crown should financially support colonists' efforts to produce iron, pitch, or tar, rather than forcing producers to seek their own markets. Their clamoring for Crown support was met with silence.

Despite these early setbacks, Virginia colonists did not abandon metalworking or manufacturing altogether, but the projects they undertook represented a very different economic vision for the colony. Archaeological evidence from Jamestown indicates the presence of glassmaking and copperworking infrastructure. English colonists, however, manufactured both glass and copper beads to use as trade goods with the neighboring Powhatan and other peoples in the area. These enterprises oriented manufacturing inward to the North American continent rather than east across the Atlantic. Glass and copper beads aided in trade for goods that might be shipped across the Atlantic; they were not themselves objects to be shipped across the sea.[16] Virginia's woods were to serve local needs and fuel enterprises aimed at continental trade rather than as resources bound into networks of transatlantic commerce.

Changes to the Virginia Company leadership helped reignite plans to create commodities from Virginia's woods. Since the early 1610s, after John Rolfe introduced a new strain of tobacco to Virginia, the plant had dominated Virginia's export economy. Smoke provided the profits that the company's investors so desperately craved, but, by 1618, both the Virginia Company and its backers were growing increasingly skeptical about tobacco. These doubts led to Edwin Sandys's 1619 election as treasurer of the Virginia Company on a promise to diversify Virginia's economy. He immediately enacted a number of diversification schemes that would enable Virginians to build an economy on what he viewed to be a firmer foundation.[17]

Invocations of catastrophic scarcity in England and Virginia's abundance had shaped many of the Virginia Company's earliest plans. Sandys's new projects demonstrated a more sophisticated approach. The Virginia Company appears to have recognized that its enterprises needed to compete with domestic and colonial commodities and were unlikely to receive substantial support from James's government. Virginia investors and colonists would need to justify their actions in commercial rather than political terms. To do so, they sought experts from England and the European continent.[18]

Sandys's program to diversify the economy saw substantial efforts to resume plans to exploit commodities from the woods that had been attempted or suggested a decade earlier. The Virginia Company sent Polish artisans to set up production of pitch and tar from the pine trees they had identified in Virginia's woods. They soon encountered issues. In 1620, John Pory, secretary of the Virginia Company, wrote to Sandys informing him that the Polish workers had produced the desired commodities but warning that he should not expect large quantities of them. The workers informed Sandys that Virginia's pine stands grew only in small groves and that gathering enough trees to start the industry would result in "great labor and great loss."[19] In their response to inquiries from company officers in London, the governor and council in Virginia downplayed Pory's assessment of the colony's woods. The issue, they claimed, was labor: the cost was high and the Polish workers had grown recalcitrant after being made freemen.[20]

Timber production was less sensitive to forest structure than pitch and tar manufacturing, but this project also struggled. As it had done to produce pitch and tar, the company drew on European artisans, in this case sawyers from Hamburg (although they occasionally were described as Dutch in contemporary sources). Failure to provide beer rations and difficulty locating appropriate streams to power a mill slowed the enterprise, but multiple correspondents warned the company that, even after these issues were ironed out, transportation costs were greater than the value of timber or boards.[21] Unlike Ireland, where planters could turn profits selling pipe staves to European and English merchants, distance and transportation costs limited the exploitative possibilities for Virginians.

The attempts to produce silk under Sandys's diversification plan suffered from similar problems as plans for pitch, tar, and timber—a misunderstanding of the composition and organization of Virginia's woods and conflicts with experts designated to aid in the enterprise.[22] John Smith had offered the most detailed description of mulberry trees in 1612. He listed two places to find mulberries: "Some great mulberry trees," he wrote, stand "by the dwelling of the Savages"; others grew in "pretty groves."[23] Smith's report, though optimistic, hinted that the quantity and concentration of mulberries might be a barrier to commercial production. In December 1618, James I met with the newly appointed governor of Virginia, George Yeardley, to hear a report on the colony and give orders to be carried out after Yeardley's transatlantic voyage. James had long displayed great interest in sericulture and ordered Yeardley to resume action on James's 1612 orders to Lord De La Warr (Thomas West, twelfth Baron De La Warr, governor from 1610 to 1611). The king's instructions attributed problems with silk production and silk grass cordage to the insufficient supplies of mulberry trees and silk grass. His injunction to plant more mulberry trees suggests that he and some of the company leadership had come to doubt earlier reports of abundant mulberry groves. Nonetheless, his orders, which the company repeated in its own instructions to Yeardley and which the General Assembly in Virginia codified the next year, assumed that colonists simply needed to plant more mulberry trees and silk grass in order to create a profitable commodity.[24]

Others within the Virginia enterprise appeared to cast doubt on these assertions. In 1619, Nicholas Ferrar, Sandys's ally in Parliament and another leader of the Virginia Company, complained that John Rolfe's optimistic assessment of Virginia's commodities was "but an ornament to the thing of substance." Nicholas urged his son William Ferrar to "keep a perfect day book" in which he recorded his observations of Virginia's commodities and climate. Finally, Nicholas requested silk grass "to make experiment here."[25] Pory's 1620 letter on Virginia commodities informed Sandys that the colony needed men trained in sericulture in other countries, "for there belong great curiosity to it." Sandys did not heed this information from Virginia and noted his disagreement in the margin. Sericulture, he wrote, was but a "plain thing" to be learned by all, including children.[26]

Despite Sandys's protestations, experts had already gone to Virginia. Vignerons, men skilled in growing vines and making wine, claimed knowledge of silk making as well, but this expertise also was subject to challenges. A Mr. Chanterton had come to cultivate vines and possibly begin sericulture as well. John Bonoeil, a Huguenot refugee who had been involved with royal sericulture efforts since 1611, became one of the most important foreign experts in the colony. Sometime around 1615, Bonoeil became involved in Virginia, though he would not come to prominence there until 1620. Contrary to James I and Sandys, Pory maintained that Virginia already had "as many mulberry trees as in Persia." The issue, Pory argued, was that Virginia lacked true experts in sericulture. He urged Sandys to look to the Low Countries. At least some of his objections appear to have been on confessional grounds. In June 1620, Pory again wrote Sandys, pleading for experts. Chanterton, Pory claimed, "smelled too much of Rome." Rather than skillfully develop commodities, the vigneron "attempts to work miracles with his crucifix," showing "much zeal in maintaining his senseless religion."[27]

Different understandings of Virginia's woods informed these conflicting analyses. Orders and acts to increase the cultivation of mulberry trees and silk grass suggested that colonists had failed by relying on natural bounty rather than by cultivating mulberry trees as a crop. In contrast, Nicholas Ferrar's requests for better knowledge and Pory's pleas for reliable experts suggested that the issue was skilled cultivators, not natural resources. Both undermined the promises of easy returns in promotional writing. Planting trees in Virginia and waiting for them to mature would require time and costly labor, just as James's mulberry-planting plans for England required. The earliest proclamations had assumed that colonists could easily turn plants that Carolina and Virginia Algonquians had used into commercial crops. If silk making was a "great curiosity," that suggested that it was unique and complicated, an object for natural philosophical study and explication, something perhaps requiring secret or obscure knowledge.[28] The hunt for experts left the settlement vulnerable to charlatans peddling false optimism or superstition.

Beginning in 1620, around the same time that Sandys disputed Pory's call for more experts, the king and the Virginia Company embarked on a new course of action. In 1620, John Bonoeil became the colony's chief expert on silk making. That year, the company paid Bonoeil for sending seven or eight French vignerons alongside Englishmen who "have been trained up therein." The king also endorsed Bonoeil's expertise by granting him lands in Virginia.

Royal and company favor extended beyond payment and lands. In 1620 and 1622, Bonoeil published treatises detailing his method for setting up a silk-producing enterprise. The company not only sponsored the publication of the works, it also mandated that copies be sent across the Atlantic. Individual adventurers also endorsed the work, sending copies to agents in Virginia as instruction manuals.[29] These actions made it clear that the dominant attitude at the company had shifted. Experts on the ground and Bonoeil's texts had become the sole authorities on Virginia sericulture.

Despite expectations that Bonoeil's skill would finally enable Virginia to produce silk in profitable quantities, Bonoeil's writing cautioned that Virginia colonists needed to plant many more trees. According to Bonoeil, one ounce of silkworm seed required one thousand-weight of leaves to produce approximately six pounds of silk. He claimed that roughly twenty or twenty-five trees would produce one thousand-weight of leaves, though one "old and great" tree might produce that much. A "good husband" required two- or three-thousand trees. Moreover, simply harvesting leaves from existing stands did not work. Colonists needed to plant trees with ample space between them or cut down surrounding plants to ensure that the mulberries received sufficient light. Bonoeil warned against anything less than intensification: "It is only for women wantonly to keep a few silk-worms with a few mulberry trees, more for pleasure, than for profit."[30]

In 1622, Bonoeil altered his advice to suggest that Virginia could produce silk without such a dramatic transformation of the landscape. In the new version, Bonoeil argued that some Virginia mulberries were so large that one tree could produce enough leaves to make five pounds of silk. He also suggested that colonists might make good use of stands of mulberries in the woods by building silk houses among the trees. Nonetheless, his work continued to suggest that problems faced any enterprise based on harvesting wild leaves. Mulberry trees, he claimed, were like olives. Laborers needed to dig their roots open and manure them. He also added that mulberry leaves should only be harvested every other year. More frequent harvesting risked damaging the plants.[31]

The economics of silk production in the colony further cemented the need for large-scale cultivation. In 1623, Sir Edwin Sandys's brother, George, sent a request to Bonoeil to send vignerons that reported the wages George was willing to pay—twenty marks per year plus victuals or twenty pounds "if they will accept of our Virginia payment." According to the list of commodity prices Bonoeil included at the end of his 1620 tract, one pound of raw silk sold for one mark. A letter from Virginia colonist Thomas Newce the next year grumbled that a pound of silk cods (cocoons) sold for only 2s 6d, less than a fifth of Bonoeil's price. Even at Bonoeil's rates, the colony needed to produce 140 pounds of raw silk per year to cover only the wages of the seven Frenchmen sent in 1622. According to the ratio of trees to leaves Bonoeil provided, that would require between 466 and 583 trees, unless sufficient "old and great" trees could be found to reduce the ratio. The number doubled if the colonists followed Bonoeil's advice to only harvest leaves once every two years. Moreover, once the cost of additional laborers was factored in, silk production at anything other than a massive scale became unprofitable. Newce complained that a Virginia laborer "who hath no other way but to dig and delve" earned 3 shillings per day and that it might require forty laborers per day during the busiest times of the silk growing season.[32]

The failure of these renewed efforts to exploit the cornucopian abundance of Virginia's woods reveals deep uncertainties about the landscape and about producing goods for commercial markets. The presence of some pines or some mulberries had piqued the interest of promotional writers and company officers. Without a clear sense of the scale and density of those trees, Virginia's ligneous abundance was purely hypothetical. To produce profits would require scarce, expensive labor either to gather the resources or to create tree plantations. Colonists determined that neither was feasible.

The diversification scheme most likely to turn Virginia's woods to profit was iron-making. Shortly after achieving control of the Virginia Company, Sir Edwin Sandys launched ambitious plans to manufacture iron in Virginia that sought to overcome the issues that had stymied production in 1609. In November 1619, just days after the Privy Council had hampered Richard Boyle's ironworks with a £1,000 settlement and a significant materials loss, Sandys told the other leaders of the Virginia Company that he intended "very shortly to sett in hand with Iron-workes." Instead of turning to the East India Company, Sandys and the other company leaders looked to English iron producers. Benjamin Bluett and David Middleton were both from extensive Sussex families with iron-manufacturing backgrounds. Both families were in the process of expanding their iron businesses beyond Sussex and Kent. Bluett's records show that he had been visiting members of the Virginia Company since 1618, but that he began preparation for the ironworks "in Earnest" sometime in 1619, composing a report for the chief adventurers of the company and investigating sources of men and materials at several English ironworks. The timing was particularly good for Middleton, whose erstwhile business partner, the holder of a valuable monopoly selling guns, had taken over a forge from him without compensation or notification.

Middleton's relations had set up a blast furnace in Leicestershire at the beginning of the seventeenth century. Other family members began building ironworks in Staffordshire at roughly the same time that Middleton committed to the Virginia enterprise.[33] Middleton and Bluett appear to have drawn on these connections to source the workers, materials, and examples of existing ironworks to emulate. According to the accounts they submitted to the Virginia Company, Bluett took several trips to Staffordshire to view slitting mills and to recruit colliers. On these trips, he contracted with John Bluett and Abraham Bluett to find workers, though Benjamin Bluett's exact relationship with these two men is unclear. Middleton purchased iron tools, stones, and building materials from Sussex. In addition, Middleton and Benjamin Bluett brought some Sussex iron with them to Virginia, perhaps to test the furnace they intended to build or to compare the quality of Virginia ore.[34] Middleton and Bluett's plans and receipts indicate that they intended to construct a large, technologically advanced ironworks that would be able to rival the East India Company's Irish operations and many works in England.

Sandys's actions demonstrated a far more sophisticated sense of the contours of domestic and colonial iron markets. He had abandoned the state-centered vision of political ecology endorsed in the Virginia Company's promotional materials. Instead, the partnership with Middleton and Bluett attempted to use English experts with experience and connections in the domestic iron industry to build ironworks in Virginia. The plan did not rely on James's curtailing domestic ironmaking to avoid wood scarcity. Sandys, Middleton, and Bluett seemed to believe that Virginia iron could compete with English and Irish metal.

An odd set of circumstances helped the fledgling project. In February 1620, as Middleton and Bluett's ship prepared to sail, an anonymous donor, writing under the pseudonym "Dust and Ashes," gave the company £550 for the "Converting of Infidels to the faith of Christ" by establishing a religious school for Native children forcibly taken from their families. The company initially delegated the task to Southampton and Martin's Hundreds, but neither group wanted it. Martin's Hundred claimed "their [Plantation] was sorely weakened and as then in much confusion." Southampton Hundred offered to add £100 to the grant so long as they were not responsible for the endeavor. "Finding no other means how to set forward that great work," the company decided to allow Southampton Hundred to use the funds to cover some of the costs in setting up an ironworks. The Hundred promised to provide a "ratable [portion]" of its profits "for the educating of 30 of the Infidel[']s Children in Christian Religion."[35] The expedition now had a source of funding, experienced ironmasters, and a market opportunity created by the disorder in Munster as lawsuits halted Richard Boyle's ironworks.

Fate intervened before Middleton and Bluett could test their skill in Virginia's woods: Both took ill on the voyage and died, along with many of the ironworkers who had accompanied them. The deaths threw the enterprise into disarray. Virginia governor George Yeardley wrote that Bluett's demise "will give a great blow to the staggering of that business." Yeardley vowed to keep the surviving workers busy, but a year later he could only repeat his promise "to set the work in what a forwardness we can."[36] There is no indication that other Sussex men attempted to restart the enterprise.[37] The loss of Middleton and Bluett threatened to stymie Virginia iron production before it began, yet, as we have seen, attempts at pitch and timber production also encountered difficulties as a result of labor disputes and cost issues at roughly the same time.

Several other leaders emerged to fill the void left by Bluett and Middleton, testifying to contemporaries' sense that Virginia offered a valuable opportunity to produce iron. One potential candidate, Michael Lapworth, a confidant of the Ferrars in Virginia, offered to write to ironmasters he knew in Herefordshire or to Sir Edward Wintour in the Forest of Dean to recruit new leaders and workers to restart the works. Lapworth provided a blunt assessment of the state of the ironworks in an open letter to Southampton Hundred in 1621. Only twenty-five ironworkers survived, Lapworth wrote, and the dead were "the most material men." None of the Sussex men behind the original proposal showed an inclination to restart the project and, without skilled leaders, Lapworth argued, the enterprise would go nowhere. His plan to restart the ironworks leveraged new sources of expertise, moving away from Sussex to the Forest of Dean and the surrounding counties of Herefordshire and Gloucestershire. But his help came with strings attached. Lapworth, still stung from being denied a place on the Virginia Council, railed against the company's attempt to have him manage the works for a lower rate than his predecessors. "Money be not the follower [but] the stream which drives all the wheels about," he wrote. His point was clear: He would spill no ink until he had been paid.[38]

Lapworth's request went over poorly. The company assigned the works instead to John Berkeley of Beverstone, a distant relation to the noble Berkeleys (whose landholdings included a tract on the opposite bank of the Severn River from the Forest of Dean), who had by 1620 acquired a reputation as a competent ironmaster. Lapworth's proposal and the company's decision to award the ironworks to Berkeley pointed to a shift in its search for expertise from Sussex to Gloucestershire—in particular, the region surrounding the Forest of Dean—to spearhead the development of iron forges in Virginia.[39] In 1621, Berkeley arrived in Virginia with company support, twenty skilled laborers, and family and commercial connections with the recently founded Berkeley Hundred plantation.[40] Berkeley chose a site on Falling Creek just upstream of its confluence with the James River and just below the fall line that divides Virginia's piedmont from its coastal plain. The site offered all the ingredients necessary for early modern iron manufacturing. Falling water from the creek provided energy to turn a waterwheel. Nearby deposits of bog iron—limonite formed as iron precipitates out of water, sometimes with the aid of bacteria—provided ore. Limestone provided flux. Falling Creek's riparian habitat near an ecological borderland meant that the forest contained a diverse array of trees, which likely included stands of the oak and hickory that were preferred for manufacturing charcoal.[41]

Members of Berkeley's extended family and their partners in a Virginia plantation, George Thorpe and Richard Throckmorton, were extremely familiar with the politics of ironworks in the Forest of Dean. Throckmorton had been part of attempts to establish ironworks in the forest since 1610, and Thorpe served on James I's commission to investigate wood stores that followed the protests against the Earl of Pembroke's ironworks. In 1618, another member of the Throckmorton family, Sir William Throckmorton, brought a complaint against the royal ironworks in the Forest of Dean, prompting countercomplaints that Throckmorton had been absconding with protected trees and ultimately leading James I to order that all ironworks in the forest be temporarily shut down. In 1621, the king dealt Throckmorton and his partners' hopes in the forest a blow when he granted Richard Challoner, part of a family involved in iron production since the 1590s, a license to smelt iron.[42] Members of the Berkeley Hundred group had been a part of the battles over ironworks in the Forest of Dean for a decade. They were sophisticated investors willing to ignore or merely pay lip service to Virginia Company diversification schemes that they felt yielded little chance of profit and they were well aware of the promise and pitfalls of early modern ironmaking.[43]

Challoner's license to build an ironworks in the Forest of Dean was a setback for the Berkeley Hundred group, but Challoner's actions after establishing his enterprise indirectly aided the Virginia enterprise. Forest iron quickly captured the market in Bristol, in part because of its superior quality. Challoner, who had previously purchased Irish iron, led the campaign against it, complaining that the Irish product was "proving far worse than our Forest Iron." He was hardly a disinterested party, but other Bristol merchants agreed with his assessment. They informed Boyle that they would not deal with any further shipments unless the iron was "good and well drawn." Once Challoner's forge began producing, Boyle's iron sat unsold.[44] Failures in the Bristol iron market further threatened Boyle's ironworks, already weakened after the unfavorable judgment in his legal proceedings with the East India Company ironworks and the collapse of his partnership with Thomas Ball. If Virginians could produce iron with a reputation for higher quality, they would have an opportunity to supplant Munster.

The Berkeley Hundred group moved to establish its ironworks in Virginia with a full awareness of the promise and limitations of colonial ironworks. Berkeley's backers were intimately connected with the networks of trade in iron that connected the Severn River across the Irish Sea. The Berkeley Hundred group had stocked its supply ship for Virginia in Bristol, Ireland, and the Forest of Dean. They had a sense of both the current struggles facing Irish ironworks and of the past and present issues facing producers in the Forest, and they believed the moment was ripe for Virginia iron. Other Bristol merchants, seeing similar opportunities to move production across the Atlantic Ocean, proposed to build an ironworks in Newfoundland using the Forest of Dean's ore. Colonial projects in Newfoundland had existed since the sixteenth century and enjoyed support from powerful and connected patrons. Although nothing came of this particular proposal, contemporaries might easily have assumed it had the potential to succeed, not the least because Sir Francis Willoughby, who had been involved in English ironmaking and Irish colonial projects, was involved. The powerful influence of Irish ironworks was apparent in the proposal for Newfoundland works, which justified the shipment of ore from the forest by claiming that similar projects had succeeded in Ireland.[45]

The Berkeley Hundred group was able to react swiftly to the deaths of Middleton and Bluett because the group had considered ironworks from the outset of the enterprise as part of its purported interest in developing diverse profitable commodities, a program that was launched at the same time as Middleton and Bluett's forge. An inventory of the goods it sent to Virginia in 1619 included saws, bellows, hammers, wedges, and "iron for the mills," but the Berkeley group ordered colonists to select a site suited to diverse economic activity. The group wrote that the lands chosen for the settlement needed healthy air, good access to water, and rich soil. They should also be stocked with "iron ore, silk grass, mulbery trees for nourishing of silk worms, apt for vines, English wheat, maize and other Virginia corn and for rice, Aniseeds flax [oade] oil seed and the like, rich also in meadow and pasture for cattle and in timber for shipping and other uses." The Berkeley Hundred adventurers outlined a vision that conformed to Sandys's plan for diverse economic activity, though, as historian Lorena S. Walsh has observed, the adventurers' actual policies may have belied their rhetorical endorsement of a broad-based economy. Therefore, it is notable that they actually provided tools and materials for ironworks in 1619, and it is likewise worth recognizing that, after the Sussex ironworkers died, the Berkeley Hundred adventurers turned aggressively to building a blast furnace. In 1621, Thorpe wrote to London, reporting the poor state of the remainder of Bluett's workers and offering to supply a "mason of my own that hath built many Iron furnaces in England." By the beginning of the next year, the Virginia Company received reports that the works were in "great forwardness."[46]

For the first time, conditions in England and Ireland justified iron production in Virginia. Members of the Berkeley group were poised to take advantage of the opportunity. They had experience with ironworks and connections with merchants in Bristol. They selected a site at Falling Creek well supplied with water, wood, and ore. And the Irish competitors who had foiled previous attempts to produce iron in Virginia were struggling. Amid the failure of simultaneous projects to erect sawmills and produce naval stores, Falling Creek provided the best opportunity for Sandys to prove that Virginia's economy need not be built on a foundation of smoke.

That opportunity ended on the morning of 22 March 1622, when Powhatan warriors launched a surprise attack on the fledgling ironworks. Twenty-seven English men, women, and children perished in the assault, including the ironmaster and all of the workers on-site. According to an inventory taken afterward, the warriors shredded bellows, hurled iron tools and building stones into the river, and slaughtered the draught animals. The Powhatan raid on Falling Creek followed a decade's worth of intermittent skirmishing and was part of a broader attack—dubbed "the Massacre" by English colonists—against the Virginia colony, which was in response to the continuous expansion of English settlements and the colonists' habits of supporting the Powhatans' enemies and kidnapping Powhatan children for forced conversion. The attack led King James I to revoke the Virginia Company's charter in 1624 and prompted English leaders in Virginia to wage a sustained war against the Powhatans. During lulls in the fighting and then again throughout the remainder of the seventeenth century, governors sought to promote ironworks in Virginia, but no efforts on the scale of the Falling Creek blast furnace advanced beyond the planning stage until the eighteenth century.[47]

Uncertainty surrounds the construction and operation of the blast furnace. Surviving documents hint that ironworkers may have begun operations before the onset of war in 1622 but do not offer definitive evidence, leading some historians to doubt that the furnace ever produced iron. Archaeological evidence is similarly unclear.[48] Regardless of whether the furnace was ever operational, the surviving documentary sources testify to the project's ambitious scope. An inventory taken after 1622 reported losses of laborers and materials consistent with a blast furnace and a forge (either a finery or hammer forge) capable of not only casting ordnance but also making bar iron. Moreover, earlier projectors had visited a slitting mill (a watermill for slitting bars of iron into rods) in Shropshire while planning their Virginia ironworks. Had they succeeded in erecting a slitting mill, it would have introduced a technology to Virginia that would have competed with the most advanced works in England and Ireland.[49] The efforts that began in 1619 to make iron in Virginia pointed toward a grand vision for Virginia's place in the English Atlantic where Virginia iron, made by men with commercial connections to centers of English ironmaking in Sussex or Gloucestershire, could compete in a transatlantic market.

The Virginia Company's failure to restart the enterprise at Falling Creek suggests that the project was doomed to be abandoned. But the records detailing the destruction of the furnace, the company's financial and political status after the onset of war in 1622, and the broader context of European trade show that this was not the case. The Powhatans' attack gutted the infrastructure at Falling Creek and killed Berkeley and most of the other skilled laborers. To restart the works, the company would require hammermen, founders, miners, finers, filers, master colliers, carpenters, masons, workers for casting ordnance, potters, and twenty general forge laborers, all of whom (apart from the laborers) were skilled workers. The company would almost certainly have had to offer special inducements to convince these artisans to leave the relative comfort and safety of England. Moreover, the scales and bellows would need to be rebuilt. The draft animals and carriages required to move the raw materials and iron would need to be replaced. Tools for processing the wood and mining the ore prior to its being put into the furnace would need to be replenished.[50] Ironworks were capital-intensive projects, and those that thrived had strong connections with English and European merchants. Historian Richard S. Smith estimates that establishing an ironworks cost at least five hundred pounds—a figure that Sir Francis Willoughby's agents only arrived at through some creative accounting on the cost of timber.[51] The onset of war consumed the initial outlay of materials and labor. To restart would require another large investment.

In the wake of the attack, the Virginia Company was in no position to offer the money needed to restart the project. The company had suffered from declining investments since 1619, and its debts had grown dramatically since its inception. Moreover, the decline in investment was most pronounced among merchants. Finally, despite his stated opposition to tobacco, Sandys had negotiated a contract with James in 1622, granting the Virginia Company a monopoly on tobacco imports and offering handsome stipends to Sandys, the Ferrars, and a few other well-placed company members to administer the contract. In 1624, James I launched *quo warranto* proceedings against the Virginia Company, which led to its dissolution and Virginia's transformation into a royal colony.[52]

As Sandys attempted to reorient Virginia back toward tobacco and the company struggled financially and politically, James's government revised its trade policies in ways that removed incentives to produce iron in Virginia. While Berkeley built the ironworks at Falling Creek, James's government had sought to promote English manufacturing by restricting trade with the Baltic; however, after Falling Creek was destroyed, the government significantly softened these restrictions. In 1623, the Privy Council granted Plymouth, Dartmouth, and other, unnamed, "Westerne Porte Townes" the right to purchase Baltic goods from Dutch ships as they had done prior to the bans on Dutch traders launched two years earlier.[53] This proclamation allowed Baltic iron carried cheaply on Dutch vessels back into the English market. As the 1620s progressed, structural changes began to take place in the Swedish iron industry that would permit it to dominate the English market by the eighteenth century. The Swedish state privatized ironworks. Among those who purchased the valuable Swedish works were Dutch merchants with a keen interest in boosting exports. As a result, English and colonial iron makers faced new competition from the Baltic.[54] Old sources of competition also continued to produce iron: In addition to Boyle's enterprises and those of the East India Company, at least twenty other ironworks were operating in Ireland from 1620 to 1641, when the 1641 Rebellion in Ireland destroyed many of them.[55]

While the Irish iron industry rebounded and Baltic iron exports grew in the 1620s, Virginia's government recast the surrounding woods as sites for war, not commercial enterprise. Following the dissolution of the Virginia Company, the new royal government adopted policies toward Virginia's woods that imagined them as a dangerous shelter for the Powhatans with whom the English were at war. Francis Wyatt, the first governor of the newly created royal colony, focused on war against the Powhatans. Historian James D. Rice argues that Wyatt and other Virginia leaders adopted a policy of "ecological warfare" by timing their attacks to coincide with the ripening of corn. Other sources suggest that Wyatt adopted a similar attitude toward woods. He ordered colonists to build "a strong Palisade from martins [Martin's] Hundred to Cheschiacqia to Plant Pawnenka." He neatly summed up the purpose of the barrier: the "winning of the Forest." By 1626, Wyatt and the council in Virginia had further developed the idea. The span of the proposed wall had decreased to six miles, but the phrase "winning of the Forest" remained. The plan identified Virginia's wooded landscape as an asset for the Powhatans and a danger to the colony, and it recommended agricultural policies and land grants designed to deforest the region. The council argued against granting large swaths of the newly palisaded territory to any lone individual lest sloth, illness, or death leave the valuable new territory untended waste. Wyatt and the council called for the woods to be "stocked, immediately with Cattle, horses, & Asses, as the foundation of all other great works."[56] Early promotional literature for Virginia cast the abundance of Virginia's forests as a profitable solution to England's scarce woods. The proposals to win the forest instead treated them as an impediment to settlement to be slowly eroded by pasturing animals and then cleared to make room for farms.[57]

In the same letter in which Wyatt and the council described their plans to wall off the colony, they disparaged continued calls for Virginians to diversify their economy. The overwhelming number of diversification schemes, they claimed, prevented any serious efforts from moving forward: "But all Commodities, are not to be set upon at Adventures which are esteemed such in populous Countries, but a Choice must be made, as wine, Silk, Salt, Fish and Iron, and it were better seriously to apply our Selves, to the most hopeful and beneficial, than to grasp all at once, and these are rather to be referred, to the industries of private men, than the public stock, to be expended upon them, only an extraordinary reward would be proposed to those that should first bring them to perfection." In the meantime, they concluded, though individuals debated which commodity to choose, "it is necessary that the price of Tobacco be upheld by prohibition of all other, but ours, and the Sommer Ilands [Bermuda]."[58] Wyatt and the council did not outline how an ironworks, which depended on steady supplies of charcoal for fuel, would coexist with their broader plan for deforestation through agriculture, nor did they mandate that Virginia's woods be used to produce commodities for the transatlantic market. They did not oppose ironworks but offered no support for them, leaving the future of manufacturing in Virginia's woodlands to the "industries of private men."

Wyatt's government was similarly lukewarm on the other woodland products that had been celebrated in early promotional writing and revived as a part of Sandys's diversification efforts. Wyatt reiterated orders to plant vines and mulberries while complaining that colonists had ignored previous orders to do so, despite evidence to the contrary in colonist George Sandys's letters.[59] Yet there seems to have been little effort to enforce this and, within the next few years, Wyatt's government and the Virginia Council were openly resisting diversification efforts. They demanded that authorities in England select a single commodity for colonists to pursue, rather than attempting to produce the cornucopia promised in promotional writing. In 1628, Charles I made his choices clear. His instructions to the colony made no mention of silk or silk grass.[60]

As in England and Ireland, changing political regimes prompted reassessments of economic and agricultural policies and new investigations into the state of landscapes. During his tenure as governor in the last year of Virginia Company rule, Francis Wyatt complained about commissioners sent to seek out "the present estate of the colony, what hopes may be conceived of it, and the directest way to those hopes." The faults in the English settlements, Wyatt claimed, stemmed from the company's failure to pay for supplies, not from ignorance of the natural world. After arriving in Virginia in 1630, Governor John Harvey wrote that he proposed to set out "surveilling the Country" to search for the best locations and commodities. Harvey's surveillance coincided with his broader distrust toward preexisting Virginian political elites. Harvey, however, was also not immune to skepticism. Just one year after appointing Harvey governor, Charles I launched a commission to investigate potential commodities in the colony.[61] Nearly twenty-five years after the first colonists landed on the James River, colonists, governors, and the Crown could not agree on what they had found.

The inability to agree on the potential yields from Virginia's landscape hampered attempts to establish the diverse commodities promised in promotional tracts. In England, surveyors disputed the number and quality of trees in royal forests and forest officials and governments under Elizabeth, James, and Charles all struggled to translate the variegated quantitative, qualitative, and cartographic representations of English woods into consistent policies. In Ireland, the situation was even worse. Contemporary accounts about the state of Irish woods varied wildly, making regulation difficult. Despite persistent calls to protect Irish trees to serve the navy, there were significant gaps between surveys. In Virginia, colonial governors encountered a similar problem. They were unable to assemble information about Virginia's landscape required to support particular projects or regulate resources, and changes in government led to calls for new assessments of the colony's potential commodities. Colonists had encountered a rich and diverse physical environment but were unable to translate it into the abundant, valuable commodities they sought.

The attempts to produce timber and naval stores failed because of high labor costs, competition, and the structure of Virginia's woods, which made the timber uneconomical to export. Attempts at sericulture foundered against conflicting expertise and difficulties achieving supplies of raw materials large enough to produce commercially viable quantities of silk. Iron production stood the best chance of overcoming these difficulties and producing a commodity for export using Virginia's woods. Tudor and Stuart promoters had cast North America as a solution to purported chronic scarcity in England. Despite their rhetoric, however, many contemporaries questioned the role colonies should play in filling England's needs. Examining the attempts to produce iron in Virginia demonstrates that projectors understood that purported scarcity did not guarantee their success. Instead, they had to justify their projects' profitability by exploiting opportunities created by royal regulation and lawsuits to gain traction against competing enterprises. English colonists did not simply discover abundance across the Atlantic: they needed to create it.

Charles had heeded the Virginia government's urgings to reconsider sericulture, but he did not completely abandon plans to spur commercial uses of Virginia's woods. "To our dishonor and the shame [of] our people," he wrote, "it is and may be truly said, that this Plantation is wholly built upon Smoke." Despite earlier reports to the Virginia Company regarding the difficulties of producing pitch, tar, and sawn timber in Virginia's woods, Charles ordered the Virginia government to produce naval stores, set up sawmills to produce pipe and barrel staves, and build ironworks. He discounted all previous reports about Virginia's environment, asserted that Virginia possessed a "Multitude of Pinetrees," and ordered the colonists to build ironworks using materials sent over "in the time of Lord La Ware [Thomas West, twelfth Baron De La Warr, governor from 1610 to 1611] or other times." The king appeared to disregard previous warnings about the salability of timber products across the Atlantic.[62]

Charles's policy may have been motivated by his attempts to sell off England's royal forests while simultaneously building new ships for the navy.

At the beginning of Charles's reign, projectors urged him to adopt replanting schemes and to reform forestry practices to conserve English woods. Instead, Charles and his government began disafforesting lands—releasing them from the strictures of the Forest Laws and allowing them to be sold and farmed—and granting generous rights to fell timber in royal forests. These policies quickly generated controversy because they threatened the common rights of the poor and middling sort, as well as the gentry and nobility's positions as forest wardens and keepers.[63] Amid domestic strife, Charles I's government may have seen the appeal in renewed exploitation of Virginia's woods, a hint at practical efforts to craft a royal political ecology that stretched across the Atlantic alongside Thomas Wentworth's efforts to exert royal control over woods as Lord Deputy in Ireland.

The government in Virginia, however, was unwilling to enact these policies. Instead, it responded, as the governor and council had done under the Virginia Company, by listing the environmental and economic constraints on the commercial exploitation of Virginia's woods. Their colony possessed numerous pines, they wrote, but the stands were scattered and the colonists were unable to carry felled trees to a central location without quickly pushing the cost of the pitch and tar above their potential return. The 1622 attack on English settlements had destroyed the infrastructure for ironworks and the costs of reestablishing it were too high without other means of support. Moreover, sending workers into the woods risked "incursions of our enemies the Indians."[64] The Virginia government's reply reflected the same attitude as that displayed in the proposal for "winning of the Forest:" Virginia's woods were a dangerous place because of war with the Powhatans, and colonists should not risk their lives for commodities unlikely to yield a profit.[65] If Charles and his government wanted colonists to manufacture iron, then the state would have to fund the enterprise.

The same cycle of encouragement for economic diversification that encompassed woodland products for export and explanations for why such endeavors could not succeed continued into the 1630s. Ironworks stood out to contemporaries as the most promising option for profiting from Virginia's woods. In 1630, Governor John Harvey wrote that the Falling Creek site held excellent stores of wood, water, and ore, but he failed to follow his praise with an effort to rebuild the blast furnace.[66] In 1634, Sir John Zouche and his son, fleeing the hostile takeover of their ironworks in Derbyshire, attempted to establish an ironworks in Virginia, but the project failed as Zouche's son became implicated in the political battle between Harvey and the Virginia burgesses over control of the colony.[67] The Zouche enterprise was the most serious attempt to build an ironworks since the destruction of Berkeley's blast furnace, and it shared many characteristics with the Berkeley enterprise. Like Middleton and Bluett and members of the Berkeley group, the elder Zouche had experience with English ironworks. The major difference was that Zouche came to Virginia fleeing chronic debts and hostile takeovers of his works in England, not as part of a new enterprise to form a plantation in Virginia. Without financial support from the Crown, company, or colonial government, the underfunded project withered amid political turmoil.

*   *   *

Virginia colonists and investors struggled to find profits in Virginia's woods through the first three decades of the seventeenth century. Their travails point to the need to reexamine abundance and scarcity in the English Atlantic. The diverse trees in Virginia astounded some early modern English observers. Promoters saw the variation within woods and imagined a dizzying array of commodities that would allow the colony to supplant trade with Spain, the Ottoman Empire, and the Baltic. But they failed to consider the quantities and densities of trees required for commercial production. Experts imported to help produce pitch and silk complained that Virginia's varied, spacious woods failed to provide sufficiently concentrated mulberries and pines to supply their enterprises. The variation that inspired promotional writers left Polish pitch makers lamenting that the pines they needed were scattered too far apart to enable efficient production.

Promotional writers, citing anxieties about English and Irish wood scarcity, imagined that ironworks in Virginia would prove immediately profitable, but the East India Company's decision to site a new ironworks in Ireland rather than across the Atlantic in 1610 belied this claim. The projects to produce iron from 1619 to 1621 suggest that contemporaries saw potential profits in Virginia's woods, but that those who ventured over did so as part of a broader trend of expansion in the English domestic iron industry. They were not fleeing scarcity at home; rather, they were seeking to expand on their domestic efforts. The failure to restart an ironworks following the destruction of Falling Creek in 1622 demonstrates that, as conditions changed around the Atlantic and the Baltic, the appeal of Virginia's woods also shifted. Promoters had imagined that domestic scarcities and colonial abundance would yield quick and easy profits with the application of small amounts of European labor, but the issues of cost, scale, and competition that shaped domestic projects followed colonists across the Atlantic. North America was not a new world free from these constraints, just a new venue for them.

Throughout the first decades of the English colony in Virginia, investors in the Virginia Company and, later, governors of the royal colony sought to justify a place for Virginia in the English Atlantic that looked beyond profits. Appeals to force ironworks abroad to protect the navy and later calls for royal investments and guaranteed markets for pitch, tar, and other naval stores defined a political ecology centered on the state in which the Crown regulated woods across the Atlantic world for its own benefit. Charles's government had made gestures toward such a vision with his efforts to reform management of royal forests and the Earl of Strafford's attempts to curtail the exploitation of Irish woods. Orders to Virginia governors to explore pitch and tar production and ironworks in Virginia, suggest that the king and his advisers had, at least to some degree, sought to integrate Virginia into their broader plans to manage woods. The cash-starved monarch was unable to support these plans with investment. At the beginning of the seventeenth century, colonists and investors looked to scarcity, abundance, and the state to forge connections between Virginia's woods and England, but all failed to do so.

CHAPTER 4

Conservation and Commercialization
in Bermuda

Unlike Ireland or Virginia, Bermuda did not factor into plans to shore up England's wooden walls or to meet its hunger for iron and naval stores. Nonetheless, from the moment in 1609 when a hurricane forced the *Sea Venture*, destined for Virginia as a supply ship, onto Bermuda's reefs, English colonists remarked on the character and utility of the islands' trees. In one of the first reports to circulate on the islands, William Strachey wrote an open letter that circulated among the leadership of the Virginia Company detailing the dramatic story of the *Sea Venture*, offering a description of Bermuda, and providing a report on the English settlement at Jamestown. In his description of Bermuda, trees stand out for their utility for colonists and their potential to yield rich commodities for transatlantic trade. Strachey compared Bermuda's flora to biblical examples and to the Spanish Caribbean colonies. Yet he also noted the presence of "other kinds of high and sweet-smelling woods there be and divers colors, black, yellow, and red, and one which bears a round blue berry, much eaten by our own people, of a styptic quality and rough taste on the tongue like a sloe, to stay or bind the flux."[1] Bermuda's wooded landscape offered trees that, if not quite the equals of biblical cedars or Spanish colonial palms, nonetheless offered utility for colonists and adventurers alike as food, shelter, medicines, and commodities for export.

In Ireland, Virginia, and, to some degree, England, much friction between political ecologies of wood resulted from questions of state security and the production of bulk commodities. Contemporaries debated whether it was better to produce ship timber, naval stores, and iron at home or in colonies and whether those supplies might be purchased from abroad without harm. Yet, other commodities were also important to early modern ideas of political economy. The seventeenth-century merchant and economic and monetary theorist Edward Misselden, for example, lamented that England's purportedly unbalanced trade with continental Europe threatened domestic social order and enabled Catholic kingdoms to threaten the security of Protestant England through economic rather than military means. Misselden's critique focused on goods that he believed were unnecessary—Spanish raisins, Levantine currants, and Italian silks. While some critiques of consumption inveighed against these goods, successive English monarchs sponsored projects to promote the production of luxuries.[2] Colonial promoters, particularly those writing on Virginia, Bermuda, and Barbados, emphasized their ability to produce these luxury goods for England, thereby alleviating the political economic anxieties behind Misselden's critique. Promoters, governors, and colonists in Bermuda claimed that they had found some of these luxuries in the islands' woods or that they might easily transform the wooded landscape to provide them.

Over the course of the first four decades of the seventeenth century, English colonists attempted to both exploit the existing wooded landscape in Bermuda and to introduce or expand cultivation of non-native trees to produce exportable luxury commodities for sale in European markets. Some projects, such as plans to plant orchards of mulberry trees for sericulture, echoed programs aimed at Virginia's colonists, a result of the overlapping personnel who governed through the Virginia and Sommer Islands Companies, the joint-stock ventures that governed the islands for much of the seventeenth century, and the breadth and range of one form of ecological imagination for New World colonies. Bermuda, however, stands apart from the pattern of woodland exploitation and regulation in early Virginia. In contrast to Virginia colonists' repeated failures in woodland enterprises, trees became central to Bermuda's early export economy. Bermuda cedars became luxury commodities used in specialty construction and furniture making; their high value overcame issues of transportation cost that hampered Virginia timbering projects. By the 1630s, orchard trees, particularly oranges, lemons, and citrons, provided fruits that came to occupy a key place alongside tobacco in rental payments between landlords and tenants. Both the Sommer Islands Company and local authorities sought to regulate the use of trees in Bermuda to a far greater degree than had authorities in Virginia.[3] These regulations demonstrate that, as in Ireland, English forestry techniques could cross oceans. At the same time, regulations in Bermuda show that early modern English colonists sought to adapt wood regulations in response to locally specific environmental concerns. Moreover, regulations on woods aimed at controlling the behavior of the poor took on new meaning and forms as colonial authorities increasingly relied on labor from enslaved African and Afro-Caribbean people.

In Bermuda, competing political ecologies developed that, in many cases, turned on claims about waste and scarcity, even though the colony was never part of plans to secure English woods through colonial expansion. As in Ireland and Virginia, there were frictions between transatlantic commerce and local demands on the landscape. English attempts to exploit, transform, and govern Bermuda's landscape for transatlantic commodity production often ignored or undercut local patterns of use. Adventurers and Sommer Islands Company administrators in England often saw trees or types of wooded land that might be immensely useful to colonists as impediments to commercially valuable land uses. On the islands, colonists fought over differing visions for the landscape and incompatible understandings of natural limits and productive capacity. Because of Bermuda's relatively small size, environmental feedbacks and pressures were often more pronounced than elsewhere. As a result, the colony saw early efforts at preservation paralleling those adopted in England and Ireland. These efforts to combat colonial scarcity likewise grew out of competing political ecologies.

*   *   *

Bermuda is the product of accretions and migrations. The islands sit on top of a submerged volcano, though the landmass visible in the early modern period and today is the product of roughly a million years of limestone formation from coral and calcareous algae, a type of seaweed with hard bodies. As the limestone forged of millions of dead plants and animals hardened into a cap, winds draped sand and dust over the islands, forming dunes and allowing plant life to grab hold. Over the last 100,000 years, the combination of rain and the plants led to the cementation of the dunes into another layer of limestone. The soil atop this rock has likewise been shaped by migration, with areas of rich red soil formed from depositions of sand and dust from as far away as the Gobi and Sahara Deserts. Bermuda's soil, sand, and stone exist in a constant state of flux, undergoing periods of dune formation, cementation, and erosion back to sand.[4]

Bermuda's plant and animal communities were the result of both slow processes and rapid transformations. The warm waters of the Gulf Stream bathed the islands in a steady flow of marine and terrestrial organisms. Steady westerly winds carried spores, seeds, insects, and birds to the islands. Many of these plants and animals failed to establish a place on the islands or

their surrounding reefs. Bermuda's distance from other islands and the mainland meant that larva, spores, and seeds needed to be able to endure long-
distance travel by wind or sea to have a chance to survive. Once they reached
the islands, limited numbers and kinds of habitats prevented some species
from establishing themselves. At the same time, as ecologist Martin Thomas
notes, the processes of succession—the patterns of formation of biological
communities—differed in Bermuda. Unlike other oceanic islands, where sediments only accumulate after a period of slow colonization of bare rock by
hearty plants and animals, sediments were present in Bermuda as the land
emerged from the sea. As a result, Bermuda experienced the slow process of
biological colonization on bare rock and the relatively rapid development of
plant and animal communities simultaneously.[5]

Bermuda's ecosystems evolved in isolation from human influence yet
simultaneously were exposed to diverse plants and animals carried by the
winds and ocean currents. Dense woods blanketed the islands. Red mangrove (*rhizophora mangle*) and black mangrove (*avicennia nitida*) grew in
muddy, marshy coastal areas. In drier locations, the Bermuda palmetto (*sabal
bermudana*) and the Bermuda cedar (*juniperus bermudiana*) were the dominant plant species. These dominant species created habitats where smaller
trees, shrubs, and grasses grew. The plants that made up Bermuda's woody
landscape were a mixture of endemic species like the palmetto and cedar
and native plants carried from the North American mainland and the Caribbean.[6] Bermuda's wooded landscape formed through both the slow processes
of evolution into endemic species and the rapid colonization of plants carried
ashore by wind, water, and birds.

In the early modern period, humans joined wind, water, and the digestive
tracts of animals in shaping Bermuda's landscape. The Portuguese mariner
Juan Bermudez first came upon the islands that bear his name in 1505. For the
remainder of the sixteenth century, European ships sailing to the New World
shaped the islands through deliberate and accidental actions. Shipwrecks and
deliberate landings introduced pigs and rats, who devoured native plants and
animals unaccustomed to these introduced predators. Upon their first arrival,
English colonists reported the presence of fig and olive trees that were likely
introduced by the people or animals who temporarily came ashore during the
sixteenth century.[7] Humans had substantially altered Bermuda's landscape
before any permanent settlers set foot on the islands, but much of this history
of environmental change was invisible to the waves of English colonists who
landed on the islands after 1609. For them, the presence of figs, olives, and
other potentially useful trees signaled the natural presence of luxuries.

The earliest reports on Bermuda's trees, like the earliest reports on Virginia, emphasized the cornucopian range of potential commodities to be found in the islands' woods. In practice, however, two endemic trees defined early English attempts to exploit Bermuda's existing landscape—the cedar and the palmetto. The Bermuda cedar (*juniperus bermudiana*) is, in botanical fact, not a cedar at all but a juniper. It was, at the time of English settlement, the most dominant tree in Bermuda. The Bermuda palmetto (*sabal bermudana*) is a species of cabbage palmetto related to those common in the southern United States. Each species had adapted to Bermuda's unique environmental conditions, developing root systems, bark, and leaves tolerant of high winds and salt spray and, by the early modern period, they dominated the islands' woodlands.[8] English colonists on the islands immediately developed distinct uses for the plants, but the different economic niches each filled led to dramatically different systems of regulation and valuation. Tracing the exploitation of these native trees reveals how different visions for the islands' landscape and economy shaped the physical environment, contributed to efforts and social regulation, and helped define visions for labor.

*   *   *

Although colonists would ultimately come to focus on the Bermuda cedar and palmetto as the two most important endemic trees in the seventeenth century, they initially attempted to turn the islands' other trees into profitable commodities. The anonymous author of a 1612 addition to Sylvester Jourdain's description of Bermuda, which was published the next year, attempted to sum up the islands' arboreal potential. The palmetto was very tall and provided food. The Bermuda cedar and a hitherto unknown tree yielding "a very fine wood, of color yellow" offered excellent timber. The remainder of the islands' trees merited only this succinct dismissal: "Other kind of trees there be, but no timber trees they are." The lone exception were mangroves, which "grow very strangely and would make a man wonder to see the manner of their growing."[9] Early efforts to turn the mysterious tree with yellow wood and the islands' mangroves to profit reveal struggles, like those in Virginia, to turn trees deemed potential commodities in promotional writing or early descriptions into goods with value in transatlantic trade.

After the initial interest in the tree with yellow-colored wood (perhaps *zanthoxylum flavum*, more commonly known as "Yellowood," "Yellow Wood," or "West Indian Satinheart"), the tree disappears from Bermuda's surviving records until 1632, when Governor Roger Wood issued a proclamation against the waste of timber. This order, which reaffirmed a 1622 injunction against destroying woods, extended protections to "yellow wood boards, clefts, chests, planks, or the like." The proclamation suggested that the tree had found uses as a material in construction, furniture, or packaging, but offered no explanation for why the tree only merited explicit mention in a proclamation created a decade after the initial prohibitions against wasting woods. Wood's condemnation suggested that some offenders might have targeted the tree seeking profit from trading trees, planks, and chests, but he simultaneously complained that others merely engaged in "wasting, burning, and consuming."[10] Despite the initial interest in the hitherto unknown tree, including the suggestion that it might produce timber similar to *lignum vitae* (the extremely hard wood from *Guaiacum officinale* or *Guaiacum sanctum*, which had important medical uses in Europe throughout the early modern period), its chief value in transatlantic trade seems to have been as a container for other commodities.[11]

By 1617, the initial fascination with the strangeness of mangroves appears to have worn off. In a letter to Sir Nathaniel Rich, Robert Rich, his agent in Bermuda, wrote, praising some recently purchased land. The newly acquired shares were "very good, beyond my expectation" but were overgrown with "few palmettos and many little cedars, worth nothing, and great store of mangroves." These woods, in Robert's estimation, were not commodities but merely an impediment to productive agriculture. To realize the value of the land, "it will cost much labor in the clearing."[12] The only recorded attempt to turn them into a commodity came from Governor Daniel Tucker, who tried to cultivate a diverse array of plants and trees on his lands. According to Governor Nathaniel Butler, who despised Tucker and opposed his vision for the agricultural life of the colony, Tucker had ordered "a trial to be made for the tanning of the raw hides with the bark of a mangrove tree and to that end framed divers cisterns of cedar and appointed one or two of the Colony people (who professed most for themselves and their skills, that way, to take that charge in hand)." The results were disastrous: "Not only the labor but many of the hides were utterly lost and spoiled to the extreme enraging of the Governor and the punishment of some of the boasting tanners."[13] Butler condemned Tucker as the author of "vain and impossible [plans] and so known by himself," particularly measures for widespread sugar cane cultivation. Any attempt to profit from mangroves, he suggested, was equally ill informed and foolish.[14]

At the same time as these failed efforts to exploit yellowood or mangroves, colonists experienced some early success with Bermuda's cedars and, as a result, regulations quickly emerged to protect them. As they did for yellowood, the first English reports on Bermuda cedars painted them in glowing terms. William Strachey wrote that Bermuda's cedars were "fairer than ours here in Virginia," although they were not the famous cedars of Lebanon described by Peter Martyr. Strachey relied on comparison with examples outside England to explain Bermuda's trees. Bermuda's cedars, he lamented, were not equal to the type most esteemed by early modern natural philosophers. Nonetheless, he wrote, they produced a pleasant berry, which he compared to a currant, and might become a valuable resource for colonists. Sylvester Jourdain was even more optimistic: Bermuda's cedars were "the fairest, I think, in the world." Fortunately, Jourdain noted, there were "an infinite number" of the trees for colonists to exploit.[15] Despite Strachey's measured assessment of the trees, the colonists who followed Strachey across the Atlantic found the islands' cedars useful as timber both for local construction and transatlantic sale and for building barrels, casks, and other vessels for shipping goods. Unlike in Virginia, where attempts to establish a timber trade quickly foundered, in Bermuda the cedars became part of a small but readily discussed trade. Quickly, however, colonists and colonial authorities discovered that the trees were not "infinite" and passed measures to protect the trees. Throughout the first five decades of the English colony, these regulations reflected attempts to protect property and the market for commercial cedar timbers often at the expense of providing fuel or shelter from strong winds.

There was never a period of rapid, uncontrolled exploitation of Bermuda cedars. Colonists and the Sommer Islands Company quickly recognized the value of the Bermuda cedar for commercial timbering and nearly simultaneously, authorities attempted to control cedar felling. The first record of commercial cedar exploitation for a transatlantic market came in early 1616, when the company ordered colonists to load squared cedar timbers onto a whaling vessel for shipment back to England. That same year, Governor Daniel Tucker lamented "great spoil and waste" of timber and the spoiling of fences. Tucker's proclamation signaled an early concern with the islands' trees but one predicated on his desire to experiment with the islands' natural resources to discover profitable commodities and his concern with social discipline. Tucker's proclamation focused on timber—commercially salable wood to be used in construction—rather than on trees or woods more generally. Moreover, his edict on timber was just one part of a wide-ranging proclamation condemning pilfering, lewd speech, and illicit trade. He railed against bands of unsupervised young men and boys and ordered them to be put to work. Tucker's action in response to purported spoiling of timber was to order anyone felling timber trees or fences to first obtain permission from the bailiff "whereby such enormities may be avoided."[16] Tucker's proclamation recognized the value of timber trees, but it offered no program for replanting, coppicing, enclosure, or any of the other forestry methods used in England. Instead, it relied solely on an administrative process (notifying the bailiff) to limit felling.

Other colonists seem to have shared Tucker's focus on trees as a commodity (timber). In 1617, Robert Rich, who served as a steward in Bermuda for Sir Nathaniel Rich and Robert Rich, later Earl of Warwick, wrote to Nathaniel describing several shares purchased from another adventurer. The lands were densely wooded but only with "few palmettos and many little cedars, worth nothing." "Little cedars" not valuable as timber, were considered merely an impediment to be cleared away to access good agricultural land.[17] Nonetheless, it is clear that colonists did take protections for certain trees seriously. In 1618, four men were brought before the assizes in a civil case for illegally felling cedar.[18]

Tucker's proclamation protecting timber trees and the 1618 civil suit represent the earliest recorded actions taken to protect trees in Bermuda. These were limited and predicated on the commodification of trees as timber. The *Orders and Constitutions* (1622) set forth by the Sommer Islands Company and printed in 1622 point toward a more expansive understanding of Bermuda's woods. Like Tucker's earlier proclamation, the *Orders* sought to protect trees as commodities, ordering "special care of the preservation of timber" and emphasizing the importance of property by prohibiting felling without the owner's written consent. It expanded on earlier attempts to control the market for timber by banning any exports without the governor's warrant. Unlike the earlier measures, the *Orders* sought to ensure that Bermudians would continue to enjoy timber in the future and threatened "grievous penalties" to anyone who felled "young cedar trees, before they be come to their growth."[19] These regulations continued to protect trees as commodities but did so with an eye for future production.

Three additional orders further strengthened colonial authorities and the rights of large landowners. The company prohibited any "timber wood" from being used as firewood. It banned tenants and servants from cutting timber trees, "but upon a survey and setting out thereof by the overseers, respectively; which timber so cut down, shall be laid up and preserved for the building of houses, and other necessary uses with the owner's consent." Finally, the *Orders* prohibited the transportation of any timber without the landowner's consent but made a provision for the company or colonial government to take wood so long as it compensated the owner at a price to be set by a jury.[20] Each of these acts focused on timber rather than on trees. The acts sought to control use of and access to a valuable resource through surveillance and the strict defense of property rights.

Another order, however, suggests that the leaders of the Sommer Islands Company had come to value the islands' trees as more than just sources of timber. "Care also shall be taken," they ordered, "that all sorts of trees, which defend the Islands from winds and tempests, be preserved and maintained." Trees, they observed, were crucial to protecting the island from fierce storms and, as a result, had value beyond the quantity of timber they produced. Like the earlier regulation for timber trees, this order likewise emphasized regrowth. In areas "where decay hath been" colonists were to replant seedlings. These were to be "cherished."[21] By recognizing the importance of "all sorts of trees" and promoting replanting, the company offered a conception of Bermuda's woods that moved beyond the crudest commercial impulses.

Other sections of the *Orders and Constitutions* reinforce the sense that the company leadership's concern with Bermuda's environment moved beyond purely functional or commercial interests. They ordered the governor and council to enact measures to preserve Bermuda's birds by "reserving to them those Islands whereunto they resort." The same order also called for the preservation of young "tortoises" (likely, sea turtles).[22] Turtles and birds both served as food sources for Bermudians, so the measures to protect them stemmed, in part, from an effort to ensure the continued presence of valued sources of meat and eggs. At the same time, the creation in the *Orders* of reserved islands for birds marked a departure from regulations on age, size, sex, or hunting season.

The attempt to preserve habitats rather than just regulating quantities and methods for hunting followed the pattern used to preserve deer, boar, and other game animals hunted by elites in England. In doing so, the preservation orders hinted at a conception of the relationship among humans, animals, and landscapes that differed from other contemporaries. For example, John Smith praised the "strict inhibition for their preservation" that protected the cahow ("Bermuda petrel," *Pterodroma cahow*) after "there hath been such havoc made of them [that] they were near all destroyed." Smith's sense of "havoc," however, focused on the quantity of birds taken and hunting practices. He noted that at night "if you but whoop and hollow [holler], they will light upon you, that with your hands you may choose the fat and leave the lean." The ease with which the birds were captured enabled Bermudians to kill huge numbers of them—Smith claimed that Richard Norwood had taken "twenty dozen of them in three or four hours."[23] Smith focused on a hunter's choice between fat and lean animals and on the quantity taken, rather than on the destruction of nesting grounds.

The company's orders to preserve diverse stands of trees as windbreaks and to set aside islands exclusively for birds gesture toward a conception of preservation that moved beyond the articulation of property rights. Each order placed limits on the ability of individuals to control space. Instead, the company set out lands and preserved plants to serve broader communal ends. Preserving trees as windbreaks assigned value based on the trees' capacity to protect colonists rather than just their ability to yield timber. The recognition that mature standing trees, not just favored or commercially valuable ones, protected the islands suggests that at least some of the colonists and company leaders believed that the preservation of Bermuda's landscape as it existed prior to colonization was crucial to ensuring the success of the colony. In contrast to visions of improvement that saw human intervention and control as universally beneficial, these orders gesture at an acknowledgment, however slight, that there might be limits to the utility of human action.

The actions of the company and authorities in Bermuda following the *Orders* did not uphold this more holistic sense of preservation and instead focused largely on cedars as valuable property. The same year it published the *Orders*, the company issued a directive to the master of the *Barnstable* to refuse "any planks or chests of cedar wood, full or empty . . . without the Governor's special warrant." This action, like several of the *Orders* and regulations of cedars since 1616, focused on supervision and permission. It was not an outright ban on exporting cedar planks or furniture. In 1625, the company forwarded a request from several adventurers to fell cedar trees on their lands and ordered the governor to have the trees shipped back on the next vessel to England.[24]

The company worked to control the market for cedar timber, but issues with wind continued to plague the colony. In a 1627 petition, an anonymous group of inhabitants of the islands explained their pattern of land use and the differences in agriculture between England and Bermuda:

> [In England,] the husbandman hath his land ready for the plough, and his houses built; we no such thing. He hath his beasts of labor to plough his land, we none but our hands, his wheat being sown his labor and charge is little or none till harvest ours is daily and hourly, his crop being housed his care and charge is ended, then is our care greatest and our danger most, yea of so [f]ickle and dangerous a nature is this Tobacco, in the house, that one hours neglect or the least

want of help may spoil a whole year's crop, neither is it in the power of man to prevent it when it is come to that pass.

Labor, they argued, could overcome some of the ecological issues that had plagued the islands. Later in the petition, the authors displayed detailed knowledge of the winds that "blasted" their crops. The winds arrived late in the season and came from "north west-north, north east, or at east which is common." Farmers who avoided the winds, the petition noted, had enough labor to get their crops in the ground early and harvest them quickly.[25]

The commercial market for cedars became crucial to Bermuda's economy in the years following the acts to preserve trees. As Bermuda's tobacco declined in quality and price between 1622 and 1626, adventurers often received only small shipments of potatoes, oranges, and plantains. Without tobacco, cedar planks appeared to be one of the few truly valuable commodities the islands could produce. Through these tough years, Bermuda's governors took steps to prohibit unlicensed cutting.[26] But, by the 1630s, this system of regulations began to show cracks. In 1632, the council reiterated the 1622 acts preserving woodlands.[27] It did so with good reason. Two tenants of the London adventurer William Lecroft—James Ragsdall and John Trimmingham—found themselves in a dispute over the cedar on their shares. Trimmingham and Ragsdall negotiated a lease with Lecroft, specifying that each should receive a division of land with equal timber. Upon finding that Trimmingham's share contained more timber, Ragsdall began felling trees. The alarmed Lecroft wrote the council, repudiating the entire agreement and ordering Ragsdall to cease and desist immediately.[28]

The continued commercial failure of Bermudian tobacco put a strain on regulations designed to conserve cedars. As the 1630s progressed, tenants began harvesting cedars and other trees with greater vigor, despite regulations prohibiting felling. In Paget's Tribe, colonists battled churchwardens to prevent them from chopping down all the trees on their common land. Another tenant in Paget's "turned cooper," leaving the land "impoverished of timber." Nathaniel Rich pressed both the governor and his tenants to procure him four cedar trees for construction in England.[29] Even tenants under Rich's watchful eye wound up destroying woodlands. In 1635, Rich lamented to Thomas Durham that his tenants at Crawl had "unnecessarily wasted" the trees and urged him "hereafter to prevent all injurious course in that kind." Nonetheless, he continued to ask after cedar boards.[30]

Slightly more than a decade earlier, adventurers, the company, and the government in Bermuda had passed regulations aimed at preserving

Bermuda's woodlands, recognizing the important role that trees played in protecting the islands from the full brunt of Atlantic storms. Just three years after the council in Bermuda reiterated the preservation measures, Rich's motivation appears to have shifted. In the face of failing tobacco revenues, cedar planks became a crucial source of income. The increased commercial importance of the trees did not eliminate regulations of felling them. Instead, landlords and the Bermudian government sought to control felling to ensure that adventurers, whose hopes of tobacco profits were proving illusory, could still continue to derive some value from their island holdings.

Efforts to preserve cedars for transatlantic shipment and elite consumption shaped leases in the 1620s and 1630s. A 1629 lease between Francis and Anne Arnold, a London haberdasher and his wife, and Captain Thomas Stokes, who had previously been convicted of drunkenly abusing his post, granted Stokes fifty acres of Bermudian lands for twenty-one years. The lease gave Stokes broad permission to exploit the woods on the shares, including cedar trees. Stokes was entitled to fell, sell, and ship any and all trees. Nonetheless, the lease took measures to ensure that the lands would not be completely and permanently deforested. Stokes was required to leave "competent and sufficient number of wavers called standers or storers for the increase of wood to be thereof at felling time and times left standing and growing according to the use and custom of the said Country." This clause for regenerating felled woods mirrored long-standing policies in English grants and leases. In contrast, the London grocer George Smith reserved all standing and growing timber for himself in a 1639 lease.[31] As cedar became an increasingly valuable part of any Bermudian holding, landowners used lease conditions similar to those found in England or in Boyle's leases in Ireland to regulate access and use of their woods and set forth policies that they hoped would ensure the continued presence of the valuable trees on their lands.

The story of Bermuda's cedars is not one of careless destruction followed by a recognition of their value. Instead, as in Richard Boyle's efforts to manage woods on his Irish estates, the regulations propounded failed to stave off fears of scarcity. Less than a decade after the shipwrecked crew of the *Sea Venture* dragged themselves ashore, governors and the company began passing laws and issuing proclamations to protect trees. However, the deforestation of the islands and consistent English anxieties about impending destruction of Bermuda's cedars reflected the character of these regulations. For the first forty years of English settlement in Bermuda, restrictions on cutting cedars were designed to protect property and reinforce the authority of the islands' governors. These rules permitted company leaders and landowners in England to order their tenants in Bermuda to fell trees and, as the tobacco economy suffered, many landowners chose to do so. Alongside policies to protect trees as property, though, the company and authorities in Bermuda began to enact some of the most assertive preservation and restoration policies in England or its colonies.

*   *   *

Efforts to protect cedars stemmed from their commercial value in transatlantic trade as well as their utility protecting crops from damaging tropical winds. Profit and pragmatism theoretically coexisted. In contrast, transatlantic profits and pragmatic concerns clashed around the palmetto; as a result, no tree provoked a wider range of reactions. Palmettos proved immediately useful to English colonists and continued to provide food, shelter, construction materials, wind protection, and drink throughout the first half of the seventeenth century. Palmettos were an essential and omnipresent part of life in English Bermuda, but they did not yield any commodities salable in transatlantic markets. At moments of anxiety over disorder caused by government corruption, the purported presence of religious radicals, or the fear of slave and servant uprisings, Bermudian authorities sought to regulate access to and uses of palmettos as a means of social control. At times, these regulations condemned the trees alongside whatever group threatened trouble; in other cases, authorities claimed that the useful, valuable trees needed protection from the lurking agents of disorder. The shifting perceptions and regulations of palmettos demonstrate that plants, politics, and economics were consistently intertwined from the beginnings of the English colony.

William Strachey's widely circulated description captured the range of opinions about Bermuda's palmettos. His account vacillated between a disappointed comparison with the riches of the Spanish empire, lamentations of valuelessness, and a glowing description of the trees' utility. The palmettos were, unfortunately, "not the right Indian palms, such as in San Juan, Puerto Rico." They did not bear coconuts or figs and had a trunk "sappy and spongious, unfirm for any use." Moreover, Strachey connected the edible hearts of the palm to the dietary habits of poor and unsophisticated colonists. "Our common people, whose bellies never had ears ... murder[ed] thousands of them" indifferent to the gastrointestinal aftereffects that plagued more refined digestions. Yet the leaves proved excellent shelter against "the greatest storm," the bark could be peeled and dried to form paper, and, most fantastically, Strachey claimed that he had spotted "silkworms" among the leaves, which he confusedly claimed were similar to the cochineal insects found on the prickly pear cactus described by José de Acosta.[32] Strachey's conflation of two prized insects for early modern Europeans betrayed his promotional anxiety. The palmetto may have been incredibly useful for anyone settling in Bermuda, but investors demanded profitable commodities for trade not comfortable conditions for colonists.

Another early dispatch from the islands abandoned Strachey's attempt to link palmettos with rich fabrics and dyestuffs. Instead, the author lauded the palmettos as a source of food and drink. The anonymous addendum to a 1612 manuscript copy of Sylvester Jourdain's account of Bermuda, wrote that the top of the palmetto was "a great deal sweeter and wholesomer than any cabbage." Just a page later, the pamphlet returned to the tree. "Of necessity," the author effused, "I must needs mention the palm tree once again, I have found it so good." Cutting into the bark with an axe or boring a hole with an augur yielded "a very pleasant liquor, much like unto your sweet wine." Moreover, the palmetto "bears likewise a berry in bigness of a prune and in taste much like." Palmettos were "no timber," but their ability to supply food, liquid that might be made into alcohol, and shelter made them an extremely useful plant for colonists.[33]

The palmetto proved this utility during times of distress. Richard Norwood, the islands' eventual surveyor, hinted that supplies of food were low in 1613. By 1614, "the whole country was in great necessity for want of victuals." Dearth drove Norwood to consider abandoning the islands altogether. His hunger pushed him "to think and determine of going from hence in a boat to some of the Cariby [Caribbean] or Bahama Islands uninhabited, where was store of victuals," a voyage of at least 700 miles. Instead, Norwood fell back on the survival strategies that Strachey and the first accidental English inhabitants aboard *Sea Venture* had used in 1609. He built an unstable dugout canoe and paddled sixteen miles across Bermuda to collect "some palmetto berries for relief." Ultimately, Norwood wrote that his status as surveyor did more to preserve him than any foraging skills and thanked God that Governor Richard Moore frequently wished to dine with him, for "there were many in those times that died daily for want of victuals."[34]

For Bermudians without standing invitations at the governor's table, palmettos were essential for warding off hunger. Around the same time as Norwood desperately paddled in search of berries, Edward Dun, tenant to Sir Robert Rich, later Earl of Warwick, outlined the difficulties colonists faced. Dun delicately apologized for "having so small a beginning for the planting of corn." But there was little the tenants could do. Each had only "1 &

1/2 [pounds?] to a man, the which corn was not good." The fledgling colony was in a precarious position. Any ecological disturbance could not only cause one harvest to fail but also could eliminate the seed reserves needed for future crops. The disturbance came ashore from a seized Spanish vessel laden with meal in 1614. Norwood reported that a few rats swam ashore from the captured frigate. Within weeks, "they overspread all the country, devouring all that was planted, neither could we by all the means we could use hinder the increase of them, much less destroy them."[35] As the rats ravaged agriculture, foraged food, particularly trees, became crucial supplements for hungry colonists. In his history of Bermuda, Nathaniel Butler, who would govern the islands from 1619 to 1622, accused colonists at this time of "over-clearing St. George's Island . . . by cutting down the palmetto trees to have their heads for food (a chief relief of the people at that time)."[36]

Within a few years, colonists and writers had clearly abandoned Strachey's optimistic, if muddled, claims about the insects growing on the palmetto and instead continued to laud its functional value for food and shelter. But, despite this clear utility for colonists living in Bermuda, adventurers in London and some colonial officials had deemed palmettos "unprofitable" because of the lack of any salable goods to be generated from it. Butler recommended that adventurers order their tenants to dig up palmettos and instead plant olives and mulberries. By replacing the functional but not commercially viable palmettos with trees that produced commodities for transatlantic markets, Butler wrote in 1620, "what a little Paradise would your sweet islands prove."[37]

Butler's push to plant trees that would yield commercially viable commodities reflected the complex political ecology of wood in Bermuda. In his later history of Bermuda, Butler echoed earlier praise for the palmetto's functional utility. He lamented that in 1614, colonists had cleared away the palmettos from St. George's, seeking food. Doing so led to "such a disabling of the place for Tobacco (which is as yet the staple commodity) as that not only to this day, but for many years to come, it must needs feel the weight of that stroke." Butler understood that palmettos were essential to agriculture in Bermuda. The islands were subjected to "huge, great winds and thereby frequent blasts." "For remedy to hope in fences," he warned Sir Nathaniel Rich, "is to lean on a broken reed, for the best fences, we find, will not sufficiently safe guard our Tobacco." But palmettos could serve as windbreaks. The issue, however, lay in the plant's profitability. In a 1620 letter to Nathaniel Rich, Butler made it clear, with his characteristic bluntness, that the purpose of the colony was profit and that profits required the transformation of the landscape.

"Assure yourself," he cautioned, "that if you place your hopes of these Islands only or chiefly upon the expectation of in-bred commodities you will find yourselves deceived and abused."[38] Butler acknowledged that the palmetto was a useful tree for food, for shelter, and as a barrier against strong tropical winds, but he nonetheless sought to replace it with ostensibly more profitable mulberry and olive trees.

Butler's claim that the islands' native plants could not sustain a profitable colony was part of a broader effort to reorient Bermuda's political ecology. The sense that commodities might be extracted from already existing resources on the land and sea or through agricultural experimentation had brought the first people of African descent to islands beginning in 1616. Governor Daniel Tucker and Robert Rich, agent for the lands of Sir Nathaniel Rich and the Earl of Warwick, sought out agricultural skill and expertise from people of African descent, likely those with experience in the Spanish Caribbean. Although the English had suffered setbacks exploiting the wealth of nature, many retained hope in the islands' promise and believed that skilled individuals would allow them to achieve it. Butler did not. He argued that the islands' limited space required a focus on a cash crop—tobacco—and food production. Labor, not the skills fancied in adventurers' "discursative courts" or Tucker's experiments, was crucial to achieving this vision. As a result, Butler wrote, "Slaves are the most proper and cheap instruments for this plantation that can be." "Another thing I find would be very useful in these parts," he added in the next line, "is the labor of Asses." Butler's sense of Bermuda's productive potential had ramifications not only for its trees but also for the pattern of slavery on the island.[39]

Butler had articulated a vision for Bermuda's landscape to maximize profits in a limited space through the exploitation of coerced labor and by uniting profit and pragmatism by replacing palmettos with trees valued in the transatlantic trade. Strong winds forced Bermudian colonists, investors, and governors to abandon part of this vision and to treat woods as a crucial part of the agricultural landscape, not merely as resources to be exploited or husbanded. Butler had not been the first Bermudian to report on damaging winds. As early as 1617, colonists began complaining that strong gusts had "blasted" their corn and tobacco, leaving them with shortages of food and no commodities to send to England.[40] In 1622, the company took steps that differed from Butler's recommendations to mitigate the destructive effects of wind. They required colonists to protect "all sorts of trees" because they "defend the Islands from winds and tempests." Although Bermudians had deemed the palmetto unprofitable, the company appeared to recognize that they served an important purpose as windbreaks. Moreover, the company's action recognized the long life cycles of trees. Newly planted trees needed time to grow large enough and root deeply enough to withstand the battering of a tropical storm or hurricane. Nonetheless, the company did not completely abandon commercial timbering. Instead, it attempted to create a system of oversight to ensure that the company could exercise tight control over felling. One act prohibited anyone from cutting down trees unless an overseer had surveyed the land and approved the action. Another regulation banned anyone from exporting trees, except to owners in England.[41]

There appears to have been little immediate enforcement of the ostensible protections against felling palmettos. The only record of legislative or judicial attention to palmettos in the 1620s came in 1627, when the council passed an act prohibiting anyone from felling palmetto trees to make "bibbie" (or "bibby"), a cheap liquor fermented from the hearts of the palmettos. The purpose of this legislation was social control, not the preservation of property or protection against the wind. The authors of the act complained, "Servants and other ill-disposed persons . . . spend much time and thrift in drinking thereof to the prejudice of their masters and undertakers and evil example unto other good inhabitants of this plantation."[42] Palmettos, the act suggested, not only failed to offer any profits for the company or adventurers, they undermined public order and sobriety by yielding a cheap liquor to distract colonists from more profitable pursuits.

The attempt to control the behavior of "servants and other ill-disposed persons" coincided with broader anxieties about order and authority in Bermuda. In March 1627, the General Assembly convicted Captain Thomas Stokes, commander of the castle and its garrison of soldiers of a series of offenses ranging from neglect of long-standing orders to repair a highway to drunkenly firing off a barrel and a half of gunpowder during a celebration, leaving the islands' gunpowder supply greatly diminished. The frequently intoxicated Stokes, they concluded, had sown drunkenness and disorder throughout all ranks of the garrison. The General Assembly went on to try several of Stokes's associates and the former governor for misappropriation of gunpowder, embezzling labor for public projects to private ends, and seditious speeches. The breadth of the allegations and the convictions of several "Captains" suggested an atmosphere of disorder marked by abuses of power.[43]

A 1627 letter to the company in England from the assembly and the new governor, Philip Bell, made the extent of this crisis clear. After outlining the proceedings and charges against Stokes and the other tainted officers, the letter's signatories asked that the company bar any of the convicted men from holding office in Bermuda again. They backed this demand with a threatening request. If the company saw fit to reappoint anyone who the assembly had just convicted to a position of authority, the authors asked that any freemen in Bermuda be permitted to buy out their obligations to the company investors and return to England.[44] The possibility that Bermuda's most prosperous inhabitants might simultaneously leave for England threatened to undermine the entire colony.

The authorities in Bermuda paired their firm stance with the company with a crackdown on dissent in the islands. In March 1627, the governor and council ordered harsh punishments for seditious speech in favor of former governor Henry Woodhouse. The Reverend Mr. Staples was sentenced to sit "bestride a piece of ordnance being fully laden and so discharged." Captain Miles Kendall, who served as an agent for the powerful Ferrar family and Sir Edwin Sandys in Bermuda, was sentenced to "be carried to the Gallows Island with a rope about his neck as if he went to execution and be there fastened to the Gallows twenty-four hours."[45] The governor and council imposed such public punishments against relatively prominent colonists to send a clear message that any challenge to their authority, even simply speaking favorably of the previous government, would be dealt with harshly.

Yet these measures did not curb colonists' disruptive behavior. In June, Governor Bell issued a proclamation in response to "general heart burning and contention betwixt certain inhabitants of several Tribes in the Summer Islands, by reason of discontents for their seating in their churches, and other such petty controversies unworthy to be remembered or once mentioned amongst Christians in their congregations." Bell ordered them to "behave themselves lovingly and respectfully."[46] Charges of swearing, drunkenness, and sexual libertinism at the July assizes so alarmed Bell and the council that they issued a new regulation making reporting officers subject to a fine double that for swearing and drunkenness if they failed to report malcontents in their tribes. It was at this council meeting and within the context of this general anxiety about order that the council passed its ban on felling palmettos to produce bibby.[47]

The spate of convictions at the beginning of 1627 focused on the islands' government and elites—governors, captains, and reverends—but the measure to prohibit felling palmettos was targeted squarely at poor laborers. The proclamation from Bell that reiterated the council's prohibition against felling palmettos was part of a broader attempt to police the behavior of servants. Bell's proclamation barred apprentices and servants receiving wages from keeping turkeys or hogs (enslaved people would have their liberty to hold animals removed in a separate measure). A lesser restriction on keeping turkeys extended to small householders on fewer than eight acres of land, who could only keep two of the animals.[48] These restrictions on keeping animals were clearly designed to regulate the behavior of Bermuda's poorest residents.

The ban on felling palmettos followed the same pattern. The purpose of the ban was "for the general good of these Islands and to hinder vain persons in their unlawful meetings to drink bibby whereby their time and thrift is much consumed." The proclamation made no mention of windbreaks, only an attempt to protect ponds and fences from abuses. Its main purpose was not protecting agriculture but controlling the behavior of waged servants and apprentices. Bell made the mission of social control clear by permitting bibby production so long as one owned the trees in question or had permission from the landowner or the tribe. The closest he came to addressing the epidemic of intoxication over which he and the council had previously fretted came in a general ban against selling bibby or bartering it for tobacco, potatoes, and other agricultural goods, which applied to all the islands' inhabitants.[49]

In the efforts to serve a transatlantic market and at the local level, the palmetto's utility made it a problem for authorities. The tree provided an emergency source of food; materials for shelter; windbreaks for crops; and a cheap, locally available raw material to produce alcohol. Yet, aside from offering protection for commercial crops from strong winds, these uses were adjacent to the Atlantic commercial economy. Amid concerns about limited space or the drunken disorder of servants and enslaved people, palmettos became a nuisance despite their utility. These were not merely conflicts over social order; they were battles over which vision of political ecology would shape Bermuda's landscape.

By the 1650s, Bermudian authorities began to soften their attitude toward palmettos, but even as their opinion on the trees improved concerns about the palmetto's connections with social order remained. A series of new regulations in the 1650s shows this new paradigm, as well as hardening ideas about difference between Bermudians of European, African, and Native descent. In 1650, the council ordered that "servants, as well English as Negroes or Indians, that cut Bibby [Palmetto] trees shall receive public punishment for every time that they shall so offend." An earlier ban on bibby-making had focused on the behavior of waged servants and apprentices, most of whom likely hailed from England. In contrast, the 1650 order explicitly acknowledged that the term "servant" encompassed a much wider range of people, including free laborers, indentured servants, and slaves. The 1650 order also sought to make order the responsibility of masters, mandating forfeitures of property for each offense committed by the "servants." Unlike earlier efforts to curb bibby-making, which had focused largely on disciplining Bermuda's poor and curbing drunkenness, the 1650 order argued that "the destroying of the Palmetto is a general prejudice to the public weald."[50] The council had again sought to curb the production of alcohol from palmettos, but this time its justification stemmed from the desire to preserve a "useful tree" (as members of a grand jury called it in a 1651 presentment) for the public rather than solely the desire to regulate behavior.[51] These actions in 1650 and 1651 reflected a renewed interest from Bermudian authorities in palmettos as functional trees that, despite their lack of utility as commercial exports, were essential to the colony.

In 1652, the panel of the grand jury again took up the matter of making bibby and felling palmettos. "This cutting of Bibby was forseen by the last grand jury," they complained, "and presented at the Assizes, yet we see no redress nor remedy thereof but rather increasing of their work." The jurors offered more specific allegations about the nature of bibby production on the islands and the culprits for increased spoil. Making bibby was "at the first innocently done by them who would drink a cup or the like, and then but of trees growing upon waste places." In years since, however, "time and experience [had brought] things to perfection" and production now threatened the islands. Instead of targeting trees on waste grounds, the jurors complained that now "they say the highest trees yield the sweetest Bibby so that none are safe and the best trees are cut." They warned that, unless the government took some swift action, "all of our trees will be destroyed."[52] Butler had complained about excessive localized clearing of palmettos in the early 1620s at the same time as the company took steps to preserve trees as windbreaks, but subsequent legislation had focused mainly on the perceived social ills of drunkenness at a time of elevated anxieties about disorder. The order to preserve the trees in 1650 refocused regulations around palmettos to social utility, but it was only with this presentment in 1652 that anyone raised the specter of shortage.

The grand jurors argued that technological shifts in the alcohol being produced drove this new, dangerous consumption. "At the first," they reiterated, "cutting of Bibby was done but in moderation for to drink a cup or the like." "But now," they warned, "they have learned to distill it into aquavitae and so for to make more of it that they now cut Palmetto trees in all manner of places." According to the jury, the shift from fermented bibby to distilled aquavitae had also prompted a marked increase in production and offered new opportunities for those "aiming at self ends by making a profit of Bibby by Aquavitae." The jury's attempt to assign responsibility for these developments offered a muddled picture. First, they blamed the increased palmetto felling on "idle negroes," who "in all parts of the Islands cut most." Subsequently, however, they indicted "all the Inhabitants [who] know well of what great uses these palmetto trees are of in this plantation and that we could not live without it, yet they [are] not regarding posterity."[53] The presentment clearly identified a technical culprit—the shift from fermentation to distillation—in increased felling, but, unlike earlier proclamations against bibby, which cast drunkenness as a problem of the poor, this presentment vacillated between blaming enslaved Africans and indicting a much larger portion of Bermudian society. When Governor Josias Forster issued a proclamation in response to the presentment, he declined to blame any specific group, instead assigning responsibility to "men and women [who] did presume to proceed therein more than formerly by distilling it into aqua-vitae" and requiring "all manner of persons not to proceed herein especially in distilling."[54] Forster focused on technical process rather than on the identity of the consumers or producers to preserve palmettos.

The link between slavery, ideas about differences between people of African and European descent, and English attitudes toward Bermuda's environment began long before the debates on palmettos and bibby in the 1650s, but actions by the assembly and grand juries in the 1650s point toward a shift in attitudes toward labor and identity in the islands. The grand jury's 1652 presentment reflected not only general anxieties about bibby production and purported moral decline that had been present since the 1620s but also the continued development of ideas about Afro-Bermudians' labor, skill, and status. The same jurors lamented "what a profane condition the Island is fallen into since we have been destitute of preaching ministers" where inhabitants went "to sail and go abroad in their boats on the Lord's days to the great dishonor of Almighty God." They railed against "the great increase and multiplying of all manner of disorders of late years and amongst these the sin of drunkenness," decried swearing, and worried that "the great sin of lying . . . doth exceedingly abound in these Islands." Blasphemy abounded.[55] At the same time, the jurors expressed panic about sexual relations between Bermudians of African and Bermudians of European descent. They presented Henry Gaunt for being "unnecessarily conversant" with Afro-Bermudian women and giving them gifts, calling their relations "abominations." They likewise presented and tried Thomas Higginbotham and "Sarah the Mulatto," servants of Captain Turner for fornication and sentenced them to acknowledge their sin before the parish church. They presented two "servants," Margaret Holmes and "John, a Negro man" for fornication. They also presented

Holmes for lying to midwives and claiming that her child's father was a Dutchman. Both were sentenced to receive thirty-one lashes.[56] That these presentments accompanied moaning about blasphemy, swearing, and general moral decline suggested that Bermuda's authorities feared that social and sexual bonds between free wage laborers, indentured servants, and slaves posed a threat to order.

Through the 1650s, Bermuda's governors had sought to erect firmer boundaries between Bermudians of African and Bermudians of European descent. In 1656, after allegations of a conspiracy among Afro-Bermudians led to the convictions of nine purported leaders, two of whom were executed and the rest exiled, the council issued a series of orders designed to exert greater control over Afro-Bermudians. The council sought to clearly link African descent with slavery. All free Afro-Bermudian men and women were to be banished from the islands immediately. The council also sought to curtail freedom of movement by requiring all Afro-Bermudians to carry a pass from their master if moving after dark. Finally, they sought to isolate Afro-Bermudians by prohibiting them from carrying on any sort of trade and banning them from attending parish churches.[57]

In the coming years, however, the council expressed worry that drink might undermine these attempts at segregation. In 1659, the council bound the wife of John Bailie to appear at the next assizes "for being drunk and for using immodest gestures in her drunkenness towards a Negro man called John Forse." The next year, they ordered "that if any of our English housekeepers or others shall take upon them to put out any strong drinks to any Negroes to make sale thereof, they shall lose such strong drinks and the Negroes are to be whipt."[58] Alcohol threatened to create the types of sexual, social, and commercial bonds that assize judges, grand juries, governors, and councilors had tried to prohibit.[59]

These attempts at segregation failed most spectacularly in 1661. That year, Governor William Sayle issued a proclamation warning of an impending revolt. "There has been a dangerous plot or combination of the Irish and Negroes," he warned, "that if the Irish cannot have their freedom, they intend to cut the throats of our Englishmen." Sayle and the council were "loath to have our citizens destroyed as these bloody people have done to English Protestants in Ireland." He ordered constables to seize any arms in the possession of African or Irish people and to prohibit any assemblies. If any of the islands' officers saw "any Irish or Negroes congregating, even in numbers of two or three, they are to be whipped from constable to constable while they run home to their master's houses."[60]

The attempts at the beginning of the 1650s to curb felling of palmetto trees reflect how Bermudian authorities tried to create order. Unlike the 1627 prohibition against felling palmettos for bibby, the actions from 1650 to 1652 did not merely focus on Bermuda's poorest laborers or solely target drunkenness. The presentments and proclamations cast palmettos as public resources, essential to survival in Bermuda, and they painted alcohol consumption as a threat, not solely to public order due to drunkenness but also to the resources that enabled the colony's existence. At the same time, between 1650 and 1652, Bermuda's authorities displayed an increasingly firm idea of difference buttressed through regulations. Over the course of two years, the council, grand jurors, and governor portrayed restrictions against cutting palmettos as a way to control all servants independent of status as free laborers, indentured servants, or slaves; as a solution to issues stemming specifically from the threat of rebellion by Afro-Bermudians; and as a necessary corrective against a problem created by new technology. Drink created opportunities for commercial, social, and sexual interactions that threatened the authorities' ideas of order. Classifying palmettos as public resources reflected an evolving sense of value for trees that extended beyond transatlantic markets. At the same time, the shifting views on palmettos created new space for authorities to clarify and maintain barriers between masters and servants and, with intensifying rigidity, between African, "Indian," and English Bermudians.

* * *

Clearing and felling did much to transform Bermuda's woods and efforts to set and redefine uses for native plants did much to define the political ecologies of early Bermuda, but English colonists also introduced new trees. These introduced species became critical to plans to improve Bermuda and produce rich commodities for transatlantic export. Introduced trees were crucial tools in efforts to define Bermuda's landscape. Despite differences in climate, soil, size, and demography, the Sommer Islands Company often drew on a similar set of proposed projects to Virginia, particularly sericulture, but the Sommer Islands Company and Bermudian governors and landowners also sought plants from the Spanish Caribbean. These plans suggest that visions of Bermuda's landscape as Virginian and Caribbean coexisted. Introduced species also played an important role in local politics. Figs became, like palmettos, sites of conflict over status, order, and authority. Finally, attempts to produce valuable commodities by introducing new trees to Bermuda demonstrate that issues of price and transportation cost shaped colonists' actions for orchard trees as well as for timber.

Early descriptions and the company's first instructions emphasized the identification and exploitation of readily available resources, but they also suggested that the islands might be transformed over a longer period of time through the introduction of valuable trees. Strachey wrote that it was likely that lemons, oranges, and "commodities of other western islands would prosper there." The anonymous addition to Jourdain's account noted the successful introduction of new trees. The author of the addition described Bermuda's soil in glowing terms. It was "the richest ground to beare forth fruit, (whatsoever one shall lay into it) that is in the world." Despite this sense of flexible fertility, the author made no mention of Caribbean trees. Instead, the author focused on sources for commodities that came through the Mediterranean— mulberry and olive trees—echoing claims in promotional tracts describing Virginia.[61] Imported trees, according to early descriptions, were to play an important part in developing a profitable colony in Bermuda, but the source of these imports remained unclear.

In the 1610s, the company hoped that colonists would successfully introduce English, Continental, Asian, and Caribbean plants. As colonists struggled to fend off the hordes of rats and to retain enough corn to use for seeds the next growing season, the company pushed them to experiment with more diverse crops to help build the islands' commerce. The company's 1616 commission listed the plants the company sent to Bermuda along with instructions for their cultivation. The company sent vines both whole and in cuttings. It included aniseeds, seeds for mulberry trees, "sweet fennel seeds, commine seeds, Marjoram, Basil and Onion seeds . . . orange seeds, lemon, and citron." The company ordered colonists to use this stock of seeds to create a self-sustaining crop, sending some seeds and produce back to England each year, retaining enough store to sow the following year. They also sought to improve tobacco cultivation and trade by contracting with Mr. Tickner, "a skilfull planter & curer of tobacco," to teach the colonists his method and, later, by purchasing Fernando, an enslaved man renowned for his talents curing tobacco. The company contracted with a Mr. Wilmot to bring plants from other Caribbean islands for trial in Bermuda.[62]

Even as rats ravaged the corn in 1617, these actions began to bear fruit. Several letters praised Robert Rich for his skill with vines, some of which Tucker shipped to England. Rich turned one acre of ground into a vineyard, fenced it with fig trees and planted five hundred vines. He sowed indigo, which he planned to distribute throughout Bermuda the following year. His garden contained pineapples, lemons, and cotton trees. Beyond that, he had made headway as a beekeeper. Robert Rich's garden and vineyard seemed to be islands of prosperity compared to the destruction that the rats brought forth on the rest of Bermuda. Yet he also offered evidence that some of his tenants were making small gains as agriculturalists. Rich claimed that his tenants in Port Royal had planted corn, tobacco, and potatoes. Some of Rich's plants had likely come ashore with Wilmot, who Rich acknowledged in his dispatch home.[63]

African and Afro-Caribbean agricultural expertise played a key role in these efforts at diversification. Rich moved one of his servants and an unnamed man of African descent to two shares occupied by Goodman Wethersby. The lone word Rich used for these shares was "barrenness." Yet he looked to this enslaved man for the knowledge and skills to cultivate "West Indian plants, wherein he hath good skill." Rich's writings suggest he felt that African men, likely those who had been enslaved in the Spanish Caribbean, could transform barren lands into productive shares. His confidence in African or Afro-Caribbean skill extended to one of Bermuda's key cash crops: tobacco. Robert Rich asked his brother Sir Nathaniel to procure Francisco, an African man owned by another colonist, whose "judgment in the curing of tobacco" made him more valuable to Rich than any other African in Bermuda. Rich must have gotten his wish fairly quickly. Francisco appeared on a list of people resident in Southampton Tribe from March 1618, one month after sending his letter requesting that Sir Nathaniel purchase Francisco.[64]

Tucker's settlement at the Overplus—the plot of land left over after Richard Norwood's survey of the islands—cultivated many of the agricultural goods that the company had endorsed in previous years. Tucker reported to Sir Nathaniel Rich that his vines prospered. Pineapples, plantains, and sugar cane also thrived. He reported that the last crop fared so well that he would have sufficient seed to supply Robert Rich, Nathaniel's agent on the islands, with sugar cane for the next year. Tucker did not believe this success was replicable everywhere. Sugar cane, he wrote, could only thrive with abundant water. Tucker's four men at the Overplus had found a well. If Sir Nathaniel and Robert Rich, Earl of Warwick wanted to plant canes, Tucker told them they would need to purchase land at Brackish Pond, a settlement in Devonshire Tribe with access to water.[65] Tucker's caution suggested that limits on fresh water confined sugar production to a few locations. Despite Tucker's warning, Robert Rich planted sugar cane alongside his plantains on the Rich lands at Port Royal. Rich wrote that the crops did "greatly fructify." His fig trees also continued to thrive. He pleaded with Sir Nathaniel to trade shares with the Earl of Southampton, to allow Robert Rich to stay on the shares he had accidentally settled before the division of land was clear. Robert Rich complained that the vines "do better flourish delighting in a reddish mold than those do in black and white." The soil at his shares at Port Royal were "not yet fitting for them."[66]

Robert Rich and Tucker pursued a diverse agricultural mixture that included grain, commercial crops of sugar and tobacco, and orchards containing imported Caribbean trees. At the same time, each also used introduced trees outside the orchard, planting figs as fences. Unlike Virginia, where plans focused either on silk or on bulk woodland commodities like timber, iron, and naval stores, Bermudian colonists saw imported fruit trees as a crucial aspect of the islands' agriculture during the first years of settlement.

Under Butler's governorship, tobacco was to be king. Nonetheless, despite his hostility toward Tucker's projects involving sugar cane and vines, Butler praised figs and Caribbean fruit trees. In his history of Bermuda, Butler recounted with evident pride that he shipped two cedar chests full of "figs, pomegranates, oranges, lemons, plantains, sugarcanes, potato and cassava roots, papoes [perhaps pawpaw or papaya], red pepper, the prickle pear and the like" to Virginia. He also sought to reinvigorate plans for silk and olives. Like colonists in Virginia, Butler lamented that Bermudian sericulture schemes suffered from incompetent and duplicitous experts. In a letter to Sir Nathaniel Rich, Butler complained that the Earl of Warwick had entertained "that French Peter." He also complained that the purported expert was a dishonest fraud who went around London proclaiming that "there are not better trees in the world" than in Bermuda but "killed and starved the worms of purpose to get home again." With honest and true experts, however, Butler believed that mulberries and silkworms would thrive on the islands. He expressed a similar need for expertise and skill in his comments on olives.[67]

Butler's comments on olives reinforced his skepticism about the profitability of Bermuda's native plants. In another letter to Nathaniel Rich, Butler warned him, "If you place your hopes of these Islands only or chiefly upon the expectation of in-bred commodities you will find yourselves deceived and abused." Butler's plans for olives depended on the radical transformation of a native Bermudian plant. He first came to believe that olives might prosper in Bermuda after "having of late discovered some wild olive trees which bore a small harsh berry." Based on his description, Butler likely had encountered the Bermuda olivewood (*Elaeodendron laneanum*), an endemic species that grew in small, scattered numbers and that derives its name from its small fruit similar in appearance to a green olive. He recognized that the trees he had found differed from European olives, even if they bore fruit with a similar color and shape. These trees, he warned, were not "the true olive tree," and it was only "by skillful usage [that] they would soon be reduced."[68]

Butler clearly valued Caribbean orchard fruits, mulberry trees, and olives, but he saw them as secondary concerns to corn and tobacco. Butler worried about the limited space on the islands. He objected to planting vines because "[they] must necessarily take up too much room for us to rest in any ease." Despite his optimism about mulberries and olives, he made it clear that they were to be set as fences and not as commercial plantations. Planting these trees was justified only because they "will require no more ground than the unprofitable palmetto." He envisioned a predominantly agricultural land-scape with valuable trees in "hedges" not a wooded world.[69]

Even as hedges and fences, figs and other fruit trees generated controversy. Fig trees were important parts of public projects and status markers for governors and prominent planters. In 1618, Captain Thomas Stokes was brought before the assizes in the first of his many brushes with Bermuda's courts for failing to build a promised path between Tucker's Town and the king's castle. Stokes was ordered to clear the path and plant it with fig and pomegranate trees. Robert Rich reported that Tucker took six of the ablest men in Bermuda to build his house, clear the land, and fence and plant his garden. Rich added bitterly that Tucker forced his tenants to build a thirty-foot-wide path lined with fig trees to his new settlement. Rich complained that his men needed to neglect their own planting "only for a prospect to [Tucker's] house."[70] Enhanc-ing the governor's aesthetic pleasure did not justify loss of colonists' labor. During the colony's first decade, as the colony contended with rats, winds, and the difficulties establishing agriculture in previously untilled soil, demands to plant fig trees generated grievances among both elites like Stokes and the agents of important company members like Robert Rich.

The most active adventurers in the Sommer Islands Company saw fig trees as a valuable public amenity that symbolized their commitment to sound husbandry practices. A petition from May 1623 recorded a dispute between groups of adventurers and colonists over a new taxation plan. The most active colonists, whose interests the petition represented, accused adventurers who had left their lands uncultivated of propagating "mere fic-tion." Instead of owning up to their sloth, they pretended to forbear planting "out of a care of preserving the Islands because, as they pretend, the mould of the earth will, by cultivating of it, wear away, and so no ground left for Corn and provisions hereafter to maintain the Inhabitants." The authors of the petition offered two challenges to their opponents. First, they argued that cultivation did not deplete Bermuda's soil: "Even those grounds which bear Tobacco (which as they pretend doth most suck out the heart of the earth) after they have been so employed for some years and the rankness of the earth thereby taken away, they do then bear exceeding good corn. And if after 2 or 3 crops taken they be let to lie fallow a year or two, they will again bear good Tobacco, and so, for ought we ever heard, like forever to continue, especially they have a good Marl for Compost, if occasion be, to mend with them." Second, the petitioners argued that tobacco cultivation only occupied one to 1.5 acres of each 25-acre share. The rest of the land was dedicated to "corn, Victuals, and Provisions" and fenced with pomegranate and fig trees, "the fruit whereof serve exceedingly for the relief and comfort of the Inhabitants."[71] Amid concern that tobacco cultivation was ruining Bermuda's soil and risking the sustenance of Bermuda's residents, the petitioners pointed to fences of fig and pomegranate trees as evidence of their concern with improving the landscape and the fertility of the soil.

As the decade went on, however, Bermudian authorities began to question exactly what rights Bermudians had to fig trees. In 1627, Governor Philip Bell issued a proclamation alleging that "the straggling and going abroad of our swine" had caused the figs at St. George's to begin to fail. No swine, he wrote, should "be kept tied up with lines or strings or otherwise than in their said styes." Later in the proclamation it became clear that Bell's personal loss to both animals and people drove this proclamation. "Not my figs only but pomegranates also are already pillaged and taken away," he bitterly exclaimed, "and so those few oranges and lemons are in like danger to be purloined and what else I shall plant for my own or the public benefit which practice is more befitting Indians and salvages than a colony of Christians." These purloiners, who "dishearten all Industrious people," forced Bell to impale his vineyard.[72]

Bell forced the council to revisit regulation of fig gathering in 1630. Bell claimed that under his predecessor, Governor Henry Woodhouse, the council had passed a law attempting to prevent the islands' inhabitants from gathering figs and pomegranates with baskets. The order failed, however, to stop the practice, and "divers insolent persons have abused the said order by their wrong interpretations." Bell and the council issued a clarification forcefully banning anyone from gathering figs "growing upon any man's particular land" with a basket or any other vessel. Nor could anyone gather figs from any public or private path without license from the colonial government or the landowner. A person could only take figs for immediate eating.[73]

Bell's attempt to curtail fig gleaning was part of the broader crackdown on the behavior of the poorest Bermudians at the end of the 1620s. His first

injunction against pigs and people destroying his orchards and fences coincided with the first attempt to control bibby production and restrictions on
owning pigs and poultry targeting poor artisans, slaves, and servants. During
that same period, the council enacted measures to curtail nearshore fishing.
The stated aim of the measures was to preserve large, valuable fish, but, in the
process, it removed another source of sustenance from Bermuda's poor.[74] At
the beginning of the 1620s, Bermuda's most active planters and investors had
cited the public benefit of fig trees as a justification for their vision of Bermuda's landscape and their husbandry practices. By the end of the decade,
Bermuda's governors were curtailing those rights as part of a broader wave
of actions designed to control the behavior of the poor, the enslaved, and the
bonded laborers.

This new emphasis on controlling access to fruit trees as common
resources stemmed from the failure of Bermuda's tobacco economy. During
his governorship, Butler claimed, "There will be never found any true
ground of hope of any commodity growing here anyway half so beneficial as
Tobacco."[75] Yet, reports from 1620 indicate that his vision of a landscape dominated by tobacco faced serious issues from the moment he articulated it. In
January, Thomas Durham wrote Sir Nathaniel Rich with a frank assessment of
his estates. John Day and John Williams, who occupied Rich shares in Southampton Tribe, "planted little Corn and potatoes, but never cared for raising
any profit planting tobacco more than for their own use." Cooke and Cre-
swell, two servants, "made away" for want of victuals. The tenants on shares
at Heron Bay included "Edward Athens [Athen] and Thomas Turner, politike
fellows." Athen in particular drew Durham's ire as "a famous man and a great
practitioner in phisicke and all not worthy a straw but flattering and dissimu-
lation." Mr. Needham "intendeth to plant corn and potatoes upon [his shares
at Brackish Pond, Devonshire] to raise no profit out of them planting tobacco."
The Richs' most "painful [painstaking]" and "lusty" tenants had not yet
reached their productive potential. They would, Durham wrote, "raise great
profit" if only they had a "boy" or two to labor in the fields. The only group
Durham wrote that had actually produced anything were enslaved Africans.
As a group, they produced 1,350 pounds of tobacco.[76]

In an account from February 1620, Nathaniel Rich informed Warwick of
the value of his Bermudian holdings, £110 12s 7d. Of this sum, only £56 16s 3d
were liquid revenues from sold tobacco. Just less than half the value was debt
repayment owed by Warwick's Bermudian tenants, including his cousin Robert, who managed many of Warwick's affairs on the islands. Thomas Durham,
another tenant who corresponded with Warwick, sent a 26-pound bundle

of tobacco that still left him 8*s* 9*d* in debt to the earl.[77] This ratio of debts to cash was not a problem so long as Warwick had sufficient liquid assets and credit to manage his affairs in England and tenants like Durham continued to chip away at their debts. And evidence from Warwick's accounts suggests that his tenants were doing so. In 1619, all those who held land from him, save Durham, had repaid the earl for the cost of the goods he sent over.[78]

In their attempts to create a thriving tobacco economy in Bermuda, however, colonists ran against environmental consequences from the clearing of Bermuda's native woods. Clearing trees was essential to creating fields for tobacco, but, in doing so, colonists exposed their crops to the ravages of tropical winds. John Dutton, Sir Nathaniel Rich's agent in Bermuda, wrote to describe the hardships hampering tobacco cultivators: "Perhaps we may plant four or five times and not get them [to] stand, being eaten up with worms. When they do stand, want of rain may starve it in, or burn it off the ground. Or else when it is near ripe the wind torn [tore] it up by the roots, besides all danger of losing it when it is in the house. . . . None of the best shares in the Islands will admit past eight or nine acres to be fallen of any use. In some of them, five or six, others not singly to be lived on."[79] The picture Dutton painted was bleak. Less than half of a twenty-five-acre share could support tobacco cultivation. Pests and droughts killed many plants. Whatever plants happened to survive would be ripped from the ground by tropical storms.

In addition to his concern about the threat of winds, Dutton worried that soil exhaustion was beginning to plague some colonists. The men at Heron Bay, Dutton complained, gave leave to other colonists to fell and clear their land to plant two crops of corn in order to earn enough to leave their tobacco fields fallow in an attempt to save them. Without these desperate measures, Dutton estimated that their tobacco grounds "cannot else last out 2 or 3 years."[80] Heron Bay had been under cultivation since at least 1618. In earlier years, the oldest tenants had fared best, but now the formerly fortunate appeared to suffer. "In a few years," Douglas Helms, historian at the United States Department of Agriculture writes, "Annual plants used up . . . the nitrogen, phosphorus, potassium, calcium, and magnesium, which the deep-rooted trees had taken up, concentrated, and stored in trunks and limbs over several decades."[81] Early Chesapeake farmers could expect three years of tobacco and three years of corn, which has a deeper root system to draw on a new layer of nutrients, followed by a twenty-year fallow period in unmanured soil.[82] Even after this fallow period, nutrients remained trapped in deeper soil layers, placing longer-term limits on the relatively nutrient-poor soils of the North American piedmont and coastal plain.[83] Bermuda's thin soil had slowly gathered over millennia. Nutrient-depleting crops like corn and tobacco and erosion from the strong winds quickly ate into the sparse nutrient reserves in Bermuda's soil. Even after the nutritive booster shot of decaying plant matter that followed land clearances, commercial agriculture threatened to exhaust the soil. Allowing other colonists to clear and cultivate ground bought the Heron Bay tenants a few years for fallowing, but it removed their ability to cultivate other parts of their holdings and leave their tobacco grounds fallow for a long period of time.

By 1622, the failure of tobacco to deliver profits pushed the company to change course and echo plans aimed at Virginia's colonists to diversify their economic activities. The company ordered colonists to reduce their dependence on tobacco. Two separate regulations simply urged colonists to "apply themselves ... to more stable and solid commodities" without giving any specific instructions as to what those commodities might be.[84] In 1626, the adventurers blamed intercolonial and international competition. Bermudian tobacco could not compete with "Virginia tobacco far better than it was wont to be, also store of Spanish by license and from St. Christopher's Islands which is very good." In response to this competition, the company ordered all colonists to immediately halt tobacco production. The order prompted vitriolic reactions from each of the tribes, who claimed that they could not survive without tobacco revenue.[85] In the years that followed, however, colonists attempted to move away from tobacco cultivation, and trees were at the center of many of their schemes.

The worries about the failure of Bermudian tobacco led the leaders of the Sommer Islands Company to reassess Bermuda's landscape and climate. They wrote Captain Henry Woodhouse, the islands' new governor, with a long list of projects the company wanted pursued. The colonists needed to pursue "pieces of ground in two several tribes fit to plant sugar canes." They lamented that colonists' "eagerness about their tobacco causeth them to neglect both that and all things else so that they cleared their canes so soon as they came to be fit for swine before they came to ripeness." "Surely," they contended, "your climate which ripens figs and other fruits cannot choose but ripen grapes exceeding well." The company outlined a detailed and ambitious project to set up silk works. The ship bearing the company's letter carried seeds from the "great black and best sort of mulberry, the leaf strong and hearty for the silkworms the fruit very wholesome and good, and it is the same fruit as whereof in Spain they make their great quantities of Alegant [Alicant] wine." The company again informed the colonists that weather should not hamper the enterprise: "We suppose your climate to be ordinary good and fitting for this work inasmuch as the Summer is early and brings forth food, whereby you may bring forward worms betimes in the year which is the only sure help to that business, and that they may have finished their spinning before the midst of May." The optimistic reassessments of Bermuda's climate and the wisdom that pests "would destroy all if painful and diligent prevention were not used" carried an implicit accusation that diligent labor was lacking.[86] As in Virginia, fears that tobacco might no longer supply profits, led adventurers in England to push plans for silk and wine. Unlike Virginia, however, adventurers moved beyond these plans and experimented with commodities drawn from imported trees.

In the 1630s, adventurers resumed their search for imported trees that would serve as windbreaks but also allow for the production of profitable bulk commodities. In 1632, colonists attempted to cultivate "oil seeds," likely castor oil plants (*Ricinus communis*), which the council immediately protected with an injunction against "purloiners" stealing oil trees. The next year, Governor Roger Wood shipped a box of seeds back to England with a letter requesting an oil press to refine them in Bermuda.[87] Despite this auspicious beginning, correspondence from 1634 revealed a confused mess of production, refining, and sale. One of Wood's letters lamented low output of seeds as the result of Bermuda's lingering malady—tobacco overproduction. In another, he proudly exclaimed, "We have planted and gathered so much seed as it may be likened to Joseph's provision for corn in Egypt." Wood sat on this abundance unable to find a press to extract the oil, a complaint he repeated in another letter that year. This technical limitation was the least of Wood's problems. "Before I will put a finger to a press to make this oil for 12*d* a gallon," he spat, "I will pluck up all my trees and burn them." Wood issued this threat for good reason. He wrote the adventurer Thomas Cumberford that one of his tenants in Paget's tribe, John Carter, had planted no tobacco, only oil seeds. He had so many that "no men will buy them of him nor can he make [oil] himself for all the Tribes' estates will not erect a mill and press for that business." The other tenants in Paget's learned from Carter's mistake and tore up their trees to plant tobacco, lest the low price of oil "make us all beggars." On John Woodall's shares in Paget's, tenants simply left their homes, convinced that the leases for half tobacco and half oil would leave them destitute. The problems with oil occurred in other parts of the islands. Wood reported that, in Smith's tribe, "most men pull up their trees and intend to plant Tobacco [in] their places for they cannot sell their seed rough." It would be better, Wood wrote, "the land should lie fallow than worn out for no profit."[88]

In 1634, William Jessop ordered his agent in Bermuda to cease renting Rich shares in Hamilton tribe for tobacco, which was "like to be of small value." Instead, Jessop, Warwick, and Nathaniel Rich all implored their tenants to pursue junipers and "juniper juice," which was "likely to be of good value." Like the oil trees, they required a press, which only one tenant had built. Like the oil trees Wood described, Warwick lamented that the juniper juice sold poorly. Despite Rich's, Warwick's, and Jessop's encouragement of juniper, their tenants apparently responded the same way as their fellow Bermudians and tore out their trees. Unlike annual crops of corn or tobacco, trees, even shrubby ones like juniper, take years to mature and bear fruit. The Earl of Warwick correctly deduced that planting and destroying them in a few years prevented "more accurate trial . . . of the commodity."[89] After such an abysmal start to the enterprise, Rich continued actively promoting it in 1635. He praised Christopher Parker's efforts and offered him refining machinery and labor and chastised Thomas Durham for not working hard enough "although as yet your encouragement be small and the price uncertain."[90] Rich's message was clear: Tenants who followed the patterns of cultivation he desired would be rewarded with access to resources and labor.[91] Those who did not would be left to fend for themselves.

Despite these spectacular failures, smaller attempts at planting citrus orchards proved more successful. Rich's, Warwick's, and Jessop's tenants sent back oranges, lemons, pineapples, and plantains. Although the pineapples and plantains came back spoiled, the London recipients expressed their pleasure with the goods and expressed the hope that more would be forthcoming.[92] The next year, more oranges made it back to England and were met with further encouragement from Rich and Jessop, who pressed colonists to add pomegranate, citron, and other trees to their shares.[93] Despite the enthusiasm for pomegranates and citrus in their correspondence, adventurers continued to offer leases that required their tenants to produce tobacco.

Adventurers in London received mainly fruits, trees, and vegetables from their tenants. In 1637, Jessop, Rich, and Warwick received potatoes, plantains, pineapples, and oranges. Shipboard spoilage and delays reduced the potatoes and pineapples. Colonists desperate to show that they had done anything sent back peas. Juniper planks were the most profitable good sent back. The woodlands destroyed at the Crawl provided Jessop with timber on two separate occasions—four shaped boards, eight trees, and forty-five planks in total.[94] In 1638, Edward Montagu, Viscount Mandeville, who took over the recently deceased Nathaniel Rich's shares, praised the quality of oranges he received from his tenants. In two letters that year, Warwick mentioned tobacco and oranges in the same breath, thanking his tenants for "the tobacco and token of oranges." Warwick forbore commenting on the tobacco but instructed both agents to send along as much fruit as possible, "especially of oranges which I do mightily value."[95] The correspondence over the latter half of the 1630s from Rich, Warwick, and Jessop demonstrates their knowledge of the poor quality of Bermudian tobacco. Nonetheless, other than their failed attempts to cultivate junipers, none sought to change the Bermudian economy.

Their inaction spoke to a larger trend among landowners at the end of the 1630s. Leases and rentals from across the islands between 1637 and 1641 demanded rents in tobacco in amounts that even experienced tenants like Hugh Wentworth failed to produce. In the light of the correspondence between Bermudians and English adventurers and the decreasing quantities of increasingly poor tobacco straggling to market in London, these agreements represented fantasies or attempts at outright exploitation. The Kentish adventurer William Ewen leased "two shares of land containing by estimation 50 acres" to William Farmer. Ewen's ignorance of the actual size of his holding is telling. The terms of this agreement demanded Farmer produce 400 pounds of "good, sufficient, and merchantable of the best sort of Bermudas Tobacco." Moreover, Farmer was to send "good potatoes and two hundred of good oranges and one hundred of good lemons." These amounts were impossible given the state of the shares' orchards, so the agreement added that Farmer must "at his own charge set and plant upon the leased premises yearly during the said term twenty orange trees and twenty lemon trees apt and fit to grow." A lease of fifty acres in Paget's tribe demanded "250lb of Tobacco of the best sort and also half a hundred of oranges and lemons of the biggest size there growing, and a barrel of potatoes to be paid and delivered yearly." In five leases across Warwick's and Sandy's tribes, George Smith demanded between 250 and 400 pounds of tobacco and 100 to 200 pounds of potatoes for rent. In a 1638 codicil to a lease, Bennet Mathew ordered his tenant Hugh Beard to search out drugs. If he found any, Beard was to cultivate them and receive a generous share of two-thirds produce for himself.[96] Mathew's vague orders may have indicated an interest in natural philosophy or they may have been an attempt to search out anything profitable on his shares. This codicil represented the lone innovation in the leases in the 1630s.

These rentals were not simply the result of custom. In 1638, the Middlesex knight Sir William Killigrew found himself in dispute with Henry Woodhouse over six shares of land in Hamilton tribe. Woodhouse owed "100 oranges, 100 lemons, and one hundred of potatoes at the feast of the Annunciation of the Blessed Virgin Mary" every year, beginning in 1634. Unlike other leases,

Woodhouse owed no tobacco. Nonetheless, he had not paid his rent since 1637. Killigrew ordered his attorney to force Woodhouse to farm his shares or to lease the land "to the said Thomas Wood for the first 3 years of the said 21 the yearly rent of 300 of the best oranges, 100 of the best potato roots, and 350 weight of Tobacco, and after the first 3 years are ended the yearly rent shall be 300 of the best oranges, 100 of the best lemons, and four hundred-weight of Tobacco."[97] In one sense, Killigrew's lease was more reasonable than many others, requiring the same amount of tobacco from six shares that other adventurers demanded from two. Yet, the addition of tobacco to the agreement at all is puzzling. Why not instead encourage his tenants to do something else to raise his profit?

The documents tentatively suggest that adventurers' conviction that labor could overcome purported natural limits was to blame. In 1638, Warwick turned down the lease offers of Thomas Wills and several other tenants for shares near the Crawl, which had been recently deforested. Warwick wrote, "The rent offered by him for those shares was so small that I cannot by any means accept thereof."[98] He would rather let his shares lay uncultivated than accept a low rent. In the first correspondence between Mandeville and his tenants, Mandeville chastised them for sending back less tobacco than he was owed. Mandeville informed his correspondents that he intended for them to make up this shortage in the next shipment. After years of declining quality and volume, Mandeville's request was wishful thinking.

*　*　*

Attitudes, policies, and actions toward Bermuda's wooded landscapes stand out in the history of wood in the Atlantic colonies. Although Virginia occupied a more prominent place in metropolitan conceptions of political ecology and plans to alleviate purported wood scarcity in England, both transatlantic and local timber trades developed in Bermuda to a far greater degree and held greater economic importance than in early Virginia. Likewise, despite the cornucopian promises of promotional literature, Bermuda, not Virginia, managed to create commercial orchards serving elite investors and landowners in England. The Sommer Islands Company, Bermudian governors, and landowners recognized the value of products from Bermuda's woods and orchards and set out to protect them with evolving rules and regulations. Despite all this, Bermuda's timber trade, orchards, and tree plantations did little to assuage English fears of wood scarcity nor did contemporary promoters of the islands even suggest they might.

Nonetheless, the trade in and policies toward the islands' trees are crucial to understanding the complex political ecologies of wood in this period. The demand for luxury commodities shaped early assessments of the cedar and palmetto, defining one tree as a valuable luxury and the other as a nuisance, despite its importance to colonists' everyday activities. It was only the rise of fears about deforestation and the destructive force of oceanic winds that elevated the palmetto to a plant worth preserving. Despite this, the palmetto's associations with drunkenness and disorder lingered. Even without concerns about naval supply and relief for domestic woodlands, colonists, the governors, and adventurers created policies and practices to consciously shape Bermuda's woods and to address questions of scarcity.

Until the 1640s, English adventurers advanced a political ecology focused on serving metropolitan demands. When the Bermuda tobacco suffered in the London market, they ordered rapid changes to the wooded landscape, seeking new commodities for long-distance trade. Issues of transportation and cost plagued attempts to cultivate fruits or oils, just as they did bulk commodities in Virginia and Ireland. Bermuda, however, stands out for the rapid planting and destruction of several introduced species as adventurers grew increasingly desperate for profits and as their tenants grew increasingly frustrated with ill-informed projects from afar.

In Bermuda, colonists, governors, and adventurers struggled to balance concerns about profit, noncommercial uses for plants, and choices between commodities in a geographic space they understood as limited. From the first attempt at permanent settlement, the company, governors, landholders, and their agents set out rules and restrictions to protect potential resources while they (drawing on both English and African and Afro-Caribbean experts) experimented to see what might work. By 1622, the *Orders* formalized a relatively holistic vision for preservation that looked beyond trees solely as commodities. In their rules, proclamations, and estate management, colonists clearly rejected promotional rhetoric about inexhaustible resources. The deforestation, rapid changes in the landscape, and efforts to introduce new tree species that occurred resulted from the quest for profits, even when contemporaries acknowledged that doing so would rob colonists of valuable and utilitarian trees.

CHAPTER 5

Deforestation and Preservation in Early Barbados

In 1631, Henry Colt decried Barbados as a wretched place full of lazy masters and disobedient servants. This sense of the social disorder was reflected in the landscape. "Your ground & plantations shewes what you are," he scolded, "They lie like the ruins of some village lately burned." Colonists lived among charred stumps, unconcerned with digging and weeding for "beauty" while vaingloriously boasting that their thin soil of decaying leaves and ashes was the best in the world. There were few "great trees" amid the mass of shrubby underwood "not hard to be cleared" but left standing because of the constant bickering of querulous masters and idle servants.[1] Scorched stumps and weedy shrubs served as constant reminders of the colony's moral rot.

Colt's disgust with the woody landscape provides an example of a colonial attitude toward the environment. Like English writers who railed against the Irish woodkern and the dark, terrifying forests that enabled Irish rebellion or the Virginia government's plan to wage war against the forest during the Second Anglo-Powhatan War, Colt equated Barbadian woods with degeneration and decay. His condemnation implied a plan for the island: Virtuous masters and diligent servants should clear away trees and stumps to create an aesthetically appealing agricultural landscape. Their acts to cleanse the landscape would, in turn, reinforce a harmonious social order. His was an ecological and political fantasy that demanded total transformation.

Barbados, in contrast to and more than any place else in the English Atlantic, has served as the example of the scale and scope of environmental degradation that accompanied colonial expansion. Between 1627, when the first permanent English colonists landed on the island, and the 1670s, most of the native woods had been removed and sugarcane fields dominated the landscape. For both early modern observers and modern historians, the pace and extent of ecological change sparked concern. At best, reports of mass deforestation in Barbados and complaints about consequent soil erosion and climate change from the 1660s through the early eighteenth century led to rigorous legal protections for woods around the English Caribbean. The staggering transformation of Barbados served as an impetus for what historian Richard Grove called "green imperialism." Others have taken a far bleaker view: The sugar plantations of the English and Dutch Caribbean were uniquely horrifying manifestations of "a colonial attitude toward the environment" that blithely razed preexisting landscapes to cultivate a monoculture maintained only through the brutal exploitation of enslaved people or they were one of the earliest examples of "ecocide" in the early modern period. Scholars critically assessing the concept of the "Anthropocene"—a geological epoch defined by human influence over the earth's bio-geo-chemical systems—have argued that, to more appropriately attribute causation, the time period should instead be named the "Capitalocene" and that the sugar complex that spread across the Atlantic World and transformed Barbados was a foundational moment or have claimed that early modern social and ecological transformations in the plantation system were so crucial that the entire period should be called the "Plantationocene."[2] In these accounts, deforestation in Barbados was not just a facet of early modern history but a transformational moment that either birthed environmental consciousness or served as an early manifestation of the system of exploitation and degradation that has culminated in the staggering, interconnected threats of climate change, mass extinction, and toxicity that define our world today. These accounts suggest that colonists, at least initially, embraced Colt's vision, with devastating consequences for the physical environment.

Despite its importance, it is difficult to tell the environmental history of early English Barbados. Unlike Bermuda, Virginia, or Ireland, where records from joint-stock companies, large landholders, or local governments survive in significant quantities, deeds and leases comprise the majority of surviving sources offering insights into how colonists understood and altered the island's environments. Plantation records detailing agricultural practices and patterns of resource management are relatively rare, even into the eighteenth century.[3] Deeds and leases, necessarily emphasize property and commercial value in their description of land; other conceptions of value for trees or landscapes appear briefly, only hinting at the presence of multiple and complex political ecologies. Nonetheless, as in Ireland, property records tell an important story about resource management that complicates contemporary narrative accounts of destruction and waste.

Closer examination of the early history of Barbados reveals a much more ambiguous picture of colonial political ecologies and of colonists' early impact on the island's woods. Deforestation of the island as a whole and on individual holdings did not happen immediately; it was both a consequence of shortages of labor and tools and a result of deliberate actions to preserve both individual trees and forested lands. The desire to protect property was at the heart of these measures; nonetheless, they show that early English colonists considered both specific trees and wooded lands natural resources to be managed, rather than simply nuisances to be cleared. These actions were not merely the result of economic distress as colonists flailed between cotton, indigo, and tobacco. Instead, they coincided with relatively successful plantation economies that already depended on the labor of enslaved people of African descent.[4] Individual trees and wooded land continued to be valued even after sugar began to be cultivated. Large-scale deforestation nonetheless accompanied the boom in sugar production, but it did so amid regulations and customs that protected and valued individual trees and woods, not in their absence.

Moreover, these transformations occurred in the presence of an appreciation for Barbados's forests that went beyond a concern for property and utility. The colonist Richard Ligon's *A True and Exact History of the Island of Barbados* (1657), which has served as an essential source for historians of early English colonization on the island, articulated an emotional, experiential, and aestheticized appreciation for wooded landscapes separate and distinct from their economic value. Ligon, while not necessarily representative of widespread attitudes among colonists, nonetheless provides a unique opportunity to examine those aspects of colonial environmental thinking less visible in the property records, which constitute the majority of surviving sources addressing Barbados's landscape in this period. Ligon's fondness for and ascription of aesthetic pleasure to woods untouched by European cultivation or management were rare in early modern England and its colonies, where much of the discussion of early modern wood scarcity and management focused on legal, social, and economic matters.[5] Ligon provided one of the richest accounts for aesthetic and affective environmental thinking in the seventeenth century, but, despite his celebration of Barbados's forests, he ultimately welcomed the work of the axe.

The dramatic transformation of Barbados from a wooded island to a landscape dominated by sugarcane took place deliberately. As in Bermuda, the earliest property records in Barbados reflected colonists' and adventurers' uncertainties about what resources and commodities the island might provide and, as a result, sought to protect potentially valuable woods. The initial vision for Barbados's colonial society reflected a political ecology of local self-sufficiency and transatlantic export. It included colonists practicing diverse professions to create a functional society while still producing commodities. Food production, the manufacturing of household goods, coopering, and carpentry all required wood, and property records show efforts to ensure that there would be sufficient supplies to do so. The first sugar production took place within this paradigm of self-sufficiency. Expanding it required a shift in political ecology from one emphasizing local production of basic necessities to one depending on resources harvested from outside the island or supplied from other English colonies. This shift in political ecology enabled the intensive sugar monoculture that came to dominate, and, in the 1650s, it had only just begun to emerge.

*   *   *

Barbados lies at the edge of the Caribbean, the easternmost of the Windward Islands in the Lesser Antilles. Unlike the volcanic islands in this chain, Barbados emerged as sedimentary rock was pushed upward at the subduction zone where the Caribbean Plate overrode the South American Plate. Coral formed colonies on the deep-water sedimentary rocks now visible in the Scotland District. Over time, these too were exposed, creating limestone terraces from the island's high point down to the current shoreline. The slow seeping of water through these limestone formations has created systems of caves, some of which collapsed to form gullies. Patterns of precipitation, temperature, and wind exposure emerged around these geological features, creating conditions for diverse small ecosystems.[6]

Barbados was uninhabited when English colonists arrived in 1627, but it had not always been so. Although the island is a geological and geographical outlier within the Windward chain, it was closely integrated into the broader human geography of the Caribbean. Peoples referred to by archaeologists as either "Paleo-Indians" or "Lithic/Archaic Age Amerindians" may have left material traces on Barbados nearly 4,000 years ago, though this evidence is disputed and sparse relative to other Caribbean sites. By the later phase of the Early Ceramic Age, material remains of human habitation appeared in patterns suggesting sparse settlements. Pottery types, such as the artifacts classified as Barrancoid-influenced Modified Saladoid found in Barbados, point to connections between the South American mainland and other Caribbean islands. At the same time, the island's relative isolation produced some distinct ceramics, differing from those of other Windward islands. By the Late Ceramic Age, the density of sites on Barbados increased and included inland settlements, suggesting a more extensively inhabited landscape.[7] Movement through trade and migration connected islands with each other and with the South American mainland. Yet, within this web of material and cultural entanglements, there was considerable diversity.[8]

English colonists did not, therefore, encounter an untouched landscape, even on a then-uninhabited island. The dramatic changes to the Barbadian landscape from English colonization have done much to obscure the pre-colonial landscape. Only one stand of trees, Turner's Hall Wood, may offer insights into pre-European vegetation and, as geographer David Watts noted, the site's relative isolation and location in an ecological niche make generalizations difficult and force us to rely on textual descriptions left by English colonists to do any reconstruction.[9] As a result, it is difficult to precisely assess how indigenous peoples shaped Barbados. The similarities between Caribbean and South American environments point to processes of transmission through wind and water, but deliberate introduction and the exploitation of species by Native peoples over a long time period must also be considered.[10]

There are several fundamental ambiguities in tracing how English colonists transformed Barbados from a largely wooded world to an island of cane plantations in the seventeenth century. Early maps and deeds provide inconsistent information about the extent of island-wide English settlements. At the level of individual holdings, rates of clearance varied. Of the roughly 20 percent of surviving deeds between 1633 and 1660 mentioning woods or trees, a significant proportion described the lands being sold as "fallen or unfallen" or variations thereof. Ownership did not equal clearance. Few deeds indicated the proportion of fallen to unfallen land, but those that did suggest that significant portions of estates retained forest cover, including those where sugar was grown. Behind these uncertainties were, unquestionably, issues surrounding the supply of labor from English, Irish, and Scottish indentured servants and enslaved African, Afro-Brazilian, and Afro-Caribbean people. But conditions attached to deeds also indicate that colonists did not simply clear all the land they could. Instead, they took measures to preserve specific types of trees for construction material and exported dyewood. Moreover, others reserved patches of forested land to supply fuel. Colonists carried across the sea practical concerns and customs for preservation common in England and Ireland and similar to those that took hold in Bermuda.

The first visual depiction of Barbados reflected the uncertainties about the interior of the island. "A topographicall [Description and] Admeasurement [of the Yland of] Barbados" (Figure 9) accompanied Richard Ligon's 1657 history of the island, drawing on surveys from a Captain Swan/Swann who first came

Figure 9: This map, "A topographicall [Description and] Admeasurement [of
the yland of] Barbados," thought to have been drawn from an original from
Barbados's early surveyor, John Swan was included in Richard Ligon's *A True
& Exact History of the Island of Barbados* (London, 1657). It depicted the distribution of English settlements in Barbados simultaneously showing an island
already populated with colonists and blank spaces into which future settlements might be placed or natural wonders might exist. Courtesy of the John
Carter Brown Library.

to the island in 1628.[11] Most named settlements cluster on the leeward (west)
side of the island. Blank spaces or narrative images, such as the one depicting
a light-skinned figure on horseback pursuing two dark-skinned figures, cover
significant portions of the interior and windward coast. Depictions of cattle,
asses, and camels suggest that colonists, with the aid of animal transportation,
were exploring these lands and turning at least some of them to use as pastures. Yet the images of boar, light-skinned figures on horseback firing guns,
and a man wearing little clothing and holding a longbow, who may represent
the Native people brought to the island, suggest wilder space where animals,
people, and activities associated with the forest reside.

The ambiguous, comingled symbolism of settlement and wildness in the
map corresponds to tensions between the map and early deeds. Historical

geographer Frank Innes has noted the existence of a 1647 deed from inland St. Philip in a space Ligon left blank, suggesting that the map may have under-represented the extent of English settlement. Deeds from St. Andrews and St. Lucy predating Ligon's 1647 arrival support this intuition. It is unclear, how-ever, whether these omissions were intentional. The deed Innes cited noted that the land was "fallen and unfallen" and forty-four deeds in St. Andrew and St. Lucy preceding Ligon's arrival bear similar notations or other indication that land remained forested.[12] Even with these omissions, Ligon's map still pointed toward significant portions of wooded land in the 1640s.

Drawing on the map printed along with Ligon's history, geographer David Watts created a modern visualization showing the extent of cleared and uncleared land in 1647, based on approximations of cleared land surround-ing each plantation (Map 1). His approximations likely correct for some of the omissions in the seventeenth-century map, showing significantly less for-ested land than the blank spaces left in the 1657 map. Moreover, classifying all the land surrounding plantations as "Stump and plantation land," may have undercounted smaller patches of woods that remained standing. Watts's map indicates the substantial clearance that had already taken place by 1647, but it also makes clear that many parts of the island remained largely untouched.

Within thirty years, however, the island's landscape had changed dramat-ically. Philip Lea's 1685 map (Figure 10), produced from a series of surveys taken between 1676 and 1680, showed plantations throughout much of the island.[13] Small wooded areas remained but buildings representing colonial settlements now dominated in the representation. The blank spaces of the earlier map had largely disappeared, but wood had not. The descriptive text in the lower right specified logwood, green and yellow fustic, and lignum vitae, as commodities of the island. As in Bermuda, the luxury market for woods was an important part of the colonial economy, something reflected in early property records. As the text indicated, these trees retained their importance in English conceptions of the island's resources even after sugar had become Barbados's dominant export. Protections for individual tree types valued as luxury goods did not require the protection of forests. Lea's map could cele-brate the persistence of these trees in a denuded landscape.

The line between wood and woods exemplified in the disjuncture between Lea's image and text echoed a pattern found in deeds from the first decades of settlement. Land given over to plantations or captured in deeds was not blank space. The deeds reveal two things. First, they leave a profound uncer-tainty about what exactly constituted planted land. Of the approximately 2,500 deeds in the recopied deed books from the 1630s to 1660, 457 contain

Standing Timber in Barbados circa 1647

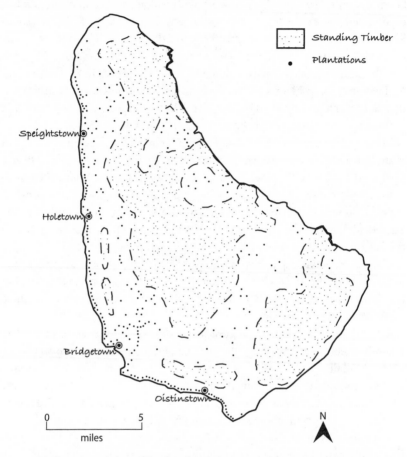

Map 1: Map of cleared land and woods c. 1647 designed by Alec Foster after David Watts, *Man's Influence on the Vegetation of Barbados, 1627–1800*, Occasional Papers in Geography 4 (Hull: University of Hull, 1966), Figure 8, p. 42.

references to reserved trees or wooded ground and information on the size of the holdings with another 14 deeds containing references to woods but no information on the size of holdings. Most often, in 73 percent of the 457, the presence of wooded land was captured in the phrases "fallen and unfallen," "fallen and standing ground," or several variations thereof.[14]

Most deeds for lands fallen and unfallen did not indicate the ratios between the two, but those that did suggest that unfallen land often constituted the

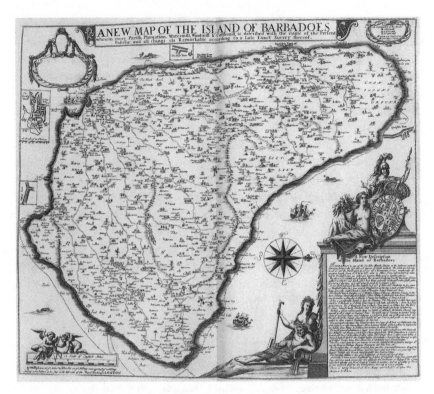

Figure 10: This map, likely based on the work of the surveyor Richard Ford, shows much denser settlements that extended through the interior, as well as the presence of mills used in sugar production, reflecting changes to the island's landscape. Philip Lea, *A new map of the island of Barbadoes* (London, 1676). Courtesy of the John Carter Brown Library.

largest portion of a holding. John Matthewes and Robert Francklin had only cleared one of their twenty acres. John Jones's 1640 deed to Robert Morgan offered 40 acres of uncleared land, Jones having previously sold his four or five acres of cleared ground. A 1639/1640 deed from St. Andrew described a similar ratio. James Simpson claimed that he had cleared four of his twenty acres in another 1640 deed. A 1647 inventory for Christopher Meltropp's estate showed that substantial quantities of uncleared woods coexisted alongside sugar production. Forty acres was "standing land" with eight already under cultivation as cane fields. In addition, there was a twenty-acre parcel of "loose land" of which six acres was fallen. Some of these acres were specifically reserved to grow palmettos, which, as the actions of Bermudian colonists demonstrated, could serve as sources of food, drink, and construction material. A 1647 survey of the lands of David Bix and Reynold Allen recorded that twenty-six of their sixty acres had been cleared.[15] Other deeds, however, indicate that the fallen portion might be significantly larger. Walter Leaw specified that he had cleared three-quarters of his 135 acres in St. James. John Powell sold 10 acres in 1651 "being the most parte thereof fallen ground."[16] "Fallen and unfallen" might indicate a wide range of landscapes, from a tiny plot of root vegetables amid standing trees to a largely cleared holding containing a small portion of wood.

The pattern of substantial forested land alongside cultivation applied to larger plantations as well. A 1646 hand-colored plot of Thomas Middleton's 300-acre plantation (Figure 11) showed three clusters of settlement and cultivation surrounded by wooded land along the leeward coast near modern-day Holetown.[17] Pasture and a "potato peece [piece]" are present at the bottom left alongside more pasture at the center of the holding. Otherwise, trees dominate. Even in the land marked as settled, trees persisted. At the upper left, trees run through a green colored portion with labels indicating "fallen land" on either side of the tree line. On a large holding of relatively flat coastal land in the area of the densest English settlement, cultivated land and pasture sat surrounded by persistent woods.

Labor availability certainly contributed to the persistence of woody landscapes, but Barbados's woods also served a wide range of quotidian and commercial uses for English colonists, and they took steps to protect those uses. They built their houses of cedar wood planks and thatched their roofs with palm leaves. Inside, colonists stored their goods in cedar chests. They ate off wooden plates and wooden trays. They fermented a liquor called "mobbie" from potatoes, ginger, and orange peel in wooden tubs that were included in deeds. They exported the fustic tree (*maclura tinctoria*) to produce a yellow dye used in cloth production. Colonists found employment as carpenters and sawyers, working to fell Barbados's trees and turn them into houses, tableware, furnishings, and pots for manufacturing drink.[18] These quotidian uses made little impression as economic exports, but behind each of these objects or professions lay systems of ownership, access, and use that inscribed value onto trees, defining who could claim or cut them. The brief mentions of domestic furnishings and wood-dependent professions suggest the presence of a political ecology grounded in local community and everyday life that coexisted alongside the protection and use of specific trees like fustic as commodities for export to Europe. Woods had value for their capacity to meet local needs, but, as in Bermuda, it was those trees with the capacity to serve transatlantic markets that registered most prominently in surviving property

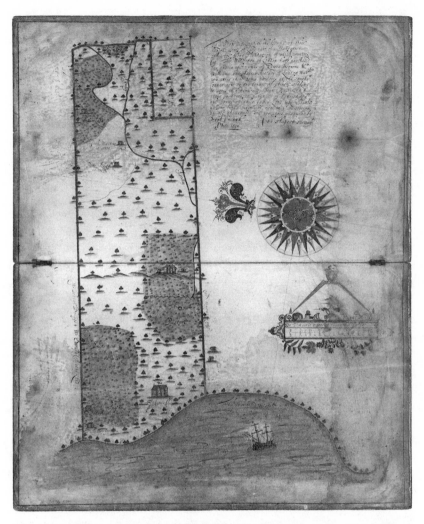

Figure 11: Manuscript map of Thomas Middleton's 300-acre Fort Plantation near present-day Holetown, including a description from surveyor John Hapcott dated 1646. The map depicted the partial nature of clearance and used the phrase "fallen land" common in Barbados's early property records. John Hapcott, Estate Plan of 300 Acres Near Holetown, c. 1647–1677, SHELF Et647 1 Ms, John Carter Brown Library. Courtesy of the John Carter Brown Library.

records. Much like the Bermuda palmetto, the patterns and rules that colonists developed for everyday and local uses fall largely outside the scope of surviving records.

Early property records, despite their limitations, show that colonists valued woods and hint at aspects of a political ecology centered on local uses and needs. Forty-seven percent of the deeds mentioning woods contain language specifically including wooded land; timber; specific trees such as fustic, mastic, or cedar; or restrictions on exploiting wood, including 24 percent of the deeds specifying fallen and unfallen land. Even planters like Thomas Stanhopp and Thomas Ware, whose deed for 130 acres in St. Andrews hinted that clearing was inevitable by granting "all grounds fallen or to be fallen," identified timber and timber trees as separate privileges included in the grant. Enumerating woods or timber as specifically included commodities in deeds suggested that both woods and specific types of trees had value for colonists. Moreover, the small proportion of deeds (5 percent) that included exemptions or restrictions on use indicate that specifically enumerated rights to wood, timber, or specific types of trees were important, lest previous owners return to exploit those resources. In leases like John Bread's 1644 agreement, the requirement that both growing and fallen timber trees would only be used on the plantation and not sold into market during the term of occupancy protected resources for his later use. Other records, however, included exemptions in sales.[19] These records indicate that timber was a critical asset for plantations. To protect it required not only restrictions on agricultural clearance but also efforts to prevent it from becoming a marketable good. Ensuring resources for local use required boundaries against the expansionist logic of commercial transactions like that which English investors had championed for the Bermuda cedar.

Hints of this commercial market for timber peek through the often-formulaic language of the deeds. In 1642, Richard Jarrett sold twenty acres of land but withheld all cedar trees growing therein, which he had previously sold to Thomas Cliffs. James Thomas's 1644 deed for thirty acres in St. James near Black Rock along the leeward coast likewise reserved fustic trees with a note that they had already been sold. In a 1640 agreement between Thomas Smith and William Chapman, Smith agreed to "go to sawing and acquiring of cedar trees and not to leave off until he hath sawn nine thousand foot of cedar boards" to satisfy a debt both men owed. Smith promised to both provide his labor and purchase trees. In return, Chapman agreed to provide an additional laborer, victuals, and 2,000 pounds of cleaned cotton. Smith likewise retained a sawyer to aid him in the enterprise.[20] Timber was not merely a commodity that landowners might profit from while clearing room for plantation agriculture. Conditions reserving cedar and fustic trees point to two separate markets for wood: local and transatlantic. Cedars were being used in construction on the island. Fustic, however, appealed to a transatlantic market in dyewoods, where yellow cloth—the color fustic produced—was one of the most heavily produced hues into the eighteenth century, if never equal in price to reds from cochineal or bluish hues of indigo.[21] Each use required skilled labor and demanded selective felling rather than the indiscriminate burning that the author of one early description cited as evidence of colonists' moral degeneracy.[22]

The interest in wood as a commodity suggests that sales for "standing wood" or other wood grounds were not automatically preludes to clearance. At least some of the deeds for wood may have indicated sales of land that colonists were unable to farm themselves, as in the case of Captain Francis Skeele. Likewise, Robert Ashmole envisioned some clearances when selling ten acres. Yet Ashmole only required that one acre be cleared and planted with roots, not the entire plot.[23] Overall, 49 percent of deeds mentioning rights to woods also included a specific, separate grant right to timber and 7 percent included separate grants to fustic, mastic, or cedar trees. Colonists did not simply value wooded land for the soil beneath it and its abstract value as acreage. Instead, many had a sophisticated understanding of wooded lands that included multiple, differentiated uses. For colonists hoping to profit from timber production; carpentry; or specialized uses for cedar, mastic, or fustic, these plots would have provided ideal opportunities to practice their trade.

There also were clear indications of preservation. Conditions in leases sought to protect both individual trees and woods. Richard Estwicke's 1641 lease reserved all cedars standing or fallen over the 21-year term. In 1656, Lawrence Parre required that Nathaniel Durant refrain from selling any trees or wood and confine any felling to necessary uses for the plantation.[24] These leases sought to preserve wood for fuel as well as for timber or dyes. In 1653, the London merchant Henry Quintyne purchased 108 acres of land being let out to tenants in St. John. The next year, Quintyne granted a lease of his own for 84 acres of the land to Giles Quintyne. The land was clearly being used for sugar production and the lease included "certain servants, Negroes, cattle and other materials incident to a sugar work." It also, however, included a clear provision to protect woods for fuel. Henry retained the rights of free ingress and egress to fell wood to fuel his brick-and-tile kiln throughout the term, an indication that the cane fields should not encroach on this liberty. Richard Bickford's 1654 lease was even more explicit. He retained the right to reenter the property at any time to cut timber or to acquire fuel for his sugar works.[25]

The presence of localized preservation measures demonstrated colonists' efforts to maintain self-sufficiency. Even as sugar came to dominate more of the landscape, the colonists did not abandon local sources of fuel and building materials. This continued presence of stores of wood on Barbados challenges historians' explanation for the connection between Barbados's sugar and North America's woods. In this account, wood scarcity in a deforested Barbados drove the search for new sources of timber. Complaints about scarcity in Barbados, however, date to the 1650s and 1660s, after the first efforts to trade timber between New England and Barbados had already been established.[26]

The misaligned chronologies for scarcity fears in Barbados and the onset of an intercolonial timber trade demand new explanations for this ligneous connection. As was the case with ironworks in Ireland and Virginia, the first efforts to trade timber relied on personal, familial, and mercantile connections. From the early days of English settlement in Barbados, there had been strong connections among the island and the New England colonies. John Winthrop had sent one son, Henry, there in the 1620s, where he quickly left after failing to cultivate salable tobacco. Samuel Winthrop, another of John's sons, went to the island at his father's behest in the 1640s after struggling to market New England commodities, including timber and pipe staves, in Tenerife. The first shipments of timber to Barbados came before Samuel's arrival; they were from Connecticut colonists in 1640–1641, who were eager to seek out new markets for the cotton trade as their commerce with England became increasingly disrupted, not at the behest of Barbadian planters. Colonists from Massachusetts followed suit the next year. As the trade grew into the 1650s, the demand was for red oak, a non-native wood.[27] The trade between New England and Barbados grew, not out of desperation amid deforestation but from New Englanders shopping around the empire and beyond for viable markets for their commodities.

The actions of the Connecticut General Court suggest that the court understood that it needed to make its timber a desirable and affordable good and could not simply rely on necessity. The colony's leaders took actions to regulate their own woods to ensure that there would be high-quality, desirable material to export. The General Court prohibited unlicensed felling of wood, including outside the boundaries of the plantation; limited the pipe-stave trade; and required quality inspections for any timber or pipe staves before export. It likewise ordered a survey of "Pequot Country" seized after the bloody struggles of the Pequot War to ensure the orderly distribution of timber there.[28] Connecticut colonists were not simply taking advantage of a natural abundance. Instead, they enacted a combined program of tighter regulation on lands already under English control and the exploitation of territory seized in war. Their actions represent one of the earliest efforts to craft a political ecology of wood predicated on intercolonial trade—exchanges between colonies—rather than on exporting commodities directly to England and an early example for the pattern of woodland regulations designed to support trade with the Caribbean that would come to dominate by the end of the century.

The origins of the timber trade between New England and Barbados lay neither in Caribbean scarcity nor in North American abundance but instead in commercial policy. The regulations that accompanied Connecticut's trade mission reveal the effort behind timber exports. Colonists were not merely harvesting a supply of trees perceived as limitless. Instead, authorities sought to control cutting to ensure the availability of a sufficient supply of high-quality wood close enough to English settlements to manage transportation and labor costs and took advantage of land seized through war to ensure an additional supply if the regulated timber became too expensive. New England colonists needed to entice cotton producers in Barbados to trade with cheap wood and they developed a program of regulation and colonial expansion to do so.

Atlantic trade would eventually lead to a shift toward a political ecology and geography of wood in Barbados, serving large plantation owners' desires to maximize sugar production by emphasizing trade and connection to acquire resources, but this did not occur immediately. Even after the timber trade with New England had begun, Barbadian colonists continued to take actions to protect future supplies of wood. A deed and a lease to Robert Hooper from 1651 and 1654 contain the most detailed conditions in the surviving property records. A 1653 revision to the 1651 lease for ten acres required five acres to be planted with corn and potatoes and two acres to be left as woods, with trees over ten inches in diameter to be cut down by the end of the five-year term. The requirement to fell trees over ten inches in diameter while preserving woodland roughly followed forestry practices in England. Trees were allowed to grow to a point of maturity when they would be felled, while smaller trees were left standing. With a constant replacement rate (a substantial assumption and one that was hotly debated in England), this would yield wood in perpetuity. A 1654 deed for forty acres in Christ Church to Robert Hooper, who had begun styling himself "Captain," reserved four acres of standing wood and allowed Francis Williams to fell any mastic trees over eight inches in diameter within six months of the property transfer. Williams sought to both preserve wood and acquire an immediate supply of timber. If Hooper wanted building timber of his own, he would need to invest the time and land to grow it to maturity.[29] As in England, landholders sought to balance between immediate and future returns. The conditions imposed on Robert Hooper mirrored those found in England and Ireland. Trade with New England for wood did not eliminate these local measures for preservation and regulation: The unusually precise lease conditions hint that Barbadian landowners may have intensified regulation as imported alternatives became available.

Even after the sugar boom was further under way, colonists, including some owners of large plantations, continued to minimize their reliance on imported wood. Henry Drax's 1679 instructions to Richard Harwood for managing Drax Hall and Hope Plantations, two of the largest on the island, ordered Harwood to avoid wood purchases "except upon absolute necessity or that you Can meet with it very Cheap." Instead, Drax likely relied on his own wood reserves, on replanted trees, and on alternative fuels, such as dried cane, to process sugar. Other Barbadian planters did experience localized scarcity and increasingly relied on dried cane husks and other "crop trash" for fuel. Archaeological analysis of wood charcoal on the island of Nevis, another site of seventeenth-century English colonization and sugar production, points to a mixture of local hardwoods, imported trees, and dried cane husks as fuels into the eighteenth century.[30] Even as colonists cleared more acres for cane and lamented the lack of trees, local woods never entirely disappeared.

Moreover, Drax's instructions reveal that local trees remained important for more than fuel. Drax provided instructions for Harwood to create fertilizer by burning lime on Drax Hall Plantation in an area with significant quantities of limestone and "the greater part of the wood." Burned lime provided "good manure for land and the Cheapest You Can use for Land that lies at Distance from the work." Whatever his anxieties about the supply or cost of wood, Drax did not believe they offset the value of cheap, portable fertilizer. In addition to using woods to produce fertilizer, Drax added instructions to turn already felled mastic and locust trees into specialized parts ("stocks or arms grafts for Shafts or rowlers [rollers]"). He noted that the sweetwood (*Nectandra membranacea*) made excellent lathes, though "Smooth & Strait grained mastke [mastic]" might be used as well. Finally, Drax understood the importance of wooded land as a windbreak and ordered that Harwood plant fiddlewoods (*Citharexylum spinosum*) along the windward boundary of all divisions in the cane fields.[31]

Necessity and cost functioned in tandem to control the use of imported wood. In Brazil, fuel might make up 20 to 25 percent of the total operating cost for sugar enterprises.[32] Barbadian colonists sought to control their dependence on New England and nearby islands for fuel. In turn, New Englanders understood the need to control their costs through regulations on felling at home. Drax's instructions made it clear that he sought to manage woods on his plantation to provide a permanent supply, requiring Harwood to "Either to let your New Land as you fall it to run again to wood or to plant the same quantity in some other piece with fiddle woods."[33] Even as plantation agriculture transformed the Barbadian landscape, colonists sought to avoid absolute scarcity, provide sustainable supplies of resources that required a minimum of costly, imported wood, and plant enough trees to preserve cane fields from howling tropical windstorms.

The measures Drax took to ensure sustainability were present from the earliest surviving deeds, while much of the island remained covered with native woods. When the Barbados Assembly passed an act in 1656 prohibiting felling of boundary trees or incursions into neighboring property to fell woods, it was not simply a response to a new and unprecedented problem.[34] Instead, it built upon a long-standing system of valuing woods and individual trees at the level of individual landowners and parish churches.[35] This context was built into the language of the act, which sought to protect individual property from interlopers. Unlike in Bermuda, where the assembly sought to protect palmettos and cedars across the islands for public use or for England or Ireland, where the Crown reserved trees through grants and laws, the Barbadian act focused on the rights of individual landowners, ignoring glebe lands or public concerns. Preservation and deforestation depended on the actions of individual planters.

The focus of this system was ensuring colonists had wood not forests. It ascribed value based on utility. Nonetheless, there were opportunities for preservation, management, and replanting, alongside efforts to produce consistent profits. Colonists took these opportunities both before and after widespread sugar cultivation. Neither the measures for preservation nor the measures for sustainability, however, prevented significant loss of pre-contact woodlands. Moreover, the broader attempts to create sustainable sugar landscapes, of which measures for wood preservation were a part, exacted a staggering human toll. According to historian Peter Thompson, Drax anticipated a 3–5 percent annual mortality rate for his enslaved laborers, resulting from unrelenting work and brutal discipline to mitigate erosion and constantly apply fertilizers to soils that Drax and other planters feared were becoming worn out.[36] This system emerged, not from a casual disregard for the Barbadian environment but rather from an intimacy with it and a desire to extract the maximum possible profit.

*   *   *

Property records in Barbados contain evidence for a pragmatic and utilitarian concern with the island's trees, but they offer little information on colonists' sense of or feelings about the landscape. This does not mean that property and pragmatism were the sole factors in the English ecological imagination. Richard Ligon, who had managed financial affairs for English elites and participated in schemes for fen drainage before joining Thomas Modyford's voyage to the Caribbean in 1647, sought to balance discussions of arboreal usefulness with reflections on beauty and pleasure in the island's woods. In *A True & Exact History of the Island of Barbados* (1657), revised while he was incarcerated for debt after his return to England, Ligon offered abundant details about the composition and the distribution of woods in Barbados. Indeed, the abundant details in Ligon's account and the paucity of surviving records for the first decades of English colonization have made it a critical source for studies of early Barbados.[37] *A True & Exact History* was also more than a history of one colony: Some contemporaries championed it as a model for a sugar-centered colonial economy to be copied in the English conquest of Jamaica and it remained a crucial text for colonial administrators in England long after its initial publication.[38]

Unlike many contemporaries, Ligon was not a crude proponent of felling a woody landscape deemed uncivil. He provided a complicated perspective that celebrated the island's wooded landscapes both for their utility and for the values that transcended economics while simultaneously suggesting that they should largely fall to provide space for sugar. Ultimately, Ligon's aesthetic and emotional connection to the environment did not prove a barrier to exploiting it. Ligon advanced a political ecology that privileged profitable enterprises but sought to avoid reckless destruction of practically and aesthetically valuable wooded landscapes.

At points, Ligon appeared, like Colt, to equate clearance with the health of the colony. According to Ligon's informants, Sir William Courteen and his crew determined that Barbados was uninhabited because it was "so

overgrown with Wood, as there could be found no Champions, or Savan-
nas for men to dwell in," leaving it eligible for English settlement. The first
ships "were sent, with men, provisions, and working tooles, to cut down the
Woods." Struggle, according to Ligon, marked the first years of settlement,
with "earthy and worthless" tobacco yielding paltry profits or none at all.
The struggle to find a profitable commodity was reflected in the landscape:
Meager food crops were "planted between the boughes, the Trees lying along
upon the ground; so far short was the ground then of being clear'd." He urged
anyone with money, goods, or credit to purchase a plantation already prepared rather than "to begin upon a place, where land is to be had for nothing,
but a trivial Rent, and to endure all hardships, and a tedious expectation, of
what profit or pleasure may arise."[39] Life "between the boughs" was ceaseless
toil for meager reward reserved for those with the least means.

Clearing the forest, however, was a valuable endeavor, both for individual
landholders and, Ligon implied, for the colony overall. The "vast height and
largeness" of trees and plants created a hot and humid climate. The moisture in the air rusted metal tools and set clocks and watches askew. It also
threatened human well-being. Ligon lamented the "close and very unhealth-
ful weather" that impeded both vitality and pleasure.[40] Deforestation, he
implied, might therefore be a means to improve the climate. Cleared land was
therefore essential not only to profit but to survival.

Ligon, however, also valued trees and wooded lands for both practical
and aesthetic reasons. At some level, this attitude reflected his attempt to
place himself into the learned discourses of seventeenth-century natural historical and philosophical writing, in which authors sought to demonstrate a
rich and complete knowledge of plants while consciously distancing themselves from purely economic concerns. Unlike natural historians in Europe,
Ligon sought to advance this diverse appreciation for woods alongside pragmatic concerns.[41] Immediately counseling potential colonists to purchase a
"ready furnished" plantation, he noted that his companion had done precisely that. The 500-acre plantation contained 120 acres of wood and 70 acres
for "provisions," which included citrus, banana, and plantain trees. He wrote
favorably of the locust, mastic, bully-tree, redwood, prickled yellow wood,
cedar, and ironwood, citing their utility for building and resistance to rot.
He returned to these species in a catalog of trees and other plants, taking
up a total of eighteen pages and that includes native and introduced species
with detailed descriptions and accounts for their uses. He reported extensively on the "physick-nut." Finding that fences of felled logs rotted easily and
noting that horses, cattle, and asses avoided browsing near the physick-nut,

colonists planted nurseries full of these trees, which they then used to build hedges. Moreover, as the name implied, Ligon reported that it was an excellent purgative. These trees also produced charcoal. He offered a more mixed assessment of the poison tree, which he warned could blind both people and horses, but nonetheless noted that it provided staves for most sugar vats, the poison dissipating after the boards dried in the sun.[42]

Unlike Harriot's list of "merchantable commodities," Ligon wrote with obvious pleasure and humor about the beauty and wonder of individual trees and the joy he experienced in the woods. From the beginning of the section, he adopted a playful tone, quipping, "There are such infinite varieties, as to mention all, were to loose my self in a wood." He emphasized strangeness, noting the spikes of the macow tree, in addition to its utility for making clothing, building furniture, or producing fruits or nuts. He waxed that the locust resembled a Tuscan pillar, citing "that rare Architect, Vitruvius, taking a pattern from Trees," invoking contemporary debates on the relationship between nature and art.[43]

Even trees that impinged on the cultivated, profitable landscape might offer amusement. While lamenting the pasture-destroying annoyance of the appropriately named "gnaver," Ligon lightened his description with a scatological anecdote: "These seeds have this property, that when they have past through the body, wheresoever they are laid down, they grow. A Planter, & an eminent man in the Island, seeing his Daughter by chance about her natural business, call'd to her: *Plant even, Daughter, plant even.* She answered: *If you do not like 'em, remove 'em, Father, remove 'em.*" Colonists spent much "pain and labour" destroying the saplings deposited by cattle on their pastures, yet Ligon's treatment of them is relatively gentle.[44] Unlike the authors of husbandry and surveying guides who described weeds as diseases plaguing fields, the gnaver was an annoyance, not an existential threat.[45]

Ligon's sense of play was critical to his construction of Barbados's environment. He cultivated natural knowledge through rigorous observation and experimentation but simultaneously found symbols, allegories, and metaphors on civility, difference, violence, royal authority, and the ideal construction of society. He crafted his observations to comment on and demonstrate his command of English and of broader European debates on politics and natural philosophy. For cultural and environmental historian and critic Susan Scott Parrish, Ligon's notions of beauty and his understanding of nature reflected a search for order in the aftermath of a destructive civil war, a move that reflected broader trends in early modern English environmental thought.[46] At the same time, Ligon's political ecology was not solely grounded in the experience of political violence in England. It also reflected a political ecology of woods built, in part, on play. Punning; comingling tawdry anecdotes and analysis of Classical architecture; and his interest in novel, curious, and unusual trees, even those lacking practical value, suggest that the Barbadian woods were, like those in *A Midsummer Night's Dream*, also a space for amusement, exploration, and temporary liberation from social constraints.[47]

Cleared pastures, canes, and fields were not in conflict with the beauty and wonder of the woods in Ligon's *History*. Most of the plantations were on the leeward coast. The interior remained densely wooded. Ligon indicated that even his extensive arboreal catalog was incomplete and that opportunities for profit and discovery remained: "Strange" plants and trees grew in the woody interior, which were "no doubt medicinable in their natures."[48] The continued presence of large, dense, and unknown woods presented a challenge, not for broadax and hoe, but for "skillful men" able to coax valuable medicines from the novel trees. Sugar, however profitable, need not preclude natural philosophical inquiry.

Ligon's attitudes toward the Barbadian woods challenge the notion of a unitary English colonial attitude that eagerly sought to transform the landscape or that only responded to the shock of rapid, radical environmental change. Instead, Ligon valued individual trees and wooded areas for practical use and aesthetic pleasure. Ligon was an atypical colonist deeply engaged in European natural philosophy, who used his empirical observations of the island's flora to participate in debates on art and nature. From the surviving sources produced during the earliest decades of settlement, it is difficult to know whether Ligon's aesthetic attitudes were idiosyncratic or common. Even Ligon's own reflections suggest that planters did not always receive his comments on architecture, music, and beauty with enthusiasm. At the same time, evidence of book sales and references to Roman histories in writings about potential slave revolts belie the perception, which Ligon stoked, that Caribbean planters lacked cultural and intellectual interests.[49]

Nonetheless, Ligon displayed a regard for Barbados's woods rooted in both practical and aesthetic concerns that coincided with the sugar boom rather than resulting from it. He offered a deeply elaborated reflection on the beauty and wonder of wooded landscapes with no surviving contemporary colonial parallels and few English ones. Yet Ligon's calls to moderate the profit motive were not incompatible with plantation management. Instead, they represented efforts to make it "sustainable."[50] Detailed knowledge and appreciation for the island's woodlands and trees was not a barrier to their exploitation or even to their destruction; it simply meant that those actions would not be taken carelessly or ignorantly. Just as Henry Drax's 1679 instructions showed a plan to manage woods and soil fertility for long-term continued production, Ligon too had begun to develop a model for sustainable plantations.

Ligon offered one of the most detailed and lengthy appreciations for trees and wooded land in the seventeenth century, and this reverence helped inform his thinking on Barbadian slavery. In contemplating the beauty of nature and wandering in the shade of a plantain grove or the thick forest, Ligon began to question his assertions that people of African descent were "accounted a bloody people." He wrote extensively about a man named Macow, who "was our chief Musician; a very valiant man, and was keeper of our Plantain-grove."[51] Ligon began his account by explaining how Macow had scorned his wife after she gave birth to twins, taking it as an evil sign. In Ligon's telling, only the master's threat of hanging prevented Macow from killing his wife, a conclusion designed to reinforce his earlier claim that overwhelming English violence was necessary to suppress "bloody" tendencies.

Appreciation for Macow's skill as a musician softened Ligon's harsh assessment. While wandering amid the plantains "to refresh me in that cool shade, and to delight my self with the sight of those plants, which are so beautiful," Ligon came upon Macow carving wood into a multi-pitch percussion instrument. Just a few days earlier, Ligon reported that he had shown Macow his theorbo, a stringed instrument like a lute, and demonstrated how to achieve different pitches. In the relative seclusion of the plantain grove, Macow's instrument prompted Ligon to directly inform his readers "these people are capable of learning Arts."[52]

Although wooded, the plantain grove was a cultivated space, not wild or waste. As in Bermuda, English colonists had sought out African and Native expertise early on to cultivate unfamiliar crops and to adapt to an unfamiliar environment. Captain John Henry Powell claimed that, immediately after arriving in 1627, Sir William Courteen brought thirty-two Native people from South America "to assist and instruct" the colonists with the sugar cane, cotton, tobacco, cassava, potatoes, and pineapples that they would plant. The grove reflected the agricultural skill and environmental knowledge of Native people and enslaved people of African descent.[53] Nonetheless, for Ligon, it was not a purely functional landscape but also a site for leisure and exploration.

Ligon's most profound questions about Barbadian slavery came in dense, unfelled woods. Ligon claimed that he spent time employed in public works cutting paths to the island's churches. To navigate around impassible gullies, Ligon relied on a compass, which sparked a discussion with an enslaved man named Sambo also working on the trail-cutting. According to Ligon, Sambo was deeply impressed after learning the function of and principles behind the compass, so much so that he desired to convert to Christianity, believing that such knowledge inhered in the religion.[54] Ligon treated both the cultivated grove and the wild wood not as a fearful space but as sites to complicate his earlier assertions about the "bloody" character of African peoples.

Ligon's tales provide only highly suspect information about African knowledge and belief, revealing much more about his own attitudes and attempts to situate Barbados within broader Atlantic intellectual currents. Macow and Sambo's naïve fascination with English technologies, their gratitude for Ligon's instruction, and Sambo's immediate association between knowledge, material technology, and Christianity echo patterns historian Joyce Chaplin found in English accounts of Anglo-Native interactions in North America. Denying Macow and Sambo even ventriloquized words, Ligon merely summarized their purported questions, emotions, reactions, and motivations.[55] His interactions with enslaved people were monologues not conversations. Their transcendence beyond alleged savagery depended on their ability to fit into well-worn European archetypes for non-Christians. Yet the setting in which Ligon deployed these tropes mattered. Comfortable in the belief that he possessed superior knowledge and technology, Ligon feared neither the shaded seclusion of the plantains nor journeys through dense woods. Instead, they might serve as sites for conversion, either cultural or religious.[56]

Ligon's willingness to see Barbados's woods as a site for transformation, curiosity, and beauty stemmed from his broader views on nature. Nature need not be perfected through human artifice. Instead, it served as a medium for divine communication. Citing his skill "as an Artist," Ligon opined that "a very excellent Limner" could not paint a crucified Christ to equal the one appearing in a split fruit. The unparalleled art of nature served as a divine injunction as well as a gift for contemplation. Ligon condemned colonists "professing the names of Christians" for "denying to preach to those poor ignorant harmless souls the Negroes, the doctrine of Christ Crucified, which might convert many of them to his worship." Those colonists "will deny them the benefit and blessing of being Christians" rather than lose them as slaves. The image of the crucified Christ in the banana was divinely placed to reproach them.[57]

Ligon constructed a landscape and geography of English power. His compass created knowledge of space in the dense woods and, in Ligon's telling, Sambo immediately recognizes and desires the power to know and create geography through this European technology. Likewise, despite the agricultural expertise that enabled the plantain grove to exist, Macow and other people of African descent require preaching from English colonists to uncover the mysteries Ligon claimed were divinely encoded in the fruit. The image of the crucifixion was a rebuke to colonists, not a message to enslaved people. In this way, Ligon attempted to render people of African descent, in geographer Katherine McKittrick's term, "ungeographic"—passive recipients of English knowledge in spaces Ligon defined rather than people in posses- sion of their own spatial understanding.[58]

The map accompanying Ligon's text, however, strains against his depic- tion of African and Afro-Caribbean ignorance of landscape and geography. There are three figures in the upper left corner of the image (Figure 12) in an area without the place names or road markers delineating English plan- tations. A light-skinned figure on horseback dressed in English-style cloth- ing chases two dark-skinned individuals with light-colored cloth wrapped around their midsections. The figure on horseback brandishes a whip nearly striking one of the fleeing figures. The placement of the image suggests that people fleeing slavery took to the relatively mountainous and wooded ter- rain of Barbados's eastern, windward coast. For the mapmaker, this area was blank, unknown space, and the kinetic quality of the image suggests a

Figure 12: Image showing two dark-skinned figures fleeing a light-skinned man on horseback in English dress. This comes from a portion of Ligon's 1657 map unmarked with place names near the parishes of St. Lucy and St. Peter. Detail from "A topographicall [Description and] Admeasurement [of the yland of] Barbados" printed in Ligon, *A True & Exact History of the Island of Barbados* (London, 1657). Courtesy of the John Carter Brown Library.

headlong flight. Nonetheless, the image points toward a geography of resistance in which wooded spaces played a critical role.

Moreover, this geography persisted even as English settlers sought to reduce woods to resources. Wooded land and deep gullies were crucial spaces for runaway servants and enslaved people to evade capture and launch attacks on sugar plantations throughout the seventeenth century. Living and moving through these spaces, leaving and returning after setting cane fields ablaze, points toward the system of spatial and environmental knowledge absent in colonial sources and muted in Ligon's history. Even as the decline in overall forest cover led many enslaved people to look to the sea for freedom, woods, however patchy, remained critical spaces for resistance. Into the eighteenth century, enslaved people resisted captivity and coercion in gullies, ravines, and caves, obscured by trees and other vegetation. Even as colonists constructed a landscape of cultivation, discipline, and control, enslaved people forged alternative geographies enabling resistance.[59]

* * *

On the island that eventually would become the center of the English sugar trade, early colonists valued Barbados's trees and woods as sources of fuel and timber, as materials for farm implements and housewares, and as commodities to be shipped across the Atlantic. Trees—timber and dyewoods but also unspecified forested land—were treated as natural resources and protected. The restrictions and values attached to trees and woods in property records demonstrate that English colonists saw the landscape as more than a repository for cotton, sugar, or other cash crops. Richard Ligon offered an eloquent and detailed assessment of Barbados's woods. His history looked beyond functional concerns, praising individual trees for their beauty and seeking solace in the shade. Ligon conveyed a value in woods that transcended functionality, anticipating the aestheticized appreciation of landscapes associated with the later rise of environmentalism and demonstrating that such thinking emerged in the colonies as well as in England.[60] Neither the practical regulations in property records nor Ligon's natural philosophical values, though, halted transformations to the island's landscape or questioned the exploitation of enslaved workers that drove them. The ecological degradation that has drawn environmental historians to Barbados was not a product of careless destruction; rather, it resulted from a political ecology that valued natural resources in complex and multifaceted ways but that ultimately privileged profit.

English colonists did not transform Barbados overnight. Early settlements were limited and, even after land grants covered much of the island, groves and parcels of uncleared land remained. Clear-cutting and burning took place alongside selective felling and deliberate preservation. The early trade in mastic, fustic, and other trees used in dying or as luxury goods points toward a path not taken, in which the island's woods became sites of production for dyestuffs and furniture. Yet even as planters began to cultivate sugar, they continued to preserve individual trees and patches of woods.

Regulations to protect resources did little to protect the landscape. Ligon saw uncleared woods as sites for rest, shade, and curious inquiry, but the rules in deeds and leases protected property, not aesthetics. Enslaved people crafted geographies of resistance and freedom in which woods were key sites, alongside gullies and caves. The colonial government sought to suppress them. Colonists considered and protected resources, but landscapes are more than the sum of their functional value. As the century wore on, Barbados ceased to be a colony planted between the boughs and became a society set amid the canes.

CHAPTER 6

Toward an Atlantic or Imperial Political Ecology?

On the 5th of November 1662, John Evelyn dined with the Council of the Royal Society. After the meal, his diary notes, he proposed a "discourse . . . concerning planting his Majesty's Forest of Dean with oak, now so much exhausted of the choicest ship timber in the world."[1] Evelyn and the Society took up the issue in response to a 1662 appeal composed by navy commissioner Peter Pett. Pett offered five questions for the Society to consider: (1) whether the king should replant trees in all forests, parks, and chases within twenty miles of the sea or a navigable river; (2) how much of these lands should be planted and how the plantations should be geographically distributed in the lands; (3) whether the king should have a right of first refusal for any timber growing on private lands; (4) whether the king should ban the use of timber in home construction in London and its environs; and (5) whether every landowner should be required to plant an acre of timber out of every hundred acres of land.[2]

Two years later, the Royal Society published Evelyn's discourse, titled *Sylva*, its first printed work. *Sylva* proved immediately popular—so much so that Evelyn gloated in the second edition (1670), "More than a thousand copies had been bought up, and dispersed of the First Impression, in much less time than two-years' space (which book-sellers assure us is a very extraordinary thing in volumes of this bulk)." Moreover, he claimed that two million timber trees, "besides infinite others," had been planted in England, Ireland, and Scotland as a result of his work.[3] *Sylva* was regularly reprinted over the next 150 years and influenced a diverse range of thinkers, including Henry David Thoreau. Some historians have doubted Evelyn's most optimistic claims and questioned the work's influence, but most recognize *Sylva* as the most important work of early modern English forestry and a foundational text for English and Anglo-American environmental thought.[4]

Sylva, however, offers only a partial and limited sense of mid-seventeenth-century English thinking about wood. Evelyn sought to obscure and efface previous work on forestry, quipping that his was the first and only substantial thought on the subject except for "small sprinklings to be met withal in Gervase Markham, Old Tusser, and the Country-Farm long since Translated out of French."[5] Evelyn's claims about originality ignored generations of reforms to English forestry and nearly a century of plans to integrate colonies as sources of timber, naval stores, iron, and luxury woods. His project largely succeeded, allowing his vision to dominate subsequent discussions of scarcity. As historian Paul Warde observed, the work of Arthur Standish was "soon forgotten" while "public debate was largely framed by reissues of *Sylva* into the second half of the eighteenth century."[6] Evelyn's work was never just description; it articulated a political ecology. And despite *Sylva*'s importance, other political ecologies persisted and shaped approaches toward woods.

Sylva diagnosed an extreme wood scarcity facing England while simultaneously arguing that purely domestic actions, specifically widespread tree planting, could address it. For Evelyn, even after decades of imperial expansion, colonies occupied an uncertain place in England's wooden world. Like authors writing at the beginning of the seventeenth century, Evelyn believed in the power of improvement to produce significant quantities of new resources in England, which obviated the need to develop an imperial political ecology of resource flows from the colonies to England. Virginia and Ireland appear in the text as places where particular types of trees might be found or the location of curious practices, not places where English colonists might produce valuable woodland commodities. Virginia appears in two ways in the text. First, Evelyn noted plants that originated in Virginia. He spent the most time describing the Virginia Acacia (*Robinia pseudoacacia*; black locust), which he noted had thrived under the supervision of French gardeners and, more recently, in St. James's Park, but also mentioned two flowering plants with Virginia in their names. Second, Evelyn noted that Virginians, like New Englanders and Dutch colonists in North America, burnt pine knots as fuel, which "is something offensive by reason of the fulginous smoke which comes from it." Ireland appears only once, when Evelyn chastised English landowners for failing to plant the *arbutus* (likely the *Arbutus unedo* or strawberry tree), asking why they neglected a tree "which grows so common and so naturally in Ireland."[7] Ireland and Virginia might have unique, useful, and attractive trees, but Evelyn urged his readers to cultivate them in England—not to establish colonies or commercial ventures abroad for them.

For Evelyn, Ireland and Virginia, large colonies capable of producing substantial amounts of timber as bulk commodities, were more like Bermuda and Barbados, fascinating lands that might hold wondrous curiosities. Their role was to provide useful trees that would be assimilated into a newly verdant England, not to supplant the need for domestic wood production. That useful plants grew in these colonies was evidence that skilled cultivators should be able to produce them in England's temperate climate, not a justification for expansion abroad. After all, if the cedar could grow in "the moist Barbados, the hot Bermudas, the cold New England; even where the Snow lyes (as I am assured) almost half the year: Why then it should not thrive in Old England"? Even trees confined to the New World or remarkable for their size might be replicated in the Old World. After citing Ligon's work on Barbados's giant palms and descriptions of large trees from Juan D'Acosta and Sir Francis Drake, Evelyn promised to present trees of a similar size to those and to the largest New England mast pines "but without traveling into foreign Countries for these wonders."[8] Despite having read descriptions of colonies in the Spanish and English Atlantic, Evelyn emphatically reasserted a domestic conception of political ecology.

The closest Evelyn came to arguing that colonies had a role to play in the provision of wood, trees, or forest products to England were his discussions of pitch and tar and ironworks. In his section on pines, Evelyn published a text from John Winthrop on making pitch and tar in New England. New Englanders gathered knots from trees that had died and were decaying or those "quite consumed and reduced to ashes by the annual burnings of the Indians . . . which yet has, it seems, no power over these hard knots." Producing tar by gathering resinous knots may have seemed idyllic to English readers accustomed to strenuous labor, but the low-intensity process stemmed from economic concerns not New England's stunning abundance:

> It must not be conceived, by what we have mentioned in the former description of the knots, that they are only to be separated from the bodies of the trees by devouring time, or that they are the only materials out of which tar can be extracted: For there are in these tracts millions of trees which abound with the same sort of knots, and full of turpentine fit to make tar: But the labor of felling these trees, and of cutting out their knots, would far exceed the value of the tar; especially in Countries where Workmen are so very dear: But those knots above mentioned, are provided to hand, without any other labor then the gathering only.

New England might provide "millions of trees" fit for tar production, but European scarcity was not dire enough to enable New Englanders to overcome the high costs of labor and transportation to export their products.[9]

Indeed, by the 1670 edition, Evelyn hinted that production in America, even using this labor-saving method might not be worth the cost. At the end of this section in the 1670 edition, he wrote, "I am persuaded the pine and fir trees in Scotland, might yield his Majesty plenty of excellent tar, were some industrious Person employed about the work." Scotland here played spoiler to North American ambitions to supply England with naval stores. Yet even Scottish tar manufacturers also could not rest secure in their industry. Evelyn praised the Kent MP Sir Norton Knatchbull's "delicious plantation of pines." The trees, Evelyn claimed, had shot up more than sixty feet in height in only twenty years. Knatchbull's experiment, likely on his lands near the Kentish Downs, and Evelyn's own knowledge of the trees led him to doubt claims that such trees might not prosper in England. Later he reinforced his claims that England could grow numerous pine species, writing that fir and pine grew in large numbers in Cumberland, Cheshire, Stafford, and Lancashire because "multitudes of them are to this day found entire, buried under the earth." In addition to this petrified evidence for England's arboreal capacity, Evelyn claimed that he had successfully grown several Scottish firs from seeds sent by the Marquis of Argyle.[10]

Evelyn was far more explicit about New England's promise when describing iron production. In a section on laws and regulations for trees and forests, Evelyn wondered, "What if some of [the ironworks] were even removed into another World? 'Twere better to purchase all of our iron out of America, then thus to exhaust our woods at home." He expanded on this point in his conclusion. New England's colonists "are now become very numerous and hindered in their advance and prospect of the continent by their surfeit of woods which we want." Fortunately, they had built two iron mills that had begun "to clear their high-ways." This sort of action wasted woods at home, Evelyn wrote, but it was "now but expedient their Brethren [New England colonists] should hasten thither to supply us with Iron for the peace of our days." This transatlantic iron market would enable Charles II to become the "great sovereign of the ocean." The king's glory, however, was to stem from necessity: "This were the only way to render both our Countries habitable indeed, and the fittest sacrifice for the Royal-Oaks and their Hamadryads to whom they owe more than a slight submission."[11]

Even with this apparent endorsement for New England ironworks, Evelyn still expressed doubt about colonial ventures and a preference for domestic production. Immediately after wondering whether many ironworks should be sent off to North America, he questioned his own assertion. "I doubt not," he wrote, that ironworks in England "might be so ordered, as to be rather a means of conserving [the woods]." To support this assertion, he recounted the story of Christopher Darell, "a Surrey gent of Newdigate, that had a particular indulgence for the cutting of his woods at pleasure, though a great Iron-master." Despite Darell's exemption from regulations regarding woods and his work producing iron, his trees were well preserved. Evelyn explained that, though paradoxical, his own father had told him that ironworks might preserve woodlands, "I suppose," he mused, "by increasing the industry of planting, and care." Although he was somewhat vague on the means, Evelyn clearly described the results of his father's attitude: "What he has now left standing of his own planting, enclosing, and cherishing . . . does sufficiently evince, a most laudable monument of his industry, and rare example."[12] If English landowners could produce iron without unsustainably consuming their trees, what then justified North American iron production?

Evelyn's discussion of pitch, tar, and iron production showed that, despite his claims about "universal" English scarcity, colonial, and even Irish and Scottish production of woodland commodities, largely did not factor into his political ecology. New England, the one region for which he made a strong case, occupied a precarious position. As Evelyn's discussion of the economics of tar production showed, New Englanders operated within narrow profit margins. Increased labor costs might leave production uneconomical. This constrained the scale and technology that might be applied to New World works and it rendered colonists dependent on decaying trees and Native American fires. Domestic production launched by skilled arborists might imperil even this austere, minimally intensive model of production. Evelyn justified ironworks in more political than economic terms. His acknowledgment that domestic English producers might "order" ironworks "that they were a means of preserving" threatened to make colonial ironworks subject to the same cost pressures that undermined tar production.[13]

For Evelyn, Ireland, Virginia, Bermuda, and Barbados were barely a part of England's wooden world. They provided him interesting tree species or tales of curious practices, but, like so many other metropolitan thinkers, Evelyn struggled to explain exactly how colonies fit. Their absence in his work, however, did not reflect a lapse in attempts to exploit colonial woods. Examining both the politics of scarcity and the attempts at commercial timber exports to England and iron production in the 1650s and 1660s in Ireland, Virginia, and New England demonstrates that the competing political ecologies of wood that took shape in the late sixteenth and early seventeenth centuries persisted through the political upheavals of the Civil War and

Restoration. While much remained the same, this period saw the first signs of Atlantic and regional political ecologies of wood built on intercolonial trade rather than exchanges centered on an English metropole.

*   *   *

Although a request to help alleviate "so great a scarcity of timber for the supply of [Charles II's] navy" prompted Evelyn to write *Sylva*, he offered a complex and often ambiguous analysis of dearth throughout the work that emerged from debates on the use of woods during the English Civil War and the Cromwellian Protectorate and was entangled with concerns about royal authority. In the introductory epistle to his 1664 edition, Evelyn treated scarcity as a largely political phenomenon. Evelyn indicted Parliament and the Cromwellian Protectorate for widespread destruction. The "Usurpers," he wrote, were "prodigious Spoilers, whose furious devastation of so many goodly Woods and Forests have left an Infamy on their Names and Memories not quickly to be forgotten!" He even excused the depredations of the "Gallant and Loyal Gentry" as "deplorable necessities . . . to preserve the poor remainder of their fortunes and to find them bread." By the 1670 reprinting, however, Evelyn had effaced their infamy from his note to readers, replacing his Royalist denunciation of Roundhead deforestation with a statement on the novelty of his work and a few jabs at older husbandry guides. In just six years, Evelyn had shifted his focus from political and environmental history to his place within English agricultural and improvement literature.[14]

Despite the shift in his introductory epistles, Evelyn developed an argument about wood scarcity in his introductory chapter, text that remained constant through the first two editions. "There is nothing," he proclaimed, "which seems more fatally to threaten a weakening, if not a dissolution of the strength of this famous and flourishing Nation, than the sensible and notorious decay of her wooden-walls." England, he claimed, was doomed to decline without a navy and a merchant fleet. Here Evelyn clearly outlined the causes for deforestation. There had been an increase in shipbuilding and the construction of ironworks and glassworks. But the greatest destruction stemmed "from the disproportionate spreading of Tillage, caused through that prodigious havoc made by such as lately professing themselves against Root and Branch." Evelyn claimed that the scarcity caused by shipbuilding, manufacturing, and (overwhelmingly, according to Evelyn) conversion of woods to agricultural land by individuals who had rebelled against royal authority was "universal." In response to this kind of severe destruction, he wrote, "I conceive nothing less than an universal Plantation of all the sorts of trees will supply and well encounter the defect."[15]

For Evelyn, disobedience and rebellion had ravaged England's woods and forests; therefore, the project of restoration needed to be environmental as well as political. Charles II had called for his subjects to "bury all Seeds of future Discords and remembrance of the former as well in His owne Breast as in the Breasts of His Subjects one towards another" through wide-ranging pardons and restrictions on public acts of speech and memory.[16] But *Sylva* suggested that the landscape bore the scars of rebellion: To bury the seeds of the past required planting trees for the future. From the onset of Parliamentary opposition to Charles I through the radical Diggers to Evelyn's Royalist account, conflicting claims about appropriate use, common rights, ownership, and forest management shaped understandings of scarcity in England's woods, just as it had done from Elizabeth I's reign. Even with the destruction of trees and the collapse of forest authorities during the Civil War, anxieties about scarcity did not reflect absolute shortages. Scarcity remained a problem of political ecology and conflicting ideas about domestic shortages continued to shape broader visions for the political ecology of wood in the colonies.

Evelyn was right that the Civil War had also seen a conflict over forests, even if his association between opposition to the monarchy and greedy, wasteful, destruction masked the complexities of these competing political ecologies. Opposition to Charles I's forest policies was a small but nonetheless visible part of the grievances that moved some members of Parliament to opposition in the 1640s. In 1640, Parliament passed an act "for the certainty of forests and of the meres, metes, limits, and bounds of the forests" that repudiated Charles I's attempt to expand the Forest Laws in the 1630s. The act invalidated all presentments, judgments, awards, and perambulations taken since the twentieth year of James I's reign while approving his disafforestations and restoring common rights to inhabitants "as anciently or accustomably they have used or enjoyed." Despite this assault on Charles's forest policies, members of Parliament continued their offensive the next year. In 1641, they issued *A Remonstrance of the State of the Kingdome*, more commonly known as the *Grand Remonstrance*. Two complaints about the management of royal forests accompanied the catalog of grievances against Charles. According to the *Remonstrance*, Charles had enlarged the boundaries of royal forests "contrary to *Charta de Foresta*, and the composition thereupon." He had also enabled the "general destruction of the King's Timber, especially that in the Forest of Dean, sold to Papists, which was the best Store-house of this Kingdom, for the maintenance of our Shipping." These grievances reflect the

somewhat contradictory policies Charles pursued during his reign, expanding the enforcement of the Forest Laws and attempting to increase the areas
subject to the fines and penalties included under it while simultaneously
engaging in disafforestation and sale of royal lands, including the controversial grant to the recusant Sir John Wintour of the Forest of Dean referenced
in the *Remonstrance*.[17]

The forestry grievances in the *Remonstrance* also reflected ongoing tensions in the use and management of woods that would continue through
the Civil War, parliamentary rule, and Oliver Cromwell's Protectorate. The
Remonstrance placed its charges against Charles's forest policies alongside
grievances about monetary exactions without parliamentary consent, royal
assaults on local militias, and monopolies on "sope, salt, wine, leather, sea-
coal, and in a manner, of all things of most common and necessary use."[18] In
doing so, the authors of the *Remonstrance* reflected the multiple and potentially incompatible attitudes toward the woods. They railed against the sale
of royal forests and the extension of their boundaries, measures that both
James's and Charles's advisers had claimed would tend toward the preservation of wood while also enhancing royal revenue, but they also decried
wasted timber. Waste was a contested and politicized concept that grew out
of conflicting notions of rights and use as well as the felling of trees.

These characteristics continued to shape perceptions on the destruction
of woods, even as the conflicts between Charles I and Parliament descended
into the open conflict of the Civil War. In 1646, in the midst of the fighting,
George Oldfield, a warden for the Forest of Dean, wrote to an acquaintance
in London, describing wasted woods in Gloucestershire. Oldfield wrote that
many good oaks had been felled under the orders of a Colonel Massey and
that the foresters had destroyed beech trees "in a more abundant manner than
before." Measurement and regulation, the tools championed by reforming
foresters and surveyors from Elizabeth I's reign onward, also failed. William
Winbury, who had been sent to measure the woods, "proved a very knave."
Oldfield wrote that he and "divers other gent[lemen] of this country of public
spirits" were "perplexed" about why these officials would threaten their own
"profits and good" with these actions. He wrote to the House of Commons
pleading for some measure to preserve the forest and prevent further spoils.[19]
Oldfield's report cast spoil as both an ecological and bureaucratic problem.
Trees, he claimed, were being felled more abundantly, but one of the major
issues was incompetent administration.

Two years later, Parliament passed an ordinance for the preservation of
timber that again indicated the politicized nature of waste. The ordinance

opened by decrying the "great Spoil, Waste, and Destruction of Timber, made of late Years throughout the whole Kingdom." The most damaging actions, according to the ordinance, had taken place in the Forest of Dean. In response, Parliament banned all felling of oak, ash, elm, or beech "upon any pretense whatsoever." Nor was anyone to lop, top, or otherwise trim trees. Provision for continued use of the woods was nonetheless embedded in this otherwise stringent set of restrictions. The navy was to have all use of downed and remaining timber. Anything left over was to be sold to pay the Earl of Salisbury for debts the state owed.[20] A year later, Oliver Cromwell reported to the Council of State that public goods were "in danger to be embezzled." The 1648 ordinance for the Forest of Dean had championed preservation to secure naval stores and pay state debts. Cromwell and the Council of State articulated more specific recommendations for forestry practice and a more ambiguous statement about the utility of parks, chases, and forests. Timber was only to be felled at "due seasons and in convenient proportions" to build and repair the Commonwealth's ships, but also for "such public uses as they shall judge necessary."[21] Instead of treating former royal assets solely as the province of the navy or as tools to service state debt, Cromwell and the Council of State suggested that they be treated as public goods.

As the new republic sought to take stock of its resources following the execution of Charles I at the beginning of 1649, there was considerable concern about the destruction of wood and impending scarcity. The actions that the state took in that year show that the Council of State and the officials sent to investigate particular forests understood the destruction of wood at least in part as a problem of order. As a result, the new government took actions that were designed to impose order, which they often framed as attempts to preserve woods. Statements on the need to preserve timber prefaced orders to sell wood to pay debts. Ironworks were to be closed to preserve wood for other ironworks. Problems in England's woods, the government suggested, could be solved through honest officers and an obedient populace.

Throughout 1649, the Council of State issued numerous orders to use and protect woods that displayed their concern with ensuring order, but they revealed the ambiguities in what exactly a necessary public use entailed. The Commons reiterated blanket restrictions against felling trees in the Forest of Dean, and the Council of State ordered the governor of Chepstow Castle to preserve ship timber "it being the only place in those parts where there is any timber for the use of shipping, which is also very much decayed in most places in England and therefore ought to be preserved with so much the greater care." In the same order, they allowed the continued operation of ironworks, so long as the proprietors took greater care to preserve the coppices that fueled them. By the end of the year, the Council of State authorized the surveyors and preservators of the Forest of Dean to sell "short cords," trees that they determined would not produce adequately sized timber for sale, so long as they kept detailed accounts showing profit for the Commonwealth notwithstanding all of the previous restrictions on felling. Elsewhere, the Council of State took steps to preserve traditional timber rights for forest officials. They ordered navy commissioners in Waltham Forest and another unspecified location to preserve "livery wood" and ensure that rights to gather fuel and construction material were respected when combing through lops and tops for elbows and other bent timber for the navy. In June 1649, the Council of State ordered that oaks and beeches in Windsor Forest deemed fit only for firewood be sold off for the state's benefit. Here officers were tasked with judging the quality of trees. In the fall, they issued orders to fell timber to build frigates for Clarendon and Theobalds Parks and gave a general warrant to the navy commissioners to seek out supplies where they saw fit. At the same time, Lord Thomas Grey, the parliamentary commander and regicide, ordered all ministers of the peace in Northampton and Buckingham to conduct searches for greyhounds, crossbows, and other implements for poaching in the areas surrounding Whittlewood Forest after "divers disorderly and dangerous persons" killed deer, rabbits, and other game there.[22] Public goods included shipbuilding, iron production, provision of fuel and other common rights. It meant that trees unfit for naval use could be sold for revenue, but it also meant that military officers would order actions to preserve forests as hunting preserves.

The state's policies, particularly the emphasis on profits and revenue for the Commonwealth, provoked resistance, most dramatically expressed in the Digger Gerrard Winstanley's *Declaration of the Poor Oppressed People of England* (1649). Winstanley expressed his opposition to sales of common woods in unambiguous terms, warning anyone intending to do so, "You shall not do it." The woods, according to Winstanley, were the common resource of the "poor oppressed," not those "who have, by the murdering and cheating law of the sword, stolen the land." Winstanley's attempt to preserve the woods from private individuals grew out of his concerns about the distribution of resources not the preservation of trees. Winstanley articulated a vision that seemed to suggest universal tillage and, aside from the ownership and distribution of the newly plowed land, mirrored that of radical improvers, while simultaneously hinting that such a transformation might leave stores of trees. "Our purpose," he wrote, "is to take those common woods to sell them, now at first, to be a stock for our selves, and our children after us, to plant and manure the Common land withal." He focused on the rights of the poor to decide how to benefit from wood sales, offering the ambiguous note that the transactions would take place "quietly [and] without diminution." His invocation of future generations and his claim that these transactions would not result in "diminution" suggest a desire to maintain woods, but that is difficult to reconcile with the expansion of agriculture implied in his call to "plant and manure."[23] Even for the period's most radical thinker, crafting a political ecology that served the commonwealth and posterity proved a challenge.

The records of the Council of State also make it clear that resistance was not confined to radicals. The unrepentant Royalist and former Worcestershire MP Sir Ralph Clare claimed right to "waste and spoil of timber" in Bewdley Park, Worcestershire, preventing the state from profiting from the sale of the felled wood. The Council of State blamed the poor for wastes in Clarendon Park and ordered the Town of Salisbury to provide them with "maintenance" to prevent the spoil. Failing that, they authorized the local army commander, "If the numbers should be great and their meeting amount to a riot, that you cause them to be proceeded against as such." The Council of State took accusations of spoil by the poor seriously. In 1650, they ordered troops to Surrey to suppress wood-stealing and illegal felling. Failing to punish disobedience in the woods "encourageth that looser and disordered sort of people to the greater boldness in other designs against the Commonwealth." The threats to disorder came not just from Royalist elites and disordered commons but also from dishonest officers of the state. The Council of State also worried that the purveyors assigned to procure ship timber for the navy were entrusted with a great responsibility and urged the navy commissioners to draw up an oath to better ensure the purveyors' trustworthiness.[24]

A report on the state of the woods in the Forest of Dean from the end of the year revealed the difficulties formulating coherent forest policies. The report's authors Colonel J. Brownwick and Captain George Bishop opened with a staggering statistic. Since 1641, according to the report, more than 50,000 trees were known to have been destroyed. Of these, 30,000 were "the best and primest trees of the Forest." The remainder of the document points to the uncertainty beneath these quantifications. Brownwick and Bishop attributed some of the blame to the Royalist Sir John Wintour, reiterating the charge leveled in the *Grand Remonstrance*, but it also indicted forest officers, the very people tasked with monitoring and counting. As the report put it: "The honest officers are put out and knaves put in." The charges leveled against these "knaves" show the difficulties the state faced assessing the situation in its forests. Foresters cropped trees, an action that might result in serious damage but also a charge long leveled at forest officials by forestry reformers who sought to ensure trees were used for commercial timber rather than as browse for deer. The officers allowed overly large cordwood to be sold with false measurements. They forged markings on trees unfit for naval service and allowed the best to remain unmarked. Armed men threatened observers sent to survey and view the forest. Those who reported spoils were accused of being Royalist delinquents subject to fines and punishments.[25] These charges make it clear that the state was operating on the basis of irregular, chaotic, and often contradictory information.

Brownwick and Bishop's own attempts to define destruction in the forest suggest that they too operated according to somewhat contradictory principles. They lamented that "great quantities of iron, furnaces, woods, and watercourses of other men's forcibly taken, kept, destroyed to very great value and no satisfaction given, nor dare the poor men ask for it." In this point, the destruction of Dean's iron industry was part of the broader story of waste in the forest. In the very next point, however, they appeared to reverse course on ironworks. Twelve furnaces and forges were still operating. These works defrauded the state of £20,000 by failure to pay for appropriate licenses. Iron-works unleashed "destruction of so much timber and the goodliest Forest in England." Those responsible were "pretended Parliament servants and formerly Commissioners and entrusted to prevent such destructions." The only solution, Brownwick and Bishop claimed, was to ban all ironworks until the knotted mass of competing claims could be untangled in court lest "the whole Forest will be suddenly destroyed."[26] Ironworks were both victims and authors of Dean's destruction. Brownwick and Bishop's report identified disorder and disobedience as the major threats to the Forest of Dean. Commercial timbering and iron production caused problems when "knaves" supervised them.

Their report displayed two characteristics common to reports about the state of woods under the Commonwealth: ambiguous language about the scope and scale of destruction and concern with problems of order and authority. According to Brownwick and Bishop, Dean had been destroyed and stripped of its best timber. At the same time, urgent actions were needed, indicating that the woods were at least somewhat salvageable. Their language about future spoil called into question the scale of waste they had already invoked. Yet the ability to save the battered but nonetheless valuable forest faced numerous struggles. Reliable information was scarce. Disordered and defiant crowds threatened surveyors. The officers tasked with protecting woods were "knaves."

Some observers responded to the difficulty regulating woods with calls for radical action. The agricultural improver Sylvanus Taylor argued in *Common-good* (1652) that enclosure was the solution to England's agricultural and silvicultural woes. Taylor argued that common rights were simply incompatible with timber production. Bushes and weeds choked off trees. Anything that somehow survived would not fare any better: "[The surviving trees] must suffer a remove, either to the fire, or to the hedge, or to some other such uses. But if it happily escapes all these, yet it is still liable to such lopping and topping, that it commeth to be but a knotty pollard, and at last after it hath long cumbered the ground, it serves for no more at best but for a doted log to lie behind the fire." He argued that the traditional common rights accorded to forest dwellers—fireboot, hedgeboot, houseboot—and those given to forest officers—cutting browse for deer by lopping—threatened to leave England with no valuable timber. Only the security of enclosure would encourage private individuals to convert the disease-producing commons bearing thorns, briars, and moss into tree plantations "whereby our Shipping may be for ever maintained, and our Nation thereby (so far as means can go) made strong and safe."[27]

Taylor's solution for erstwhile royal forests revealed issues in his approach. Taylor, unsurprisingly given his consistent clamoring for enclosure, argued that forests should also be enclosed. He railed against the Forest Laws, claiming that they were a tool to protect deer and leave the unenclosed cornfields of forest dwellers subject to destruction. At the same time, he complained that sheep were not commonable animals in many forests. Finally, he argued that the commonwealth's supply of wood had been gravely threatened. Enclosure, he claimed, would ensure that "the Forest of Dean, so famous for Ship-timber (not to be paralleled) might again flourish with goodly trees, which to waste comes not far short of Treason." At the same time, enclosures would allow "that goodly Forest of Waltham, so apt for Wood and Grass and lying so convenient to a Navigable River" to produce abundant cattle and "gallant Timber." "That Upland and now-Bushy Chase of Enfield," he claimed "will then be loaded with Corn and Sheep."[28] Enclosure would somehow ensure increases in timber production while simultaneously guaranteeing the common rights of pasture and the advance of tillage that earlier foresters, surveyors, and government officials had blamed for much of the spoil. Without going into any further details, Taylor asserted that enclosure would enable uses to productively coexist that at least some contemporaries felt were incompatible. His optimism perhaps stemmed from his understanding of how spoil occurred. The Forest of Dean, he claimed, was destroyed by "Rome's agents" John Wintour and Sir Basil Brooke, who had at one point held a grant to produce iron in Dean. These "notable Popish politicians" had "designed" the destruction of timber.[29] Without their nefarious influence and with the panacea of enclosure, problems would cease to exist in England's forests and chases.

Resistance from above and below, difficulty assessing and maintaining resources, and pressing financial issues appear to have shaped the government's decision to engage in mass disafforestation and sale of timber in 1653. The parliamentary act authorizing sales of former royal forests explicitly sought to provide for the needs of the poor who were unable "by work or otherwise, to maintain themselves and families." It also acknowledged the thicket of overlapping rights claims by individuals and towns that included pasturing rights, rights to fuel and building materials, pannage for pigs, and rights to turf. The act, however, sought to quarantine that complex system of claims and uses. Each group was to present its case to newly appointed, oath-bound trustees. After the trustees allocated these rights, remaining timber was to be valued and sold. The land was to be enclosed and improved.[30]

Through the act, the government sought to impose order where preexisting regulations and forest officers had failed, but issues remained. Carey Mildmay's report from Waltham Forest in Essex noted that the new law failed to quell disorder. Since the act of disafforestation, the foresters had daily committed "great spoil" and their destructive example had, according to Mildmay, led other inhabitants astray. "No person of trust," he claimed, was "empowered to punish offenders and preserve the just rights and customs of the inhabitants." Moreover, the questions about title and right raised by the act had led some people to simply take wood: Once the parcel called "Wallwood" was "questioned," there was "great spoil made in timber."[31] In 1657, surveyors John Kinsey, Thomas Watts, and George Sargeant lamented that "great waste had been made of the wood and timber" in Needwood Chase in Staffordshire. At the same time, there was still hope that they might prevent "destruction of one of the best forests in England." They described these depredations as problems of authority. Inhabitants ignored the laws, refused to pay taxes and fees, and felled timber day and night without regard for authority. They urged Cromwell to send them cavalry so that they might collect taxes and fees and they requested a warrant to sell any timber they seized.[32] Attempts to impose order in forests, parks, and chases through sale, enclosure, and the selective use of military force failed to stem the complaints about destruction. Instead, local officials marshaled anxieties about the destruction of woods to support requests for troops to aid in tax collection or to clarify titles to property.

Natural philosophers also sought to take advantage of fears of scarcity under the Commonwealth to promote their own projects. In 1653, Ralph Austen published a tract titled *A Treatise of Fruit-Trees* that offered practical guidance for planting and grafting trees in an orchard and provided extensive advice on manufacturing cider. In his dedicatory letter to Samuel Hartlib, the author of numerous works on agricultural improvement and the leader of a correspondence circle that brought intellectuals and natural philosophers, including John Evelyn, together during the period, Austen claimed fruit trees were "the chief means to enrich this Commonwealth." Wood scarcity was not part of his case. Instead, he wrote, by consuming more cider and perry, England could cease sending money overseas for French wine. In addition to benefiting trade, planting fruit trees in enclosed fields would provide work for the poor and spare them from "idleness, beggary, shame, and consequently, theft, murder, and (at last) the gallows."[33] By 1656, however, Austen offered a different justification for his work. England suffered "great scarcity of fuel in many places but also of timber for building." He wondered how future generations might build ships to defend the country and asked, "What preparation is there for a future supply?" The answer, he wrote, lay in his book. The rules for planting fruit trees applied just as well to oak, ash, and elm. Talk of timber scarcity, according to Austen, filled the "news books," and he saw an opportunity to make his work relevant. He asked Hartlib to help persuade members of Parliament, the Lord Deputy of Ireland, and the Lieutenant of the Tower to read his *Treatise*. He even authored, with Hartlib's assistance, a petition to Parliament.[34]

The text of his petition made it clear, however, that Austen was attempting to persuade MPs to tack text about fruit trees onto a law about timber. "There hath been," he noted, "of late years, a great destruction of wood and timber." Fruit trees were, he claimed, part of the solution since they would ensure bark for tanners while making fuel plentiful across England. Austen never explained how planting and tending producing fruit trees would simultaneously allow sufficient quantities of bark and fuel to ease national scarcity. Instead, he dwelled on his long abiding interest, the production of cider and perry. Austen's petition, like his *Treatise*, extolled the health virtues of these English drinks. "Judicious physicians" had found those spirits to be the most "healthful liquors." Again, he promised that mass planting of fruit trees would busy the idle hands of the poor. The petition made a vague attempt to connect fruit trees with fuel and timber scarcity, but, in a letter to Hartlib about the petition, Austen acknowledged that there was little connection between the two and that planting timber was "more necessary."

Nonetheless, he hoped Parliament might see the wisdom in a national plan to promote perry and cider orchards.[35]

The ambiguous and often politicized claims of spoil and scarcity make it difficult to assess the scale of damage in England's woods during the period, but the history of ship-timber production in the Forest of Dean offers some insights into the disjuncture between claims of destruction and scarcity and the realities of commercial and naval forestry. In 1648 and 1649, the Commonwealth government consistently invoked a destroyed Forest of Dean, but the actions of that government over the course of the 1650s complicate the earlier claims of widespread ruin. In 1650, the Council of State ordered the destruction of all ironworks in the Forest of Dean under military supervision, but three years later they issued a grant to Major John Wade to restart the ironworks to supply the navy.[36] Records detailing the supply of naval stores show that Dean continued to be a major source for ship timber throughout the 1650s. In 1654, even as shipwrights complained about scarcity, perhaps as a result of demands to supply the fleet headed forth to conquer Spanish territories in the Atlantic or as a consequence of war with the Dutch, a group of navy officers wrote to the admiralty commissioner that even after factoring in the cost of labor and transportation, timber from the Forest of Dean could be sold in the shipyards at Chatham, Deptford, and Woolwich for between £1/5s and £1/15s profit per load and recommended a supply of 400–500 loads be sent over.[37] The allegedly impending scarcity had not halted iron production or the profitable export of ship timber.

Wade, who, by the end of the 1650s, had established himself as a considerable ironmaster and provider of naval stores in the Forest of Dean delivered one of the most scathing indictments of Commonwealth forestry in 1657. He seethed in response to the 1657 act governing the Forest of Dean. The act repudiated the forest policies of Charles I, accusing him of having violated the "rights, liberties, and privileges" of Dean's inhabitants and conspiring for the "destruction" of Dean by granting it to Sir John Wintour. In response, the act forbade more than one-third of the forest to be enclosed at any time, allowed inhabitants to fell trees without supervision and warrant, and made provision for the "improvement" of lands by converting them to tillage while simultaneously restoring the boundaries that existed during James's reign. The government framed the act as a salve against the spoils of the deposed king, but Wade saw the act as an invitation to flatten the forest. He accused the government of authoring a proclamation allowing "all the waste, spoil, and destruction [to] be done and committed upon the Forest of Dean as the hearts of wicked people can invent or imagine to do." He asked the Admiralty Commissioners to free him of his obligations and buy him out of his contract "for it cuts the very heart and mind of me to see the barbarous dealings that are done in this forlorn, disowned piece of ground so much talked of and so little cared for in reality." The provisions against enclosure were at the heart of his complaint. Without enclosures to protect his woods from grazing animals, Wade feared that his ironworks and tree plantations would be gnawed to ruin.[38]

Despite Wade's dire predictions, records regarding Dean after the act show that it continued to produce timber. In 1660, not long after Wade forecast Dean's utter destruction, Daniel Furzer wrote from Lydney in the Forest of Dean requesting permission to establish an ironworks and describing shipments of trees for the navy too large to fit into the vessels in port, and a report from Furzer in 1661 indicated that Dean continued to produce naval stores the next year.[39] There were some complaints about scarcity, but close examination of these complaints demonstrates that claims of shortages from Dean stemmed from difficulty securing transportation for felled wood. In 1659, there were complaints that the Forest of Dean was not producing sufficient timber, yet that year Wade reported felling 1,200 tons of ship timber in the Forest of Dean in addition to making more than 12,000 tree nails. A letter to the navy commissioners explained that the issue lay not in wood supply but in labor and transportation. Timber carriers were unwilling to work because they had not sown their barley crops and would not do so until mid-May. So long as transportation laborers were involved in agricultural work, carriage rates for timber hit twelve shillings per ton, a rate the navy deemed unacceptable. The same issues had plagued production in Dean since 1657.[40] Materials scarcity in naval shipyards reflected not only the supply of trees in England but also transportation and labor. From the end of the Civil War, the Commonwealth government expressed anxieties about the Forest of Dean. Surveyors and forest officials wrote that it had been wasted. Yet, through the Restoration, navy suppliers and ironmasters continued to find timber there, often at prices cheap enough to justify sales as far away as shipyards in Kent. Complaints about waste and destruction did not devastate forest industries.

Through the Civil War and Restoration, wood scarcity was a persistent but slippery issue. Often contradictory complaints about the nature, scope, and causes of destruction poured in from across England. These accounts, like Evelyn's claims about scarcity in *Sylva*, did not separate political and environmental issues. Disobedience and deforestation swirled together. Natural philosophers and agricultural improvers promised solutions to the problem, as others had done since the sixteenth century. Evelyn argued that he was the first person to seriously consider the problem of wood scarcity. In

reality, he was only another entrant into a long-standing debate. The problem remained one of political ecology and, as had been the case since the
late sixteenth century, this had consequences for if and how colonies fit into
proposed solutions.

*   *   *

In Evelyn's account, Ireland barely figured, but, like England, it had seen considerable violence in the 1640s and 1650s. As in England, contemporaries
sought to understand the effects of war on the landscape. During the conflict,
Royalists, supporters of Parliament, Catholics, and, ultimately, Cromwellian
governors hurled accusations of woodland destruction, and provisions for
the protection of valuable woods were part of an early, unsuccessful treaty
attempt. Alongside laments about the arboreal impacts of war, accounts pro-
liferated about rebels lurking in dense, impenetrable woods, which invoked
older discourses about woodkerns and disorderly landscapes.[41] The same
conflict that drove Evelyn's analysis of scarcity in the first edition of *Sylva* had
produced similar complaints and allegations in Ireland. It is a testament to
the Anglo-centric character of his political ecology that these did not surface
in the text.

Other contemporary writers did attempt to understand the effects of war
on Ireland's landscape and the consequences for continued English projects to reform the island's people, politics, and economy. In *Ireland's Natural
History*, first published in 1652, the Dutch physician and natural philosopher Gerard Boate offered an uneven assessment of the state of Irish woods
after the 1641 Rebellion, war, and Cromwellian conquest.[42] In the heading
for one section, Boate wrote, "Great part of Ireland very bare of woods at
this time." The very next section was titled "Many great woods still left in
Ireland." Boate's contradictory descriptions stemmed from his deeply ambiguous opinions about the best uses of Irish land. His major source of anxiety
was the inability of Ireland's inhabitants to find sufficient firewood or timber
for construction. The difficulties procuring firing prompted some people to
"make shift with turf, or sea-coal, where they are not too far from the sea."
For construction timber, "they are necessitated to fetch it a good way off, to
their great charges, especially in places where it must be brought by land."
However, Boate echoed the commentary of generations of English writers
describing Ireland, complaining that the woods were a haven for "thieves and
rogues" and an impediment to profitable land use. "Woods in most part of

Ireland," he wrote, "may be reduced not only to very good pastures, but also to excellent arable and meadow." At the same time, he noted that English planters had created a "mighty trade . . . [which] brought great profit to the proprietaries."[43] Ireland's woods existed in a state of flux in Boate's description. They had been destroyed and continued to stand. They were nuisances and necessities. They were signs of Irish sloth and sources for English profits. His uncertainty was representative of English writings on Ireland during the 1640s and 1650s.[44]

Despite these vacillations, Boate was clear about who had felled Irish woods: the English. Citing Gerald of Wales, the twelfth-century clergyman and author of a justification for the contemporary Anglo-Norman invasion of Ireland, Boate claimed that from these first settlements onward the English "did by degrees greatly diminish the woods in all the places where they were masters." The greatest destruction, according to Boate, had come between 1603 and 1641 during a period of peace as English planters sought "to make merchandise of [the woods] and for the making of Charcoal for the Ironworks." At the height of production in Ireland, pipe-stave manufacturing consumed "thousands of trees" and ironworks "infinite number of trees, all the loppings and windfalls being not sufficient for it in the least manner."[45]

Even so, Boate recognized that the English did not strip Ireland entirely bare, even in the areas of greatest exploitation: "In Munster, where the English, especially the Earl of Cork, have made great havoc of the woods during the last peace, there be still sundry great forests remaining in the Counties of Kerry, and of Tipperary; and even in the County of Cork, where the greatest destruction thereof hath been made, some great woods are yet remaining, there being also store of scattered woods both in that County, and all the Province over."[46] Boate's description reflected the results of the tension between tales of scarcity and destruction and the efforts from Boyle and other planters to use coppicing, lease restrictions, lawsuits, and other methods common in English wood management to protect natural resources. His repetition of "great" to describe the scale of both deforestation and survival reveals the difficulty early modern people experienced in explaining human interactions with wooded land. The only sense of scale Boate offered outside of greatness was his lone reference to "scattered woods." Moreover, the moral valence of this description remains unclear. Did the persistence of great swaths of wooded land indicate the failure of centuries of attempts to render the recalcitrant landscape civil and profitable? Did his decision to describe English actions as "havoc" indicate disapproval for the deforestation he had encouraged paragraphs earlier? Or were the great woodlands that survived an invitation to the next generation of English settlers to profit from intensive and profitable industries?

The lone exception to Boate's Anglo-centric account of Irish forestry was Ulster, where the counties Down, Monaghan, Cavan, and Armagh were "almost everywhere bare, not only of Woods, but of all sorts of Trees, even in places which in the beginning of this present Age, in the War with Tyrone, were encumbered with great and thick Forests."[47] Unlike his previous description, where even great havoc might leave great, or at least scattered, clusters of trees, he depicted Ulster as a completely denuded moonscape. Again, Boate's language left room for considerable ambiguity. Was the totalizing scale of destruction evidence for the unprecedented intensity of Irish rage in the 1641 Rebellion and its aftermath? Or did such destruction present an opportunity for English settlement unencumbered by these wooded barriers to abundant tillage and rich pastures?

Other sources give reason to doubt the extremity of Boate's description of Ulster. A 1654 memorandum on Hastings lands in Ulster lamented that "our woods both in Tyrone and Fermanagh are mightily wasted since the beginning of the late Rebellion." Yet, they were still salvageable if "some good course be taken to preserve them," namely restrictions on access and use and the vigorous prosecution of trespassers. An anonymous letter sent to Lucy Hastings, Countess Huntingdon, sometime between 1655 and 1679 provided advice on how to manage her lands in Ulster. In it, Hastings's correspondent noted that the countess's woods were in somewhat dire straits. "A great many" of the trees had been "barked"—had their bark stripped from them, likely killing the tree. Others were "past thriving," a problem stemming from lack of timely felling rather than rampant exploitation but an issue nonetheless for a landowner seeking to maximize value. Faced with old trees with no value as timber, there was no reason "for her honor to let those woods stand to her loss." The woods were in a delicate state, but Hastings's adviser offered two solutions aimed at the long-term preservation of afforested land. First, she might grant a multi-year lease for the woods, including barked trees but that reserved "spring wood or samplers or saplings." Later, the writer warned that leasing the woods, even with reservations for spring wood, risked "posterity for her honor" because there were "few or no samplers there but what are barked and few trees but what will come within the verge of the taker's choice." Both letters referenced destruction but largely cast it as reversible or as a future state.[48]

Although the letter did not specify the exact location of the lands, Hastings held lands in Armagh, Monaghan, Cavan, Tyrone, and three of the counties Boate had claimed were completely deforested, as well as in Fermanagh where Boate noted that great woods remained.[49] Hastings's correspondent offered a picture of destruction but not at the scale of Boate's description. Wounded trees remained standing alongside aged and decayed trees. Some spring wood may have existed, either in the form of regenerating trees that had been wounded or, most optimistically, as healthy green shoots sprouting amid the wreckage. The woods may have been damaged, her correspondent asserted, but they were salvageable through careful management of leases.

The mass destruction of woodlands does not appear in the 1641 depositions—testimonies largely from displaced Protestants collected by clergy and appointed commissioners in the 1640s and 1650s. Most of the deponents who mentioned wood or timber in their statements described the loss of either construction timber or household fuel. For example, in 1642, Percy Smyth of County Waterford told the commissioners that rebels had stolen squared timber that he had intended to use for building.[50] Where the timber lost was not already felled or being used for a trade like tanning, deponents did not specify whether the woods were physically destroyed or whether the deponent had simply lost possession of them.[51] Only two deponents explicitly referenced rebels destroying woodlands. In 1642, Edward Bloud of County Meath told the commissioners that he had been robbed of £20 "by the cutting down and spoiling of timber, hedges, gardens, and orchards." Richard Stevens of Clonshire Beg in County Limerick complained that he had "one nursery of trees digged up and taken away by the rebels to his damage & loss of ten pounds."[52] Both of these depositions suggest that rebels aimed their violence at orchards, hedges, and nurseries—trees used in enclosures or deliberately planted to produce fruit or other commodities—rather than attacking woodlands that may have been used for iron or pipe-stave production.[53]

Other depositions suggest that some of the destruction that Lucy Hastings's woods suffered may have come at the hands of English planters. James Redferne from Magherafelt in County Derry told the commissioners that he had paid for the right to bark oak trees in three and a half townlands in Ardboe, County Tyrone. Redferne claimed only that the rebellion had inhibited his ability to bark the trees; he offered no comment on whether they had been stripped.[54] Other deponents lamented that the struggles of war had forced them to fell trees. John Brereton claimed that during a siege in County Laois they were forced to extreme measures: "They have been enforced to feed upon the flesh of horses, dogs, cats, and crows, and to drink water all the time, but therein also were often scanted, and for about 8 weeks or above were forced to feed upon the very leaves of beans, potatoes, and weeds, and when extreme want enforced them desperately to adventure out and fall trees in the orchard for fuel."[55] Again, the trees destroyed here were orchard trees planted to produce fruit as part of the demesne land of a castle, not the wider woods. Moreover, Phillip Bisse, one of the commissioners responsible for collecting depositions, reported that English people might destroy orchards simply through negligence. He complained that John Perry had destroyed the Lord Primate's orchard by letting his forty cows spoil the trees "with rubbing" and had "made it a bog."[56]

Records of ironworks from the second half of the seventeenth century also point to problems with the narrative of destruction. Historian Eileen McCracken found two ironworks in County Down—one of the areas in which Boate had claimed rebels failed to leave even lone trees standing—that showed some signs of operating in the 1650s and 1660s.[57] Historian Toby Barnard's analysis of the Enniscorthy ironworks in County Wexford and Sir William Petty's ironworks in County Kerry show that many of the dynamics that shaped Irish ironmaking prior to 1641 continued to operate after the end of the 1641 Rebellion and Cromwell's conquest. Barnard argues that general wood scarcity was not a major problem for either Petty or the Enniscorthy syndicate. Instead, fuel supply became an issue because of the tight margins under which Irish ironmakers worked. Exhausting the trees located closest to water or needing to purchase cordwood from neighbors threatened to render these projects unprofitable, precisely the issue that had plagued Boyle's works and contributed to his conflicts with the East India Company. The problem was not that Irish timber cost more than English timber but that the cost of Irish wood needed to be extremely low to offset higher rates for labor, transportation, and importing suitable ores.[58]

As was the case with Boyle's ironworks, strong connections with the Forest of Dean for raw materials and the need to find ready and reliable markets defined success and failure for Irish ironworks. As Barnard shows, English merchants did not come to Ireland out of desperation at domestic shortages. Indeed, Petty struggled and never succeeded in finding a reliable English or Irish market for his iron. The Enniscorthy investors found markets in Dublin; made smaller sales to other Irish cities; and, by the 1660s, had integrated into networks of production and sale focused on the Forest of Dean while simultaneously selling small portions around the Atlantic. Yet, as Barnard argued, the Enniscorthy syndicate forged its connections with raw materials suppliers and merchants along the Severn as a result of preexisting commercial connections.[59] No amount of purported scarcity in England guaranteed the success of Irish ironworks: Irish producers succeeded or failed based on their ability to access existing commercial networks.

* * *

Evelyn's failure to mention Virginia as anything other than a source of rare or unique trees likewise ignored the continued attempts to integrate Virginia into transatlantic trade in woodland commodities. At the same time, his unwillingness to treat Virginia as anything more than a source for exotic plants may have reflected his opinion that these schemes were little more than projectors' bluster. At some level, such a skeptical view was warranted. Claims about a diversified economy built on woods and woodland commodities justified by invoking English scarcity followed a long and hitherto unsuccessful paradigm. At the same time, plans and actions taken under Governor William Berkeley suggest that Virginia colonists were attempting to situate their woods into a new, Atlantic political ecology in which New World trees would serve intercolonial and interimperial trade and not just as resources for England.

Evelyn was not the only English thinker to dismiss Virginia's capacity to supply England with wood. The colony did not register as a source of timber in discussions by Parliament, the Council of State, or various committees and offices responsible for the navy during the 1640s or 1650s. The most sustained commentary on Virginia's woods came from the work of the natural philosopher Samuel Hartlib investigating sericulture. Through the 1650s, Hartlib published two versions of a tract on sericulture in Virginia that blended his own writings on the subject with published letters from his correspondents. Hartlib praised Virginia for "the Climate being the same with China, from whence the infinite quantity of silk comes, but abounding (as it doth) with mulberry-trees naturally growing there, and exceeding it by the silkworm-bottoms found in her woods." Yet he made it clear that colonists should not depend on this natural bounty. The text, where it dealt with mulberry trees, focused overwhelmingly on methods for planting them in commercially viable concentrations. He later made it clear that English Virginians should not spend their time scouring the woods. It was best to "encourage the Savages, when they find any bottoms in the woods, to bring them to you, that you may get of the race and seed to increase it." Virginia's sericulture, according to Hartlib and his correspondents, should not be founded on foraging, particularly not foraging by English colonists. Instead, Virginia's woodlands were to be sources for trees and insects to be propagated in commercially viable quantities within the confines of English settlement.[60]

Hartlib did conclude his text with a statement referencing Virginia's role in England's imperial political ecology. Virginia, he claimed, would provide commodities at "a very reasonable rate and price, much cheaper then now we have them, and are fain to fetch them with great hazard from doubtful friends, or heathen nations, to their great enriching and our own impoverishing." Among the "doubtful friends" he listed were Baltic and Eastern European countries that provided England with timber, masts, pitch, tar, and other products derived from trees. Hartlib reinforced this point in the same section, noting that Virginia possessed everything for "building and rigging of a Navy in all complete manner from top to toe."[61] This, however, was the only mention of other commodities in this text and Hartlib did not take up this point elsewhere in his published work.

The most enthusiastic proponent of Virginia in Hartlib's circle was the Herefordshire clergyman, agricultural writer, and natural philosopher John Beale. Beale was a frequent correspondent with Hartlib, eventually publishing their letters in *Herefordshire Orchards, a Pattern for all England* (1657). Scarcity played little role in these writings. In *Herefordshire Orchards*, the only reference to dearth came in the form of praise for Lord John Scudamore, who Beale called "a great preserver of woods against the day of England's need." Instead, most of Beale's writing focused on methods for planting and tending trees. In 1658 and 1659, however, as Beale was reading Arthur Standish's *Commons' Complaint* (1611) and preparing to publish an edition of the text with a new foreword by Hartlib, he began to write about the relationship between the Virginia colony and England's woods.[62]

Beale wrote of wood scarcity as an impetus for exploiting colonial woods, but he also thought about issues of colonial development and the appropriate relationship between colony and metropole. Virginia and New England "have land enough, yet their land wants culture." Beale hoped that culture would take the form of trade in "wine, currants, navigable vessels, and iron-ordinancy, which would now be a necessary relief to these nations, which have almost consumed their store of Timber." Like other writers, Beale wondered whether the potential fruits of English colonies could be produced at home. He wrote to Hartlib that the "cotton tree" (perhaps either the Eastern cottonwood, *Populus deltoides*, or a biogeographically ambitious claim for *Ceiba pentandra*, the cotton tree common in the Caribbean) and "silk grass" (likely milkweed, *Asclepias syriaca*) "if our soil could kindly bear them" would be "considerable improvements." Likewise, he sought to develop a method for cultivating mulberry trees. Yet he wondered whether such commodities were better developed in the colonies themselves: "These curiosities are but a wantonness in England, but a relief in a foreign plantation."[63] Scarcity might make a compelling case to move production to North America, but Beale also showed a willingness to distribute commodities around the English Atlantic, perhaps even if doing so would increase the cost, to ensure the viability of English colonies.

Beale never resolved the relationship between domestic wood scarcity, the desirability of colonial development, and the need to make colonial products cost effective. In his letter to Hartlib outlining their reprinting of Standish, Beale inquired about iron production in Virginia and New England. He had "often heard at random, and upon uncertain grounds" that there were proposals to supply the entirety of England with steel and iron "better than we make and as cheap as ours." If these rumors were true, Beale opined, "it were a great help to those concerned plantations and the only or main relief to our timber, if iron works were forbidden here, as plantation of tobacco is forbidden." Beale's statement showed his conflicted views on the appropriate economic and environmental relationships between England and its North American colonies. He cast a ban on domestic iron production as the best or only solution to impending domestic wood scarcity. At the same time, his persistent references to cost and quality suggested that such a preservationist measure only made sense if English consumers could maintain access to similar or better iron at similar or lower costs. Even if price and quality drove English iron consumers to buy from North American colonists, Beale still believed that some sort of state intervention was necessary to ensure that domestic production would halt, drawing an analogy to the (occasionally circumvented) ban on domestic tobacco growing.[64] Wood scarcity might push iron production across the Atlantic but only if colonial producers could compete on cost and quality and only if the state were willing to aid the effort.

It is significant that Beale's arguments on wood scarcity and colonial development in Virginia did not appear in *Sylva* because it suggests that Evelyn had consciously ignored them. Evelyn and Beale were both correspondents in Hartlib's circle, where members wrote open letters through Hartlib. Moreover, Hartlib had made an effort to connect Beale and Evelyn, offering them shared recommendations for works on reformed husbandry. Finally, Evelyn and Beale remained correspondents, even after Hartlib's death. As literary scholar Michael Leslie has shown in his analysis of Evelyn's unpublished (at the time) gardening treatise "Elysium Britannicum," Evelyn took different intellectual paths than Beale, even though they directly corresponded.[65] All

of this suggests that Evelyn's decision to ignore concrete attempts to establish an iron industry and gestures toward the development of naval stores in
Virginia at the beginning of the 1660s was a conscious choice rather than an
omission wrought of ignorance. Hartlib and Beale had envisioned Virginia's
woods and woodland commodities in a political ecology of wood that placed
England at its center, but they saw colonies as useful and necessary to protect
domestic resources; Evelyn's vision was also imperial and metropolitan, but
Virginia had no place in it but as a source of trees.

Although the projects to profit from Virginia's woods bore many similarities to earlier colonial efforts, colonists had begun to situate them in a different
political ecology. At the heart of this shift was William Berkeley, who served as
governor of Virginia from 1642 to 1652 and from 1660 until his death in 1677
and was the key figure in attempts to develop industries based in Virginia's
woods. According to his biographer, historian Warren Billings, after suffering
military, political, and financial setbacks as a courtier to Charles I, Berkeley
saw only limited opportunities if he remained in England, so he engineered a
commission to serve as governor of Virginia, involving generous subsidies to
the popular ousted governor Sir Francis Wyatt. Despite these machinations,
Berkeley quickly proved himself a capable and ambitious leader. As Billings
recounts, Berkeley dedicated himself to diversifying Virginia's economy both
by engaging in improvement projects and agricultural experiments on his
Virginian lands and by advocating for trade policies that he believed would
enable Virginians to find a market for commodities besides tobacco.[66]

Trees were a central part of Berkeley's attempts to demonstrate how a
diversified estate might function. Berkeley planted an orchard and developed
methods for cultivating orange and lemon trees despite Virginia's cold win-
ters. He actively sought to produce silk and planted a grove of mulberry trees
to support the endeavor. In 1663, he wrote to the Earl of Clarendon that he
had produced potashes and wrote enthusiastically that he alone would be
able to ship 200 tons "besides what the country will do." Virginia, he claimed,
might supply all of England's needs for "but a few coarse cloths and some servants which we keep at our own charges as garrison soldiers for his Majesty
whenever his occasions shall require them in these parts of America."[67]

Berkeley's letter to Clarendon, however, also revealed that he viewed discussion of diversification schemes based in Virginia's woods as a tactic to
advocate for otherwise loosely related trade concessions. The purpose of his
missive to Clarendon was to beg the earl for protection since Berkeley was
attempting to stall a royal commission, which he claimed would leave the
colony devoid of servants. Without that labor, Berkeley argued, "all our great

intended undertakings vanish into wishes." He proffered his optimistic talk of potash production to illustrate what England stood to lose if Berkeley did not get his way. This was a common tactic for Berkeley. In a 1662 petition to the Council for Foreign Plantations, Berkeley opened with a list of the commodities Charles II had dispatched him to Virginia to promote: "silk, hemp, flax, potashes, masts, and timber for shipping." Of his six demands, however, only one related to the production of these commodities, a plea for £500 to pay "some few skillful men that are able to teach us the nearest the cheapest way to produce [them]." The remaining requests sought to secure debt forgiveness, secure titles against lawsuits, clarify the procedures for land sales, create a system for compensating colonists who had accidentally cleared land that was later proved to belong to another colonist, and process future debts in commodities besides tobacco.[68]

Berkeley's most comprehensive description of his vision for Virginia's new economy was his *Discourse and View of Virginia* (1663). The *Discourse* first circulated in manuscript form in January 1662 to coincide with his visit to lobby the Privy Council and the Council for Foreign Plantations to support his plan for Virginia.[69] The *Discourse* was a text deliberately designed to persuade Charles II to invest Crown resources in Virginia. It is telling then, that Berkeley described Virginia's natural commodities almost entirely as forest products: "iron, lead, pitch, tar, masts, timbers for ships of the greatest magnitude, and wood for potashes." The Crown should invest in Virginia and grant it free trade privileges, Berkeley argued, because Virginia would provide England with naval stores and with commodities like iron that wasted woods. These commodities were, he claimed, far more important and valuable than Barbadian sugar. Goods like tobacco or sugar might yield some profit, but the foundations of England's wealth and its empire were wooden.[70]

Berkeley had developed a complex political ecology of wood that was simultaneously imperial and Atlantic. Virginia's woods were a critical resource to protect domestic forests and ensure England's security, but they could only be provided by granting Virginians the rights to trade with other colonies and with European merchants. From this vision, he developed an ambitious set of proposals. Ignoring the earlier attempts at diversification under Sir Edwin Sandys while echoing the rhetoric used in early Virginia projects, Berkeley argued that Virginians languished in tobacco-dependence because of neglect and deleterious trade policies. Iron production and shipping failed because "there was never yet any public encouragement to assist the planters in those more chargeable undertakings." The failure of the Crown to provide a public stock for recruiting experts had undermined production of staple commodities. Berkeley raised the specter of English wood shortages to justify his opposition to the trade restrictions of the Navigation Acts. Ships built in Virginia should be allowed to trade at any port so that "the excellency of their timber and masts (of both which there is now a visible scarcity in England) would be known." Granting free trade to Virginia would ensure that "the timber of England might be spared for many years." Yet, even as Virginian ships traded with other European powers, benefits would redound back to England since "ships of the greatest magnitude [could be] built [in Virginia] cheaper than possibly they can be in England."[71] Berkeley attempted to justify a radically different policy than the earliest Virginia colonists, promoters, and adventurers, but he still marshaled the language of English scarcity to justify his position.

Berkeley's focus on Virginia's potential to produce naval stores and iron proved effective. Instructions to colonial governors throughout the seventeenth century had urged them to set up production of timber, naval stores, and iron. In the midst of his own political difficulties, Charles I nonetheless instructed Berkeley in 1641 to take special care preserving cattle "that much people may come thither for the setting up of iron works and other staple commodities." By 1662, however, Berkeley succeeded in getting the state to commit to investment in developing ironworks across the Atlantic. That year, Charles II agreed to support an ironworks in Virginia because the matter was "above a private undertaking." Berkeley was to return to Virginia and debate the matter with the council there. Berkeley and other Virginia leaders were to assess the quantity and quality of Virginia's ore. If it seemed good enough to exploit, they were to instruct Charles "how [he] may best undertake it, what [he] must transport from hence to that purpose, & all things that are necessary thereunto."[72] In roughly two decades, the Crown's position on ironworks had shifted from something that colonists could undertake alone once they had secured their food supply to something that only the state could handle.

Berkeley's proposals represented a remarkable moment in Virginia promoters' attempts to use wood to define the shape of an English Atlantic World. He argued that concern for English trees required the state to support a fledgling iron industry in Virginia while simultaneously allowing Virginia-built ships to freely trade with foreign powers. And he nearly succeeded. But Charles II's support began to crumble almost as soon as Berkeley had secured it. Opposition from London merchants, Maryland colonists, and other groups led the Privy Council to delay and deny Berkeley's requests. By 1664, he had suffered a reversal of fortune. The plans for diversification idled through the 1660s. By 1671, Berkeley had changed his assessment of the possibilities for Virginia iron, saying "We have admirable mast and very good oaks but for iron ore I dare not say there is sufficient to keep one iron mill going for seven years."[73]

After the Restoration, Virginia leaders advanced similar arguments to those set forth in the first Virginia Company pamphlets. Products derived from trees—silk, timber, pitch, tar, potash, and iron—were the appropriate foundations for a colonial economy. Virginia provided an opportunity to avoid pouring funds into foreign coffers, to protect decaying English woods from further destruction, and to take advantage of the cheap timber that Virginia's abundant woods offered. Berkeley's pleas for free trade added a new wrinkle to this argument by appealing to English self-sufficiency while requesting the right for Virginians to operate outside a closed imperial economy. Nonetheless, wood scarcity and abundance remained central to these arguments. The results, however, were similarly disappointing for Virginians. Despite Charles II's offer to personally support Virginian ironworks, the proposal went nowhere.

Plans to use Virginia's woods to relieve English scarcity and to relieve dependence on foreign sources for critical materials had again come to naught, but in the coming decades the intercolonial trade Berkeley championed would provide a market for the colony's trees. In the 1670s and 1680s, Barbados and other West Indian colonies began purchasing timber, naval stores, pipe staves, and many of the other long-imagined woodland commodities from Virginia.[74] Since the sixteenth century, there had been efforts to situate Virginia into an Anglo-centric, imperial political ecology—one in which the colony's woods derived their value from the condition of England's forests. Ultimately, they only became commodities through networks of Atlantic exchange.

* * *

Evelyn suggested that New England had the largest role to play of any colony, but the same Anglo-centric and imperial political ecology that reduced other colonies to mere sources of curious plants shaped his vision for New England's woods. Evelyn offered a tepid and inconsistent endorsement for New England ironworks and naval store manufactures but obscured the small but otherwise unparalleled role that New England played in addressing the problems of naval supply that ostensibly drove Evelyn and the Royal Society to first investigate trees. Instead, Evelyn described New England as a repository of excessive trees impeding colonial progress and recommended using it as a sacrifice zone for an iron industry that he suggested had ravaged English woods.[75] Evelyn's treatment of New England mimicked arguments proffered by colonial ironworks promoters since the late sixteenth century. But by deploying an argument based on scarcity, Evelyn minimized New England's place in an already existing Atlantic timber trade, misrepresented the relationship between colonists and woods, and misunderstood the forces that established ironworks in New England in the 1640s.

Unlike Virginia, the New England colonies had successfully developed a transatlantic trade for wood commodities with England. Throughout the 1650s, New England served as an occasional source of masts for naval shipbuilders, but shipwrights and other naval officials remained uncertain about relying on the colony for masts and did not mention it as a source for other types of ship timber.[76] New England masts found a market due to their uniquely large size; however, naval shipwrights and timber merchants sometimes rejected them, even during times of purported scarcity, because of cost concerns or their excessive bulk for certain types of vessels. Their actions demonstrate that even the group most responsible for the discourse of wood scarcity in the 1650s and 1660s did not uniformly treat shortages as an impetus to look to North American colonies for wood. Instead, they treated New England as a source for a niche commodity, which was valuable enough to justify shipping heavy objects across the Atlantic.

New England masts had appeared in England in small quantities since the mid-1630s but struggled to find a market, a pattern that continued through the 1650s. Tension and the eventual outbreak of hostilities with the Dutch may have provoked the Cromwellian government to seek to exploit New England naval stores in 1651 and 1653.[77] The initiatives petered out because of neglect and structural issues. In 1653, David Yale complained to the navy commissioners that earlier that year he had outfitted a ship for New England in response to the government's plan to procure masts and tar there. By November, however, Yale was unable to get any response to his pleas at Parliament or from the Council of State. When he went back to the unspecified men "from whom I had my first orders," they simply told him that the state "had so many and so great businesses to transact that they had not time in that space to peruse [his]." Nor was Yale alone. In October 1654, a report on another voyage to New England for masts noted that the voyage's sponsor had laid out a considerable sum of money and was "very importunate with us to pass his accounts."[78] The costs of transatlantic voyages were considerable and merchants' inability to recoup their expenses from the state likely discouraged further voyages.

Issues with shipping infrastructure and security also discouraged trans-atlantic mast trade. Henry Roach, Jonathan Wright, and William Wood also received a contract to fetch New England masts in 1653, but their program languished after they discovered that the only two ships capable of fitting the massive New England trees were captured Dutch prizes. The navy commissioners informed them that the state would follow the usual procedures for selling prize vessels. In December of the same year, reports came into London that privateers had attacked two ships bearing New England masts. One managed to escape, but the other was taken to Brest. General George Monck wrote to the navy commissioners urging against military action to recapture the vessel, instead suggesting that they act on a rumor that the masts would be sold at Brest and "think of some way that they might be bought there, supposing they may be had at a reasonable rate."[79] Establishing a mast trade with New England required that the state pay merchants, procure appropriate vessels, and protect those ships in the midst of hostilities with the Dutch. Monck made his opinion clear: It was easier to just purchase masts from European merchants.

The intermittent and uncertain quality of the mast trade undermined the confidence of English shipwrights in New England masts. The Portsmouth shipwright Francis Willoughby made it clear that New England woods were an unreliable solution for the problems facing English shipyards. In August 1654, he urged the navy commissioners against depending on New England ships for masts, complaining that they would not put into Portsmouth because of contrary winds. By December of the same year, he had grown increasingly frustrated. "I have several times made a demand for great masts," he complained, "and the answer propounded was that when the ships came from New England we should be fully supplied." Clearly dissatisfied, Willoughby noted that the answer provided still left him wanting and wrote to "renew my former desires that so we may be thought on and provided for." Lest they miss his barbs, he made it clear that he desired the commissioners propound a new solution. When New England ships arrived in the harbor, he noted with evident pique, "you cannot but be sensible of the expense occasioned by transportation." Willoughby's complaints were all the more remarkable because he made them immediately before declaring that a wounded frigate lay in port that "wants main masts and not one tree in stores to make one."[80] He rejected New England masts because of their excessive costs even as he lamented the complete desolation of his stores.

Two years later, a letter from Willoughby to the commissioners suggested that little had changed. Willoughby was in the midst of negotiations with a timber merchant offering New England masts, but the prices were simply too high. Worse still, the merchant demanded payment in ready money. Willoughby refused to complete the negotiations alone, leaving the final decision on the offer to the commissioners.[81] The expense and uncertainties of transatlantic voyages prompted merchants dealing in New England timber to charge greater rates and to expect swift repayment or transactions in ready money. For Willoughby, these conditions made New England masts a choice of last resort, even in the midst of purported scarcity.

The size and cost of New England masts also created issues for shipwrights that prevented them from regularly using the New World timber. Another shipwright, John Taylor, noted that New England masts were large, expensive, and most fit for the biggest ships. As a result, he was hesitant to use them for smaller ships. "Such actings," he wrote, "are against my principles as such masts are yet wanting." He would only divide the New England timber into smaller masts with written permission from the commissioners. Other shipwrights apparently lacked his principles. In 1655, Taylor lamented that workers at Deptford had "converted" four large masts. Taylor could only express his disbelief at the waste. The masts that were not cut down to fill immediate needs might easily be lost to negligence. Taylor worried that workers were keeping masts out of water without using them in ships, impeding the seasoning process designed to weatherproof the timber for long service. Their incompetence would leave the expensive wood "crusty and short not fit for service."[82] Taylor understood the rarity and expense of the largest masts and urged them to be carefully husbanded for use in special projects, not for the majority of smaller ships being built.

While English shipwrights expressed doubts about New England masts or saw them as rare products to be carefully maintained for particular projects, some New England merchants still attempted to establish a timber trade. In 1656, Daniel Gookin, who had emigrated from the plantation lands of Munster to Virginia before landing in New England; Francis Norton; and Thomas Broughton took advantage when the weather-beaten *Falcon* limped into port in New England. The men "conceived it would be acceptable service to his Highness and the States of England when he turned, to embrace a freight of masts." They claimed that "the constant sending of ships from England hither for such masts" persuaded them that loading their cargo aboard the *Falcon* was a gesture of "usefulness, if not necessity." Besides, they noted, their unsanctioned lading would save the state the money of outfitting another ship, "a prudent improvement of this reasonable opportunity." A receipt of the ship's contents shows that they had broader ambitions than simply providing masts to serve the state. The New Englanders also shipped over 3,000 pipe and hogshead staves.[83]

The boldness of these New England entrepreneurs impressed at least one naval official—Peter Pett, the shipwright who would later author the request for assistance to the Royal Society that spawned Evelyn's *Sylva*. In December 1656, Pett wrote that Broughton ought to be rewarded with a yearly contract to deliver masts and other timber products. Pett's endorsement of New England, however, came with a crucial caveat. Pett noted that the project required controls on price, controls that he claimed would only come through his ability to "make such reasonable demands in price for each sort [of timber]." New England could provide for the navy, but only if the prices and quality were right. Two years later, Pett supported a contract bid for the shipwright John Taylor, who had written about his principles for conserving New England timber. In his letter of support, Pett noted the presence of New England masts at the shipyards at Chatham amid a broader scarcity. Nonetheless, when outlining conditions for the contract, Pett wrote that Taylor should provide "all Swedish wood to be new and sound."[84]

Ultimately, as would become the case in Virginia, New England merchants found the best markets through intercolonial trade. In 1661, the Commissioners of Customs recognized the failure of New England timber products to find a market in England. The chief products of the region were "clapboard, pipestaves and other timber, fish and such gruff commodities." These goods were "better vended in other parts than here." New Englanders had developed a burgeoning Atlantic trade, supplying Madeira and Barbados with diverse timber products. England had failed to integrate New England's woods into a transatlantic political ecology and now, the commissioners warned, "Commodities of great value have from Spain and other parts been usually imported into England and his Majesty thereby much disadvantaged in his Revenue." The commissioners, though reciting the language of the Navigation Act of the previous year, nonetheless sympathized with the merchants' "equitable case" and petitioned the Lord Treasurer to consider an exemption.[85] In ignoring the actions of Pett, whose questions had first justified his presentations on woods, Evelyn suggested an entirely new position for New England in a domestically focused political ecology of wood.

Evelyn called New England's woods a "surfeit" that "hindered [colonists] in their advance and prospect of the continent," echoing Virginia planter Edward Waterhouse's comment nearly forty years earlier that "wasting of woods is an ease and benefit to the planter."[86] Promoters had deployed the trope of colonial woods as a nearly inexhaustible impediment to English expansion since the sixteenth century, but the actual policies toward woods in the New England colonies belie this simplistic, exploitative conceit. In repeating it, Evelyn ignored the legal history of the New England colonies and the actions that had enabled its settlement and trade in wood products. As early as 1626, the General Court of the Plymouth colony set out regulations to prevent "such inconveniences as do and may befall the plantation by the want of timber," a law that was reaffirmed in 1658. This law restricted unpermitted transportation and sale of wood in any form "how little soever the quantity be." Other laws and regulations from the 1620s and 1630s and the actions of the Court of Assistants in the Massachusetts Bay colony laid out rules for exploiting wood on public land designed to protect valuable timber, ensure access to firewood, and promote the careful management of a communal resource.[87] William Bradford wrote of English colonists' shock looking around and seeing nothing but a "hideous and desolate wilderness ... full of woods and thickets [that] represented a wild and savage hew." The laws, regulations, and acts of colonial governments in the 1620s and 1630s show that colonists quickly transformed their conceptualization of these spaces from repositories of "wild beasts and wild men" to repositories of community resources to sustain their settlements.[88]

Regulations in Plymouth, Massachusetts Bay, and Connecticut colonies were designed to promote multiple uses of colonial woods. Colonial governments granted rights to woodlands for sawmills and iron manufacturing, but they sought to curtail wasteful cutting. Statutes in Plymouth and Connecticut enacted in the 1650s required colonists to convert felled trees on common lands to pipe staves, timber for construction, or some other commercial use.[89] Towns set aside tracts of wooded land to serve as pastures for cattle and sources of wood for townspeople to draw upon freely "provided it be without waste or spoil thereof." Restrictions also appeared in grants that allocated specific rights like the ability to take wood for fencing.[90] Records of presentments and fines for illegally felling wood on individual lands of another settler and on a town's commons in 1647 and 1651 suggest that there were at least some efforts to enforce these restrictions.[91]

New England colonial authorities promulgated and enforced restrictions on wood use for three reasons: securing supplies for towns and cities, ensuring resources would be available for future settlements, and preserving diplomatic relations with Native peoples. Evelyn's comments on New England, like those of many early modern English commenters on North America, conveyed the sense of a vast expanse. On the ground, geographies of politics, trade, and labor all constrained where and how English colonists could access wooden resources. In 1641, Hugh Peter and Emmanuel Downing wrote to Governor John Winthrop, asking for his help "suppressing pipe staffs [pipe staves], rivers, and clapboards in our town." Peter and Downing were building two or three ships and they argued that other timbering operations threatened to undermine their enterprise and asked that "within 2 or 3 miles near any river they may not fell great timber fit for shipping, for they may as well cut it further of it being so portable, and ship-timber being so heavy." Likewise, when the inhabitants of Taunton, a settlement located between Plymouth and modern Providence, Rhode Island, petitioned for increased common pasture and woods, the General Court of Plymouth refused their request for more woodland. Granting additional woods would be a "great detriment to another plantation intended below [their boundaries]."[92] The difficulties and costs of transportation and the need for settlements to have access to fuel and construction materials shaped the geography of woods in England. These constraints did not disappear on the other side of the Atlantic.

The political geography of interaction with Native American peoples also shaped the restrictions on wood use in New England. In 1661, Daniel Gookin, who had also attempted to establish a timber trade with England, and Amos Richardson negotiated an agreement with the Pequot leader Tumsquash to acquire Pequot lands in exchange for "some convenient portions for their subsistence" located elsewhere. Gookin and Richardson, according to English records, showed "a willingness that the Indians might some time enjoy their labors" and offered rights of ingress and egress to continue to "usual places" by the river and the sea. Yet they specified that the Pequots were not to use any timber.[93] Rather than seeking cleared land by appropriating Native settlements, as Virginia colonists wrote of doing, Gookin and Richardson sought to limit the Pequots land use to preserve woods so that English colonists might later fell the trees.

Colonists' hunger for woods also shaped relations between New Englanders and the Wampanoags. In the same 1643 response to Taunton colonists' petition where the court forbade settlers from buying woods planned for use in future plantations, they encouraged the inhabitants to procure pastures from two English men living across the river or, failing there, urged them to negotiate with the Wampanoag leader 8sâmeeqan (known in contemporary English sources and in recent commemorative statues as "Massasoit") to purchase the land. Despite the injunction to preserve woods and negotiate with 8sâmeeqan for lands, the inhabitants of Taunton and nearby Rehoboth made inroads into Wampanoag woods over the next twenty years.

In 1661, the court ordered the constable of Taunton to arrest anyone coming up the river to fetch timber and to seize their goods and to crack down on trade for woods with neighboring Wampanoag people. These actions were ineffective, and the next year they ordered a Captain Willett to travel to Taunton to restore order. His actions appear to have had little effect on the colonists. In 1664, 8sâmeeqan's son, Metacom, who was referred to as "Philip" in English documents, complained to the General Court that the English at Rehoboth were cutting down timber in a swamp that was Wampanoag territory.[94] Since 1643, colonial authorities in Plymouth had sought to curtail colonists' incursions onto Native American lands by prohibiting the purchase of land or timber rights and fining offenders at five times the value of the purchase. A few years later, Connecticut's General Court issued a similar order that "no particular person whatsoever shall buy of the Indians, either directly or indirectly any timber, candlewood, or trees of any sort or kind within this jurisdiction, though it be without the bounds of the several towns."[95] Clearly, these laws failed to have the desired effect. Worse still, Metacom's complaint about illegal felling on Wampanoag lands suggests that colonists simply took wood when they could not trade for it.

Negotiations to preserve timber, prohibitions on unlicensed timber trade with Native peoples, and conflict over colonists' incursions onto Native land to fell trees all show the role woods played in defining relationships between English colonists and Native peoples. As historian Virginia DeJohn Anderson argued, the steady stream of trespasses and encroachments onto Wampanoag land escalated to the point where Metacom launched a war to defend their territory and sovereignty. Animals, as Anderson showed, were central players in this conflict, but woods as commons, pastures, and sites for sawmills and other manufacturing activities also played an important part.[96] Colonists and colonial governments each treated woods as vital assets for developing settlements, not as irritants to be cleared away. Recognizing this does not undermine the broader history of North American deforestation, but it does force us to reconsider its causes. New England colonists clamored for access to Wampanoag and Pequot territory and felled wood illicitly in so-called swamps cast as colonial commons because they valued wood and wooded land for diverse uses, not simply to advance the march of enclosed, individual private property.[97]

The development of New England's transatlantic timber trade and colonial governments' policies toward woods demonstrate the distance between the rhetoric of scarcity and the politics and economics of wood in New England.

Examining future Connecticut governor John Winthrop Jr's successful project to erect an ironworks in New England, the endeavor that prompted Evelyn to contemplate the possibility of relocating the English iron industry to North America, shows that here, too, scarcity fails to explain colonial actions in the woods. Like similar projects in Virginia and Ireland, the New England iron industry grew out of its founders' ability to leverage experience and commercial connections for investment in the enterprise and markets for their iron. In New England, the actions of the ironworkers, the investors, and the government of Massachusetts Bay colony emphasized access to quality ore, community infrastructure, and available labor over cheap timber. Cheap wood did not define the project.[98]

From the start, John Winthrop Jr's New England ironworks were bound up with similar projects in Ireland. Around 1643, as Winthrop was searching for investors, he hand-copied Sir Charles Coote's description of iron in Ireland. The account contained notes on the type of ore and iron, comparing them to deposits in Sussex and the finished product from Spain. It tabulated fuel costs and provided advice on situating a furnace. In addition to this intellectual inspiration, Winthrop made connections with investors tied to ironworks in Ireland and the Forest of Dean and to merchant networks in Bristol and London. Two of the principal investors in Winthrop's Company of Undertakers of the Ironworks in New England, John Becx and Joshua Foote, were involved in Irish ironworks near Dublin and in Clare, respectively. Becx had been involved in ironworks in the Forest of Dean. Another investor, Thomas Foley, had a slitting mill in Gloucestershire and was involved in other ironworks and mines in the counties of Gloucester, Monmouth, and Hereford. Foote also sought out ironworkers in Ireland in 1643, but he lamented that an informant "tells me that times are so in Ireland that he thinks they are killed or dead, for he can hear of none."[99] Neither Winthrop nor Foote remarked further on the Rebellion in their correspondence on the ironworks, but their knowledge about the dislocation and destruction to the industry there may have had some influence over their decision to look across the Atlantic, as Bristol investors had contemplated during troubles with Munster's iron industry in the 1620s.

The actions of Winthrop's company and the government of Massachusetts Bay both made it clear that neither group considered cheap wood to be the major asset for the project or that they treated New England's woods as a disposable impediment to settlement best consumed as charcoal. Around 1644, Winthrop wrote a report on potential sites for the ironworks. He had searched several locations and evaluated them "for the ore and the conveniency of waters for furnace and forge, and woods for supply of coals for both works." In the end, he advocated for the works to be sited at Braintree. The area had ore "of the same sort which they call in Ireland the bog mine" and which he claimed had produced good iron. Braintree, however, only had "wood enough for present to be procured near by purchase, and for future to belong to the works to be fetched further off" since it was located "in the heart of all the English colonies." Other sites located further from major settlements might offer similar ore, albeit in lesser quantities, and abundant trees, but Winthrop urged against them because they necessitated construction of housing, clearing of farmland, and provisions of cattle that would leave "greatest part of our stock expended in such occasions before we begin." Worse still, these sites would leave the works without ready access to laborers, driving up costs for workers.[100] Winthrop made it clear that he prioritized ore, labor, and the costs of building housing and farms over access to the most minimally regulated timber.

Despite Winthrop's calculus, the leaders of Massachusetts Bay granted the project permissive rights to cut timber. In 1644 and again in 1645, the General Court granted them the right to mine ore, cut timber, and gather other materials "in all places of wastes or land not appropriated to any town or person." This grant ensured that the colliers and ironworkers would have access to timber without purchasing it. It did not, however, imply that the General Court saw that timber as valueless. In 1646, in response to a letter from an agent of the ironworks, the General Court attacked the project. The ironworkers, they complained, only sold their wares for ready money and the colony lacked specie, save a few Spanish coins floating around coastal areas. If colonists could not purchase the iron made in New England, the project would "hardly recompense the wood and timber which, being in the heart of the towns, would have been of some worth to us, if but to save the carriage of fetching it so much farther."[101] The Massachusetts Bay government was willing to make large grants of wood, but it did so in the knowledge that depleting woods near colonial settlements carried consequences. Framing their complaint in terms of carriage costs and effort suggested that members of the General Court perceived the continent's supply as large, but that they recognized that even a nearly infinite store far inland could not eliminate nuisance for timber-starved townspeople near the coasts.

The ironworks investors and colonial government supported the ironworks not simply to clear timber but also to generate profit and provide a resource for colonists. In the end, the ironworks crumbled because it could not generate profits. By 1652, lawsuits from unpaid creditors plagued the project, leading to slowdowns in production and changes in ownership. Sometime around 1670 the works had ceased production. One factor undermining the colonial works, the historian Edward Hartley noted, was competition from English iron imported into New England.[102]

Evelyn looked across the Atlantic, when he bothered to look beyond England at all, and saw a densely wooded continent. Ironworks, as he saw them, were a crude means to expanded settlements. Standing on the ground in New England provided a different view. The geography of wood across the Atlantic, as in England, was local and defined by different uses. New England colonists had developed their own colonial political ecology. From the 1620s onward, New England colonies regulated access to woods to provide common pastures, firewood, and construction materials while also allotting lands to sawmills and ironworks. The labor and costs of transportation provided other limits, both economic and practical. Politics both between individual colonists and towns and between the English and the Wampanoags and Pequots created other boundaries. Individuals and groups might transcend these barriers, but there were consequences ranging from presentments and fines to war. New Englanders had attempted to establish trade with England for masts, pipe staves, and iron. These efforts produced limited results. Colonial masts might appear in English shipyards and colonial ironworks could find English and Irish investors, but New England failed to become a major source of wood in England. Evelyn imagined a political ecology that united "Mother Old England" and her "Brethren" across the seas in the service of Charles II, "the Great Sovereign of the Ocean." Freeing England from want at home would be the "fittest sacrifice" for colonial trees.[103] Necessity alone was not enough to realize this vision and the Crown did not begin regulating New England woods to protect ship timber and naval stores until the end of the century.[104]

As in Virginia, the failure to create a booming timber trade with England did not mean the absence of a trade in wood and woodland commodities. The New England colonies became a critical source for timber and pipe staves around the West Indies and a center for North American shipbuilding. In the process, colonists began to develop an Atlantic political ecology that envisioned New England's woods bound into networks of intercolonial exchange, but, by 1660, many of these connections were still fleeting and uncertain. It would take until later in the seventeenth century that New England colonists could proclaim Caribbean dependence on their woods. With the development of more intensive local, regional, and Atlantic economies, New England colonists expressed hostility toward efforts at royal regulation rather than gratitude at their inclusion in an imperial and royalist political ecology like that envisioned by Evelyn.[105]

*   *   *

Caribbean demand was essential to the changed landscape of wood in the English Atlantic. Rather than competing for space in domestic English markets, the intercolonial trade in timber, pipe staves, naval stores, and other woodland commodities gave value to woods in Virginia and New England that fears of domestic scarcity had never provided. Colonists in Bermuda and Barbados pursued distinctive strategies as this new Atlantic trade emerged. In Bermuda, colonists renewed and intensified efforts to protect and regenerate trees on the archipelago. In Barbados, although local wood supplies persisted, imported wood became increasingly important. Even as commercial connections eroded efforts for self-sufficient stocks of wood, Barbadian colonists pursued alternatives to dependence on continental timber merchants. Bermudian and Barbadian colonists pursued distinct strategies, but colonists' actions from both islands reflected the new possibilities for intercolonial trade. Their acts of both preservation and deliberate destruction reflected political ecologies designed to navigate new and emerging connections and networks.

In the 1650s, Bermudian authorities began a new wave of efforts at cedar preservation that emphasized the trees' local utility and importance in transatlantic trade. The company's 1650 letter to Governor Josias Forster complained that the company's tenants had allowed houses to decay but had "wasted and destroyed" the woods and cedars on the same land. It ordered him to set the tenants to work repairing the neglected dwellings but demanded that "no waste or delapidations of houses, cedars, and other woods be made upon the said Islands." In the same letter, the company sought to curtail trade in cedar timbers, ordering a ban on any cedar exports except as chests, hogsheads, or other containers for tobacco or other commodities and voiding any previous warrants to sell cedar timber. In 1653, Forster issued a proclamation in response to "the great abuse of destroying cedar and how often it is conveyed and carried away by several persons by ships without the providence of the owners of land who desire to have it preserved." Captains of ships were only permitted to take cedar timber on board with a warrant from the company in London. Moreover, colonists were to plant and care for young cedars. Forster closed by demanding that "prices [for cedar] between neighbors be also carefully maintained and preserved." In 1655, the company reiterated its ban on cedar exports while granting a license for free trade provisioning ships and it tightened the earlier exemption for chests and hogsheads, ordering Forster and the council to ensure that boards used to pack the islands' commodities not exceed one and a quarter inches in thickness.[106]

These bans appeared to broadly attack trade in cedar timber, but the company's subsequent actions show that, like earlier regulations, the bans instead were means to ensure that exploitation of cedars benefited English investors and the company. In 1656, the company issued a warrant to ship twenty-two tons of cedar to England for the Earl of Warwick and other company officials.[107] By maintaining cedar prices for local trade in Bermuda, requiring permits for timber exports, and restricting the size of boards used in barrels and chests, the company and Forster sought to ensure that cedar timber would remain a profitable and reliable trade. But to do so, they attempted to limit its scale.

At roughly the same time, landowners continued to take measures to preserve cedars on their lands. In 1651, John Bassett of Cornwall issued a lease to a Captain Godheard for thirty-one years that required no payment in tobacco. Instead, Godheard was to pay forty shillings of "current English money, so many cedar planks to be the value of the said money, if they can be shipped, and also two boxes of oranges and lemons packed up in cedar boards, and two cedar casks of potatoes if they can or may be possibly shipped." Moreover, Bassett required Godheard to "plant orange trees, lemon trees, pines and other fruits in convenient places such as the island will produce upon the demised premises."[108] Bassett envisioned a profitable landscape yielding timber, fruit, and potatoes. Few of his contemporaries, however, completely abandoned tobacco, and many other leases continued to seek payment in smoke.[109] Nonetheless, by the 1650s, Bermudian landowners consistently articulated the importance of trees. The same leases that called for rental payments in tobacco also carried injunctions against wasting woods while gathering fuel or repairing buildings and requirements that tenants plant lemon and orange trees. Thomas Way of London urged his Bermudian correspondent to take special care of his woods, noting that he valued the trees more than rent.[110]

These leases adopted measures, common among English and Irish landholders, that sought to ensure the reproduction of valuable woods. John Oxenbridge's 1651 instructions for the caretakers of his properties in Bermuda sought to replace the allegedly troublesome and neglectful Mrs. Taylor with a tenant that would "keep the house in repair, and not suffer it to sink into ruin" but that would also "be careful of the wood, especially the

young cedars."[111] Like Governor Forster, Oxenbridge identified the relationship among home construction, maintenance to fences and buildings, and
threats to the islands' cedars. His instructions were future-oriented—they
focused on young trees that would, upon maturity, produce usable timber.
At the same time, they pointed toward the common tension in all efforts to
regulate woods between perceived needs like maintaining dwellings and the
materials needed to meet those needs.

Even with government and private measures to protect cedars, scarcity
anxieties continued. In 1658, it was presented at the assizes that "through
the waste of timber both young and old trees there is likely to ensue great
evils thereby to posterity." The court ordered colonists and landowners alike
to engage in both replanting and preservation measures. Over the next
two years, the company alleged that the permitting system to control cedar
exports had been a failure. It consistently complained that its permitting system had been subject to consistent abuse and it claimed that cedars had been
illicitly shipped to Barbados and other destinations and ordered Governor
William Sayle to investigate incidents of illicit felling and export. By 1660,
Sayle issued a sweeping ban that "prohibited all men from transporting any
timber either for England or any other place."[112]

Sayle's proclamation warned of dire consequences caused by deforestation. "Half the land in the Island," he warned, "hath not wood to serve for
fuel, and yet do I perceive that few, or none looketh after their own good
or after generations to come." Sayle blamed this shortage on negligence and
poor husbandry, not on the timber trade. Colonists used fire to clear their
lands, "which if men had public spirits they would not dare to do." He blasted
them for sloth, claiming that burning instead of felling and saving trees they
intended to clear destroyed "abundant firewood that might, with little labor,
be saved for their own benefit, and the benefit of them that shall spring up
after them, as all good commonwealth's men would do." Worse still, Sayle
alleged, these timber spendthrifts "do burn up the cedars that might by the
blessing of God be fit for any use, which the inhabitants will in a short time
stand in need of." Sayle concluded with a stark warning that echoed the words
of Arthur Standish: "Without timber we cannot subsist."[113]

Unlike the regulations of the 1650s, which focused on supervision, oversight, and trade regulations, Sayle called for a widespread program of reforestation. He reiterated the long-standing order to replant and care for young
cedars. He ordered colonists to plant cedars along every fence line, "so by
that means the fruits of the earth may be preserved from blasting; and as
the old timber doth decay, the young trees may grow up for the use of the

land."[114] Sayle's order harkened back to the *Orders* of 1622. Bermuda's cedars were more than timber. Instead, Sayle called for rows of cedars as permanent, consistently replenished windbreaks that existed outside any market for commercial timber. In doing so, he advanced a political ecology of trees centered on local self-sufficiency rather than on imported supplies or transatlantic trade.

This concern with local uses, landscapes, and needs explains Sayle's dismissive attitude toward efforts to cultivate trees as commodities for English markets. In 1662, he wearily noted that the company had suggested that olives should thrive in Bermuda despite four decades of failure when attempting to do so. He had informed the company of this history but to no avail. He ordered two olive trees planted on each twenty-five-acre share.[115] It is unclear whether the "olives" that had failed were the endemic olivewood trees or whether colonists had since imported "true" olive trees from the Mediterranean. Nonetheless, it is clear that Sayle had no intention of giving the company's directive anything more than lip service.

Sayle's actions marked a broader shift in political ecology. For the first decades of the colony, adventurers based in England had sought out pearls, tobacco, and other commodities valuable in transatlantic trade. Cedars had been a part of their vision for the island and had been protected as a result, but the trees had needed to coexist alongside land-hungry commodity production. As tobacco profits and cultivation declined, Bermudians increasingly focused on local concerns and reoriented the colony toward the sea.[116] A secure, renewable, regulated source of ship timber was essential for the small archipelago to participate in a maritime economy; selling small quantities of olives or olive oil to English merchants was not.

Ultimately, this had a dramatic effect on Bermuda's landscape. With the final collapse of the tobacco economy and a complete reorientation toward maritime trade in the 1680s and 1690s, land-use patterns shifted, reflecting the emergence of a new political ecology. Nathaniel Butler had worried decades earlier about allowing sufficient space for trees while accommodating commercial crop production. By the eighteenth century, as historian Michael Jarvis has found, up to nine-tenths of the islands' land was set aside for woodlands to supply materials for shipbuilding.[117] This dramatic reversal from earlier clearances to support agriculture emerged from Bermuda's deep connections in intercolonial and transatlantic trade, the same forces that would help accelerate deforestation elsewhere. Unlike in those places, however, Bermudian authorities took increasingly elaborate steps to protect the islands' woods, particularly cedar trees.

These acts of local preservation did not eliminate the desire to exploit woods as luxury commodities. Even as Bermudians enacted measures to ensure a steady supply of high-quality timber on the islands, they began to develop an expansionist political ecology of wood that sought to exploit what Jarvis has called "Atlantic Commons." In 1658, Bermudians sent out a voyage to the Bahamas to search for brazilwood, a tree used to create a rich red dye that had been a part of European trade with the Americas and the iconography of Brazil on European maps. This was part of a broader pattern of exploitation that began in the 1640s and would continue well into the eighteenth century as Bermudians pursued valuable dyewoods and luxury timber around the Greater Caribbean.[118] Anxieties about the consequences of deforestation from the overexploitation of cedars for transatlantic markets had led to aggressive preservation measures in Bermuda but drove its colonists to fell trees far from home and without the protections that operated on their islands.

Similar forces shaped shifting political ecologies in Barbados during the 1650s and 1660s even as they produced dramatically different results. Colonists there also looked beyond their island but sought fuel as well as dyes and luxury woods. Leases from the 1650s indicate that, even after intensive sugar cultivation had taken hold, landholders continued to take efforts to preserve woods as sources of fuel and trees that could produce dyes and other luxury woods. At the same time, trade with New England colonists offered new sources of timber and fuel to supplement the local supply.[119] For colonists in Barbados, reliable supplies of wood to use for fuel in cane refining and as packaging for sugar for export presented opportunities to open new land to cultivation of cash crops. Rather than scarcity creating trade, the increasing development of an intercolonial trade in wood could serve as justification for abandoning rules to ensure local self-sufficiency—in effect, trade acting as a justification for local scarcity.

In practice, however, Barbadians showed that they were unwilling to leave their wood supply entirely in the hands of merchants in North American colonies, even if they sought to look beyond woods on the island. During these decades, colonists sought to expand control over timber resources over the island of St. Lucia and on the South American continent in Surinam. These projects sought to secure easily accessible timber sources under the control of Barbados. The goal, as in Bermuda, was to create exploitable "hinterlands." Unlike Bermudians' search for trees to serve markets for luxury woods and dyes, Barbadians imagined their hinterlands as repositories for necessary resources, such as fuel, that would reduce their need for trade or preservation. This was, as the historian Justin Roberts argues, a colonial project, but it was a vision that lay outside of and at times in conflict with London's imperial aims. Colonial promoters in England had long claimed that expansion would solve domestic wood scarcity. Similar rhetoric animated Barbados's colonial plans. According to Roberts, Governor Francis Willoughby, the person most responsible for the colony's expansionist program, "dramatically exaggerated the environmental challenges that the plantation elite faced in Barbados in order to elicit support from Charles II for Barbadian expansion." Unlike English plans to solve domestic scarcity in colonial woods, which had largely failed, shipments of timber and fuel from Surinam quickly began appearing in Bridgetown, and Barbadian ships carried crews of loggers to St. Lucia into the eighteenth century.[120] A political ecology designed to address scarcity fears through colonial expansion had quickly achieved its aims, but it was one centered on Barbados rather than England.

*   *   *

Historians have hailed Evelyn's *Sylva* as a foundational text for English environmental thought, but it should also be understood as a work of political ecology. Evelyn, like writers on English forests working before the Civil War, wrestled with complicated and conflicted ideas about scarcity and the role of colonial woods in an English empire. Although he claimed to be the first author to systematically treat the subject, his account of the nature and causes of scarcity in England showed that he was entering into a debate that began with the *Grand Remonstrance*. Like surveyors, natural philosophers, forest officers, and woodland inhabitants, Evelyn deployed the idea of scarcity to advance his vision for the best uses of England's woods. He also provided an argument about colonial woods and English empire. Evelyn selectively endorsed colonial projects, favoring ironworks in New England while treating Ireland, Virginia, Bermuda, and Barbados solely as sources for interesting arboreal specimens. Even there, he ignored New England's history of providing masts and attempts to establish a broader trade in timber and naval stores during the 1640s and 1650s. His account wavered between full-throated calls for an English empire and concerns about cost and efficiency in the provision of timber.

Evelyn's vacillations reflected the reality of projects depending on colonial woods. From Elizabeth I's reign onward, promoters, colonial officials, and investors deployed the language of scarcity and necessity to justify their endeavors. Irish plantations and Atlantic colonies would buttress the wooden walls of England's empire. They would provide rare and useful trees that would ease dependence on foreign imports. They alone could absorb the destructive energies of English iron and glassworks. Beyond the rhetoric, however, these endeavors struggled. As Evelyn glanced across the Atlantic in the 1660s, he saw a world that reflected long-standing uncertainties about natural resources and English empire. But while Evelyn pondered whether pressures on England's woods might require certain industries to be pushed across the sea, colonists were busily creating their own wooden worlds.

ARCHIVES CONSULTED

Barbados National Archives
Bodleian Library, Oxford
British Library
Chatsworth House Archives, Bakewell, Derbyshire
Gloucestershire Archives
Huntington Library, San Marino, California
Lambeth Palace Library
The National Archives (UK)
National Library of Ireland
National Maritime Museum, Greenwich, London

NOTES

Introduction

1. Arthur Standish, *The Commons Complaint* (London, 1611), pp. B, 2; Steve Hindle, "Imagining Insurrection in Seventeenth-Century England: Representations of the Midland Rising of 1607," *History Workshop Journal* 66, no. 1 (21 September 2008): 21–61.

2. Arthur Standish, *New Directions of Experience Authorized by the Kings Most Excellent Maiesty, as May Appeare, for the Planting of Timber and Fire-Wood* (London, 1614), pp. A2r, 1.

3. Standish, *The Commons Complaint*, pp. A4, 3–5, 7–20, 29–30.

4. Standish, *New Directions of Experience*, pp. 3–4.

5. Standish, *The Commons Complaint*, 2.

6. Standish, *New Directions of Experience*, 4–5.

7. Questions about natural limits to human consumption and growth have been a longstanding and ongoing concern for environmentalists. These debates took on particular prominence in the eighteenth century, but many of the same issues I discuss throughout persisted. See Fredrik Albritton Jonsson, *Enlightenment's Frontier: The Scottish Highlands and the Origins of Environmentalism* (New Haven, CT: Yale University Press, 2013).

8. R. I. [Robert Johnson], *Nova Britannia* (London, 1609), p. 16 (unnumbered); Council for Virginia, "A True Declaration of the Estate of the Colonie in Virginia [. . .]," in Peter Force, ed., *Tracts and Other Papers*[. . .]. (Washington, DC, 1844), 3:23–25 (quotation from p. 25). For more on Johnson, see Andrew Fitzmaurice, "The Commercial Ideology of Colonization in Jacobean England: Robert Johnson, Giovanni Botero, and the Pursuit of Greatness," *William and Mary Quarterly* 64, no. 4 (2007): 791–820.

9. Dudley Digges, *The Defense of Trade* (London, 1615), 28, 30–33; Thomas Mun, *A Discourse of Trade* (London, 1621), 29–30. On Digges and the Virginia Company, see Susan Myra Kingsbury, *The Records of the Virginia Company of London, 1609-1622*, 4 vols (Washington, DC: Library of Congress, 1933), 1:224, 3:67–68; "The names of his Ma[jes]t[y']s Counsell for Virginia," 1619, Ferrar Papers (hereafter, FP) 120, Old Library, Magdalene College, Cambridge, currently available in digitized form through Virginia Company Archives (hereafter, VCA), https://www.amdigital.co.uk/primary-sources/virginia-company-archives. For an argument that acknowledges waste but nonetheless questions scarcity, see E[dward] S[harpe], *Britaines Busse* (London, 1615), E3v; on Digges, Mun, E. S., and debates about the East India Company, see Rupali Raj Mishra, *A Business of State: Commerce, Politics, and the Birth of the East India Company*, Harvard Historical Studies (Cambridge, MA: Harvard University Press, 2018), 119–45. Mishra discusses a different aspect of Digges's arguments about wood scarcity on p. 133.

10. These questions largely echo those Fredrik Albritton Jonsson argues that improvers and projectors asked about the Scottish Highlands more than a century later. Jonsson,

Enlightenment's Frontier, 5. Here and throughout, I use the term "state" to describe the English government that emerged in the sixteenth century. In doing so, I follow Steve Hindle's argument that the English state emerged in this period and that it did so through social and economic processes, as well as through political and institutional ones. I build on Hindle's argument by incorporating the management of natural resources/environment into that broader process of state formation. Steve Hindle, *The State and Social Change in Early Modern England, c. 1550–1640*, Early Modern History (New York: St. Martin's, 2000), 1–36.

11. For example, the historical sociologist Jason Moore argues for the demolition of a boundary between "Nature" and "Society." See Jason W. Moore, *Capitalism in the Web of Life: Ecology and the Accumulation of Capital* New York: Verso Books, 2015), 33–49. For a discussion of the difficulties defining wood scarcity in the early modern period, see Paul Warde, *The Invention of Sustainability: Nature and Destiny, c. 1500–1870* (New York: Cambridge University Press, 2018), 65–78; Paul Warde, "Fear of Wood Shortage and the Reality of the Woodland in Europe, c. 1450–1850," *History Workshop Journal* 62, no. 1 (21 September 2006): 28–57. In another piece, Warde argues that wood-scarcity fears were "mediated through the social milieu in which it was articulated," but that the crises of wood scarcity could be categorized into three ideal types—allocation (political disputes about resource distribution), entitlement (moments when lack of spending power limited access to necessary materials), and crises of the state (fears that resource shortages were an "existential threat" to government—that overlapped during specific crises. Paul Warde, "Early Modern 'Resource Crisis': The Wood Shortage Debates in Europe," in *Crises in Economic and Social History: A Comparative Perspective*, ed. A. T. Brown, Andy Burn, and Rob Doherty, People, Markets, Goods: Economies and Societies in History Series 6 (Rochester, NY: Boydell Press, 2015), 141–42.

12. On the importance of memory and the construction of the past, see Andy Wood, *The Memory of the People: Custom and Popular Senses of the Past in Early Modern England* (New York: Cambridge University Press, 2013).

13. Peter C. Mancall, "Tales Tobacco Told in Sixteenth-Century Europe," *Environmental History* 9, no. 4 (October 2004): 648–78; Londa L. Schiebinger and Claudia Swan, eds., *Colonial Botany: Science, Commerce, and Politics in the Early Modern World* (Philadelphia: University of Pennsylvania Press, 2005). See, esp., Chandra Mukerji, "Dominion, Demonstration, Domination: Religious Doctrine, Territorial Politics, and French Plant Collection," in *Colonial Botany: Science, Commerce, and Politics in the Early Modern World*, ed. Londa L. Schiebinger and Claudia Swan (Philadelphia: University of Pennsylvania Press, 2005); E. C. Spary, "Of Nutmegs and Botanists: The Colonial Cultivation of Botanical Identity," in *Colonial Botany: Science, Commerce, and Politics in the Early Modern World*, ed. Londa L. Schiebinger and Claudia Swan (Philadelphia: University of Pennsylvania Press, 2005), 187–203; Joyce E. Chaplin, *Subject Matter: Technology, the Body, and Science on the Anglo-American Frontier, 1500–1676* (Cambridge, MA: Harvard University Press, 2001); Mauro Ambrosoli, *The Wild and the Sown: Botany and Agriculture in Western Europe, 1350–1850*, trans. Mary McCann Salvatorelli (Cambridge: Cambridge University Press, 1997); Brian William Cowan, *The Social Life of Coffee: The Emergence of the British Coffeehouse* (New Haven, CT: Yale University Press, 2005).

14. Eric H. Ash, *Power, Knowledge, and Expertise in Elizabethan England* (Baltimore: Johns Hopkins University Press, 2004).

15. Paula Findlen, *Possessing Nature: Museums, Collecting, and Scientific Culture in Early Modern Italy* (Berkeley: University of California Press, 1994); Paula Findlen, "Inventing Nature: Commerce, Art, and Science in the Early Modern Cabinet of Curiosities," in *Merchants and*

Marvels: Commerce, Science, and Art in Early Modern Europe, ed. Pamela H. Smith and Paula Findlen (New York: Routledge, 2002), 297–323.

16. James C. Scott, *Seeing Like a State: How Certain Schemes to Improve the Human Condition Have Failed* (New Haven, CT: Yale University Press, 1998), see, esp., pp. 23–26. Eric Ash has made this argument about early modern fen drainage and state formation. See Eric H. Ash, *The Draining of the Fens: Projectors, Popular Politics, and State Building in Early Modern England*, Johns Hopkins Studies in the History of Technology (Baltimore: Johns Hopkins University Press, 2017), 4–5.

17. For examples of the multiple definitions of political ecology, see Darcy Tetreault, "Three Forms of Political Ecology," *Ethics & the Environment* 22, no. 2 (Fall 2017): table 1; for early modern works that use the term explicitly, see Mark William Hauser, "A Political Ecology of Water and Enslavement: Water Ways in Eighteenth-Century Caribbean Plantations," *Current Anthropology* 58, no. 2 (3 March 2017): 227–56; Elisabetta Novello and James C. McCann, "The Building of the Terra Firma: The Political Ecology of Land Reclamation in the Veneto from the Sixteenth Through the Twenty-First Century," *Environmental History* 22, no. 3 (July 2017): 460–85; Molly A. Warsh, "A Political Ecology in the Early Spanish Caribbean," *William and Mary Quarterly* 71, no. 4 (October 2014): 517–48. I follow Warsh's use of the concept, particularly her emphasis on conflicts between imperial policies and local conditions and questions about knowledge and expertise. Christopher M. Parsons, *A Not-So-New World: Empire and Environment in French Colonial North America*, Early American Studies (Philadelphia: University of Pennsylvania Press, 2018); Parsons emphasizes the role of knowledge production and of agricultural cultivation in colonial political ecology, see, esp., pp. 6–7.

18. Other historians have pointed toward the sophisticated politics of natural resource thinking in the early modern period. See David Cressy, "Saltpetre, State Security and Vexation in Early Modern England," *Past & Present* 212, no. 1 (1 August 2011): 73–111; Karl Richard Appuhn, *A Forest on the Sea: Environmental Expertise in Renaissance Venice* (Baltimore: Johns Hopkins University Press, 2009); John T. Wing, *Roots of Empire: Forests and State Power in Early Modern Spain, c. 1500-1750*, Brill's Series in the History of the Environment 4 (Leiden: Brill, 2015). On seventeenth-century political economic thought, see Ted McCormick, *William Petty and the Ambitions of Political Arithmetic* (Oxford: Oxford University Press, 2009); Steve Pincus, "Rethinking Mercantilism: Political Economy, the British Empire, and the Atlantic World in the Seventeenth and Eighteenth Centuries," *William and Mary Quarterly* 69, no. 1 (1 January 2012): 3–34; Philip J. Stern and Carl Wennerlind, eds., *Mercantilism Reimagined: Political Economy in Early Modern Britain and Its Empire* (Oxford: Oxford University Press, 2014); Susan D. Amussen, "Political Economy and Imperial Practice," *William and Mary Quarterly* 69, no. 1 (1 January 2012): 47–50; Cathy Matson, "Imperial Political Economy: An Ideological Debate and Shifting Practices," *William and Mary Quarterly* 69, no. 1 (1 January 2012): 35–40; Margaret Ellen Newell, "Putting the 'Political' Back in Political Economy (This Is Not Your Parents' Mercantilism)," *William and Mary Quarterly* 69, no. 1 (1 January 2012): 57–62; Abigail Leslie Swingen, *Competing Visions of Empire: Labor, Slavery, and the Origins of the British Atlantic Empire* (New Haven, CT: Yale University Press, 2015). Swingen makes the critical point that political economy and expansion were always subjects of intense contention.

19. Joachim Radkau, *Wood: A History*, trans. Patrick Camiller (Malden, MA: Polity, 2011); see ch. 2, esp. pp. 65–97, 101–3; Warde, "Fear of Wood Shortage and the Reality of the Woodland in Europe, c. 1450-1850"; Warde, *The Invention of Sustainability*, 61-65 (on multiple uses), 65-78 (on scarcity). Vin Nardizzi has shown how scarcity concerns emerged in early modern English

drama and in the actions of theatrical companies. Vin Nardizzi, *Wooden Os: Shakespeare's Theatres and England's Trees* (Toronto: University of Toronto Press, 2013).

20. William M. Cavert, *The Smoke of London: Energy and Environment in the Early Modern City*, Cambridge Studies in Early Modern British History (Cambridge: Cambridge University Press, 2016), 17–31. According to Cavert, London's coal use grew from a mid-sixteenth-century baseline of 10,000–15,000 tons to more than 283,000 tons in 1637-1638 (p. 24). Standish, *The Commons Complaint.*, 1–2, 16–17.

21. John Manwood, *A Treatise of the Lawes of the Forest* (London, 1598), fols. 1–2.

22. Ibid., fol. 2. On Manwood's definition of the forest and concern with "vert" and hunting, see Nardizzi, *Wooden Os*, 62–69.

23. Manwood, *A Treatise of the Lawes of the Forest*, fols. 44–45.

24. Ibid., fol. 15v. On Manwood's vision for the forest and preservation, see Jeffrey S. Theis, *Writing the Forest in Early Modern England: A Sylvan Pastoral Nation* (Pittsburgh, PA: Duquesne University Press, 2009), 129–32. Warde finds that tradition and custom dominated practice and shaped new laws to address scarcity across early modern Europe. Warde, *The Invention of Sustainability*, 84–86.

25. William Salisbury, ed., "A Treatise on Shipbuilding, c. 1620: From a Manuscript in the Admiralty Library," in *A Treatise on Shipbuilding and a Treatise on Rigging, Written about 1620-1625* (London: Society for Nautical Research, 1958), 4–9.

26. Manwood, *A Treatise of the Lawes of the Forest*, 42.

27. William Lawson, *A New Orchard and Garden* (London, 1626), 37–38, 42–47; John Evelyn, *Sylva* (London, 1664), 14.

28. Evelyn, *Sylva*, 195.

29. For example, see Philip A. J. Pettit, *The Royal Forests of Northamptonshire: A Study in Their Economy, 1558-1714* (Gateshead [County Durham]: Northamptonshire Record Society, 1968), 5. Indeed, as Cavert points out, transportation helped give coal some key advantages in early modern London. Cavert, *The Smoke of London*, 20.

30. Walter Prescott Webb called North America "a great tree constantly casting down on the people of Europe windfalls, benefits which exacted little more than the exertion of getting out early, finding, and carrying away the boon." Webb, *The Great Frontier* (Austin: University of Texas Press, 1964), 180. For historians who also used the metaphor, see Eric Jones, *The European Miracle: Environments, Economies, and Geopolitics in the History of Europe and Asia*, 3rd ed. (New York: Cambridge University Press, 2003), 84; Donald Worster, *Shrinking the Earth: The Rise and Decline of American Abundance* (New York: Oxford University Press, 2016), 11–25; for the use of the word "windfall," see p. 14. For other works that define New World abundance against Old World scarcity, see Edward B. Barbier, *Scarcity and Frontiers: How Economies Have Developed Through Natural Resource Exploitation* (New York: Cambridge University Press, 2010), 254–75; William Cronon, *Changes in the Land: Indians, Colonists, and the Ecology of New England*, 1st rev. ed. (New York: Hill and Wang, 2003), 107–8; Jason Moore, "Silver, Ecology, and the Origins of the Modern World, 1450-1640," in *Rethinking Environmental History: World-System History and Global Environmental Change*, ed. Alf Hornborg, John Robert McNeill, and Juan Martínez Alier (Lanham, MD: AltaMira, 2007), 123–42; Jason W. Moore, "Madeira, Sugar, and the Conquest of Nature in the 'First' Sixteenth Century: Part I: From 'Island of Timber' to Sugar Revolution, 1420–1506," *Review (Fernand Braudel Center)* 32, no. 4 (1 January 2009): 345–90; Moore, *Capitalism in the Web of Life*; Even Michael Williams, who expressed skepticism at early modern scarcity complaints, nonetheless wrote that the idea of scarcity "took Europeans a long way along the road

to global domination." See Michael Williams, *Deforesting the Earth: From Prehistory to Global Crisis* (Chicago: University of Chicago Press, 2003), 144. On the importance of North America in modern ideas of limitless natural resources, see Fredrik Albritton Jonsson, "The Origins of Cornucopianism: A Preliminary Genealogy," *Critical Historical Studies* 1, no. 1 (March 2014): 151–68. Karl Appuhn has, to a degree, challenged notions of "European" exploitation of nature as a consequence of expansionist states and commercial markets, arguing that Venice took a distinct path focused on conservation; see Appuhn, *A Forest on the Sea*, 9–15.

31. Kenneth Pomeranz, *The Great Divergence: China, Europe, and the Making of the Modern World Economy* (Princeton, NJ: Princeton University Press, 2000), 244.

32. Nardizzi makes a similar point, citing literary scholar Jeffrey Theis, arguing instead to examine how concepts of knowledge and experience shaped scarcity. Nardizzi, *Wooden Os*, 13–15. I differ from Theis by arguing that scarcity was not solely a perception of diminishing supply but was instead grounded in conflicts over uses and rights. Theis, *Writing the Forest in Early Modern England*, 16–17. Efforts to explain how colonial environments aligned with or departed from European models was always a fraught enterprise. As Christopher Parsons argues, "The ecosystems of North America were presented as assemblages of recognizable plants" during early French colonial efforts before colonists and French authorities increasingly began to call for transformations of the North American environment through the imposition of new plants and people. See Parsons, *A Not-So-New World*, 30 (quotation), 15–41 (on early descriptions of the environment), 97–124 (on increasing emphasis on novelty), 128 (on the transplanted plants and colonialism).

33. Swingen, *Competing Visions of Empire*, 1.

34. I am drawing on Carla Gardina Pestana's definition of the English Atlantic as a creation of both migration and the development of ties (commercial, material, or otherwise) between plantations and colonies and not just with the European metropole. See Carla Gardina Pestana, *The English Atlantic in an Age of Revolution, 1640–1661* (Cambridge, MA: Harvard University Press, 2007), 3.

35. Nardizzi, *Wooden Os*, 55–58, 118–21.

36. On the EIC as a sovereign power, see Philip J. Stern, *The Company-State: Corporate Sovereignty and the Early Modern Foundations of the British Empire in India* (Oxford: Oxford University Press, 2011). On the EIC as an institution with a complicated and ambiguous relationship with the English state, see Mishra, *A Business of State*; Mishra argues that the EIC needs to be a part of the story of English empire and that dealing with it complicates a largely territorial sense of the imperial project, see pp. 12, 308–11.

37. Jonathan Eacott, *Selling Empire: India in the Making of Britain and America, 1600–1830* (Chapel Hill, NC: Omohundro Institute of Early American History and Culture and the University of North Carolina Press, 2016), 14–39.

38. In arguing this, I both build on and challenge Karl Appuhn's arguments about Venice and early modern wood scarcity. I concur with Appuhn that there was no monolithic European response to resource crises, but I argue that efforts to promote local conservation also occurred in England and that the search for timber in "ever-more-distant locales" (11) remained an uncertain and usually unsuccessful project in sixteenth- and seventeenth-century England. Appuhn, *A Forest on the Sea*, 9–15.

39. On confusion as a defining feature of early modern expansion and natural philosophical and environmental thinking, see Benjamin Breen, *The Age of Intoxication: Origins of the Global Drug Trade* (Philadelphia: University of Pennsylvania Press, 2019), 18–19; Alison Games, *The Web*

of Empire: English Cosmopolitans in an Age of Expansion, 1560-1660 (Oxford: Oxford University Press, 2008). On English cosmopolitans as men traveling largely without their wives and children, see Games, *The Web of Empire*, 22. Games and others have argued that these global connections challenge the popular paradigm of Atlantic history. See Alison Games, "Beyond the Atlantic: English Globetrotters and Transoceanic Connections," *William and Mary Quarterly*, 3rd ser., 63, no. 4 (October 2006): 675–92; Stern, *The Company-State*; Philip J. Stern, "British Asia and British Atlantic: Comparisons and Connections," *William and Mary Quarterly* 63, no. 4 (October 2006): 693–712; Eacott, *Selling Empire*; Nicholas Canny, "Writing Atlantic History; or, Reconfiguring the History of Colonial British America," *Journal of American History* 86, no. 3 (December 1999): 1093–114.

40. S. Max Edelson, *Plantation Enterprise in Colonial South Carolina* (Cambridge, MA: Harvard University Press, 2011), 2–3 (on regional variation and environmental adaptation), 13–52 (on shifting environmental understandings and economic visions). Like Edelson, I have argued for the importance of "improvement" literature in English agrarian and environmental visions for their colonies; see Keith Pluymers, "Taming the Wilderness in Sixteenth- and Seventeenth-Century Ireland and Virginia," *Environmental History* 16, no. 4 (1 October 2011): 610–32. On the value of place-based Atlantic and environmental histories and the value of "local particularities," see Strother E. Roberts, *Colonial Ecology, Atlantic Economy: Transforming Nature in Early New England* (Philadelphia: University of Pennsylvania Press, 2019), 8–11. Unlike Roberts, I have worked with "political abstractions" (13) because those abstractions helped shape colonial approaches to physical environments.

41. On competition between domestic improvement schemes and colonial projects, see Nicholas Canny, "The Origins of Empire: An Introduction," in *The Origins of Empire: British Overseas Enterprise to the Close of the Seventeenth Century*, ed. Nicholas P. Canny, The Oxford History of the British Empire (New York: Oxford University Press, 1998), 1:6–11. On the Newfoundland ironworks, see Keith Pluymers, "Atlantic Iron: Wood Scarcity and the Political Ecology of Early English Expansion," *William and Mary Quarterly* 73, no. 3 (July 2016): 418.

42. On the Atlantic as a theater for war and revolution bound up with interlocking conflicts in England, Ireland, and Scotland, see Pestana, *The English Atlantic in an Age of Revolution*.

Chapter 1

1. Standish, *The Commons Complaint*, fol. Bv–B2r. Paul Warde argues against viewing Standish as an origin point for sustainability because of the tepid English state support for his proposals and the absence of a quantitative system for measuring wood. See Paul Warde, "The Invention of Sustainability," *Modern Intellectual History* 8, no. 1 (3 March 2011): 160–63; in a more recent work, he argues for the importance of "posterity" as a concept in the early modern development of sustainability, see Warde, *The Invention of Sustainability*, 90–101.

2. On population anxiety, see Robert Gray, *A Good Speed to Virginia* (London, 1609), B2–4; on overpopulation in colonial literature, see Timothy Sweet, "Economy, Ecology, and Utopia in Early Colonial Promotional Literature," *American Literature* 71, no. 3 (1999): esp. pp. 402–3; Standish, *The Commons Complaint*, fols. B–B2.

3. Beginning with Henry VIII, Tudor monarchs introduced new positions in the exchequer responsible for supervising forests that frequently served parallel functions to preexisting warden and constable positions. See below for details.

4. Early Modern Research Group, "Commonwealth: The Social, Cultural, and Conceptual Contexts of an Early Modern Keyword," *Historical Journal* 54, no. 3 (September 2011): 659–87.

5. Buchanan Sharp, *In Contempt of All Authority: Rural Artisans and Riot in the West of England, 1586-1660* (Berkeley: University of California Press, 1980), 4–5, 208. The Victoria County History for Gloucester lambastes James and Charles for ruthlessly exploiting woods: A. P. Baggs and A. R. J. Jurica, "Forest of Dean: Forest Administration, " in *A History of the County of Gloucester: Volume 5, Bledisloe Hundred, St. Briavels Hundred, the Forest of Dean*, ed. C. R. J. Currie and N. M. Herbert (London: Victoria County History, 1996), 354-77, https://www.british-history.ac.uk/vch/glos/vol5/pp354-377. David Thomas, in contrast, blames the incompetence and corruption of Elizabethan governors for selling wood rights and disafforest-ing without even knowing the value of the land they sold. See David Thomas, "The Elizabethan Crown Lands: Their Purposes and Problems," in *The Estates of the English Crown, 1558-1640*, ed. R. W. Hoyle (Cambridge: Cambridge University Press, 2002), 67-68. John Langton and Graham Jones argued against this view, seeking to show the continued existence and importance of royal forests through the nineteenth century as part of a large research project that, unfortunately, did not receive funding from the Economic and Social Research Council; see John Langton and Graham Jones, eds., *Forests and Chases of England and Wales, c.1500 to c.1850: Towards a Survey & Analysis*, rev. ed. (Oxford: St. John's College Research Centre, 2008), vii (on funding), xi (on the narrative of neglect and forest disappearance in the early modern period).

6. George Hammersley has made a version of this point in "The Revival of the Forest Laws Under Charles I," *History* 45, no. 154 (June 1960): 88.

7. Pettit, *The Royal Forests of Northamptonshire*, 26–32; Charles R. Young, "Conservation Policies in the Royal Forests of Medieval England," *Albion: A Quarterly Journal Concerned with British Studies* 10, no. 2 (Summer 1978): 95–103; Charles R. Young, "The Forest Eyre in England During the Thirteenth Century," *American Journal of Legal History* 18, no. 4 (October 1974): 321–31. On the much earlier efforts at production and an account that de-emphasizes the role of hunting, see Dolly Jørgensen, "The Roots of the English Royal Forest," in *Anglo-Norman Studies 32: Proceedings of the Battle Conference 2009* (Rochester, NY: Boydell and Brewer, 2010), 114–28.

8. An Act for the Preservation of Woods, 1543, 35 Hen. VII, c. 17; An Act that Timber shall not be felled to make Coals for the making of Iron, 1558, 1 Eliz. I, c. 15; An Act for the Reviving and Continuance of certain Statutes, 1571,13 Eliz. I, c. 25.

9. For accounts of these protests, see Sharp, *In Contempt of All Authority*.

10. On the murky distinction between royal and nonroyal forests and royal efforts to retake lands, see John Langton, "Royal and Non-Royal Forests and Chases in England and Wales," *Historical Research* 88, no. 241 (August 2015): 381–401. See also John Langton, "Forests in Early-Modern England and Wales: History and Historiography," in *Forests and Chases of England and Wales, c.1500 to c.1850: Towards a Survey & Analysis*, ed. John Langton and Graham Jones, rev. ed. (Oxford: St. John's College Research Centre, 2008), 1–9. Langton and Graham Jones have developed a project website with a gazeteer and preliminary map of forests at their greatest extent, at http://info.sjc.ox.ac.uk/forests/Index.html. Paul Slack, *The Invention of Improvement: Information and Material Progress in Seventeenth-Century England* (Oxford: Oxford University Press, 2015), 15–16, 44. Slack discussed this point more fully in Paul Slack, "Government and Information in Seventeenth-Century England," *Past & Present* 184, no. 1 (1 August 2004); for a brief note on forests as part of broader sixteenth-century efforts to manage royal holdings, see 38–42. See also Ash, *The Draining of the Fens*; the chronology Ash outlines for early modern Fen drainage largely parallels the chronology I outline in this chapter for scarcity fears and reformed forestry.

11. Warde notes that these estimates do not prove the existence of widespread timber famines, but they do indicate that there was a material basis to anxieties about access to firewood and fuel. Paul Warde, *Energy Consumption in England & Wales, 1560–2000*, Series on Energy Consumption 2 (Napoli: Istituto di Studio sulle Società del Mediterraneo, 2007), 32–40; Williams, *Deforesting the Earth*, 186–93.

12. Warde argues that scarcity was a state concern across Europe and must be viewed within the context of broader efforts for states to control aspects of everyday life. Warde, "Fear of Wood Shortage and the Reality of the Woodland in Europe, c. 1450–1850," 42. Elsewhere, he argues that scarcity fears focused on royal forests as a result of strains to royal finances. See Warde, *The Invention of Sustainability*, 73; Nardizzi, *Wooden Os*, 47–52 (on rumors and their literary and dramatic afterlives); 102–5 (on the political and existential anxieties about deforestation).

13. John Richards makes much of these sales, casting Elizabeth as a timber spendthrift. See John F. Richards, *The Unending Frontier: An Environmental History of the Early Modern World* (Berkeley: University of California Press, 2003), 225–26; In contrast, Sylvie Nail adopts a much more nuanced narrative. See Sylvie Nail, *Forest Policies and Social Change in England*, World Forests (London: Springer, 2008), 13.

14. An Act that Timber shall not be felled to make Coals for the making of Iron, 1558, 1 Eliz. I, c. 15.

15. *Journal of the House of Commons* (London: Stationery Office, 1802), 1:18, 60–63, 124–25; David Dean, *Law-Making and Society in Late Elizabethan England: The Parliament of England, 1584–1601* (New York: Cambridge University Press, 1996), 144–46.

16. Cavert, *The Smoke of London*; William M. Cavert, "The Environmental Policy of Charles I: Coal Smoke and the English Monarchy, 1624–40," *Journal of British Studies* 53, no. 2 (April 2014): 310–33.

17. "Taverner, Roger," History of Parliament Trust, http://www.historyofparliamentonline.org/volume/1509-1558/member/taverner-roger-1523-7882; Andrew W. Taylor, "Taverner, Richard (1505?–1575)," *Oxford Dictionary of National Biography*, online ed. (Oxford University Press, 2004); Grant to John Taverner, 28 January 1572[/1573?] State Papers (hereafter, SP) 15/21, fol. 18, The National Archives of the UK (TNA); a modern copy of Roger Taverner's *Book of Survey* can be found at Land Revenue Records and Enrolments (LRRO) 5/39, TNA.

18. For an example, see Roger Taverner, "A Survey of the Forest of Chute," 1589, Lansdowne 62, fol. 3, British Library (hereafter, BL).

19. Roger Taverner, "Book of Survey" [copy], LRRO 5/39, 19, TNA.

20. Ibid., 4.

21. Sandrine Petit and Charles Watkins, "Pollarding Trees: Changing Attitudes to a Traditional Land Management Practice in Britain 1600–1900," *Rural History* 14, no. 2 (October 2003): 160; John Taverner, "The Allowances to the Feefoster Within the Forests of Shotover and Stowood, Oxfordshire," 1585, Lansdowne 43, fol. 150, BL. On the basics of coppicing and pollarding, including the standard height of trunks for pollarded trees, see Oliver Rackham, *Woodlands* (London: HarperCollins, 2012), 10. Surveys of private land holdings followed a similar pattern, see R. Gulliver, "What Were Woods Like in the Seventeenth Century? Examples from the Helmsley Estate, Northeast Yorkshire, UK," in *The Ecological History of European Forests*, ed. K. J. Kirby and C. Watkins (New York: CAB International, 1998), 137. Shotover and Stowood were some of the few forests to have species other than oak or beech identified in Taverner's survey, see LRRO 5/39, 63–64.

22. Radkau, *Wood*, 70–76; Warde, "Fear of Wood Shortage"; Robert Greenhalgh Albion, *Forests and Sea Power: The Timber Problem of the Royal Navy, 1652–1862* (Cambridge, MA: Harvard University Press, 1926), 1–10. See Certificate by John Hawkins and other shipwrights of trees needed to repair four ships and the locations of those ships, 1593, SP 12/245, fol. 118, TNA, for contemporary discussion on the types of trees needed to build a ship.

23. An account of the wood and timber growing in the Forest of Canke [Cannock] in Staffordshire, 1588, Lansdowne 56, fol. 94, BL.

24. John Taverner, Account of the woods of Canke Forest [Cannock] Staffordshire, November 1588, Lansdowne 56, fols. 96–97, BL.

25. Ash, *Power, Knowledge, and Expertise in Elizabethan England*, 8. Ash's case studies analyze the numerous ways that early modern people contested expertise.

26. On iron production, see Pluymers, "Atlantic Iron," 396–97. Estimate of the expense of making a ton of iron in Canke Forest [Cannock, Staffordshire], 1588, Burghley Papers, Lansdowne 56, fols. 100–104, BL.

27. The inquiries into customs in the Forest of Dean were similar to those Taverner conducted into Bringewood Chase, see David Lovelace, "Bringewood Chase and Surrounding Countryside" (Hereford, UK, 2017), 14, http://www.bosci.net/iw/BringewoodReportDLJan2017 .pdf. Lovelace began this report as part of a study sponsored by the River Wye Preservation Trust and Natural England, but he has continued to perform archival research and update the reports independently (personal correspondence 5 November 2017). Lovelace's work on Bringewood Chase was also part of Langton and Jones's grant-funded study of English and Welsh forests and chases; see David Lovelace, "Bringewood Chase and Its Surrounding Countryside: A GIS Survey," in *Forests and Chases of England and Wales, c.1500 to c.1850: Towards a Survey & Analysis*, ed. John Langton and Graham Jones, rev. ed. (Oxford: St. John's College Research Centre, 2008). For Taverner's list of offenses in Dean, see Inquisition into the customs of the Forest of Dean, 1565, Bond family of Newland papers, D2026/X3, Gloucestershire Archives; Legal Questions Concerning the Forest of Dean, c. 1550s, Bond family of Newland papers, D2026/L4; John Guyes or Gwies v. Geo. Ketchmaye and others, E 134/25 and 26Eliz/Mich17, TNA; Certificates of Regarders for Dean, 1569–1570, E101/141/2, TNA.

28. "A true recital and declaration of such matters of substance as were proved and set forth in evidence on her Majesty's behalf upon a trial taken at the Exchequer barr the last Easter term," 1586, Hall and Gage families of Newland papers, D1677/GG/1173, Gloucestershire Archives.

29. Records for the broader Elizabethan inquiries into Berkeley's forest holdings can be found in Star Chamber Extracts on Forest Rights and the Berkeleys, Berkeley Castle MSS, General Legal Papers (hereafter, GLP) 277, Gloucestershire Archives [microfilm] and Order to prevent Henry Lord Berkeley from Felling Trees in Michaelwood, 24 November 1584, GLP 65.

30. Berkeley Castle MSS, GLP 15, Gloucestershire Archives. For a note on Taverner's involvement, see Captain Edward Fitzgerald to Salisbury, 2 May 1610, SP 14/54, fol. 15, TNA. For Norden's commentary, see John Norden, "Observations on the cause in question between his Majesty and others in the forest of Kingswood," Cecil Papers (hereafter, CP) 132/169, Hatfield House; "Notes with respect to the Forests of Kingswood and Filwood in cos. Gloucester and Somerset," c. 1612, CP 132/167. For a summary of events in Kingswood in the sixteenth century, see A. Braine, *The History of Kingswood Forest: Including All the Ancient Manors and Villages in the Neighbourhood* (E. Nister, 1891), 51–61.

31. CP 132/169, Hatfield House.

32. Warde, *The Invention of Sustainability*, 2018, 90–101.

33. On history, memory, and the sense of the past in customary rights and landscapes, see Wood, *The Memory of the People*. For an alternative perspective on Norden, see Katarzyna Lecky, "Archiving Ordinary Experience: Small-Format Cartography of the English Renaissance," *Journal of Medieval and Early Modern Studies* 47, no. 2 (May 2017): 366–74; for the critique of Wood's reading of Norden, see p. 369. My analysis aligns with and reinforces Elly Robson's argument that Norden and other surveyors and improvers attempted to radically reconfigure property relations, use rights, and social relations in royal forests. See Elly Robson, "Improvement and Epistemologies of Landscape in Seventeenth-Century English Forest Enclosure," *Historical Journal* 60, no. 3 (September 2017): 597–632.

34. Lecky argues that Norden's small-format maps and cartographic prints were aimed at a broad public of middling travelers. The critical distinction in my argument is between local knowledges (including conflicting ones between the poor, middling sort, and elites) and that of outsiders, including those from nonelite backgrounds. Lecky, "Archiving Ordinary Experience," 367–68. The distinction I draw between local and outside knowledge in forests shares similarities with Eric Ash's interpretation of contemporaneous struggles in the Fens. See Ash, *The Draining of the Fens*, 50–108.

35. Lovelace, "Bringewood Chase and Surrounding Countryside," 21–28.

36. Berkeley Castle MSS, GLP, 277–324 (legal documents related to cases in multiple courts, including the Star Chamber relating to deer-stealing and other forest offenses, 1575–1602), 577–80 (legal documents relating to a case against Sir Thomas Throckmorton for deer-stealing and enclosure breaking).

37. Berkeley Castle MSS, GLP, 39–40 (Petition from Lord Berkeley and other documents related to a court case involving his servant William Brown vs. Richard Tyndall), 230 (information regarding intrusion by Sir Thomas Throckmorton), 321–22 ("Henry Berkeley to the Queen testimony on the death of William Oliffe killed in New Park 1601").

38. Ibid.; Beaver H. Blacker, *Gloucestershire Notes and Queries; an Illustrated Quarterly Magazine Devoted to the History and Antiquities of Gloucestershire* (London: William Kent & Co., 1884), 2:201–8; John Smyth, *The Lives of the Berkeleys, Lords of the Honour, Castle, and Manor of Berkeley*, ed. John Maclean (Gloucester: John Bellows, 1883), 2:263.

39. Berkeley Castle MSS, GLP, 65; Letter from the Earls of Warwick and Leicester to the rangers of Michaelwood forbidding Lord Berkeley from felling or removing timber, 26 September 1573, General Miscellaneous Papers (hereafter, GMP), 62.

40. John Norden, *The Surveiors Dialogue* (London, 1618), 1–26.

41. John Norden to Lord Burleigh and Sir Walter Mildmay, April 1585, Lansdowne 43, no. 58, BL. See also Lansdowne 43, no. 59, for Norden's complaint about the system of assessing fines.

42. James I, Notes on the Sale of Crown Houses and Lands, SP 15/36, fols. 16–19, TNA. For the specific conditions on sale, see fol. 18v.

43. Articles to be observed by the Park Keepers and others, for preservation of the timber in the King's woods and forests, 1609, SP 14/43, fol. 98, TNA.

44. On earlier concerns about beauty in forests and its relationship to hunting, see Nardizzi, *Wooden Os*, 64–66.

45. Notes on Behalf of the King Regarding Hunting, 1604, SP 15/36, fols. 181–82; James I to the freeholders of Braden Forest, 6 September 1604, SP 14/9A, fol. 71; James I to the Earl of Shrewsbury regarding Forest Laws in Galtres Forest near York, 11 March 1607/1608, SP 14/31, fol.

168; Articles to be observed by the Park Keepers and others, for preservation of the timber in the King's woods and forests, 1609, SP 14/43, fol. 98, TNA.

46. Hastings Manorial Records (hereafter, HAM), box 48, folders 20 (Instructions that deer may be either chased from private grounds or must be allowed to remain unmolested, 18 February 1613), 22 (Order to Henry, Earl of Huntingdon to prevent the killing of deer in Leicester Forest, 9 May 1613), 24 (Order regarding breaking of hedges in the Forest, 1613), 25 (Order to enclose certain chases within Leicester Forest, 19 May 1615), 32–34 (Instructions regarding game in the Forest, 20 August 1624; Letters concerning the effect of Hawking and Shooting upon the deer, 26 August 1624; Warrant to take action against persons having dogs, 27 August 1624), Huntington Library, San Marino, CA. For more on the ritual importance of hunting in English elite life, see Daniel C. Beaver, *Hunting and the Politics of Violence Before the English Civil War* (New York: Cambridge University Press, 2008).

47. John Norden to the Earl of Salisbury on the state of Alisholt [Alice Holt] Forest, 11 May 1609, CP 132/55, Hatfield House.

48. Wm. Glover, Surveyor of Norfolk and Suffolk, to Salisbury, 2 May 1609, SP 14/45, fol. 8, TNA.

49. For more on Salisbury's plan to reform Jacobean forestry, see Pettit, *The Royal Forests of Northamptonshire*, 57–58.

50. Similar concerns seem to have shaped management outside of royal forests, as evidenced by the presence of both intensively managed coppices cut to "optimise returns" and trees allowed to stand beyond their ideal harvest date, likely for landscape and aesthetic purposes in a 1642 wood survey. See Gulliver, "What Were Woods Like?," 150–52.

51. John Norden, Particular, and money account, of trees sold in the Forests of Aliceholt and New Forest, 30 June 1609, CP 132/108, Hatfield House.

52. Ibid.

53. Pettit, *The Royal Forests of Northamptonshire*, 59–62. For an example of these allegations, see Remembrances as to the King's Woods, July 1609, CP 128/76, Hatfield House.

54. Interrogatories Administered to Richard Tyler et al. concerning their knowledge of his Majesty's Forest of Dean, 1611, E178/3837, TNA.

55. Pettit, *The Royal Forests of Northamptonshire*, 61–62, For a similar argument, see also George Hammersley, "The Crown Woods and Their Exploitation in the Sixteenth and Seventeenth Centuries," *Historical Research* 30, no. 82 (November 1957): 136–61.

56. Description by John Norden of Northwood Coppice, New Forest, 1612, CP 132/176, Hatfield House.

57. In this, I agree with Paul Warde, who has argued that efforts to manage woods were essential to the early modern development of the idea of sustainability, while maintaining that such an ideal had not yet emerged during the seventeenth century. See Warde, *The Invention of Sustainability*. Most of the regulations here constitute what Conrad Totman called the "Negative Regimen" of controlling uses of woods. Suggestions for scattering acorns and beech nuts suggest some effort at regeneration but a significantly less developed one than was practiced under the Tokugawa Shogunate in Japan. See Conrad D. Totman, *The Green Archipelago: Forestry in Preindustrial Japan* (Berkeley: University of California Press, 1989), 83–115 ("The Negative Regimen") and 116–29 (on silviculture).

58. John Norden to the Lord Treasurer regarding the King's Woods, 1612, CP 132/145, Hatfield House.

59. See, for example, the work of Miyazaki Antei, described in Totman, *The Green Archipelago*, 118. Antei likewise called for trees to be sown and farmed like crops.

60. John Norden, "The maner how to rayse Copices and timber trees," before 24 May 1612, CP 132/146, Hatfield House.

61. William Slingsby to Salisbury on the king's woods, 1612, CP 132/148, Hatfield House.

62. SP 14/141, fols. 43 (License to Sir Wm. Slingsby, And. Palmer, Edwd. Wolverston, and Rob. Clayton, to make furnaces, etc., with sea and grit coal, 28 July 1610) and 142 (License to Sir Giles Mompesson and others to convert sea coal, stone coal, and other fuel, excepting wood, into charcoal, 25 April 1620), TNA; Simon Sturtevant, *Metallica* (London, 1612), 5–9; Dud Dudley, a later projector claiming to have discovered a means to make iron with coal, charged that Sturtevant and several others had failed to deliver on their patents. See Dud Dudley, *Metallum Martis, Or, Iron Made with Pit-Coale, Sea-Coale* (London, 1665), 3–4; George Hammersley wrote that Dudley may have had some success using coal in an ironworks, but that the development did not immediately lead to widespread adoption of the process. See G. F. Hammersley, "The Charcoal Iron Industry and Its Fuel, 1540-1750," *Economic History Review* 26, no. 4 (1 January 1973): 611. For discussion of James's disastrous grant of wood rights to Mompesson, see Pettit, *The Royal Forests of Northamptonshire*, 61–62.

63. On Churche's importance to surveying and discourses of improvement in royal forests, see Robson, "Improvement and Epistemologies of Landscape," 602, 606, 615–18.

64. R. C. (hereafter, Churche), *An Olde Thrift Newly Revived* (1612), A3r. The English Short Title Catalogue attributes authorship for the work to Rooke Churche but notes that Robert Chalmers and R. Churton are sometimes also listed as authors. Robson cites the author's name as "Rocke Churche."

65. Churche, *An Olde Thrift Newly Revived*, A3; James I, *Articles to Be Performed by Vertue of Our Commission of Sale Annexed, Touching Forrests, Parkes, and Chases* (London, 1609); James I, *Wheras Heretofore by Vertue of Sundrie Commissions and Warrants by vs and Our Progenitours Made, Giuen, and Graunted in That Behalfe, Diuers Woods and Trees Haue Beene Fallen, Cutte Downe, Soulde and Giuen, and Are to Be Fallen [. . .]* . (London, 1610).

66. The objections raised by the surveyor's opponents in Churche's dialogue did reflect grievances raised in resistance to disafforestation. See Robson, "Improvement and Epistemologies of Landscape," 618 (on ventriloquized dissent), 628-32 (on resistance on disafforestation).

67. Churche, *An Olde Thrift Newly Revived*, 2–3, 19, 33.

68. Ibid., 9, 35, 38.

69. Ibid., 15.

70. Ibid., 10, 14–15, 34. The reference to hops suggests that R. C. was familiar with broader literature of improvement; for example, Reginald Scot, *A Perfite Platforme of a Hoppe Garden* (London, 1578).

71. Churche, *An Olde Thrift Newly Revived*, 3, 6–11, 14, 16, 19-21, 24–25, 27.

72. Ibid., A3v, 5. Fears about coal exhaustion return in the eighteenth century and again become bound up in questions of political economy. See Jonsson, *Enlightenment's Frontier*, 181–87.

73. Churche, *An Olde Thrift Newly Revived*, A3v, 30.

74. For example, the 1642 Wood Book for the Helmsley estate in Yorkshire only counted oak and ash. See Gulliver, "What Were Woods Like?"

75. Churche, *An Olde Thrift Newly Revived*, 48, 50, 59, 66.

76. Ibid., 49–50, 67.

77. For discussion on the so-called riots greeting the Earl of Pembroke's ironworks, see Northampton to Rochester, SP 14/70, fols. 99 (14 August 1612) and 112 (20 August 1612), TNA. For an example of royal regulation of the Forest of Dean, see Brief of the King's title to the woods and lands called Pirton Purlew, in the Forest of Dean, claimed by Sir Edw. Winter, c. 1612, SP 14/194, fol. 50. For the case between Pembroke and the free miners see Exchequer Rolls Bills and Answers, 1613-1614, E112/83/411, TNA. H. R. Schubert, *History of the British Iron and Steel Industry from c. 450 B.C. to A.D. 1775* (London: Routledge and Kegan Paul, 1957), 185, 188-91; Cyril E. Hart, *Royal Forest: A History of Dean's Woods as Producers of Timber* (London: Clarendon, 1966), chs. 4-5; Sharp, *In Contempt of All Authority*, 190-200. Complaints about ironworks show up outside of Dean as well. In Bringewood, grievances came not from free miners but rather from users of commons for pasture and fuel gathering; see Lovelace, "Bringewood Chase and Surrounding Countryside," 32-35.

78. E126/1 fol. 270, TNA, as transcribed in Cyril E. Hart, *The Free Miners of the Royal Forest of Dean and the Hundred of St. Briavels* (Gloucester: British Publishing Company, 1953), 166-68; "Petition of Many Thousand of the Poor Inhabitants of the Forest of Dean," Bond family of Newland papers, D2026/X9, Gloucestershire Archives.

79. Warrant to the Constable of the Forest of Dean and George Marshall, 22 November 1613, Privy Council Records (hereafter, PC), 2/27 fol. 103, TNA; Hart, *Royal Forest*, 87-99; Grant to Richard Challoner and others of all ironworks in the Forest of Dean, 6 April 1621, SP 14/141, fol. 158, TNA; Peter King, "The Iron Trade in England and Wales 1500-1815: The Charcoal Iron Industry and Its Transition to Coke" (PhD diss., Wolverhampton University, 2003), http://archaeologydataservice.ac.uk/archives/view/peterking_phd_2004/downloads.cfm, 81; Lansdowne 166, fols. 380-82 (Edward Coke on the Forest of Dean, 21 February 1618/1619), 388 (Comparison of ironworks agreements, 23 February 1618/1619), BL; Order from Fulk Greville to the farmers of the king's ironworks, March 1618[/1619?], D9125/1/3031, Gloucestershire Collection archives, Gloucestershire Archives.

80. Suggestions on the best method of supplying timber for the navy, out of the King's own woods, c. 1625, SP 14/189, fol. 148; Copy of the petition presented to the late king [James I], December 1625, SP 16/12, fol. 168; Petition of Richard Daye to the king, 7 July 1627, SP 16/70, fol. 69, TNA.

81. Information about the injury sustained by the king in the woods in Hainault, SP 16/229, fol. 209, TNA.

82. Instructions to the commissioners for Gillingham Forest, 4 April 1627, SP 16/526, fol. 63, TNA.

83. HAM, box 48, folders 27 ("The contents of several grounds within the Forest," 14 September 1621), 29 (Copy of a commission to inquire of assarts, parprestares, and other things within the Forest of Leicester, 7 July 1623), 38 (Petition of Henry, earl of Huntingdon, to the Privy Council, May 1628). His claim about impositions on neighboring lands refers to Instructions regarding deer, 18 February 1612/1613, HAM, box 48, folder 20, Huntington Library, San Marino, CA.

84. Copy decree: Sir John Wintour, Benedict Hall and others, inhabitants of the Forest of Dean v. The Attorney General, 11 February 1628, Probyn family of Huntley and Newland papers, D23/E30, Gloucestershire Archives.

85. Ibid.

86. Bargain and sale by Surveyors of His Majesty's Woods to Sir Jn. Wynter and Benedict Hall, 1627, Bathurst family of Lydney papers, D421/E2, Gloucestershire Archives.

87. Sharp, *In Contempt of All Authority*, 95; Answers of Benedict Hall to William Noye's bill of complaint on behalf of the king, n.d. [c. 1631-1634], Hall and Gage families of Newland papers, D1677/GG/1178, Gloucestershire Archives.

88. Survey of trees in the Forest of Dean, July 1633, SP 16/245, fols. 27-39, TNA.

89. Nicholas Herbert, ed., *The Forest of Dean Eyre of 1634*, Gloucestershire Record Series (Bristol: The Bristol and Gloucestershire Archaeological Society, 2012), xvi–xxi, xxxvii.

90. Ibid.; for one set of notes on the proceedings, see 6–7, 9–11, 12–13, 16–17; for Finch's notes, see 24–27; for some specific presentments involving ironworks and fine amounts, see 43–48; for presentments relating to forges or furnaces, see 95–97. The value of the fine differs within and between sources, ranging from £57,939 16s 8d to £59,400. Among those presented was Richard Challoner, the Bristol merchant whose actions would play a critical role in Boyle's Irish ironworks and in the effort to build ironworks in Virginia. For the presentments against Challoner, see pp. 44–45, 48. On his role in Dean, see n. 79 above. On Virginia and Ireland, see Chapters 2–3.

91. Herbert, *The Forest of Dean Eyre of 1634*, see pp. 61–69 for presentments and fines for building unlicensed cottages. Fines for building cottages also appear in the section of presentments on purprestures (54–61), such as the £4 fine against laborer William Collier for building a cottage and small garden on the king's waste (55). For offenses against "vert," see 75–93. Baddam's presentment can be found on p. 90. For wage rates of men and women, see Jane Humphries and Jacob Weisdorf, "The Wages of Women in England, 1260–1850," *Journal of Economic History* 75, no. 2 (June 2015): table A1, p. 432.

92. Herbert, *The Forest of Dean Eyre of 1634*, 24.

93. For more on the legal scandals that erupted in the Forest of Dean in the 1630s, see Hammersley, "The Revival of the Forest Laws Under Charles I," 95–100. For Wintour's records of the legal dispute, see Contract relating to timber in the Forest of Dean, c. 1634; Hall and Gage families of Newland papers, D1677/GG/1545/1; Articles of Agreement between Sir John Wintour of Lidney and Benedict Hall, 25 June 1635, D1677/GG/800; Legal papers Rex v Sir John Wintour, 1615–1679, Bathurst family of Lydney papers, D421/E3, Gloucestershire Archives.

94. SP 15/21 fol. 18; Matthew Baker and Phineas Pett to unknown recipient, 13 February 1614/1615, SP 15/40 fol. 132, TNA.

95. Report of Richard Hore and Richard Parne, 25 November 1629, SP 16/152, fol. 93, TNA.

96. Ibid.

97. From the Privy Council to the Oxfordshire Justices of the Peace, 9 July 1630, PC 2/40, fols. 69, 417; Warrant to William Willoughby, 29 June 1631, PC 2/41, fol. 59; Orders to prevent the felling of wood, September 1630, SP 16/199, fol. 28; Officers of the Navy to the Lords of the Admiralty, 20 May 1631, SP 16/191, fol. 113, TNA.

98. TNA SP 16/191, fol. 113; Affidavit of Robert Smythe, 1633, SP 16/241, fols. 134–36; Peter Pett to the Officers of the Navy, 17 May 1632, SP 16/216, fol. 98; "Parishes: Shotover," in *A History of the County of Oxford: Volume 5, Bullingdon Hundred*, ed. Mary D. Lobel (London: Victoria County History, 1957), 275–81, http://www.british-history.ac.uk/vch/oxon/vol5/pp275-281.

99. "Necessary remembrances concerning the preservation of timber fitting for building and repairing his Majesty's ships," 1632, SP 16/229, fol. 212, TNA.

100. "Answer to objections made as touching the timber lately in Shottover and Stowewood," 1638, SP 16/406, fol. 109, TNA.

101. Hammersley, "The Revival of the Forest Laws Under Charles I"; Sharp, *In Contempt of All Authority*; D. J. Stagg, ed., *A Calendar of New Forest Documents: The Fifteenth to the Seventeenth Centuries*, Hampshire Record Series (Winchester: Hampshire Record Office for

Hampshire County Council, 1983), 5:51, 76. Stagg noted the focus on shipbuilders and foresters in his introduction on p. x.

102. Hammersley, "The Crown Woods and Their Exploitation"; Pettit makes a similar point about the failures to profit from wood or land sales. See Pettit, *The Royal Forests of Northamptonshire*, 54–62.

103. In arguing that colonial promoters had begun to reimagine English as well as colonial landscapes in service of their projects, I am expanding on hints at this connection in my earlier work, specifically the relationship between the literature of improvement and of colonization. See Pluymers, "Taming the Wilderness." The connection between colonial enterprise and domestic improvement was not solely an English phenomenon. See Parsons, *A Not-So-New World*, 48.

104. For an example of the potential costs associated with governing Irish woods, see "A declaration of the length and breadth of all the principal woods within the province of Munster," 1580, Carew Papers, MS 635, p. 117, Lambeth Palace Library (hereafter, LPL); see also Notes and discourses, chiefly touching the province of Munster out of Sir Francis Walsingham's notes, MS Cotton Titus B XII, fols. 158-66, BL.

105. "A discourse on the Reformation of Ireland," 1583, Carew Papers, MS 621, fol. 105r, LPL; for claims about revenue, see fol. 100. Such justifications were common throughout the sixteenth and early seventeenth centuries. See Carew Papers, MS 627, fol. 165 ("The manner of the woods where great trees and timber mete for building are," 4 November 1584); MS 614, fols. 254-55 (John Perrot, "Certain notes for the right honorable treasurer of Ireland to consider," 1585); MS 607, fols. 110-11v ("Short notes to be considered upon for the reducing and settling of Munster," 1584).

106. Edmund Spenser, *A View of the Present State of Ireland*, CELT Electronic Edition (Cork, Ireland: Corpus of Electronic Texts: A project of University College, Cork, 2003), http://www.ucc.ie/celt/published/E500000-001/index.html. Spenser's rather extreme views on Irish woods should give historians pause before accepting Canny's argument that Spenser is representative of the theory of plantations. See Nicholas Canny, *Making Ireland British, 1580-1650* (Oxford: Oxford University Press, 2001), ch. 1.

107. Richard Hakluyt, *Discourse of Western Planting*, ed. David B. Quinn and Alison M. Quinn, Hakluyt Society Extra Series, no. 45 (London: Hakluyt Society, 1993), chs. 2, 4. The "Discourse" was conceived while Hakluyt was in Paris. On Hakluyt's Paris years, see Peter Mancall, *Hakluyt's Promise: An Elizabethan's Obsession for an English America* (New Haven, CT: Yale University Press, 2007), 102-55. Mancall describes Hakluyt's views on economics, trade, and population on pp. 140-45.

108. Hakluyt, *Discourse of Western Planting*, 16.

109. Karen Ordahl Kupperman, "The Puzzle of the American Climate in the Early Colonial Period," *American Historical Review* 87, no. 5 (December 1982): 1262–89. Sam White has modified Kupperman's argument, showing that encounters with American climates had led to questions about this model; see Sam White, "Unpuzzling American Climate: New World Experience and the Foundations of a New Science," *Isis* 106, no. 3 (1 September 2015): 544–66; Sam White, *A Cold Welcome: The Little Ice Age and Europe's Encounter with North America* (Cambridge, MA: Harvard University Press, 2017). For White's discussion of Hakluyt, see pp. 103-8. White argues that Hakluyt "relied on the most highly regarded ideas and best information available to them at the time" (108). Anya Zilberstein, *A Temperate Empire: Making Climate Change in Early America* (Oxford: Oxford University Press, 2016). Camden organized his description of Ireland

almost entirely around its relative position to England and citations of Pliny and Strabo. William Camden, *Britain* (London, 1637), 61-63. The first edition of Camden's work was published in 1586; Bermuda governor Nathaniel Butler used Jerusalem as a reference point for Bermuda's climate. See Nathaniel Butler, "History of the Bermudas," Sloane 750, fol. 5/p. 1, BL.

110. Hakluyt, *Discourse of Western Planting*, 68.

111. Richard Hakluyt, *The Principall Navigations, Voiages and Discoueries of the English Nation* (London: 1589), 269. On the role of natural resources and efforts to promote a colonial venture in Newfoundland, see Karin A. Amundsen, "Thinking Metallurgically: Metals and Empire in the Projects of Edward Hayes," *Huntington Library Quarterly* 79, no. 4 (Winter 2016): esp. 571-79.

112. Gray, *A Good Speed to Virginia*, B2r-B3v; Timothy Sweet has extensively studied the uses of this rhetoric in "Economy, Ecology, and Utopia," and Timothy Sweet, *American Georgics: Economy and Environment in Early American Literature* (Philadelphia: University of Pennsylvania Press, 2002), esp. chs. 1-2.

113. Council for Virginia, "A True Declaration of the Estate of the Colonie in Virginia [. . .]" in Force, ed., *Tracts and Other Papers*, 3:23-25 (quotation on p. 25); R. I. [Robert Johnson], *Nova Brittania* (London, 1609), p. 16 (unnumbered).

114. John Smith, *A Map of Virginia* (London, 1612), 11.

115. Warde, "Fear of Wood Shortage."

116. N. D. G. James, *A History of English Forestry* (Oxford: Blackwell, 1981), 166-67.

117. Edward Waterhouse, *A Declaration of the State of the Colony and Affaires in Virginia: With a Relation of the Barbarous Massacre in the Time of Peace and League* (London, 1622), 3-5; John Smith, *The Generall Historie of Virginia, New-England, and the Summer Isles* (London, 1624), 213, 228, 248; John Smith, *Advertisements for the Unexperienced Planters of New-England, or Any Where.* (London, 1631), 4-5.

118. Digges, *The Defense of Trade*, 30.

Chapter 2

1. Arthur Chichester to the Privy Council on Irish woods, SP 63/231, fol. 55, TNA. The exact relationship between governments in Dublin and Westminster in the sixteenth and seventeenth centuries was complicated and uncertain, not the least for contemporaries. In Ireland, the English-appointed Lord Deputy and Viceroy each held considerable power, with the Lord Deputy presiding over his own council of advisers. At the same time, the Privy Council could and did directly interfere in Irish politics, particularly when dealing with issues surrounding the plantations. Ireland also possessed a hobbled Parliament that nonetheless met and was a site of political action. For more, see Ciaran Brady, "Politics, Policy, and Power, 1550-1603," in *The Cambridge History of Ireland, Volume II, 1550-1730*, ed. Jane Ohlmeyer (Cambridge: Cambridge University Press, 2018), 53-91; David Edwards, "Political Change and Social Transformation, 1603-1641," in Ohlmeyer, *Cambridge History of Ireland*, 92-129.

2. Chichester to Privy Council, SP 63/231, fol. 55.

3. Canny, *Making Ireland British*, 314-17; Raymond Gillespie, *The Transformation of the Irish Economy 1550-1700* (Dublin: Economic and Social History Society of Ireland, 1991), 34-35; T. C. Smout, *Exploring Environmental History: Selected Essays* (Edinburgh: Edinburgh University Press, 2009), ch. 7, esp. pp. 131-33. The foremost scholar of early modern Irish forests, Eileen McCracken, has offered a middle ground, pointing to evidence for wood shortages but also noting that records of timber sales from the eighteenth century indicate that the plantations did not

deforest Ireland completely. See Eileen McCracken, *The Irish Woods Since Tudor Times: Distribution and Exploitation*. (Newton Abbot, Devon: David & Charles for Queen's University Belfast, 1971). McCracken chronicles shortages throughout but explicitly warns against total woodland destruction on p. 98. Close analysis of documentary sources and historical pollen deposits have raised further questions about this chronology; see Valerie A. Hall, "Landscape Development in Northeast Ireland Over the Last Half Millennium," *Review of Palaeobotany and Palynology, Modern Pollen Rain and Fossil Pollen Spectra*, 82, no. 1 (1 June 1994): 75–82; Valerie A. Hall, "Woodland Depletion in Ireland Over the Last Millennium," in *Wood, Trees and Forests in Ireland: Proceedings of a Seminar Held on 22 and 23 February 1994*, ed. Jon R. Pilcher and Seán Mac an tSaoir (Dublin: Royal Irish Academy, 1995), 13–22; Valerie A. Hall, "Recent Landscape Change and Landscape Restoration in Northern Ireland: A Tephra-Dated Pollen Study," *Review of Palaeobotany and Palynology* 103, no. 1 (1998): 59–68; Valerie A. Hall, "Pollen Analytical Investigations of the Irish Landscape AD 200–1650," *Peritia* 14 (1 January 2000): 342–71; Valerie A. Hall and Lynda Bunting, "Tephra-Dated Pollen Studies of Medieval Landscapes in the North of Ireland," in *Gaelic Ireland, c.1250–c.1650: Land, Lordship, and Settlement*, ed. Patrick J Duffy, David Edwards, and Elizabeth FitzPatrick (Dublin: Four Courts, 2001), 207–22; Oliver Rackham, "Looking for Ancient Woodland in Ireland," in Pilcher and Mac an tSaoir, *Wood, Trees and Forests in Ireland*, 1–12; Kenneth Nicholls, "Woodland Cover in Pre-Modern Ireland," in Duffy, Edwards, and FitzPatrick, *Gaelic Ireland*, 181–206. The most forceful critique of the early modern destruction argument has come from Nigel Everett. He argues that historians have overemphasized accounts of destruction, often to fit into nationalist narratives and claims that English planters introduced woodland preservation to Ireland. Nigel Everett, *The Woods of Ireland: A History, 700–1800* (Dublin: Four Courts, 2015), 1–15.

4. Jane H Ohlmeyer, *Making Ireland English: The Irish Aristocracy in the Seventeenth Century* (New Haven, CT: Yale University Press, 2012), 361, 372–77. Ohlmeyer does not completely reject the argument that planters were "asset strippers," but she offers a far more nuanced explanation for natural resource management on their estates. David Edwards and Colin Rynne explicitly challenge this framing, writing that Boyle was "an asset-protector, not an asset-stripper." David Edwards and Colin Rynne, "Introduction: Nuancing an Archetype: Richard Boyle and His Colonial World," in *The Colonial World of Richard Boyle, First Earl of Cork*, ed. David Edwards and Colin Rynne (Dublin: Four Courts Press, 2018), 16.

5. Spenser, "A View of the Present State of Ireland."

6. Steven G. Ellis, *Ireland in the Age of the Tudors, 1447–1603: English Expansion and the End of Gaelic Rule* (London: Longman, 1998). Ellis's argument does not represent a consensus position. See Canny, *Making Ireland British*; John Patrick Montaño, *The Roots of English Colonialism in Ireland* (New York: Cambridge University Press, 2011), 103–53; on a distinction between private and state-directed colonization schemes, see pp. 143–53.

7. My discussion of the relationship between state formation, maps, surveys, and early modern ecological imagination draws on Scott, *Seeing Like a State*, 11–13, 23–24; William Smyth, *Map-Making, Landscapes and Memory: A Geography of Colonial and Early Modern Ireland c.1530–1750* (Cork, Ireland: Cork University Press in association with Field Day, 2006). There had been earlier sixteenth-century attempts to survey Ireland, but they produced contradictory accounts of the land as blank space, degenerate wilderness, and cultivated land ready to yield profits to English landholders. See Montaño, *Roots of English Colonialism*, 154–95; on the efforts to create new geographic and cartographic information and the struggles surveyors and cartographers faced, see pp. 195–206.

8. Montaño, *Roots of English Colonialism*; Canny, *Making Ireland British*.

9. John Derricke, *The Image of Irelande, with a Discoverie of Woodkarne* (London, 1581), A4v, plate 11.

10. Calls to make Irish woods useful predated the plantations; there had been efforts to identify potential ship timber in the 1570s, but these efforts seem to have produced little usable information. By the time of the plantations, according to Everett, "the true extent of Ireland's timber reserves remained one of the central mysteries of a kingdom long erratically possessed." He goes on to argue that the continued prominence of discourses condemning purported Irish barbarism and locating it in landscapes consistently populated by thick woods created "elusive woodlands" that leave it difficult to determine the extent of pre-plantation woods. Everett, *The Woods of Ireland*, 35–41, 75 (quotation), 50–55 (on English discourses about the disorderly Irish landscape and the woodkern), 83–92 ("elusive woodlands").

11. "Articles concerning Her Majesty's offers for the disposing of the lands in Munster," December 1585, SP 63/121, fol. 196, TNA; "Articles concerning Her Majesty's offers for the disposing of Her lands in Munster to the Planters," 1 March 1585/1586, SP 63/123, fol. 3; Francis Walsingham, "Articles concerning her Majesty's offers for the disposing of her Lands in Munster in Ireland," Carew Papers, MS 614, fol. 67, LPL.

12. Fenton's marginal comments are found in "Articles concerning Her Majesty's offers for the disposing of the lands in Munster," March 1585/1586, SP 63/123, fol. 91, TNA.

13. "A draft of instructions for Sir Valentine Browne concerning the province of Munster," 1587, Carew Papers, MS 611, fols. 317–22, LPL; "Instructions for Sir Henry Walloppe, Sir Valentine Browne and the rest of the Commissioners appointed to take a Survey of the Lands of such as have rebelled," 1583, Carew Papers, MS 600, fols. 83–84, LPL; MS Cotton Titus B XII, fols. 259–63 (Draft instructions for Sir Valentine Browne), 21r–22v (Abstracts of commissions for the surveying and disposing of escheated lands, 1585–1602), BL; Valentine Browne, "A note of certain things to be added to the articles of Munster," 3 June 1586, SP 63/124, fol. 139, TNA.

14. Montaño, *Roots of English Colonialism*, 199.

15. V. Treadwell, ed., *The Irish Commission of 1622: An Investigation of the Irish Administration, 1615–1622, and Its Consequences, 1623–1624* (Dublin: Irish Manuscripts Commission, 2006), 477–80.

16. SP 63/124, fol. 184 (An abstract of the articles for repeopling and inhabiting of the province of Munster in Ireland, 21 June 1586), 202 (Grant of lands in Munster, 27 June 1586), TNA. For plans for ethnic and religious segregation and limits on individual holdings came into tension with plans for economic development and improvement throughout the plantation articles and attempts to evaluate planters' success, see David Heffernan, "Theory and Practice in the Munster Plantation: The Estates of Richard Boyle, First Earl of Cork, 1602–43," in Edwards and Rynne, *The Colonial World of Richard Boyle*, 43–63.

17. "Plot of the attainted lands and how the same is allotted to the undertakers," 17 June 1586, Extracted Maps and Plans (MPF) 1/273, TNA.

18. "The plot for a Parishe in Ireland," January 1585/1586, MPF 1/305, TNA.

19. SP 63/122, TNA. The letter from Cecil, Hatton, and Walsingham in which they mention that they are enclosing instructions is at fol. 118. The map immediately followed it. The order for planting Munster immediately followed the removed map at fols. 122–23.

20. "Form of the grant to be passed to the undertakers," 27 June 1586, SP 63/124, fol. 210, TNA; Copies of grants to Sir Walter Ralegh, 1586, Lismore Castle Papers, MS 41,983/1, National Library of Ireland (hereafter, NLI).

21. Survey of lands allotted to Sir Walter Ralegh, c. 1600, Lismore Castle Papers, MS 43,308/2, NLI.

22. Certificates of lands granted in Munster, Carew Papers, MS 631, fols. 1-5, 7-12, 14, 17-22, 24-26. The only document to mention fishing was Charles Herbert's certificate (fol. 27); the four documents to mention woods were fols. 6 (Henry Oughtred and his associates), 13 (George Beston and Lancellot Bestock), 15 (Francis Walsingham and Edward Denny), and 16 (Sir Christopher Hatton).

23. The reliance on abstract measures for land despite efforts at more precise definition reinforces Montaño's sense that "the order that was intended to burst fully formed from the head of the surveyors and cartographers proved to be based less on the actual geography of Ireland than on the geography of the mind." Montaño, *Roots of English Colonialism*, 211.

24. "The Plotte of the greatt Countey of Lymbrik," 1587, MPF 1/97, TNA.

25. Map of the abbey and manor of Tralee, Co. Kerry, September 1587, MPF 1/309, TNA.

26. The questions were outlined in "Certain Articles to be answered unto by the undertakers for the peopling of Munster," 11 May 1589, SP 63/144, fols. 33-35, TNA. For the answers, which were all recorded in May 1589, see fols. 23-25 (Edward Denny), 27-30 (Henry Oughtred), 35 (Edward Phyton [Fitton]), 36 (Phane Beecher), 48 (William Herbert), 50 (George Herbert), 52 (George Bourchier), 56 (William Trenchard by his agent Richard Gill), 58-59 (Hugh Cuffe), 60 (Walter Ralegh), 70v-71r ("Thomas Fleetwood in the Behalf of Marmaduke Redmayne, Christopher Carus, John Calvert, and Himself"), 74 (Marmaduke Redmayne), 225 (Alexander Clarke), 226 (Arthur Hyde), 228v-229r (Jessua Smythes), 230a (Edmund Spenser), 231 (Roger Rice for Francis Berkley), 232 (Arthur Robyns), 233 (William Edwards on behalf of Christopher Hatton), 235 (Warham St. Leger and Richard Grenville). MacCarthy-Morrogh has already dealt with these documents; however, he used them mainly as a source for the English population in Munster, Michael MacCarthy-Morrogh, *The Munster Plantation: English Migration to Southern Ireland, 1583-1641* (Oxford: Clarendon, 1986), 109-111.

27. John White (attributed), "A topographical lineament of all such enclosed lands as are holden by Henrye Pyne, Esquire, from the Right Honourable Sir Walter Raley, Knight," 1598, Lismore Castle Papers, MS 22,068, NLI. Eric Klingelhofer performed excavations on locations derived from White's map in the 1990s, which failed to yield significant artifacts. Resistivity testing suggested that locations for settlements in the map corresponded with archaeological evidence. See Eric Klingelhofer, "Elizabethan Settlements at Mogeely Castle, Curraglass and Carrigeen, Co. Cork (Part 1)," *Journal of the Cork Historical and Archaeological Society* 104 (1999): 97-110; Eric Klingelhofer, "Elizabethan Settlements at Mogeely Castle, Curraglass and Carrigeen, Co. Cork (Part 2)," *Journal of the Cork Historical and Archaeological Society* 105 (2000): 155-174. See also Eric Klingelhofer, *Castles and Colonists: An Archaeology of Elizabethan Ireland* (Manchester: Manchester University Press, 2010), 25-26, 72-78. For a relatively positive review of Klingelhofer's findings, see Dennis Power, "The Archaeology of the Munster Plantation," in *The Post-medieval Archaeology of Ireland, 1550-1850*, ed. Audrey Horning et al. (Dublin: Wordwell, 2007), 23-36. Horning argues that the findings are unconvincing, in Audrey J. Horning, *Ireland in the Virginian Sea: Colonialism in the British Atlantic* (Chapel Hill: University of North Carolina Press, 2013), 88.

28. Leases, releases, and assignments for Ralegh's lands near Mogeely, Lismore Castle Papers, MS 43,142/2, NLI. Items within the folder are unpaginated. In particular, see Indenture between Guye Toose and Henry Pyne, 6 March 1591/1592; Edward Lochland to William Lee, 2 July 1593; Edward Lochland to Henry Morris, 30 June 1594.

29. Thomas Harriot, Plot of Lismore, 28 August 1589, Dartmouth Atlas of Ireland, P/49, fol. 29, National Maritime Museum (UK); Kim Sloan, *A New World: England's First View of America* (London: British Museum, 2007), 42–43. Sloan describes the Dartmouth map and Harriot's signature in greater detail in Chapter 3, note 32.

30. Copy of the survey of the manor of Dungarvan from 7 March 1566, c. 1600, Lismore Castle Papers, MS 43,308/5, NLI; Copy of the survey of Molana, c. 1600, Lismore Castle Papers, MS 43,308, fol. 6; Terence Reeves-Smyth, *Irish Gardens and Gardening Before Cromwell*, Barryscourt Lectures 4 (Carrigtwohill, Co. Cork: Barryscourt Trust in association with Cork County Council and Gandon Editions, 1999), 113–19.

31. Copy of the survey of Molana, MS 43,308/6, NLI.

32. Lease from Walter Ralegh to Robert Marple of Ballynetra, 20 August 1589; Edmund Coppinger's Deed to Richard Boyle, 8 October 1602, and William Flower and Richard Benson's Deed to Richard Boyle, 20 November 1602, Lismore Castle Papers, MS 43,150/2; Walter Ralegh's Lease to Dennis Fisher of London for Curraglass, 28 February 1588/1589, Lismore Castle Papers, MS 43,156/1; William Chisshull's Discharge of the Castle of Killmacow to Richard Boyle, 27 June 1604, MS 43,156/2; Walter Ralegh's Lease to Roger Owfeild, 31 January 1588/1589, and Henry Dorrell's Fee Farm of a Plowland Called Ballyghily from Sir Walter Ralegh, 5 October 1589, Lismore Castle Papers, MS 43,143/4; Edward Lochland's Deed to Richard Boyle, 9 June 1607, Lismore Castle Papers, MS 43,142/3; Edward Lochland's Discharge to Richard Boyle, 16 October 1607, MS 43,142/4; Roger Dalton's Lease to Boyle, 17 November 1607, MS 43,149/1; Dalton's Mortgage to Boyle, 17 November 1607, MS 43,149/2; MS 43, 095/2–3; "Agreement Concluded and Agreed Uppon Between Capten William Newce and Richard Boyle Touching the Town and Lande of Ballynotrae in the Countie of Waterford," 7 May 1602, MS 43,310/1; Ralegh recorded paying for a woodward in "The Rentall of Sir Walter Ralegh His Land in Ireland," n.d., Lismore Castle Papers, MS 43,307/1, NLI; Ralegh's lease of Tercullen Mor to Samuell Cowley, 4 December 1594, Additional Charters (Add. Ch.) 17352, BL. On Boyle's life and his importance in the plantations, see Nicholas Canny, *The Upstart Earl: A Study of the Social and Mental World of Richard Boyle, First Earl of Cork, 1566–1643* (Cambridge: Cambridge University Press, 1982); Edwards and Rynne, eds., *The Colonial World of Richard Boyle*. On Boyle as a typical Atlantic World elite, see Audrey Horning, "Shapeshifters and Mimics: Exploring Elite Strategies in the Early Modern British Atlantic," in Edwards and Rynne, eds., *The Colonial World of Richard Boyle*, 27–42.

33. For analysis of planters' attitudes toward estate management, see Ohlmeyer, *Making Ireland English*, 361.

34. See Chapter 1. For the results of those surveys, see Hammersley, "The Crown Woods and Their Exploitation," 143–44.

35. Privy Council to George Carew, 18 July 1601, Carew MSS, MS 615, fol. 235, LPL; Henry Pyne, "A Note of all such ships as have been freighted for Sir Walter Rawley, Edward Dodge, Henry Pyne, and Veron Martin," 3 March 1592/1593, SP 63/168, fols. 231-32, Note of such lands as have timber trees fit for building ships, SP 63/106, fol. 94, TNA.

36. Carew Papers, MS 615, fols. 197r–198v (Pyne to the Privy Council, 1601), 292 (From Lord Deputy Mountjoy in support of Pyne, 1 May 1601), 480 (Privy Council to the Lord President of Munster, 17 December 1602). This was not the first time Pyne had been accused of wasting woods. He and Ralegh had fended off condemnations of their pipe-stave enterprise in 1592 and 1593 from the Lord Deputy William Fitzwilliam, in part by claiming that their exported staves relieved a scarcity in the West Country. See Everett, *The Woods of Ireland*, 79–82.

37. "Extract of a Letter from Justice Smithes and George Thornton," 9 March 1592/1593, SP 63/168, fol. 229, TNA.

38. Chichester to Salisbury, 27 October 1608, SP 63/225, fols. 159–60, TNA.

39. Geoffrey Fenton to Salisbury, August 1608, SP 63/224, fol. 266, TNA; SP 63/225, fols. 159–60.

40. SP 63/225, fols. 46 (Pyne to Salisbury, 18 September 1608), 59 (Boyle to Salisbury, 20 September 1608); Henry Wright to Salisbury, 17 February 1608/1609, SP 63/226, fol.79, TNA. Everett briefly describes Chichester's thoughts on Irish woods and Cottingham's survey. In his account, Boyle lurks as a target of Chichester's ire, but he does not note Pyne and Boyle's interactions with Cottingham. See Everett, *The Woods of Ireland*, 95–96.

41. SP 63/225, fols. 46, 59, 159–60, 166 (Philip Cottingham to Salisbury, 30 October 1608), 249 (Thomas Yonge, Vice President of Munster, to Salisbury, 7 December 1608); SP 63/168, fols. 229–31; SP 63/226, fols. 79, 81 (Pyne and Wright's Bill of Lading for Timber, 1609), TNA.

42. SP 63/228, fols. 9–11 ("The second Conference about the Plantation of Ulster," 12 January 1609/1610), 32 (Articles between the King and the City of London for the Plantation of Derry and Coleraine, 28 January 1609/1610); "Instructions given unto the Commissioners for the plantation of the Escheated lands in Ulster," March 1609/1610 SP 63/226, fols. 163–65; Chichester to the Privy Council, 7 March 1610/1611, SP 63/231, fol.55, TNA.

43. The motivation for these grants may have been an effort to increase Crown revenue through customs duties on timber and pipe staves. See Everett, *The Woods of Ireland*, 98–101.

44. Lords of the Council to Chichester, 1 January 1610/1611, SP 63/231, fol. 2; Carew Papers, MS 629, fols. 29-39 (Titles of Acts to be Propounded in the next Parliament in Ireland, 1611), 165-66 (Arthur Chichester, George Carew, Thomas Ridgeway, John Denham, John Davies, Propositions for the increase of his majesty's revenue in Ireland, 1611); John Davies, Propositions to increase the king's revenue in Ireland, n.d. [c. 1612], MS Carte 61, fols. 78-79, Bodleian Library.

45. E. S., "A Survey of the Present Estate of Ireland Anno 1615," Ellesmere Papers, MS EL 1746, fol. 20v, Huntington Library, San Marino, CA. For a transcription of this source and a compelling argument for its authorship, see Bríd McGrath, "Unmasking 'E. S.', the Author of 'A Survey of the Present Estate of Ireland Anno 1615," *Archivium Hibernicum* 71 (2018): 7–33.

46. John Jephson to Richard Boyle, 9 June 1615, MS 13,236/5, NLI; Cork MSS, v6, no. 48 (Account of Rice Apian, John Brothers, and John Rice, 27 July 1615), 90 (John van der Bogarde, Receipt for Boyle, 16 November 1615); v9, no. 5 (Jephson to Boyle, 22 May 1618), 21 (Jephson to Boyle, 30 June 1618); v10, no. 22 (Account of pipe staves for Jephson and Boyle, June 1619), 53 (Thomas Smythe to Boyle, 26 November 1619), Chatsworth House.

47. Charles William Russell and John Patrick Prendergast, eds., *Calendar of the State Papers, Relating to Ireland, of the Reign of James I, 1603-1625: 1615-1625*(London: Longman, 1880), 5:48, 91. On the East India Company's actions in Munster, see Joseph Nunan, "Boyle and the East India Company in Co. Cork: A Case Study in Colonial Competition," in Edwards and Rynne, *The Colonial World of Richard Boyle*, 64–73.

48. Indeed, this exception suggests that Ireland existed at the blurred border between India and the Atlantic. See Stern, *The Company-State*, 6–7.

49. V. Treadwell, ed., *The Irish Commission of 1622*, 282–83, 728–29. See "An Act that Timber Shall not be Felled to make Coals for the Making of Iron" (1 Eliz. I, c. 15), which banned felling within fourteen miles of navigable rivers or streams.

50. Privy Council to the commissioners in Ireland, 3 April 1622, PC 2/31, fol. 311, TNA.

51. Raymond Gillespie, "Harvest Crisis in Early Seventeenth-Century Ireland," *Irish Economic and Social History* 11 (1984): 5–18; Raymond Gillespie, "Meal and Money: The Irish Harvest Crisis of 1621-4 and the Irish Economy," in *Famine: The Irish Experience, 900-1900: Subsistence Crises and Famines in Ireland*, ed. E. Margaret Crawford (Edinburgh: J. Donald, 1989), 75–95; David Edwards, "Out of the Blue? Provincial Unrest in Ireland Before 1641," in *Ireland, 1641: Contexts and Reactions*, ed. Micheál Ó Siochrú and Jane Ohlmeyer (Manchester: Manchester University Press, 2013), 98–99. For a description of these preparations, see Privy Council order on the Londonderry Plantation, 24 September 1624, SP 63/238/2, fol. 57, TNA.

52. SP 63/238/2, fol. 120v, TNA.

53. Henry Wright and Richard Blacknall, "A proposition for casting iron ordnance and making bar iron in Ireland," SP 63/268, fols. 24-25, TNA.

54. Ibid.

55. "Whereas his Majestie and the Board having beene informed of the great decay of Timber aswell within the Kingdome of Ireland [. . .]," 9 December 1629, PC 2/39, fol. 535, TNA. For another copy of this order, see SP 16/153, fol. 76. For details of Charles I's forestry policies in the 1620s, see Chapter 1.

56. PC 2/40, fols. 311 (Petition of Humphrey Slaney, 28 January 1630/1631), 327 (Petition of Abraham and Thomas Chamberlaine, 31 January 1630/1631), TNA.

57. Hugh F. Kearney, *Strafford in Ireland, 1633-41: A Study in Absolutism*, 2nd ed. (Cambridge: Cambridge University Press, 1989); C. V. Wedgwood, *Thomas Wentworth, First Earl of Strafford, 1593-1641, A Revaluation* (New York: Macmillan, 1962); Patrick Little, "The Earl of Cork and the Fall of the Earl of Strafford, 1638-41," *Historical Journal* 39, no. 3 (September 1996): 619–35; Michael Perceval-Maxwell, "Strafford, the Ulster-Scots and the Covenanters," *Irish Historical Studies* 18, no. 72 (September 1973): 524–51; Terence Ranger, "Strafford in Ireland: A Revaluation," *Past & Present*, no. 19 (April 1961): 26–45; Aidan Clarke, "Ireland and the General Crisis," *Past & Present*, no. 48 (August 1970): 90–91.

58. Notes on the case in the Star Chamber against the Londoners, 12 May 1635, SP 63/271, fols. 31v, 34v.

59. For more on this conflict, see Little, "Cork and the Fall of the Earl of Strafford."

60. Patrick Condon is referenced in Thomas Norris, Arthur Robins, and Francis Jobson, Survey of lands granted to Ralegh, 7 February 1588/1589, Lismore Castle Papers, MS 43,308/3, NLI.

61. Boyle had a relationship with Van der Bogarde that lasted into the 1630s; however, only leases from 1608 through 1610 mentioned Condon's land explicitly. See Note on pipe staves between John van der Bogarde and Boyle, 5 March 1607/1608; Bogarde's account of payments to Boyle, July 1609; Account between Bogarde and Boyle, June and July 1609; Account between Bogarde and Boyle, 1610; Lismore Castle Papers, MS 43,296/1, NLI.

62. Henry Pyne, Narrative of the wrongs done by Boyle, n.d., Cork MSS, vol. 7, no. 130, Chatsworth House.

63. Joshua Boyle, Notes from day book, 9 November 1638 to 7 December 1638, Lismore Castle Papers, MS 43,268/5, fols. 11-12.

64. Joshua Boyle, Report for Richard Boyle, 3 June 1639, Lismore Castle Papers, MS 13,237/23, NLI; Joshua Boyle to Richard Boyle, 20 July 1639, Lismore Castle Papers, MS 43,268/5, NLI.

65. David Heffernan concludes that contemporaries would have perceived Boyle's plantation as a successful one, even if it failed to fulfill all the goals of plantation theorists. Strafford's actions sought to draw a sharp distinction between a planter's personal success and a planter's

fealty to royal interests. David Heffernan, "Theory and Practice in the Munster Plantation: The Estates of Richard Boyle, First Earl of Cork, 1602–43;" on Boyle as a success, see p. 63.

66. Wentworth to Sir Christopher Wanderforde, 25 July 1636, MS Carte 1, fols. 130v–131r, Bodleian Library.

67. Sir Thomas Wroe to Wentworth, 1 December 1634, SP 16/278, fol. 5r, TNA.

68. Officers of the Navy to the Lords of the Admiralty, 25 March 1637, SP 16/351, fol. 10, TNA.

69. Edwards and Rynne, "Introduction: Nuancing an Archetype," 16 (quotation), 14–17. Everett argues that the case against Boyle as a spoiler of woods remains unproven, noting the presence of some preservation efforts in the printed edition of his papers. I argue that, instead, we should reorient our analysis toward how Boyle attempted to preserve woods. As the remainder of this chapter demonstrates, Boyle's own records show that his preservation measures did not always work as intended and that failures left him facing periods of scarcity and condemning acts of destruction. Moreover, I show that Boyle's actions on leased woodlands where he did not enact protection measures prompted many of the conflicts that led to allegations of waste. Everett, *The Woods of Ireland*, 119.

70. H. F. Kearney, "Richard Boyle, Ironmaster: A Footnote to Irish Economic History," *Journal of the Royal Society of Antiquaries of Ireland* 83, no. 2 (1 January 1953): 156–62; Eileen McCracken, "Charcoal-Burning Ironworks in Seventeenth and Eighteenth Century Ireland," *Ulster Journal of Archaeology* 20, 3rd ser. (1 January 1957): 123–38; McCracken, *The Irish Woods Since Tudor Times*. For examples of these restrictions, see Cork MSS, vol. 6, no. 150 (Cornelius Gaffny to Boyle, 18 March 1615/1616); vol. 8, nos. 35 (Elizabeth Harris to Boyle, 13 May 1617), 159 (William Freke to Boyle, 12 November 1617); vol. 10, no. 7 (Stephen Dawkes, Note of ship timber given to the navy, 6 May 1619); Survey of the Cork estates, c. 1630, Lismore Castle Papers, MS 43,308/7, NLI; Lease from Boyle to Robert Bateman, 18 October 1635, MS 43,153/2; Description of the woods at Ballydorgan, 25 September 1620, MS 43,268/4. For restrictions in lease terms, see MS 43,156/5, NLI, esp. leases to John Offman (5 January 1620/1621), Lawrence Ebden and his daughters Sara and Mary (3 May 1620), Walter Nicholas (5 July 1620), Henry Hull (23 October 1620), Hugh Roberts (20 March 1620/1621), Richard Bayly (23 November 1622), Edward Power (6 October 1623), Symon Randall, Henry Randall, the elder, and Henry Randall, the younger (1 May 1625).

71. Ralegh's lease to Roger Owfeild, 31 January 1588/1589, MS 43,143/4; Ralegh's lease to Dennis Fisher, 28 February 1587/1588, and Lease for the castle and manor of Shane, 8 September 1589, MS 43,156/1; Ralegh's lease to Robert Marple, 20 August 1589, MS 43,150/2; Ralegh's lease to Robert Carew for Salmon Fishing at Lismore, 29 September 1589, Lismore Castle Papers, MS 43,153/1, NLI.

72. Ralegh's lease to Owfeild and Ralegh's lease to Henry Dorrell, 5 October 1589, MS 43,143/4; Ralegh's lease to Marple, MS 43,150/2; Lease for the castle and manor of Shane, MS 43,156/1; Ralegh reported paying a woodward in "The Rentall of Sir Walter Ralegh His Land in Ireland," n.d., Lismore Castle Papers, MS 43,307/1, NLI; Ralegh's lease to Samuell Cowley, 4 December 1594, Add. Ch. 17,352, BL.

73. Floyer's deed to Myn, 1 November 1596, and Myn's lease to Richard Benson, 18 November 1596, Lismore Castle Papers, MS 43,150/2, NLI.

74. Lochland leases to John Darbishire (24 April 1589), Walter Phillys (2 July 1593), William Lee (2 July 1593), John Elwell (29 September 1593), Henry Morris (30 June 1594), Edward

Repyngall (2 July 1594), and Thomas Wallys (2 July 1594), and Colthurst's leases to Richard Whyte (20 October 1591) and Nicholas Hunte (15 December 1595), Lismore Castle Papers, MS 43,156/1, NLI.

75. Smout, *Exploring Environmental History*, ch. 3.

76. Norris's Agreement with O'Callaghan, 31 October 1593, Cork MSS, vol. 1. no. 9, fols. 30v-31r.

77. Francis Jobson, "The Province of Mounster," n.d. [c. 1595], Dartmouth Atlas, P/49, fol. 20; Map of Ireland South of Limerick, 1590, Dartmouth Atlas, P/49, fol. 27, National Maritime Museum (hereafter, NMM), Greenwich, London.

78. "Note of all such ships as have been freighted for Sir Walter Rawley, Edward Dodge, Henry Pyne, and Veron Martin," 9 March 1592/1593, SP 63/168, fol. 231, TNA.

79. Henry Beecher and John Richmond als. Shipward's lease to Nicholas Blacknall, 13 October 1610, Lismore Castle Papers, MS 43,095/2, NLI.

80. Edmund Coppinger's deed to Boyle (8 October 1602) and William Flower and Richard Benson's deed to Boyle (20 November 1602), MS 43,150/2; William Chisshull's discharge to Boyle, 27 June 1604, MS 43,156/2; Edward Lochland's discharge to Boyle, 9 June 1607, MS 43,142/3; Lochland's discharge to Boyle, 16 October 1607, MS 43,142/4; Roger Dalton's lease to Boyle, 19 December 1607, MS 43,149/1; Dalton's mortgage to Boyle, 17 November 1607, MS 43,149/2; Owen Keelties's deed to Boyle, 19 January 1610/1611, MS 43,095/2; David Roche's deed to Boyle, 16 April 1611, Lismore Castle Papers, MS 43,095/3, NLI.

81. Cork MSS, vol. 2, nos. 42 (Terlagh O'Callaghan's lease to Boyle, 23 November 1606), 43 (Conogher O'Callaghan's lease to Boyle, 22 November 1606), 44 (Conogher O'Callaghan's transfer of lease to Boyle, 22 November 1606); vol. 1. no.9, fols. 30v-31r, Chatsworth House. On "standard" trees, see Warde, "Fear of Wood Shortage," 36.

82. Boyle's lease to Christmas Heward, 27 November 1607, Lismore Castle Papers, NLI MS 43,156/2.

83. Ralegh's lease to Robert Carew, 29 September 1589, NLI MS 43,153/1; Boyle's lease to Robert Carew, 18 November 1606, Lismore Castle Papers, NLI MS 43,153/2.

84. Boyle's lease to Thomas Fitz-John Gerald, 20 March 1604/1605, Cork MSS, vol. 1, no. 130, Chatsworth House.

85. The leases that included woodland rights are Michael Burden (17 February 1605/1606), Richard Holland (14 April 1606), and Alexander Potter (20 September 1607), Lismore Castle Papers, MS 43,156/2; William Newman (17 May 1608) and Margrett Rogers (2 August 1608), MS 43,152/1. The only other restriction on woodland use was a ban on tanning in his lease to Thomas Braunch, 20 December 1605, Lismore Castle Papers, MS 43,152/1, NLI.

86. Boyle's lease to Mathew Harris, 20 May 1615, Lismore Castle Papers, MS 43,156/3, NLI.

87. Grant to Boyle, 10 May 1604, MS 43,087/2; Letters patent to Boyle, 23 May 1604, MS 43,087/4; Confirmation of deed between Ralegh and Boyle, 26 August 1604, MS 41,984/4; William Greatrakes to Boyle, 11 May 1604, MS 43,266/1, Lismore Castle Papers, NLI; John Account of iron to be Delivered to Boyle, 5 September 1604, Cork MSS, vol. 1, no. 123, Chatsworth House.

88. Thomas Ball to Boyle, 22 April 1606, Lismore Castle Papers, MS 13,236/3, NLI.

89. Cork MSS, vol. 2, nos. 75 (Pyne to Boyle, 6 October 1607), 79 ("A Note of Iron at Kilmacow," 26 June 1607), 114 (Henry Wright to Boyle, 1 May 1608), 135 [fol. 221] ("Account of Planks Cut to Anthony Hybright of Camphier in Zeeland, Mariner," 19 August 1608), 144, Chatsworth House; Articles of agreement between Cuthbert Boutze, Boyle, and Jonathan Frampton, 26 November 1607, Lismore Castle Papers, MS 43,096, NLI.

90. Cork MSS, vol. 2, nos. 125 (Henry Wright to Boyle, 10 July 1608), 138 (Wright to Boyle, 8 September 1608), 156 (Wright to Boyle, 6 January 1608/1609), Chatsworth House.

91. Cork MSS, vol. 3, nos. 92 (Boyle to the Lord Deputy and Council of Ireland, 3 May 1611), 108 (Boyle, Summary of the Dispute between Richard Boyle and Thomas FitzGerald, 1611), Chatsworth House. I discuss this dispute in a different context in Keith Pluymers, "Cow Trials, Climate Change, and the Causes of Violence," *Environmental History* 25, no. 2 (1 April 2020), 296.

92. Cork MSS, vol. 3, nos. 94 (Lord Deputy to Boyle, 7 July 1611), 128 (Thomas Fitzgerald, "Order to put Boyle in Quiet Possession of Lisfinny," 31 January 1611/1612), Chatsworth House.

93. William Kellet to Boyle, 15 August 1609, Cork MSS, vol. 3, no. 14, Chatsworth House.

94. Chichester to Salisbury, 27 October 1608, SP 63/225, fol. 159, TNA.

95. Abstract of the account between Boyle and John Van Der Bogarde, 6 July 1609, MS 43,296/1; "Such Things as Were Delivered over to Mr Colman as Parcell of the Iron Works [. . .]," 30 September 1609, MS 43,297/1; George Bicke's lease to Thomas Ball, 3 October 1609, MS 43,156/2, NLI; Account for pipe staves between Boyle and Van Der Bogarde, 6 July 1609, Cork MSS, vol. 3, no. 21, Chatsworth House.

96. Agreement between Boyle and Pyne, 1610, MS 43,310/1, NLI. See above for details on Boyle's exemption.

97. "A Proposition Being Made by Henry Wright on Behalf of Richard Boyle Unto Thomas Ball," April 1612, MS 43,281, NLI; Cork MSS, vol. 4, nos. 8 (William Greatrakes and Nicholas Blacknall, "Note on the Award of Land and Timber by Richard Boyle and Thomas Ball," April 25, 1612), 18 (Account between Boyle and Ball, 1612), Chatsworth House.

98. John van der Bogarde account of charges, 10 August 1613, Cork MSS, vol. 4, no. 155, Chatsworth House.

99. Cork MSS, vol. 5, nos. 56 (Richard Blacknall to Boyle, May 1614), 6 (Samuel de Bresine to Boyle, 26 April 1614), Chatsworth House.

100. Cork MSS, vol. 5, nos. 56, 14 (Boyle, License to Thomas Clark, 26 May 1614), 34 (Ensign Croker's Account, May 1614), Chatsworth House.

101. The following leases from Boyle restricted access to stumps and fallen trees: George Benbery (5 July 1616), Osyas Thorne (22 October 1616), Cornelius Gafney (24 January 1616/1617), Joan Ellen (28 May 1617), Thomas Warren (21 April 1618), Thomas Ellwell (20 March 1622/1623) MS 43,152/1; John Lock, 28 October 1616, MS 43,156/3; Ambrosse Marshfielde, 12 December 1617, MS 43,156/4; Walter Nicholas (5 July 1620), John Offman (5 January 1620/1621), Sergeant Walter Jones (7 April 1621) MS 43,156/5; Thomas Coffer (30 June 1627), William Bragg (5 February 1626/1627) MS 43,156/6; Richard Fleming, 14 August 1622, Lismore Castle Papers, MS 43,152/2, NLI. Boyle's lease to Fleming was the first to offer rights to both turf and wood.

102. Leases to James Foster, 14 February 1616/1617, MS 43,156/3; Henry Hull (23 October 1620), Richard Bayly (23 November 1622) MS 43,156/5; Thomas Swayn, 31 March 1628, MS 43,153/5; William Browning, 20 April 1637, Lismore Castle Papers, MS 43,156/11, NLI.

103. Cork MSS, vol. 6, nos. 112 (Thomas Buckwood to Boyle, 7 December 1615), 135 (William Cook to Boyle, 15 December 1615); vol. 5, no. 144 (Nicholas Symonton to Boyle, 13 February 1614/1615), Chatsworth House.

104. Boyle's lease to William Browning, 30 May 1625, MS 43,156/6; Lease to Browning, 20 April 1637, Lismore Castle Papers, MS 43,156/11, NLI.

105. Cork MSS, vol. 6, nos. 135, 150 (Cornelius Gaffny to Boyle, 18 March 1616), Chatsworth House.

106. Cork MSS, vol. 4, no. 160 (John Nobbes to Boyle, 21 March 1613/1614); vol. 5, no. 156 (Herbert Nichollas, 25 February 1614/1615); vol. 6, no. 36 (Nathaniel Curteys to Boyle, 20 June 1615); vol. 9, no. 139 (Walter Cooke to Boyle, 13 December 1618), Chatsworth House; Henry Becher's deed to Boyle, 14 September 1614, Lismore Castle Papers, MS 43,094/2, NLI.

107. Boyle to Chichester, 11 April 1613, MS Carte 62, fol. 137, Bodleian Library; Nicholas Barham to Boyle, 22 March 1615, Cork MSS, vol. 6, no. 155, Chatsworth House; Leases to Humphrey Fisher (20 February 1631/1632), John Binden (20 June 1634), Richard Willoughby (4 August 1637), MS 43,146; Nicholas Barham, 25 August 1637, Lismore Castle Papers, MS 43,156/11, NLI.

108. Henry Becher's lease to Richard Tickner, 15 September 1618, MS 43,156/4; Beecher's deed to Boyle, 2 May 1619, Lismore Castle Papers, MS 43,094/4, NLI.

109. Lease to John Zane (17 July 1619), William Bowlton (30 September 1632), MS 43,141/2; to William Wiseman (9 November 1620), Captain Richard Newce (8 January 1620/1621), John Turner (9 September 1631), Robert Williams (4 March 1633/1634), MS 43,141/3; Francis Barnard (16 August 1631), John West (12 September 1632), William Lowytt (4 October 1633), MS 43,156/8; Walter Haynes, 20 July 1635, MS 43,156/9. The following leases were for properties in the town and granted the right to enter Boyle's turf land to cut and dry fuel: Lease to Evan Wodroffe (3 October 1619), Christopher Burke (7 October 1619), Thomas Rowland (15 October 1620 and 11 September 1632), Nicholas Baker (6 August 1621), Richard Crofte (18 October 1621), Mary Turner (25 February 1632/1633), John Moorley (20 January 1635/1636), MS 43,141/1; Richard Dabson (3 January 1619/1620), John Fenton (13 January 1619/1620), MS 43,156/4; Edward Turner (20 August 1621), William Newman (13 September 1622), Lismore Castle Papers, MS 43,156/5, NLI.

110. Lease to John Offman, 5 January 1620/1621, MS 43,156/5; Richard Fleming, 14 August 1622, Lismore Castle Papers, MS 43,152/2, NLI.

111. Account of Boyle and Sir John Jephson's pipe-stave cutting, 1617, Cork MSS, vol. 8, no. 140. The anonymous account informed Boyle that O'Callaghan's woods were "cleared in September 1616," an indication for clear-cutting. For the agreements between Boyle and the O'Callaghans, see Cork MSS, vol. 5, no. 51 (Agreement between Boyle, Rice A. Pin, John Brothers, John Rice, Conogher O'Callaghan, and Patrick Newgent, 26 May 1614); vol. 9, no. 29 (Articles of agreement between Richard Boyle and Callaghan O'Callaghan, 24 July 1618), Chatsworth House.

112. Agreement between Callaghan O'Callaghan and Christopher Colthurst, 4 May 1617, Cork MSS, vol. 8, no. 23, Chatsworth House.

113. Cork MSS, vol. 9, nos. 5 (John Jephson to Boyle, 22 May 1618), 21 (Jephson to Boyle, 30 June 1618), Chatsworth House.

114. John Hodder to Sir Philip Perceval, Perceval Family Accounts, Add. MSS 46,924, fol. 54, BL.

115. John Brothers to Boyle, 10 July 1620, Cork MSS, vol. 11, no. 72, Chatsworth House.

116. Cork MSS, vol. 4, no. 60 (Dermod McCarthy's deed to Boyle, 10 May 1613); vol. 7, nos. 42 (Dermod McCarthy, Account, 20 May 1616), 54 (McCarthy, Agreement with Boyle, 11 July 1616); vol. 8, nos. 21 (McCarthy to Boyle, 2 May 1617), 134 (McCarthy to Boyle, 2 September 1617); vol. 9, nos. 20 (McCarthy, Agreement, 30 June 1618), 68 (McCarthy, Acquitance for pipe staves, 2 September 1618); vol. 14, no. 53 (McCarthy to Boyle, 20 June 1623), Chatsworth House.

117. J. H. Round and R. M. Armstrong, "Apsley, Sir Allen (1566/7–1630)," *Oxford Dictionary of National Biography*, http://www.oxforddnb.com/view/article/599. In addition, Apsley bore a connection to new world ventures. William Strachey dedicated his history of Virginia to Apsley.

See William Strachey, "The First Book of the First Decade containing the History of Travail into Virginia Britania," MS Ashmole 1758, Bodleian Library. Boyle had been accused in 1599 of undervaluing Apsley's lands to enrich himself, since Boyle had married Apsley's daughter and Apsley's son-and-heir had "willfully drowned himself." See "Articles to be proved against Richard Boyle," 17 February 1598/1599, Add. MSS 19831, fol. 8, BL. For more on Apsley's Virginian connections, see David Edwards, "Virginian Connections: The Wider Atlantic Setting of Boyle's Munster Estate and Clientele," in Edwards and Rynne, *The Colonial World of Richard Boyle*, 83–84. For Apsley's role in Boyle's Munster social networks, see David Edwards, "The Land-Grabber's Accomplices: Richard Boyle's Munster Affinity, 1588–1603," in Edwards and Rynne, *The Colonial World of Richard Boyle*, 166–88.

118. Note of the Arrears of Rent from Apsley, c. 1627, MS 43,298/2; Nicholas Blacknall to Boyle, 8 July 1618, MS 13,236/15; Apsley to Boyle, 30 March 1619, Lismore Castle Papers, MS 43,266/9, NLI.

119. Correspondence between Apsley and Boyle, October–November 1623, Lismore Castle Papers, MS 13,236/12, NLI; Thomas Fletewood to Sir Thomas Broland, 27 November 1623, Lismore Castle papers, MS 43,266/12, NLI.

120. Paddy O'Sullivan, "The East India Company at Dundaniel," *Bandon Historical Journal* 4 (1988), see, esp., pp. 13–14; Nunan, "Boyle and the East India Company in Co. Cork: A Case Study in Colonial Competition." Petition of William Burrell to the King, SP 63/235, fols. 110-11, TNA. For Boyle's relationship with Banaster, see Cork MSS, vol. 8, no. 33 (Banaster to Boyle, 10 May 1617); vol. 9, no. 72 (Banaster to Boyle, 9 October 1618), Chatsworth House; Banaster to Boyle, 20 September 1619, Lismore Castle Papers, MS 13,236/18, NLI.

121. Henry Wright, "An Estimate What a tonne of Barre Iron will stande [. . .]," 16 April 1619, Lismore Castle Papers, MS 43,297/2; Boyle's Answer to Thomas Ball's Complaint and Boyle's relation of the dispute with Ball, c. 1618, MS 43,280; Ball to Boyle, 16 July 1619, MS 13,236/16; Ball to Boyle, 6 October 1619, MS 13,236/18; To Boyle concerning the dispute with Burrell and Ball, 11 January 1619/1620, Lismore Castle Papers, MS 13,237/1, NLI; Boyle to the Privy Council, 12 January 1619/1620, SP 63/235, fol. 128, PC 2/30, fols. 307 (Privy Council to Boyle, 25 October 1619), 447 (Privy Council on Boyle v. Ball, 10 March 1619/1620), 459 (Privy Council to the Lord President of Munster, 23 March 1619/1620), 621 ("At the Star Chamber," 15 November 1620), TNA.

122. Gillespie, "Meal and Money," 75–95; Gillespie, "Harvest Crisis," 5–18.

123. Cork MSS, vol. 10, no. 64 (John Doughtie to Boyle, 3 February 1619/1620); vol. 11, nos. 36 (George Hellier to Boyle, 19 May 1620), 62 (Christopher Woodward to Boyle, 5 July 1620), 116 (Christian Bor to Boyle, 17 August 1620), 199 (Richard Challoner to Boyle, 14 November 1620); vol. 12, no. 33 (John Doughtie to Boyle, 3 July 1621); vol. 13, nos. 58 (Hellier to Boyle, 29 July 1622), 181 (Hellier to Boyle, 3 February 1622/1623), Chatsworth House; Hellier to Boyle, 18 June 1622, Lismore Castle Papers, MS 13,237/2, NLI.

124. Cork MSS, vol. 10, no. 90 (Hellier to Boyle, 12 March 1619/1620); vol. 12, no. 2 (Hellier to Boyle, 28 March 1621), Chatsworth House.

125. Richard Blacknall to Peter Baker, 7 February 1621/1622, Cork MSS, vol. 12, no. 136, Chatsworth House; Baker to Boyle, 4 and 9 December 1623, MS 43,266/12. On Boyle's mines, see Paul Rondelez, "The Metallurgical Enterprises of Richard Boyle, First Earl of Cork," in Edwards and Rynne, *The Colonial World of Richard Boyle*, 112–20. Rondelez discusses the water pump at Ballyregan on p. 115 and reproduces a contemporary sketch of it in Plate 9a.

126. Henry Wright to Boyle, 13 December 1623, Lismore Castle Papers, MS 13,237/7, NLI; Richard Blacknall to Boyle, 3 March 1623/1624, Cork MSS, vol. 14, no. 301, Chatsworth House.

127. Cork MSS, vol. 11, no. 26 (John Bor to Boyle, 27 April 1620); vol. 12, nos. 28 (Christian Bor to Boyle, 24 June 1621), 29 (C. Bor to Boyle, 24 June 1621), 157 (C. Bor to Boyle, 11 March 1621/1622); vol. 13, nos. 5 (C. Bor to Boyle, 2 April 1622), 27 (C. Bor to Boyle, 15 May 1622), 145 (Peter Bor to Boyle, 7 December 1622); vol. 16, no. 176 (Peter de Latfour, "Account for iron with Richard Boyle," 1629), Chatsworth House; Thomas Ridgeway to Boyle, 3 December 1623, MS 13,237/6. Boyle and Roger Jones, "Copies of letters to Roger Hooker concerning ironworks," 4 August 1631; George Hooker to Boyle, 12 July 1631; Thomas Pettyward, Edmond Trimbile, and Samuel Gott to Boyle, 21 March 1630/1631, MS 13,237/13; G. Hooker to Boyle, 23 September 1631; Pettyward et al. to Boyle, 5 November 1631, MS 13,237/14; G. Hooker to Boyle, 29 March 1631; Pettyward et al. to Boyle, 16 February 1631/1632, MS 13,266/15; Roger Pettyward to Boyle, 25 April 1632; Thomas Bourke to Boyle, 15 March 1633/1634; G. Hooker to Boyle, 30 January 1630/1631; T. Pettyward to Boyle, 14 August 1632, Lismore Castle Papers, MS 43,266/16, NLI. For Boyle's relationship with Philip Burlamachi, see Cork MSS, vol. 17, nos. 1 (Burlamachi to Boyle, 30 March 1630), 6 (Burlamachi to Boyle, 12 April 1630), 67 (Burlamachi to Boyle, 16 April 1631), 81 (Burlamachi to Boyle, 26 July 1631), Chatsworth House; A. V. Judges, "Philip Burlamachi: A Financier of the Thirty Years' War," *Economica*, no. 18 (November 1926): 285–300. Thomas Cogswell discusses Burlamachi's role in numerous deals involving Virginia tobacco; Thomas Cogswell, "'In the Power of the State': Mr. Anys's Project and the Tobacco Colonies, 1626-1628," *English Historical Review* 123, no. 500 (February 2008): 35–64.

128. William Wiseman to Boyle, 2 April 1634, MS 13,237/17; Augustine Atkins to Boyle, 4 June 1634, Lismore Castle Papers, MS 13,237/18, NLI; Atkins to Boyle, 3 February 1633/1634, Cork MSS, vol. 17, no. 191, Chatsworth House.

129. Atkins to Boyle, 27 February 1637/1638, Cork MSS, vol. 19, no. 119, Chatsworth House.

130. Several of Boyle's leases made no mention of woodlands at all. See the leases to Henry Gay (22 October 1630), William Bluett (5 January 1630/1631), William Todd (8 January 1634/1635), William Jones (21 September 1635), John Marren (22 September 1635), Thomas Carter (7 October 1635), Lawrence Lyne (17 October 1635), MS 43,152/2; John Warren (22 September 1635), Roger Bartlett (26 September 1635), MS 43,156/9; Alice Halin, 25 October 1636, MS 43,156/10; Rebecca Uphall (29 October 1636), John Sanders (5 December 1636), Richard Casey (7 December 1636), Richard Tylor (28 March 1637), MS 43,152/3. Only one lease limited wood rights to downed trees and roots: John Symonds, 10 November 1634, MS 43,152/2. Some longtime tenants retained the right to cut wood for fuel and construction without preapproval from Boyle's woodward: William Greatrakes, 24 April 1635, MS 43,156/9. Boyle required one tenant to build with sawed timber, a move away from construction with windfalls: Thomas Taylor, 17 October 1635, Lismore Castle Papers, MS 43,152/2, NLI.

131. See Boyle's leases to William Bragg, 5 February 1627/1627, MS 43,156/6; Frances Poole, 6 October 1637, MS 43,152/3; Walter Nicholas, 5 July 1620, Lismore Castle Papers, MS 43,156/5, NLI.

132. See leases to Hugh Roberts (20 March 1620/1621), Edward Power (6 October 1623), MS 43,156/5; John Lowntagh, 3 April 1628, MS 43,151; Thomas Pomfrett, 20 March 1636/1637, MS 43,156/10; Thomas Mason, 9 September 1631, MS 43,156/8; Thomas Notte to Boyle, 20 April 1624, Lismore Castle Papers, MS 13,237/9, NLI.

133. See leases from Morgan Polden to John Powell (20 June 1628), John Shulte (20 March 1628/1629), John Fowller (1 June 1629), and George Glanfield (28 August 1629), MS 43,156/7; to William Richard, 26 March 1630, MS 43,156/6; to Nicholas Shulte, 29 September 1631, MS 43,156/8; to Catherine Burlye, 18 April 1636, Lismore Castle Papers, MS 43,156/9, NLI. Three

years prior to this string of leases, Polden had granted land without any protections for young timber trees. See the lease to Robert Crosse, 8 January 1624/1625, Lismore Castle Papers, MS 43,156/6, NLI.

134. John Walley to Boyle, 28 September 1638, Cork MSS, vol. 19, no. 62, Chatsworth House; Walley, Report on estate business, 18 December 1638, Lismore Castle Papers, MS 43,266/17, NLI.

135. Cork MSS, vol. 20, no. 79* (Lieutenant Muschamp to Boyle, 16 July 1639); vol. 19, nos. 85 (Adam Waring to Boyle, 1 January 1638/1639), 97 (Moylin O'Cantry to Boyle, 19 January 1638/1639); vol. 20, nos. 11 (John Walley to Boyle, 21 April 1639), 68 (Walley to Boyle, 20 June 1639), Chatsworth House; Walley report to Boyle, 28 January 1638/1639, Lismore Castle Papers, MS 13,237/21, NLI.

136. Cork MSS, vol. 21, nos. 16 (Clopton Waldegrave to Boyle, 27 May 1640), 20 (John Walley to Boyle, 30 May 1640), 30 (John Nevelock to Boyle, 10 July 1640), Chatsworth House; Walley reports to Boyle, 13 April 1640, and 26 August 1640, MS 13,237/25.

137. John Clutterbooke to Sir Philip Perceval, 4 February 1640/1641, Add. MSS 46,924, fol. 186, BL.

138. Chichester to Salisbury, 2 October 1605, SP 63/217, fol. 165r; Chichester to James I, 31 October 1610, SP 63/229, fol. 171v, TNA.

139. SP 63/229, fol. 171v, TNA.

140. SP 63/217, fol. 165r; SP 63/229, fol. 171v, TNA.

141. Council for Virginia, "A True Declaration of the Estate of the Colonie in Virginia [. . .]" in Force, ed., *Tracts and Other Papers*, 3:25.

142. Ibid., 3:25.

143. Everett notes that Ireland did not fit easily into perceptions of landscape grounded in England or in Ralegh's Guiana and thus proved frustrating for many contemporaries attempting to govern it. Complaints about scarcity often resulted. I would add that its uncertain status also created frustrations for leaders and promoters in other colonial enterprises. Everett, *The Woods of Ireland*, 110–12.

144. Audrey Horning refers to the individuals following this pattern as "shapeshifters" and argues for their importance in defining the Atlantic World. See Horning, "Shapeshifters and Mimics," 27–34.

Chapter 3

1. Kupperman, "The Puzzle of the American Climate"; Pluymers, "Taming the Wilderness."

2. For more on the metaphor of the cornucopia and its wider ideological significance, see Jonsson, "The Origins of Cornucopianism."

3. Kathleen Donegan, *Seasons of Misery: Catastrophe and Colonial Settlement in Early America* (Philadelphia: University of Pennsylvania Press, 2014); Rachel B. Herrmann, "The 'Tragicall Historie': Cannibalism and Abundance in Colonial Jamestown," *William and Mary Quarterly* 68, no. 1 (1 January 2011): 47–74.

4. Timothy Silver, *A New Face on the Countryside: Indians, Colonists, and Slaves in South Atlantic Forests, 1500–1800*, Studies in Environment and History (New York: Cambridge University Press, 1990), 1–5; G. P. Fleming, K. D. Patterson, and K. Taverna, *The Natural Communities of Virginia: a Classification of Ecological Community Groups and Community Types*. Third approximation, Version 3.2 (Richmond, VA: Virginia Department of Conservation and Recreation, Division of Natural Heritage, 2020), www.dcr.virginia.gov/natural-heritage/natural-communities/.

5. Helen C. Rountree and E. Randolph Turner, *Before and After Jamestown: Virginia's Powhatans and Their Predecessors* (Gainesville: University Press of Florida, 2002); Helen C. Rountree, "The Powhatans and the English: A Case of Multiple Conflicting Agendas," in *Powhatan Foreign Relations, 1500–1722*, ed. Helen C. Rountree (Charlottesville: University Press of Virginia, 1993), 173–205. On the use of fire and on the construction of clearances for agriculture in a wooded landscape, see Martin D. Gallivan, *The Powhatan Landscape: An Archaeological History of the Algonquian Chesapeake*, Society and Ecology in Island and Coastal Archaeology (Gainesville: University Press of Florida, 2016), 31–32.

6. James Rice, "Escape from Tsenacommacah: Chesapeake Algonquians and the Powhatan Menace," in *The Atlantic World and Virginia, 1550–1624*, ed. Peter Mancall (Chapel Hill: Omohundro Institute of Early American History and Culture and the University of North Carolina Press, 2007), 97–118, 104–7 (on the Little Ice Age, diet, and agriculture); Martin D. Gallivan, "Powhatan's Werowocomoco: Constructing Place, Polity, and Personhood in the Chesapeake, C.E. 1200–C.E. 1609," *American Anthropologist* 109, no. 1 (1 March 2007): 85–100; Gallivan, *The Powhatan Landscape*, 88–90 (on pollen and charcoal analysis), 104–40 (for a detailed study of the Chickahominy, who remained independent from Powhatan rule), 132–39 and 164 (for a nuanced analysis of increased maize consumption). Sam White argues that the Little Ice Age shaped Wahunsenacawh's expansion and threats to it; see White, *A Cold Welcome*, 121–23.

7. Horning, *Ireland in the Virginian Sea*, 151–60; for example, John Smith simultaneously described evidence for significant agriculture and claimed that the land was "a plaine wildernesse as God first made it." See Smith, *Generall Historie*, 22; Smith adapted writings on commodities from Roanoke, see 9–15. As I have written elsewhere, contemporary husbandry guides and much promotional literature suggested that land that had proved fertile but was currently neglected was ideal for acquisition. In addition, for a discussion of the tension between easy profits and the need for labor, see Pluymers, "Taming the Wilderness."

8. Horning, "Shapeshifters and Mimics," 29. English colonization efforts along the James River first came under the auspices of the Virginia Company, a joint-stock venture that, along with other chartered merchant companies, drew on a wide range of investors beyond well-established merchants. Theodore K. Rabb, "Investment in English Overseas Enterprise, 1575–1630," *Economic History Review* 19, no. 1 (1 January 1966): 70–81; Robert Brenner, *Merchants and Revolution: Commercial Change, Political Conflict, and London's Overseas Traders, 1550–1653* (New York: Verso, 2003). On the diverse investors in joint-stock companies, particularly women, and the investment forms targeted and used by women investors, see Misha Ewen, "Women Investors and the Virginia Company in the Early Seventeenth Century," *Historical Journal*, 15 March 2019, 1–22.

9. R. I. [Robert Johnson], *Nova Brittania*, pp. 10 (unnumbered), 17 (unnumbered); Councell for Virginia, *A true declaration of the estate of the colonie in Virginia* [. . .] (London, 1610), 55; "Instructions, orders, and constitutions [. . .] to Sir Thomas Gates, governor of Virginia," MS Ashmole 1147, vol.7 no. 2, fols. 187–89, Bodleian Library. On sericulture and the Huguenot who were essential to English silk-making, see Owen Stanwood, *The Global Refuge: Huguenots in an Age of Empire* (New York: Oxford University Press, 2020), 71–103, esp. pp. 74–78. I am grateful to Owen Stanwood for sharing his work with me prior to publication.

10. Thomas Harriot, *A briefe and true report of the new found land of Virginia* (Frankfurt, 1590), 10; [Johnson], *Nova Brittannia*, 16 (unnumbered).

11. William Strachey, *The Historie of Travell into Virginia Britania (1612)*, ed. Louis B. Wright and Virginia Freund (London, 1953), 132; Smith, *General Historie*, 71–72; Edward Neal Hartley,

Ironworks on the Saugus: The Lynn and Braintree Ventures of the Company of Undertakers of the Ironworks in New England (Norman: University of Oklahoma Press, 1971), 29–30. That the EIC would be interested in and aware of actions in Virginia was no accident. There was significant overlap in investors in both companies and, by the end of the 1610s, their internal politics had grown significantly entangled; see Mishra, *A Business of State*, 97–98.

12. McCracken, "Charcoal-Burning Ironworks," 128; Chichester to Salisbury, 12 December 1610, SP 63/229, fol. 192, TNA.

13. Council for Virginia, "A True Declaration of the Estate of the Colonie in Virginia [...]" in Force, ed., *Tracts and Other Papers*, 3:26.

14. See Chapter 2.

15. For example, see William Strachey's dedicatory to Sir Allen Apsley, an Irish planter and commissioner for the navy. William Strachey, "History of Travail into Virginia Britania," MS Ashmole 1758, Bodleian Library.

16. John Ferrar and Richard Caswell, "Warrant & receipt, 3 Aug 1621," FP 298, VCA; Ferrar, "Warrant, 13 Aug 1621, & bill, 8–13 Aug [1621]," FP 301, VCA; Kingsbury, *The Records of the Virginia Company*, 3:489; Nicholas M. Luccketti, William M. Kelso, and Beverly A. Straube, "Jamestown Rediscovery Field Report 1994" (Jamestown, VA: Association for the Preservation of Virginia Antiquities (APVA), 1994), 27, 31–32; Beverly A. Straube and Nicholas M. Luccketti, "1995 Interim Field Report" (Jamestown, VA: APVA, 1996), 46–51; William M. Kelso and Beverly A. Straube, "1996 Interim Report" (Richmond, VA: APVA, 1997), 7; David Givens et al., "2007–2010 Interim Report on the Preservation Virginia Excavations at Jamestown, Virginia," ed. William M. Kelso, Beverly A. Straube, and Daniel Schmidt (Richmond, VA: APVA, 2012).

17. Wesley Frank Craven, *Dissolution of the Virginia Company: The Failure of a Colonial Experiment* (New York, 1932), 24–40.

18. Seeking experts from the European continent was common in domestic and colonial projects. See Ash, *Power, Knowledge, and Expertise in Elizabethan England*.

19. John Pory to Edwin Sandys, 12 June 1620, FP 177, VCA.

20. Governor and Council in Virginia, "Answer to the particular branches of the Charter for setting up more solid commodities," May 1621, FP 256, VCA.

21. FP 177; FP 256; Kingsbury, *The Records of the Virginia Company*, 3:486–87; 1:392–93. Conflicts with foreign artisans were extremely common. The most spectacular incident involved Italian glassmakers smashing their own furnace in displeasure; see "Horning, Shapeshifters and Mimics," 32.

22. It also faced a host of issues that made success unlikely. English investors continued to believe that the North American red mulberry (*morus rubra*) and the Asian white mulberry (*morus alba*) were variants of the same plant and believed that silkworms would gladly consume the leaves of either type of tree. Moreover, contemporary knowledge of silkworm reproduction led adventurers and other contemporary sericulturalists to treat the eggs of the domesticated silk moth as though they were plant seeds, capable of being dried, stored, and planted. Contemporaries even used the term "seed" to refer to the silkworm eggs they shipped across the Atlantic. See Charles E. Hatch, "Mulberry Trees and Silkworms: Sericulture in Early Virginia," *Virginia Magazine of History and Biography* 65, no. 1 (1 January 1957): 3–61.

23. Smith, *A Map of Virginia*, 11.

24. In his annotations of James I's instructions, Sir Edwin Sandys noted his affirmation for James's suggestion. See Edwin Sandys and Francis Carter, Copy of Instructions for Sir George Yeardley, FP 92; Richard Ferrar, "Report of Sir George Yeardlyes going Governor to Virginia,"

5 December 1618, FP 93, VCA. The Virginia Assembly ordered each settler to plant six mulberry trees per year for seven years, see Kingsbury, *The Records of the Virginia Company*, 3:166. On James's enthusiasm for silk, see Stanwood, *The Global Refuge*, 151.

25. Nicholas Ferrar to William Ferrar, 17 January 1618/1619, FP 99, VCA.

26. William Weldon to Edwin Sandys, 16 January 1619/1620, FP 145, VCA.

27. Warren M. Billings, *Sir William Berkeley and the Forging of Colonial Virginia* (Baton Rouge: Louisiana State University Press, 2004), 71; Joan Thirsk, *Alternative Agriculture: A History from the Black Death to the Present Day* (Oxford: Oxford University Press, 1997), 125–26; John Pory to Edwin Sandys, 14 January 1619/1620, FP 144; Pory to Sandys, 12 June 1620, FP 177, VCA.

28. Neil Kenny, *Curiosity in Early Modern Europe: Word Histories* (Wiesbaden: Harrassowitz, 1998); Robert Evans and Alexander Marr, *Curiosity and Wonder from the Renaissance to the Enlightenment* (Burlington, VT: Ashgate, 2006); Findlen, "Inventing Nature: Commerce, Art, and Science."

29. John Bonoeil, *Observations to Be Followed, for the Making of Fit Roomes, to Keepe Silk-Wormes in: As Also, for the Best Manner of Planting of Mulbery Trees, to Feed Them* (London, 1620); Warrant to pay John Bonoeil, 22 May 1622, FP 379, VCA; Kingsbury, *The Records of the Virginia Company*, 3:397–400, 474, 634–37; for more on these French vignerons and seventeenth century Huguenot migration and claims to expertise making silk and wine, see Stanwood, *The Global Refuge*, ch. 3.

30. Bonoeil, *Observations to Be Followed*, 12–13, 14, 16–17.

31. John Bonoeil, *His Maiesties Gracious Letter to the Earle of South-Hampton, Treasurer, and to the Councell and Company of Virginia Heere: Commanding the Present Setting Up of Silke Works, and Planting of Vines in Virginia.* (London, 1622), 2, 6–8, 31–33.

32. Kingsbury, *The Records of the Virginia Company*, 4:68; Bonoeil, *Observations to Be Followed*. See the list appended at the end of the pamphlet; Thomas Newce to Sandys, 27 May 1621, FP 251, VCA. Mine is a conservative estimate. Stanwood estimates that Bonoeil's plan called for planting 2,000–3,000 mulberry trees, at minimum. See Stanwood, *The Global Refuge*, 152. Difficulties facing the exploitation of scattered trees remained a feature for European colonists and merchants. See, for example, failed efforts to create mahogany plantations and the competitions over skill harvesting scattered trees in dense forests discussed in Jennifer L. Anderson, *Mahogany: The Costs of Luxury in Early America* (Cambridge, MA: Harvard University Press, 2012), 210–49.

33. Kingsbury, *Records of the Virginia Company of London*, 1:258 ("shortly"); Bluett, "Account for Southampton Hundred," 1619–20, FP 142, VCA. "Bluett" and "Middleton" appear frequently in the Wealden Iron Research Group's database of ironworkers; see http://www.wirgdata.org/. For work on the Middleton family, see King, "The Iron Trade in England and Wales," esp. 3n13, 5–6, 11–12, 15, ch. 4. For more on the Middleton enterprises in Staffordshire, see P. W. King, "The Development of the Iron Industry in South Staffordshire in the 17th Century: History and Myth," *Transactions of the Staffordshire Archaeological and Historical Society* 35 (1996): 59–76, esp. 64–68. On David Middleton's relationship with Sackville Crowe, who later acquired part of the royal ironworks in the Forest of Dean and was associated with the Throckmorton family's efforts to produce iron in the Forest, see Henry Cleere and David Crossley, *The Iron Industry of the Weald* (Atlantic Highlands, NJ: Humanities Press, 1985), 74.

34. David Middylton [Middleton], "Coppie of Instructions given Mr Hayle," [1619?], FP 136, VCA; Benjamin Bluett, "Account for Southampton Hundred," 1619–1620, FP 142, VCA; David Midylton [?], "Account for ironwork, 22 Jan 1619/20," 1619–1620, FP 148, VCA; John Cuff

[?] Thomas Norget, "Notes for Midleton's and Bluett's account & Reciept, 15 March 1619/20, FP 160, VCA; Charles E. Hatch Jr. and Thurlow Gates Gregory, "The First American Blast Furnace, 1619–1622: The Birth of a Mighty Industry on Falling Creek in Virginia," *Virginia Magazine of History and Biography* 70, no. 3 (July 1962): 266–67; James A. Mulholland, *History of Metals in Colonial America* (Tuscaloosa: University of Alabama Press, 1981), 22–24.

35. Kingsbury, *Records of the Virginia Company of London*, 1:307–8 ("Convertinge," 1:307), 585–87 ("sorely weakened," 1:587). The company did not inform the donor about the investment. The details only emerged in 1622 after Dust and Ashes attempted to make a second donation and asked for a report on the results from his earlier gift. Anonymous gifts to establish schools or churches in Virginia were not uncommon. See Kingsbury, *Records of the Virginia Company of London*, 3:576.

36. George Yeardley to Sandys, 7 June 1620, FP 175 ("great blow"); Governor and Council of Virginia, "Answer to the particular branches of the Charter for setting up more solid commodities," May 1621, FP 256 ("worke"); Proclamation of the Virginia Company, 17 May 1620, FP 173; Yeardley to Sandys, n.d. [November 1620?] FP 194, VCA.

37. Middleton's family and commercial connections had problems closer to home. The partnership to build ironworks in Staffordshire was dissolving amid court proceedings and attempts to sell off forge materials. King, "The Development of the Iron Industry," 64–67.

38. Michael Lapworth to John Ferrar, 26 June 1621, FP 268, VCA.

39. Lorena S. Walsh, *Motives of Honor, Pleasure, and Profit: Plantation Management in the Colonial Chesapeake, 1607–1763* (Chapel Hill: Omohundro Institute of Early American History and Culture and the University of North Carolina Press, 2010), 48–54; Instructions, 24 July 1621, FP 285, VCA; Kingsbury, *The Records of the Virginia Company*, 1:472, 476, 3:581–88.

40. Kingsbury, *The Records of the Virginia Company of London*, 1:352–53, 475–76, 623, 3:402–4; J. Frederick Fausz, "John Berkeley (ca. 1560–1622)" in *Dictionary of Virginia Biography*, ed. John T. Kneebone et al. (Richmond: Library of Virginia, 1998) 1:451–52.

41. Silver, *A New Face on the Countryside*, 1–5, 14–26; Lyle E. Browning, "Falling Creek Ironworks: Past, Geophysics, and Future," *Quarterly Bulletin of the Archeological Society of Virginia* 60, no. 1 (March 2005): 43–55; "The Natural Communities of Virginia Classification of Ecological Community Groups," *Virginia Department of Conservation and Recreation*, http://www .dcr.virginia.gov/natural_heritage/natural_communities/ncoverview.shtml. For a discussion of limonite, see D. A. Crerar, G. W. Knox, and J. L. Means, "Biogeochemistry of Bog Iron in the New Jersey Pine Barrens," *Chemical Geology* 24, nos. 1–2 (January 1979): 111–35. For charcoal manufacturing, see John Evelyn, *Sylva; or, A Discourse of Forest Trees* [. . .] (London, 1670), 191–95.

42. Smyth, *The Lives of the Berkeleys*, 2:254, 298; Hart, *Royal Forest*, 87–99; Grant to Richard Challoner, 6 April 1621, SP 14/141, fol. 158, TNA; King, "Iron Trade in England and Wales," 81; "Forest of Dean The Difference of the Bargains," 23 February 1618/1619, "Touching the business of Dean Forest by Sir Edward Coke," 21 February 1618/1619, "Waste Committed in the Forrest 1615–1618," 23 February 1618/1619, D3921/I/43, Gloucestershire Archives [Transcript and copies of "Papers relating to the Forest of Deane," Lansdowne MS 166/94, BL]; Fulk Grevill, Order to suspend cutting down timber, 29 March 1618, D9125/1/3031, Gloucestershire Archives. For details of the Berkeley Hundred Plantation, see Kingsbury, *The Records of the Virginia Company of London*, 3:109–14, 190, 207–10. See also Eric Gethyn-Jones, *George Thorpe and the Berkeley Company: A Gloucestershire Enterprise in Virginia* (Gloucester, UK: Sutton, 1982.)

43. Lorena Walsh has argued for the sophistication of the Berkeley Hundred investors. See Walsh, *Motives of Honor, Pleasure, and Profit*, 48–54.

44. Cork MSS, vol. 11, no. 199 (Richard Challoner to Richard Boyle, 14 November 1620); vol. 12 nos. 33 (John Doughtie to Boyle, 3 July 1621), 68 (Doughtie to Boyle, 29 October 1621), 99 (George Hellier to Boyle, 13 December 1621); vol. 13, no. 58 (Hellier to Boyle, 29 June 1622), Chatsworth House; Hellier to Boyle, June 18, 1622, Lismore Castle Papers, MS 13237/2, NLI.

45. Kingsbury, *Records of the Virginia Company of London*, 3:178–89, 195–96, 417–18; "Reasons to move the Privy Council to grant licence to export iron ore, & c. to Newfoundland," April 1620, Colonial Office (CO) 1/1, no. 50, fol. 162, TNA; on earlier Newfoundland proposals and their connections with metalworking, see Amundsen, "Thinking Metallurgically;" Horning also notes the failed Newfoundland ironworks and treats it as a serious effort in the context of other similar projects around the Atlantic. Horning, "Shapeshifters and Mimics," 31.

46. Kingsbury, *The Records of the Virginia Company of London*, 3:178–89 ("iron for the mills," 3:182), 207–10 ("iron oare," 3:208, brackets in original), 446–47 ("mason," 3:446–47), 1:623; George Thorpe to Edwin Sandys, 15 May 1621, FP 247, VCA. The company used the phrase "great forwardnes" to describe the state of the ironworks in a later response to critics of the company. See General Assembly in Virginia, "Answer to the Unmasking of Virginia," 16 February 1623/1624, FP 527, VCA; Walsh, *Motives of Honor, Pleasure, and Profit*, 48–54.

47. Kingsbury, *The Records of the Virginia Company of London*, 3:537 ("Massacre"), 548, 565, 670–71; Frederic W. Gleach, *Powhatan's World and Colonial Virginia: A Conflict of Cultures* (Lincoln: University of Nebraska Press, 1997), 3–4 ("corrective"), 148–58; John Sountherne, "A Liste of such Woorkmen [. . .] now wantinge for ye Supplie of The Irone Woorkes," 1622–1623, FP 449, VCA; James D. Rice echoes Gleach's analysis. See James Rice, *Nature and History in the Potomac Country: From Hunter-Gatherers to the Age of Jefferson* (Baltimore: Johns Hopkins University Press, 2009), 86–87.

48. Philip Alexander Bruce, *Economic History of Virginia in the Seventeenth Century*, 2 vols. (New York: Macmillan, 1907), 2:444–52; Hartley, *Ironworks on the Saugus*, 29–43. The narrative of the discovery of the Falling Creek site can be found in Thurlow Gates Gregory, "Iron of America Was Made First in Virginia" 1957, MSS 7:3 HD9510 G861:1, Virginia Historical Society; Hatch and Gregory, "The First American Blast Furnace." For subsequent archaeology appearing to confirm Hatch and Gregory's interpretation, see Thomas F. Higgins III et al., *Archaeological Investigations of Site 44CF7, Falling Creek Iron Works, and Vicinity, Chesterfield County, Virginia*, Virginia Department of Historic Resources Survey and Planning Series, no. 4 (Richmond, VA: Virginia Department of Historic Resources, 1995); Howard A. MacCord Sr., "Exploratory Excavations at the First Ironworks in America," in *Pots, Pipes, and Trash Pits*, ed. Edward Bottoms and Cynthia S. Hansen (Chesapeake: Archaeological Society of Virginia, 2006), 1:95–107. For subsequent histories accepting these conclusions, see Mulholland, *History of Metals in Colonial America*, 22–24; John S. Salmon, "Ironworks on the Frontier: Virginia's Iron Industry, 1607–1783," *Virginia Cavalcade* 35 (Spring 1986): 184–91; Robert B. Gordon, "Industrial Archeology of American Iron and Steel," *IA: The Journal of the Society for Industrial Archeology* 18, nos. 1–2 (1992): 5–18; Robert B. Gordon, *American Iron, 1607–1900* (Baltimore: Johns Hopkins University Press, 1996), 55; John Bezís-Selfa, *Forging America: Ironworkers, Adventurers, and the Industrious Revolution* (Ithaca, NY: Cornell University Press, 2004), 45–49. For recent work questioning these conclusions, see Geoffrey Jones, "Geophysical Investigation at the Falling Creek Ironworks, an Early Industrial Site in Virginia," *Archaeological Prospection* 8, no. 4 (December 2001): 247–56; Browning, "Falling Creek Ironworks: Past, Geophysics, and Future;" Horning, *Ireland in the Virginian Sea*, 309. At present, archaeologist Lyle Browning is developing plans to further explore Falling Creek. For current projects at the site, see "Falling Creek Ironworks," http://www.fallingcreekironworks.org/.

49. "A note of charges lead out by mee Benimain Bluet," 10 January 1619/1620, FP 142, VCA; Colin Rynne, "The Social Archaeology of Plantation-Period Ironworks in Ireland: Immigrant Industrial Communities and Technology Transfer, c.1560–1640," in *Plantation Ireland: Settlement and Material Culture, c.1550–c.1700*, ed. James Lyttleton and Colin Rynne (Dublin: Four Courts, 2009), 248–64, esp. 260–61.

50. John Southerne, "A liste of such Woorkmen, and other Necessaries as are now wantinge for the Supplie of The Irone Woorkes," n.d. [January? 1622/1623], FP 449, VCA.

51. Richard S. Smith, "Sir Francis Willoughby's Ironworks, 1570–1610," *Renaissance and Modern Studies* 11, no. 1 (1 January 1967): 100.

52. Rabb, "Investment in English Overseas Enterprise"; Theodore K. Rabb, *Jacobean Gentleman: Sir Edwin Sandys, 1561–1629* (Princeton, NJ: Princeton University Press, 1998), 356–63; Cogswell, "'In the Power of the State.'" For contemporary commentaries on the tobacco contract, see "Lord Sackville's Paper respecting Virginia, 1613–1631, II.: C. Concerning the Tobacco Contract," *American Historical Review* 27, no. 4 (July 1922): 738–65; "A Comparison In one particular betweene the Contract made by the Companies for Virginia and Summer Islands. [. . .]," n.d. [c. 1622], Egerton MSS 2978, fols. 10v–11r, BL; "Considerations Touching the New Contract for Tobacco," 1625, Add. MS 12496, fol. 420, BL.

53. Petition from Plymouth, Dartmouth, and other Western Port towns, 23 May 1623, PC 2/31, fol. 715, TNA. The attempt to ban Dutch ships carrying Baltic goods from landing in English ports began in 1620. Two members of the Virginia Company's governing council, Thomas Smyth and John Wolstenholme, persuaded the Privy Council to ban Dutch shipping. See Petition of the Eastland Merchants to the King, 26 June 1620, SP 14/115, fols. 169–72; "Report by [Sir John Wolstenholme and others], the referees on the [Eastland Company's] petition," n.d. [c. 1620], SP 14/118, fol. 236; "Reasons assigned by the Eastland merchants for the great decay in their trade," n.d. [c. 1620], SP 14/118, fols. 230–31. Order to grant the Eastland Merchant's Request, 11 July 1622, SP 14/132, fol. 48, TNA.

54. David Kirby, *Northern Europe in the Early Modern Period: The Baltic World, 1492–1772* (New York: Longman, 1990), 149; Chris Evans, Owen Jackson, and Göran Rydén, "Baltic Iron and the British Iron Industry in the Eighteenth Century," *Economic History Review* 55, no. 4 (1 November 2002): 642–65; Chris Evans and Göran Rydén, *Baltic Iron in the Atlantic World in the Eighteenth Century* (Boston: Brill, 2007), 31–32.

55. McCracken, "Charcoal-Burning Ironworks," 126–35.

56. Rice, "Escape from Tsenacommacah," 136–38 ("ecological," 136); "Sir Fr[ancis] Wiate [Wyatt] from Virginie whilst Gov[ernor]," n.d. [after 1622], Add. MSS 62135, fols. 23–24 ("strong Palisade," fol. 23v), BL; Francis Wyatt and Council of Virginia to the Privy Council, 17 May 1626, Records of the Colonial Office (CO) 1/4, fols. 21r–22v ("stockt," "wynning," fol. 21v); Samuel Mathews and William Claybourne, "A Proposition concerning the winning of the Forest," 17 May 1626, CO 1/4, fols. 28r–v ("winning," fol. 28r), TNA.

57. Philip Levy writes extensively on the relationship between the palisade and the transformation of Virginia's landscape. See Philip Levy, "A New Look at an Old Wall: Indians, Englishmen, Landscape, and the 1634 Palisade at Middle Plantation," *Virginia Magazine of History and Biography* 112, no. 3 (2004): 226–65; Philip Levy, "Middle Plantation's Changing Landscape: Persistence, Continuity, and the Building of Community," in *Early Modern Virginia: Reconsidering the Old Dominion*, ed. Douglas Bradburn and John C. Coombs, Early American Histories (Charlottesville: University of Virginia Press, 2011), 185–206. On the war against the Powhatans from 1622 to 1632, see Rountree, "The Powhatans and the English," 190–92; Gleach,

Powhatan's World and Colonial Virginia, 159–69; Rountree and Turner, *Before and After Jamestown*, 150–53.

58. Wyatt and the Council of Virginia to the Privy Council, 17 May 1626, CO 1/4, fols. 21–22 (quotations, fol. 22r), TNA.

59. George Sandys to the Virginia Company, 8 April 1623, CO 1/2, fols. 168-70, TNA; "Wyatt Manuscripts," *William and Mary Quarterly*, 2nd ser., 7, no. 4 (1 October 1927), 253.

60. Wyatt and the Council of Virginia to the Privy Council, 17 May 1626, CO 1/4, fols. 21r–22v; Charles I, Orders for Virginia, 27 February 1627/1628, CO 1/4, fol. 84.

61. Add. MSS 62,135, fols. 23–24, BL; CO 1/5, fols. 176-77 (John Harvey to Dudley Carleton, Viscount Dorchester, 15 April 1630), 203 (Harvey to Dorchester, 29 May 1630); CO 1/6 fols. 22-24 (Harvey to Dorchester, fols. 22r–23r), 135 (John Harvey to the Lords Commissioners, 27 May 1632).

62. Charles I to the Governor and Council of Virginia, 27 February 1627/1628, CO 1/4, fol. 84; Robert Heath to the Governor and Council of Virginia, November 1627, CO 1/4, fol. 86 ("tyme," fol. 86v), TNA.

63. On opposition to disafforestation, see Robson, "Improvement and Epistemologies of Landscape." See also Chapter 1.

64. "Answer of the Governor, Council, and Burgesses of Virginia, to the King's letters, concerning tobacco and other commodities," 26 March 1628, CO 1/4, fols. 118–81 ("small," fol. 120r), NA.

65. Mathews and Claybourne, "A Proposition concerning the winning of the Forest," CO 1/4, fol. 28r ("winning"), TNA.

66. Harvey to Dorchester, 15 April 1630, CO 1/5, fols. 176–77, TNA.

67. Conway Robinson, "Notes from Council and General Court Records," *Virginia Magazine of History and Biography* 13, no. 4 (April 1906): 389–401, esp. 392; Smith, "Sir Francis Willoughby's ironworks, 1570–1610," 127–28. In Virginia, Sir John Zouche and his son both spelled their surname "Zouch." For their trouble with Harvey, see "The names of such men as have been proved to be the chief heads and actors in the late faction and mutiny in Virginia. [. . .]," December 1635, CO 1/8, no. 85, fols. 220–24, TNA; "Addenda," Sir John Zouche to Sir John Zouche (his father), 5 May 1635, CO 1/32, no. 4, fols. 7–8, TNA. The archaeologists working on the Falling Creek site have indicated that the Zouches attempted to establish their ironworks at Falling Creek and have noted that they spent at least £250 on the enterprise. They write that this outlay showed "extraordinary resolve," yet the total spent does not approach the fund Dust and Ashes left the Virginia Company or the lowest estimate Richard S. Smith provided for establishing a contemporary ironworks. See "The 17th Century at Falling Creek," http://fallingcreekironworks .org/17century.html.

Chapter 4

1. Louis B. Wright, ed., *A Voyage to Virginia in 1609: Two Narratives: Strachey's "True Reportory" and Jourdain's Discovery of the Bermudas*, Jamestown Documents (Charlottesville: University of Virginia Press, 1965), 26–27.

2. Edward Misselden, *Free Trade or the Means to Make Trade Flourish* (London, 1622), 1. For more on luxury in early modern England, see Linda Levy Peck, *Consuming Splendor: Society and Culture in Seventeenth-Century England* (Cambridge: Cambridge University Press, 2005). On wood as a luxury good in the later seventeenth and eighteenth centuries, see Anderson, *Mahogany*.

3. In emphasizing the role of trees, I seek to broaden our sense of political ecology under the Sommer Islands Company to look beyond tobacco, which Michael Jarvis puts at the center of the company's actions. See Michael Jarvis, *In the Eye of All Trade: Bermuda, Bermudians, and the Maritime Atlantic World, 1680–1783* (Chapel Hill: University of North Carolina Press, 2010), 11–12.

4. Martin Lewis Hall Thomas, *The Natural History of Bermuda*, 1st ed. (Bermuda: Bermuda Zoological Society, 2004), 18, 26–32; Stanley R. Herwitz et al., "Origin of Bermuda's Clay-Rich Quaternary Paleosols and Their Paleoclimatic Significance," *Journal of Geophysical Research* 101, no. D18 (27 October 1996): 23389–400; Stanley R. Herwitz, "Quaternary Vegetation Change and Dune Formation on Bermuda: A Discussion," *Global Ecology and Biogeography Letters* 2, no. 3 (1 May 1992): 65–70; Peter R. Vogt and Woo-Yeol Jung, "Origin of the Bermuda Volcanoes and the Bermuda Rise: History, Observations, Models, and Puzzles," *Geological Society of America Special Papers* 430 (1 January 2007): 553–91.

5. Thomas, *The Natural History of Bermuda*, 33–36.

6. Ibid., 36–42.

7. Ibid., 42–48. One major casualty of these introductions has been the Bermuda petrel, a bird thought extinct in the seventeenth century but rediscovered in the twentieth century and currently the subject of an intensive preservation campaign. For more on the petrel, see Elizabeth Gehrman, *Rare Birds: The Extraordinary Tale of the Bermuda Petrel and the Man Who Brought It Back from Extinction* (Boston: Beacon Press, 2012). The nineteenth-century Bermudian governor and chronicler of the islands' human and natural history John Henry Lefroy noted that neither fig nor olive trees are native to the Caribbean or the Americas and argued that they came ashore on "some shipwrecked vessel from the South of Europe." See John Henry Lefroy, *Memorials of the Discovery and Settlement of the Bermudas or Somers Islands, 1511–1687* (London: Longmans, Green, and Co., 1877), 1:69.

8. For further information on these species, see the entries from the Bermuda Department of Conservation Services: https://www.environment.bm/bermuda-cedar/ and http://www.environment.bm/bermuda-palmetto/. See also Thomas, *The Natural History of Bermuda*, 37–38.

9. Lefroy, *Memorials*, 1:70; praise for Bermuda's other trees is on pp. 68–70.

10. Lefroy, *Memorials*, 1:528; "Yellowood," Department of Environment and Natural Resources, http://environment.bm/yellowood/.

11. On the disputed comparison with lignum vitae, see Lefroy, *Memorials*, 1:70. On guaiacum's early modern medical uses, see Londa Schiebinger, *Plants and Empire: Colonial Bioprospecting in the Atlantic World* (Cambridge, MA: Harvard University Press, 2004), 8, 38, 105, 178.

12. Vernon A. Ives, ed., *The Rich Papers: Letters from Bermuda, 1615–1646: Eyewitness Accounts Sent by the Early Colonists to Sir Nathaniel Rich* (Toronto: University of Toronto Press, 1984), 20.

13. Nathaniel Butler, "History of the Bermudas, 1609–1620," Sloane 750, pp. 88–89/fols. 48v–49r, BL.

14. Ives, *The Rich Papers*, 189. Butler railed against Tucker throughout his history of Bermuda, accusing him of failing at sugar cultivation, supporting pirates, and plotting at meetings of the Sommer Islands Company in England to reintroduce sugar cultivation and undermine Butler's plans; see Nathaniel Butler, "History of the Bermudas, 1609–1620," Sloane 750, fols. 49r, 69–70, 104v/p. 89, 130–132, 200, BL. I discuss consequences of the dispute between Tucker and Butler and the development of slavery in Bermuda elsewhere; see Keith Pluymers,

"Environmental Knowledge, Expertise, and the Development of Slavery in Bermuda," in *Atlantic Environments and the American South*, ed. Thomas Blake Earle and D. Andrew Johnson (Athens: University of Georgia Press, 2020), 176–94.

15. Wright, ed., *A Voyage to Virginia in 1609*, 23; Sylvester Jourdain (als. Jordan), *A Plaine Description of the Barmudas, Now Called Sommer Ilands* (London, 1613), C3v. The cedar's glowing reputation continued into the eighteenth century. See Jarvis, *In the Eye of All Trade*, 129. On the use of published accounts on the Spanish Empire in early English descriptions of Bermuda, see Pluymers, "Environmental Knowledge, Expertise," 178–80. These texts were important for botanical and agricultural knowledge around the English Atlantic. See Melissa Morris, "Spanish and Indigenous Influences on Virginian Tobacco Cultivation," in *Atlantic Environments and the American South*, ed. Thomas Blake Earle and D. Andrew Johnson (Athens: University of Georgia Press, 2020), 157–75, esp. 159.

16. Lefroy, *Memorials*, 1:114, 121–23. As Jarvis notes, Tucker's embrace of harsh disciplinary tactics learned in Virginia made him an unpopular leader. Jarvis, *In the Eye of All Trade*, 22.

17. Ives, *The Rich Papers*, 20.

18. A. C. Hollis Hallett, ed., *Bermuda Under the Sommer Islands Company, 1612–1684: Civil Records*, 3 vols. (Hamilton, Bermuda: Juniperhill Press, 2005), 1:11.

19. Ibid., 2:568–69.

20. Ibid., 2:581.

21. Ibid., 2:268–69.

22. Ibid., 2:568.

23. Smith, *Generall Historie*, 171.

24. Hallett, *Bermuda Under the Sommer Islands Company*, 3:536, 1:38–40.

25. Lefroy, *Memorials*, 1:433–35.

26. Ibid., 1:347, 373; Hallett, *Bermuda Under the Sommer Islands Company*, 1:40.

27. Hallett, *Bermuda Under the Sommer Islands Company*, 1:166–67.

28. Ibid., 1:205.

29. Ibid., 1:204, 206. Transcription of William Jessop Letterbook, Add. MSS. 63,854, fols. 18-19 (Sir Nathaniel Rich to Thomas Durham, 19 July 1634), 21 (N. Rich to Governor Wood, 19 July 1634), BL.

30. N. Rich to T. Durham, William Jessop Letterbook, Add. MSS. 63,854, fols. 136-37, BL.

31. Hallett, *Bermuda Under the Sommer Islands Company*, 3:73, 81.

32. Wright, *A Voyage to Virginia in 1609*, 23; Pluymers, "Environmental Knowledge," 178–80.

33. Lefroy, *Memorials*, 1:65, 69, 70; Jourdain's narrative was printed a year later. Jourdain, *A Plaine Description of the Barmudas*.

34. Richard Norwood, *The Journal of Richard Norwood, Surveyor of Bermuda*, ed. Wesley Frank Craven and Walter Brownell Hayward, (New York: Scholars' Facsimiles and Reprints for the Bermuda Historical Monuments Trust, 1945), 52–55.

35. Ives, *The Rich Papers*, 3–4; Norwood, *The Journal of Richard Norwood*, 53–54. Scientists and governments have long known that rats are one of the most dangerous invasive species for island biodiversity. See Carolyn M. Kurle, Donald A. Croll, and Bernie R. Tershy, "Introduced Rats Indirectly Change Marine Rocky Intertidal Communities from Algae- to Invertebrate-Dominated," *Proceedings of the National Academy of Sciences of the United States of America* 105, no. 10 (11 March 2008): 3800–4. Jawad Abdelkrim, Michel Pascal, and Sarah Samadi, "Establishing Causes of Eradication Failure Based on Genetics: Case Study of Ship Rat Eradication in

Ste. Anne Archipelago," *Conservation Biology* 21, no. 3 (2007): 719–30. James C. Russell et al., "Intercepting the First Rat Ashore," *Nature* 437, no. 7062 (19 October 2005): 1107.

36. Butler, "History of the Bermudas," MS Sloane 750, fol. 19r, BL.

37. Ives, *The Rich Papers*, 10, 20–21, 222.

38. Ibid., 180; Butler, "History of the Bermudas," fols. 10r; 19r-v, BL.

39. I develop this argument in more detail in Pluymers, "Environmental Knowledge." On agricultural skill and the position of enslaved Africans as a "surrogate peasantry" in the Spanish Atlantic, see David Wheat, *Atlantic Africa and the Spanish Caribbean, 1570–1640* (Chapel Hill: Omohundro Institute of Early American History and Culture and the University of North Carolina Press, 2016), 186–97; Ives, *The Rich Papers*, 179 (on the impossibility of non-tobacco commodities), 155–57 (space and climate limitations), 186 ("discursative courts"), 222 (need to focus on food production), 229–30 ("slaves" and "asses").

40. Ives, *The Rich Papers*, 49, 99.

41. Hallett, *Bermuda Under the Sommer Islands Company*, 2:569.

42. Lefroy, *Memorials*, 1:453. Restrictions on drinking were common fare for early modern English governments, particularly at times of social upheaval or economic distress. See Keith Wrightson, "Alehouses, Order and Reformation in Rural England, 1590-1660," in *Popular Culture and Class Conflict, 1590-1914: Explorations in the History of Labour and Leisure*, ed. Eileen Yeo and Stephen Yeo (Atlantic Highlands, NJ: Humanities Press, 1981), 1–27; Peter Clark, *The English Alehouse: A Social History, 1200-1830* (Atlantic Highlands, NJ: Humanities Press, 1981); Steve Hindle, *On the Parish? The Micro-Politics of Poor Relief in Rural England C. 1550-1750* (New York: Clarendon, 2004).

43. Hallett, *Bermuda Under the Sommer Islands Company*, 1:70-75, 77-82.

44. Ibid., 1:87.

45. Lefroy, *Memorials*, 1:410. For Kendall's relationship with the Ferrars and Sandys, see FP 467-68, VCA.

46. Lefroy, *Memorials*, 1:448.

47. Hallett, *Bermuda Under the Sommer Islands Company*, 1:102-3.

48. Ibid., 1:104.

49. Ibid.

50. Ibid., 1:309. "Indian" was a term with a broad meaning in Bermuda that included people from North America as well as the Spanish Empire and referred to free people, waged servants, indentured servants, and "perpetual slaves." See Hallett, *Bermuda Under the Sommer Islands Company*, 1:321, 371, 394, 488, for examples of the diverse origins and legal statuses encompassed by this term. In this section, I have avoided the term "race." As Susan Dwyer Amussen argues, English people possessed multiple ways of organizing hierarchical social relations in this period and the emergence of a division into "black" and "white" based on skin color took time to develop. See Susan Dwyer Amussen, *Caribbean Exchanges: Slavery and the Transformation of English Society, 1640-1700* (Chapel Hill: University of North Carolina Press, 2007), 11–12, 21–23.

51. This language appears in a presentment from 1651. Hallett, *Bermuda Under the Sommer Islands Company*, 1:313.

52. Lefroy, *Memorials*, 2:28.

53. Ibid.

54. Ibid., 2:34.

55. Ibid., 2:27–32.

56. Hallett, *Bermuda Under the Sommer Islands Company*, 1:325–26.

57. Ibid., 1:403–5.

58. Ibid., 1:449, 472.

59. These actions in Bermuda parallel historians' findings elsewhere in the English Caribbean and in Virginia, specifically colonial authorities' obsessions over sexual behavior between people of European and African descent and the close connection between ideas about gender and emerging ideas about race. See Amussen, *Caribbean Exchanges*, 232–33; Kathleen M Brown, *Good Wives, Nasty Wenches, and Anxious Patriarchs: Gender, Race, and Power in Colonial Virginia* (Chapel Hill: Omohundro Institute of Early American History and Culture and the University of North Carolina Press, 1996).

60. Hallett, *Bermuda Under the Sommer Islands Company*, 1:506.

61. Wright, *A Voyage to Virginia in 1609*, 24; Jourdain, *A Plaine Description of the Barmudas*, fols. C4v, F.

62. Lefroy, *Memorials*, 1:116–17.

63. Ives, *The Rich Papers*, 39, 10, 18, 25, 21, 17; Lefroy claimed that the Caribbean silk cotton tree (*Bombax ceiba*) was introduced in 1845 and that the cotton plant (*Gossypium herbaceum*) had been introduced in the eighteenth century. John Henry Lefroy, *The Botany of Bermuda* (Washington, DC: U.S. Government Printing Office, 1884), 53–54; Britton's natural history follows Lefroy's chronology but instead classifies the silk cotton tree in Bermuda as *Ceiba pentandra*. Nathaniel Lord Britton, *Flora of Bermuda* (New York: C. Scribner's sons, 1918), 240–41.

64. I discuss these examples and African/Afro-Caribbean environmental knowledge in more detail in Pluymers, "Environmental Knowledge"; Ives, *The Rich Papers*, 54, 59, 81.

65. Ives, *The Rich Papers*, 98–99.

66. Ibid., 54, 50, 56.

67. Butler, "History of the Bermudas," p. 330, fol. 144r; Ives, *The Rich Papers*, 223–24.

68. Ives, *The Rich Papers*, 180, 224; Thomas, *The Natural History of Bermuda*, 38; "Olivewood," Department of Environment and Natural Resources, http://environment.bm /olivewood/.

69. Ives, *The Rich Papers*, 223–24.

70. Lefroy, *Memorials*, 1:132; Ives, *The Rich Papers*, 94, 52.

71. Ives, *The Rich Papers*, 266–67.

72. Lefroy, *Memorials*, 1:454–55. Bell had previously brought the complaint to the assembly. Hallett, *Bermuda Under the Sommer Islands Company*, 1:67–68.

73. Hallett, *Bermuda Under the Sommer Islands Company*, 1:145; Lefroy, *Memorials*, 1:505.

74. Hallett, *Bermuda Under the Sommer Islands Company*, 1:452–53, 103, 95–96; Lefroy, *Memorials*, 1:411–12.

75. Ives, *The Rich Papers*, 180.

76. The efforts to plant provisions rather than tobacco were part of a consistent struggle between the provisioning trade and commercial tobacco production that lasted until the end of the seventeenth century. See Jarvis, *In the Eye of All Trade*, 78, 109; Ives, *The Rich Papers*, 171–73, 176.

77. Ives, *The Rich Papers*, 347.

78. Ibid., 348.

79. Ibid., 206.

80. Ibid., 234.

81. Douglas Helms, "Soil and Southern History," *Agricultural History* 74, no. 4 (October 2000): 727.

82. Lois Green Carr and Russell R. Menard, "Land, Labor, and Economies of Scale in Early Maryland: Some Limits to Growth in the Chesapeake System of Husbandry," *Journal of Economic History* 49, no. 2 (June 1989): 407–18.

83. Helms, "Soil and Southern History," 727–33.

84. Hallett, *Bermuda Under the Sommer Islands Company*, 2:570, 581.

85. Lefroy, *Memorials*, 1:398, 374, 379–84.

86. Ibid., 1:358–59.

87. Hallett, *Bermuda Under the Sommer Islands Company*, 1:166–67, 178–79. Lefroy identified "oil seeds" as a reference to the castor oil tree and noted that it had been introduced in the 1620s and extensively cultivated in the 1630s. Lefroy, *The Botany of Bermuda*, 106.

88. Hallett, *Bermuda Under the Sommer Islands Company*, 1:185, 187, 203, 209, 218; Lefroy, *Memorials*, 1:538.

89. William Jessop Letterbook, Add. MSS. 63,854, fols. 2 (N. Rich to Hugh Wentworth, 12 February 1633/1634), 5 (N. Rich to George Hanmer, 19 July 1634), 10 (Robert Rich, Earl of Warwick, to H. Wentworth, 19 July 1634), 13-15 (W. Jessop to H. Wentworth, 12 February 1633/1634), 18-19 (N. Rich to Thomas Durham, 19 July 1634), 20 (N. Rich to Thomas Kemble, 19 July 1634), 77-79 (W. Jessop to H. Wentworth, 2 September 1634), BL.

90. Ibid., fols. 133 (N. Rich to C. Parker, 1 June 1635), 136-37 (N. Rich to T. Durham, 1 June 1635).

91. Rich's June 1635 letter to Thomas Kemble praised Kemble for keeping a vineyard and promised him timber and labor to improve it. Rich also informed Kemble that his request for more laborers depended on his success with juniper. William Jessop Letterbook, Add. MSS. 63,854, fol. 134, BL.

92. Ibid., fols. 10 (Warwick to H. Wentworth, 19 July 1634), 13-15 (W. Jessop to H. Wentworth, 19 July 1634), 16-17 (W. Jessop to T. Durham, 19 July 1634), 77-79 (W. Jessop to H. Wentworth, 2 September 1634), 80-82 (W. Jessop to T. Durham, 2 September 1634).

93. Ibid., fols. 131 (N. Rich to Henry Wethersby, June 1635), 134 (N. Rich to T. Kemble, 1 June 1635), 148-50 (W. Jessop to T. Durham, 21 September 1635).

94. Ibid., fols. 232 (W. Jessop to T. Kemble, August 1637), 241 (W. Jessop to Mr. Stowe, August 1637), 236-38 (W. Jessop to H. Wentworth, August 1637).

95. Ibid., fols. 244 (Edward Montagu, Lord Mandeville, to T. Kemble and Henry Wethersby, 24 May 1638), 246 (Warwick to T. Durham, 17 July 1638), 248 (Warwick to N. Shaw, August 1638).

96. Hallett, *Bermuda Under the Sommer Islands Company*, 3:77, 80, 81–82.

97. Ibid., 3:210.

98. Warwick to T. Durham, 17 July 1638, William Jessop Letterbook, Add. MSS. 63,854, fol. 246, BL.

Chapter 5

1. Vincent T. Harlow, ed., *Colonising Expeditions to the West Indies and Guiana, 1623-1667*, Hakluyt Society, 2nd ser., no. 56 (Nendeln/Liechtenstein: Kraus Repr., 1967), 66–67.

2. Richard H. Grove, *Green Imperialism: Colonial Expansion, Tropical Island Edens, and the Origins of Environmentalism, 1600-1860* (Cambridge: Cambridge University Press, 1995), 67–71. On English anxieties about landscape degradation alongside the celebration of colonial agriculture and plantation, see Britt Rusert, "Plantation Ecologies: The Experimental Plantation in and Against James Grainger's the Sugar-Cane," *Early American Studies: An Interdisciplinary*

Journal 13, no. 2 (2015): 341–73; Joachim Radkau, *Nature and Power: A Global History of the Environment*, trans. Thomas Dunlap, 1st English ed., Publications of the German Historical Institute (Washington, DC: German Historical Institute and Cambridge University Press, 2008), 153; Stefan Halikowski Smith, "The Mid-Atlantic Islands: A Theatre of Early Modern Ecocide?" *International Review of Social History* 55, Supplement S18 (2010): 60; Moore, "Madeira, Sugar, and the Conquest of Nature"; Moore, *Capitalism in the Web of Life*; Williams, *Deforesting the Earth*, 2003, 219–21; Donna Haraway et al., "Anthropologists Are Talking—About the Anthropocene," *Ethnos* 81, no. 3 (26 May 2016): 535–64.

3. For an example of the work that can be done on these records, see Justin Roberts, "Working Between the Lines: Labor and Agriculture on Two Barbadian Sugar Plantations, 1796-97," *William and Mary Quarterly* 63, no. 3 (2006): 551–86. On the limited surviving records in Barbados and the English Caribbean, see pp. 552-54.

4. The most important work arguing for the relatively gradual deforestation of Barbados is David Watts, *The West Indies: Patterns of Development, Culture and Environmental Change Since 1492* (New York: Cambridge University Press, 1990), 154, 166–68. Conservation measures and relatively slow deforestation did not mean an absence of environmental issues. Watts identifies the introduction and expansion of invasive species and nutrient loss from careless burning of trees and cash-crop cultivation as issues that appeared relatively rapidly. See also David Watts, *Man's Influence on the Vegetation of Barbados, 1627-1800*, Occasional Papers in Geography 4 (Hull: University of Hull, 1966). On the negative reception of Barbadian tobacco in England, see Hilary Beckles, *A History of Barbados: From Amerindian Settlement to Nation-State*, 2nd ed. (New York: Cambridge University Press, 2006), 16–17; Gary A. Puckrein, *Little England: Plantation Society and Anglo-Barbadian Politics, 1627-1700* (New York: New York University Press, 1984), 40; Russell R. Menard, *Sweet Negotiations: Sugar, Slavery, and Plantation Agriculture in Early Barbados* (Charlottesville: University of Virginia Press, 2006).

5. On beauty and English forestry, see Chapter 1. Andrew McRae argues that Michael Drayton is an exception to this pattern. See Andrew McRae, "Tree-Felling in Early Modern England: Michael Drayton's Environmentalism," *Review of English Studies* 63, no. 260 (June 2012): 410–30.

6. Watts, *Man's Influence on the Vegetation of Barbados*, 4–34; Stephen K. Donovan and D. Harper, "The Geology of Barbados: A Field Guide," *Caribbean Journal of Earth Science* 38 (2005): 21–33.

7. Alistair J. Bright, *Blood Is Thicker Than Water: Amerindian Intra- and Inter-Insular Relationships and Social Organization in the Pre-Colonial Windward Islands* (Leiden: Sidestone Press, 2011), 38–39, 41–42, 72–73, 98–100.

8. On this point, see Samuel Meredith Wilson, *The Prehistory of Nevis, a Small Island in the Lesser Antilles*, Yale University Publications in Anthropology 87 (New Haven, CT: Yale University Press, 2006), 5–7. Wilson argues that "Carib" and "Arawak," categorical terms deployed by Spanish colonists, minimize the linguistic and cultural diversity of the Caribbean.

9. Watts, *Man's Influence on the Vegetation of Barbados*, 20–37.

10. Bright, *Blood Is Thicker Than Water*, 33.

11. Frank Cecil Innes, "Plantation and Peasant Farm: A Vertical Theme in the Historical Geography of Barbados, 1627-1960" (PhD diss., McGill University, 1967), 38–41.

12. Ibid., 77. Recopied Deed Books (hereafter, RB3) RB3/1, 101 (Anthony Fisher's Deed to Thomas Reace, Roland Mylton, and John Lawrence, 1 August 1643), 285-86 (Captain Thomas Stanhopp and Thomas Ware Attorneys to Captain William Woodhowse and John Hawksworth

to John Thrubarne, 20 November 1642), 40 (Edward Sheffield's Assurance of Grant for Edward Vaughan, 4 April 1643), 48-49 (Francis Godfry's Deed to Owen Williams, 2 June 1643), 773-74 (Francis Hewett to William Rowley, Ward Rowley, and George Arden, 27 August 1640), 511-12 (George Sertell to Daniell Dondee, 4 November 1644), 920-21 (George Surtail to George Younge, 13 August 1641), 957 (George Thomas to Thomas Cage, 26 August 1641), 622 (Henry Milles to Hersey Barrett, 2 June 1643), 795 (James Simpson to Peeter Fleetwood and John Pye, 31 July 1640), 439-40 (Joane Allene to Robert Cox, 1 August 1644), 465 (John Gay to Laghlin Farrell, 3 November 1643), 912-13 (John Kennecott to Thomas Pearson, 2 October 1641), 515 (John Overley to Francis Humphrys, 9 September 1644), 36 (John Vaughan and Cornelius Vadaelst Grant to Robert Hansby, 4 February 1642/1643), 581-82 (Peter Stephens, David Longe, and John Hodges to Edward and George Moore, 20 September 1644), 226-27 (Phillipp Lovell to Farford Goldsmyth, 12 August 1643), 810 (Roger Byran and William Becke to Thomas Nocke, 12 August 1640), 606 (Samuell Knight, William Freeman, and Thomas Freeman to John Scoth, 30 March 1645), 890 (Thomas Hackelton to John Barbour and Emmanuell Domminigoe, 1 August 1641), 822 (Thomas Jones to Humphrey Pritchett and Henry Barrett, 30 June 1640), 959 (Christopher Merricke to Thomas Jordon, 7 April 1641), 504 (Edward Piggott to Robert Lea, 4 February 1644/1645), 234-35 (Henry Franckland of London, Merchant, to Captain Robert Hooker, 26 May 1643), 522-23 (John Hawkins to Robert Ireland, 11 December 1644), 776 (John Whitfield and George Hopson, 29 June 1645), 650 (Matthew Sley and Henrie Saint to Leih Maycocke, 8 May 1645), 449-50 (Richard Price to Thomas Wallis, 29 August 1644), 802 (Robert Ashmole to William Douglas, 11 August 1640), 553-54 (Thomas Browne to Peter and James Hayes, 23 January 1640/1641), 241-42 (William Naylor to Henry Thornton, 2 February 1642/1643), 553 (William Walton to Mathew Key, 24 November 1644); RB3/2, 304 (Anthony Johnson to Robert Hales and Josias Goslinge, 23 August 1641), 277-78 (George Nore to William Shenn, 10 October 1647), 10 (George Roberts to George Head, 4 April 1646), 232-33 (Hugh Burrows to John Bryne, Walter Cooke, and John Brend, 23 June 1647), 233-34 (John Pryne and John Brinn to Edward Harrison, Henry Milles, and Thomas Jones, 17 January 1645/1646), 445 (John Tomlyn and William Tomlyn to Walter Follett and Henry Worthy, 30 March 1641), 230 (Robert Dawson to Robert Smith, 30 March 1647), 32 (Thomas Banke, Carpenter, to Captain [Blank], 8 September 1645), 33-34 (William Hawkesworth to Colonel William Woodhouse, 8 August 1646), 358-59 (Andrew Louther to Joseph Belgrave, 7 December 1640), 268-69 (John Mathews to Greffen Price, 12 November 1644), 272 (Ralph Booth to Robert Reynolds, 4 February 1646/1647), 406 (Thomas Godwin to Robert Meyer, 26 January 1640/1641), Barbados National Archives.

13. On the creation of Lea's map, see Innes, "Plantation and Peasant Farm," 41.

14. Barbados National Archives, RB3/1-3.

15. RB3/1, 759 (John Matthewes to Robert Francklin and Robert Atkins, 1 August 1640), 715 (John Jones to Robert Morgan, 2 April 1640), 734-35 (Thomas Rigley to Leonard Robinson and William Lymone, 21 March 1639/1640), 795 (James Simpson to Peeter Fleetwood and John Pye, 31 July 1640); Inventory of Christopher Meltropp's Estate, 28 September 1647, RB3/3, 438-40, Barbados National Archives.

16. Walter Leaw Deed to Thomas Mathew for a Quarter Part of His Plantation Known as Wind Mill, June 1647, RB3/3, 466-67; John Powell Administrator to John Merricke, Deceased, and Mary Merrick, His Child, to Robert Hooper, 31 May 1651, RB3/2, 618, Barbados National Archives.

17. "This Plott Representeth the Forme of Three Hundred Acres of Land Part of a Plantation Called the Fort Plantation of Which 300 Acres Cap. Thos. Middleton of London Hath

Purchased" (1646), Shelf Et647 1 Ms/C8210, John Carter Brown Library, http://jcb.lunaimaging
.com/luna/servlet/detail/JCBMAPS~1~1~1159~106490001:This-plott-representeth-the-forme-o
?qvq=q:C-8210;lc:JCB~1~1,JCBBOOKS~1~1,JCBMAPS~1~1,JCBMAPS~2~2,JCBMAPS~3~3&
mi=0&trs=1#.

18. RB3/1, 294 ("Captain David Bix and Captain Reynold Allen Theire Particulars Fol-
lowinge at the Suite of Captain William Hilliard for and towards Satisfaccon of Sixteene Hun-
dred Pounds Sterling," 10 March 1642/1643), 56-57 (Francis Dickenson and Robert Haynes's
Grant to Allexander Lindsay, 14 June 1643), 532-33 (John Mullins and Edward Hammond to
Thomas Baggington, 2 December 1644), 703 (Peter Gill and Thomas Whitehead to Nicholas
Kinlesow, [?], And Symons Harper, 17 May 1640), 449-50 (Richard Price to Thomas Wallis,
29 August 1644), 313-14 (Walter Fenton to Richard Hawkings, 12 March 1639/1640); William
Butland and Joseph Taylor to William Philip, Senior, 5 June 1647, RB3/2, 192-94, Barbados
National Archives. On "mobbie," see Jerome S. Handler, "Aspects of Amerindian Ethnogra-
phy in 17th Century Barbados," *Caribbean Studies* 9, no. 4 (1970): 61; RB3/1, 465 (John Gay
to Laghlin Farrell, 3 November 1643), 664 (John Morris to Henry Sliore, 14 April 1644), 279
(John Smyth to Ann Butler, 17 August 1642), 395-96 (William Bradshaw to Thomas Crosse and
John Latchilas, 21 June 1644), 753 (William Waterfield, Carpenter, to Thomas Jordan, 24 August
1640), Barbados National Archives. On fustic as a dyestuff, see Alexander Engel, "Colouring
Markets: The Industrial Transformation of the Dyestuff Business Revisited," *Business History* 54,
no. 1 (February 2012): 10-29.

19. Thomas Stanhopp and Thomas Ware to William Gibbs and Thomas Merricke, 26
March 1644, RB3/1, 327-28; John Younge to John Bread, 10 June 1644, RB3/1, 491, Barbados
National Archives.

20. RB3/1, 353 (Richard Jarrett to John Low, Clement Malin, and Edward Dines, 25 July
1642), 476-77 (James Thomas to John Kelly, 2 October 1644). On reserved fustic trees, see also
RB3/1, 669-70 (Edward Oistine to Thomas Moore[?], 13 May 1645), 706 (Thomas Smith to William Chapman, 16 September 1640); RB3/2, 404 (Joseph Purdey and John Smith's Agreement,
9 February 1640/1641), Barbados National Archives.

21. For example, see George Rowe of Cornwall, Mariner, to John Cotton of London, Merchant, 16 March 1646/1647, RB3/2, 116-17, Barbados National Archives; Engel, "Colouring Markets," 16-17, 21-22.

22. Harlow, *Colonising Expeditions to the West Indies and Guiana*, 66.

23. RB3/1, 182-83 (Arther and Rebecca Leader to Richard Raileton, n.d.), 277-78 (Ensigne
Stephen Baxter to James Allen, 22 September 1643), 504 (Edward Piggott to Robert Lea, 4 February 1644/1645), 423 (Francis Skeele to Richard Estwicke, 11 March 1641/1642), 132 (Captain
Frances Skeele to Ensigne Michaell Cooke, 9 August 1642), 802 (Robert Ashmole to William Douglas, 11 August 1640); RB3/3, 600 (Richard Hinde's Grant to John Joyce, 20 March
1649/1650), Barbados National Archives.

24. RB3/2, 408 (Agreement between Roger Jones and Robert Jones, January 1640/1641);
RB3/3, 140-43 (Indenture between Lawrence Parre and Nathan[iel] Durant, 17 August 1656);
RB3/1, 924-26 (Richard Estwicke to John Reeve and George Read, 12 December 1641), Barbados
National Archives.

25. RB3/2, 745-46 (John Pillis to Henry Quintyne, 12 July 1653), 735-38 (Lease between
Henry Quintyne and Giles Quintyne, 21 June 1654), 757-59 (Richard Bickford, Carpenter,
Lease to Samuel Capthorne via Thomas Sandiford and Thomas Martin, Attorneys to Samuell
Capthorne of Plymouth in England, 16 April 1654), Barbados National Archives.

26. Mary Draper notes that historians have remarked on the rapid pace at which Barbados was deforested while noting that such accounts may exaggerate the speed at which this transformation occurred. Draper's analysis of the records from the Colonial Office points toward the 1650s and, particularly, the 1660s as the critical period for scarcity discourses in Barbados. Mary Draper, "Timbering and Turtling: The Maritime Hinterlands of Early Modern British Caribbean Cities," *Early American Studies: An Interdisciplinary Journal* 15, no. 4 (2017): 774 n. 12 (on the narrative of rapid deforestation), 774–76 (on claims about wood scarcity from the 1660s and 1650s).

27. Larry D. Gragg, "A Puritan in the West Indies: The Career of Samuel Winthrop," *William and Mary Quarterly* 50, no. 4 (1993): 770 n. 6 (on Henry Winthrop), 769 (on Samuel's failed trading expedition in Tenerife), 770 (on Samuel's brief stay in Barbados); Charles F. Carroll, *The Timber Economy of Puritan New England* (Providence, RI: Brown University Press, 1974), 81–83; Williams, *Deforesting the Earth*, 221–22. Many of the most developed and important connections between the Connecticut Valley and English colonies in the Caribbean grew after 1660 and began to accelerate English models for colonial development and economic activity in both regions in the 1680s. See Roberts, *Colonial Ecology, Atlantic Economy*, 76–79, 130; firewood was largely a regional commodity rather than one aimed at the Caribbean in great quantities, see p. 99.

28. J. Hammond (James Hammond) Trumbull, ed., *The Public Records of the Colony of Connecticut* (Hartford, CT: Brown and Parsons, 1850), 1:60. Regulations were not solely designed to support the Caribbean export trade and reflected internal colonial issues as well. Nonetheless, regulations throughout the seventeenth and early eighteenth centuries reflected efforts to craft regulations that would serve trade with the Caribbean. See Roberts, *Colonial Ecology, Atlantic Economy*, 132–39.

29. RB3/2, 618-19 (John Powell Administrator to John Merricke, Deceased, and Mary Merrick, His Child to Robert Hooper, 31 May 1651 and 31 May 1653), 705-6 (Francis Williams to Captain Robert Hooper, 7 October 1654), Barbados National Archives.

30. Peter Thompson, "Henry Drax's Instructions on the Management of a Seventeenth-Century Barbadian Sugar Plantation," *William and Mary Quarterly* 66, no. 3 (2009): 571–72, for quotation, see 589; Sean F. Britt, "Fueling the Fire: Examining Caribbean Colonial Relations Between Humans and the Environment," *Historical Archaeology* 44, no. 3 (2010): 54–68; Roberts, "Working Between the Lines," 568.

31. Thompson, "Henry Drax's Instructions," 589, 591–92, 601.

32. Shawn W. Miller, "Fuelwood in Colonial Brazil: The Economic and Social Consequences of Fuel Depletion for the Bahian Recôncavo, 1549-1820," *Forest & Conservation History* 38, no. 4 (1994): 183.

33. Thompson, "Henry Drax's Instructions," 601.

34. Richard Hall, *Acts, Passed in the Island of Barbados: From 1643, to 1762* (London, 1764), 25–26.

35. St. John Vestry Minutes, 1649-1682, D279, vol. 1, p. 14, Barbados National Archives; Watts, *The West Indies*, 43.

36. Thompson, "Henry Drax's Instructions," 572–77; Neil Oatsvall and Vaughn Scribner analyze, at length, interactions between the brutal form of slavery used on Caribbean sugar plantations and environmental conditions and call for a redefinition of "work" to recognize this. See Neil Oatsvall and Vaughn Scribner, "'The Devil Was in the Englishman That He Makes Everything Work': Implementing the Concept of 'Work' to Reevaluate Sugar Production and Consumption in the Early Modern British Atlantic World," *Agricultural History* 92, no. 4 (2018): 461.

37. "Ligon, Richard (c.1585–1662)," Karen Ordahl Kupperman in *Oxford Dictionary of National Biography*, ed. H. C. G. Matthew and Brian Harrison (Oxford: Oxford University Press, 2004); online ed., ed. David Cannadine, January 2008; Watts, *Man's Influence on the Vegetation of Barbados*, 21–27, 38–42; David Chan Smith emphasizes Ligon's efforts to balance profit and pleasure within the context of early modern ideas of improvement. I largely concur with Smith's sense for Ligon as an improver. See David Chan Smith, "Useful Knowledge, Improvement, and the Logic of Capital in Richard Ligon's True and Exact History of Barbados," *Journal of the History of Ideas* 78, no. 4 (2017): 549–70. Smith suggests that Ligon had begun his work prior to his incarceration, see p. 552.

38. Pestana argues that English colonists and the leaders of the conquest rejected the Barbados model after experiencing limitations on food and natural resources while in Barbados. Carla Gardina Pestana, *The English Conquest of Jamaica: Oliver Cromwell's Bid for Empire* (Cambridge, MA: Belknap Press of Harvard University Press, 2017), 154 (on Ligon as a rejected model), 48–57 (on the frustrations of the expedition and Barbadian elites while the fleet resided there). Susan Dwyer Amussen treats Ligon as a key source in her analysis of English ideas about society and labor and their transformation in the Caribbean, arguing that his work is "particularly useful" for its "acute observation, great detail, and an individual perspective" as well as for its status as a reference work for the Committee of Trade and Plantations and for contemporaries' frequent citation of it. See Amussen, *Caribbean Exchanges*, 45 (quotation), 43–71.

39. Richard Ligon, *A True & Exact History of the Island of Barbados* (London, 1657), 22–24. There were considerable controversies over Courteen's position in early Barbados. See Gary Puckrein, "Did Sir William Courteen Really Own Barbados?" *Huntington Library Quarterly* 44, no. 2 (April 1981): 135–49.

40. Ligon, *A True & Exact History of the Island of Barbados*, 27–28. On early modern attempts to improve climate, see Zilberstein, *A Temperate Empire*.

41. Brian W. Ogilvie, *The Science of Describing: Natural History in Renaissance Europe* (Chicago: University of Chicago Press, 2008). For a concise statement on the importance of aesthetic pleasure and the aversion to economic concerns among early modern natural historians, see p. 270.

42. Ligon, *A True & Exact History of the Island of Barbados*, 22, 41, 66–84. On Ligon as a purveyor of "useful knowledge" in the broader paradigm of improvement writing, see Smith, "Useful Knowledge, Improvement, and the Logic of Capital," 552–56.

43. Ligon, *A True & Exact History of the Island of Barbados*, 66, 72, 76. On European debates on art and nature, see Lorraine Daston and Katharine Park, *Wonders and the Order of Nature, 1150–1750* (New York: Zone Books, 1998), 261–65, 290–300. Ligon repeatedly sought to place his text into discourses on painting. See Smith, "Useful Knowledge, Improvement, and the Logic of Capital," 557–58.

44. Ligon, *A True & Exact History of the Island of Barbados*, 71.

45. On the rhetoric of disease in seventeenth-century husbandry guides, see Pluymers, "Taming the Wilderness," 4.

46. Susan Scott Parrish, "Richard Ligon and the Atlantic Science of Commonwealths," *William and Mary Quarterly* 67, no. 2 (2010): 209. On political order, violence, and nature in English environmental thought, see Cavert, "The Environmental Policy of Charles I"; McRae, "Tree-Felling in Early Modern England."

47. For a reading of the forest in the play emphasizing struggle and danger, see Theis, *Writing the Forest in Early Modern England*, 91–120.

48. Ligon, *A True & Exact History of the Island of Barbados*, 79. Smith articulates a similar argument, though without my focus on the island's woods. He writes that Ligon's "call to balance industry and delight was not intended to discourage improvement or exploitation, but rather to make capital accumulation sustainable for the planter and justifiable to an early modern audience sensitive to the connection between avarice and commerce." Smith, "Useful Knowledge, Improvement, and the Logic of Capital," 570.

49. Smith, "Useful Knowledge, Improvement, and the Logic of Capital," 565–66; Jason T. Sharples, "Discovering Slave Conspiracies: New Fears of Rebellion and Old Paradigms of Plotting in Seventeenth-Century Barbados," *American Historical Review* 120, no. 3 (1 June 2015): 831–33 (on Caribbean planters' literacy).

50. Sukanya Dasgupta, "Drayton's 'Silent Spring': 'Poly-Olbion' and the Politics of Landscape," *Cambridge Quarterly* 39, no. 2 (2010): 152–71; McRae, "Tree-Felling in Early Modern England"; Smith, "Useful Knowledge, Improvement, and the Logic of Capital," 565 (on moderation), 570 ("sustainable").

51. Ligon, *A True & Exact History of the Island of Barbados*, 46–47.

52. Ibid., 48–49; Robert Spencer, "The Theorbo in England," *Early Music* 24, no. 3 (1996): 540–42; Parrish, "Richard Ligon and the Atlantic Science of Commonwealths," 238–39. For more on this passage, see Erich Nunn, "'A Great Addition to Their Harmony': Plantation Slavery and Musical Exchange in Seventeenth-Century Barbados," *Global South* 10, no. 2 (2016): 27.

53. Harlow, *Colonising Expeditions to the West Indies and Guiana*, 30–32. Afro-Brazilians likely provided critical expertise and knowledge on Barbadian sugar plantations. See Menard, *Sweet Negotiations*, 17. On the importance of African skill and expertise in the Atlantic World, see Judith Ann Carney, *Black Rice: The African Origins of Rice Cultivation in the Americas* (Cambridge, MA: Harvard University Press, 2001); Walter Hawthorne, "From 'Black Rice' to 'Brown': Rethinking the History of Risiculture in the Seventeenth- and Eighteenth-Century Atlantic," *American Historical Review* 115, no. 1 (2010): 151–63.

54. Ligon, *A True & Exact History of the Island of Barbados*, 49–50.

55. Chaplin, *Subject Matter*, 280–316; on ventriloquism, see also 26–27.

56. This reading complements David Chan Smith's emphasis on Ligon's concern with skill but also ascribes importance to the setting in which these musings occurred. Smith, "Useful Knowledge, Improvement, and the Logic of Capital," 567–69; Susan Dwyer Amussen has also noted the connection between Ligon's sense of nature and his views on social order and the treatment of people of African descent. Her analysis focuses on "strangeness" rather than beauty. See Amussen, *Caribbean Exchanges*, 51–67, esp. 61–62.

57. Ligon, *A True & Exact History of the Island of Barbados*, 82. On the definition and history of limning, see Katherine Coombs, "'A Kind of Gentle Painting': Limning in 16th-Century England," in *European Visions: American Voices*, ed. Kim Sloan, British Museum Research Publication, no. 172 (London: British Museum, 2009), 77–84. Here, too, Ligon sought a "moderation" compatible with colonial exploitation. As Smith notes, Ligon's enthusiasm for conversion did not imply a challenge to chattel slavery. Smith, "Useful Knowledge, Improvement, and the Logic of Capital," 568.

58. Katherine McKittrick, *Demonic Grounds: Black Women and the Cartographies of Struggle* (Minneapolis: University of Minnesota Press, 2006), viii.

59. Hilary Beckles, "From Land to Sea: Runaway Barbados Slaves and Servants, 1630–1700," *Slavery & Abolition* 6, no. 3 (December 1985): 81–82; Jerome S. Handler, "Escaping Slavery in a Caribbean Plantation Society: Marronage in Barbados, 1650s-1830s," *NWIG: New West*

Indian Guide/Nieuwe West-Indische Gids 71, no. 3/4 (1997): 190–91; Marisa J. Fuentes, *Dispossessed Lives: Enslaved Women, Violence, and the Archive* (Philadelphia: University of Pennsylvania Press, 2016); on erasure, absence, slavery, and the archive in Barbados, see pp. 13–45; on "fugitivity" and alternative geographies, see pp. 16–17. On English colonists' ignorance about African and Afro-Caribbean knowledge and practices and colonists' erroneous belief in their own understanding, see Sharples, "Discovering Slave Conspiracies," 829–31.

60. Recent scholarship on Michael Drayton has also argued for an aestheticized environmentalism in the seventeenth century. See McRae, "Tree-Felling in Early Modern England"; Dasgupta, "Drayton's 'Silent Spring.'"

Chapter 6

1. John Evelyn, *The Diary of John Evelyn*, ed. William Bray (New York: M. W. Dunne, 1901), 1:365.

2. Beryl Hartley, "Exploring and Communicating Knowledge of Trees in the Early Royal Society," *Notes and Records of the Royal Society* 64, no. 3 (20 September 2010): 229; the text of the request is on p. 245.

3. Evelyn, *Sylva*, a1v–a2r.

4. For the skeptical viewpoint, see Nail, *Forest Policies and Social Change*, 25. For positive statements on Evelyn's influence, see Jedediah Purdy, *After Nature: A Politics for the Anthropocene* (Cambridge, MA: Harvard University Press, 2015), 58–63; Oliver Rackham, *Trees and Woodland in the British Landscape* (London: J. M. Dent, 1981), 96–97; Radkau, *Wood*, 74, 137; Michael Williams, *Americans and Their Forests: A Historical Geography*, Studies in Environment and History (New York: Cambridge University Press, 1989), 373; Donald Worster, *Nature's Economy: A History of Ecological Ideas*, 2nd ed. (New York: Cambridge University Press, 1994), 87–88; Albion, *Forests and Sea Power*, 130–32.

5. Evelyn, *Sylva*, C1.

6. Warde, *The Invention of Sustainability*, 98.

7. Evelyn, *Sylva*, 56, 64, 69; J. Robert Sealy, "Arbutus Unedo," *Journal of Ecology* 37, no. 2 (1949): 365–88.

8. Evelyn, *Sylva*, 61, 81.

9. Ibid., 55–56.

10. Ibid., 53–54; Nicholas Keene, "Knatchbull, Sir Norton, first baronet (1602–1685)," *Oxford Dictionary of National Biography*, Oxford University Press, 2004; online ed., January 2008, http://www.oxforddnb.com/view/article/15703.

11. Evelyn, *Sylva*, 109, 114.

12. Ibid., 109–10.

13. Ibid.

14. Ibid., A4 (1664), C1 (1670). For commentary on Evelyn's Royalism, see Nail, *Forest Policies and Social Change*, 25; Purdy, *After Nature*, 58–63; Theis, *Writing the Forest in Early Modern England*, ch. 6.

15. Evelyn, *Sylva*, 1–2.

16. "Charles II, 1660: An Act of Free and Generall Pardon Indempnity and Oblivion," in *Statutes of the Realm: Volume 5, 1628-80*, ed. John Raithby (London: Great Britain Record Commission, 1819), 226–34, British History Online, http://www.british-history.ac.uk/statutes-realm/vol5/pp226-234. Erin Peters analyzes cultures of remembrance and forgetting in the Restoration

in Erin Peters, *Commemoration and Oblivion in Royalist Print Culture, 1658–1667*, Palgrave Studies in the History of the Media (Cham, Switzerland: Palgrave Macmillan, 2017), 23–69.

17. An Act for the Certainty of Forests, and of the Meers, Meets, Limits and Bounds of the Forests, 1640, 16 Charles I, c.16; *A Remonstrance of the State of the Kingdome*. (London, 1641), 6; Theis, *Writing the Forest in Early Modern England*, 171; Joan Thirsk, "The Crown as Projector on Its Own Estates, from Elizabeth I to Charles I," in *The Estates of the English Crown, 1558–1640*, ed. R. W. Hoyle (New York: Cambridge University Press, 1992), 350.

18. *Remonstrance*, 6–7.

19. George Oldfield to James Symes, 3 January 1645/1646, SP 46/128, fol. 10, TNA.

20. C. H. Firth and R. S. Rait, eds., "April 1648: Ordinance for Preservation of Timber in the Forest of Deane," in *Acts and Ordinances of the Interregnum, 1642–1660* (London: His Majesty's Stationery Office, 1911), 1125–26, http://www.british-history.ac.uk/no-series/acts-ordinances-interregnum/pp1125-1126.

21. Order in Parliament regarding embezzling and timber, 22 February 1648/1649, SP 25/87, fols. 16v-17r, TNA.

22. SP 25/94, fols. 53 (Council of State to Captain Nicholls, 26 March 1649), 97 (Council of State to Messrs. Holland, Smith, and Rob. Thompson, Navy Commissioners, 16 April 1649); Order of the Navy Commissions regarding Waltham Forest, 2 May 1649, SP 18/1, fol. 146; Warrant Book from the Council of State, 16 June 1649, SP 25/62, fol. 443; Council of State to Captain Ludlow, 18 October 1649, SP 25/94, fol. 495; Council of State to the surveyor and preservators of Dean Forest, 1 December 1649, SP 25/63/2, fols.168, 170; Council of State to the Ranger and Keepers of Theobalds Park, 27 August 1649, SP 25/123, fol. 51; Council of State to Navy Commissioners, 18 October 1649, SP 18/6, fol. 77; Thomas Lord Grey to all Constables, Thirdburrowes, and other ministers of the peace in counties Northampton and Bucks, 27 October 1649, SP 18/3, fol. 49, TNA.

23. Gerrard Winstanley, *The Complete Works of Gerrard Winstanley, Vol. 2*, ed. Thomas N. Corns, Ann Hughes, and David Loewenstein (Oxford: Oxford University Press, 2009), 36–37, http://www.oxfordscholarlyeditions.com/view/10.1093/actrade/9780198183433.book.1/actrade-9780198183433-book-1. Some scholars and modern journalists have attempted to cast Winstanley as a proto-Green. For a description of and rebuttal to this argument, see Ariel Hessayon, "Restoring the Garden of Eden in England's Green and Pleasant Land: The Diggers and the Fruits of the Earth," *Journal for the Study of Radicalism* 2, no. 2 (2009): 1–25.

24. SP 25/94, fols. 217 (Council of State to Christopher Worgan, Andrew Home, Thomas Berow, and Arthur Rowls, preservators of the Forest of Dean, 6 June 1649), 277 (Council of State to the Worcester Committee, 2 July 1649), 495 (Council of State to Navy Commissioners, 18 October 1649), 497 (Council of State to the Mayors and other Justices of the Peace for Sarum, 18 October 1649); Council of State to the Lord General, 23 February 1650/1651, SP 25/95, fol. 11, TNA.

25. Report, by J. Brownwick and George Bishop, of the spoils committed in Dean Forest, 19 December 1649, SP 18/3, fol. 130, TNA.

26. Ibid.

27. Sylvanus Taylor, *Common-Good: Or, The Improvement of Commons, Forrests, and Chases, by Inclosure* (London, 1652), 20–21, 24.

28. Ibid., 29–30.

29. Ibid., 33.

30. C. H. Firth and R. S. Rait, eds., "November 1653: An Act for the Deafforestation, Sale and Improvement of the Forests and of The Honors, Manors, Lands, Tenements and Hereditaments Within the Usual Limits and Perambulations of the Same. Heretofore Belonging to the Late King, Queen and Prince," in *Acts and Ordinances of the Interregnum, 1642-1660* (London: His Majesty's Stationery Office, 1911), 783–812, http://www.british-history.ac.uk/no-series/acts-ordinances-interregnum/pp783-812. It is tempting to wonder if this action was connected to preparations begun the following year on the "Western Design" to seize parts of Spain's Atlantic empire, but a definitive connection remains elusive. On the planning and preparation for the Design, see Pestana, *The English Conquest of Jamaica*, 15–39.

31. Carey Mildmay, Account of Waltham Forest, Essex, n.d. [c. 1654], SP 18/77, fol. 222, TNA.

32. John Kinsey, Thos. Watts, and Geo. Sargeant to Cromwell, 9 May 1657, SP 18/155, fol. 36, TNA.

33. Ralph Austen, *A Treatise of Fruit-Trees Shewing the Manner of Grafting, Setting, Pruning, and Ordering of Them in All Respects* (London, 1653), 1v–12.

34. M. Greengrass, M. Leslie, and M. Hannon, eds., *The Hartlib Papers* (Sheffield: Published by HRI Online Publications, 2013), https://www.dhi.ac.uk/hartlib/, 41/1/106A-107B (Ralph Austen to Samuel Hartlib, 6 March 1655/1656), 114A (Austen to Hartlib, 2 October 1656), 119A (Austen to Hartlib, 10 October 1656), 121A (Austen to Hartlib, 9 February 1656/1657), 146A-B (Austen, Petition to Parliament on Planting Fruit Trees, n.d.).

35. *Hartlib Papers*, 41/1/119A (Austen to Hartlib, 10 October 1656), 146A-B (Austen, Petition).

36. Council of State, Day's Proceedings: The case of Mr. Pury and his partners, 3 January 1649/1650, SP 25/63/2, f.235; Instructions to Major John Wade, 27 August 1653, SP 25/70, f.289; John Wade to the Chiefs of the Admiralty, 5 December 1653, SP 18/62, f.68; Jno. Hooke to the Navy Commissioners, November 1655, SP 18/117, f.172, TNA.

37. SP 18/90, fols. 225 (H. Browne and Geo. Payler to the Admiralty Commissioners, 23 November 1654), 293 (John Taylor to Commissioners of the Navy, 30 November 1654), TNA. On the intense demands for resources to enable the Western Design, see Pestana, *The English Conquest of Jamaica*, 29–31; Pestana points to contemporary anxieties about skilled labor and naval stores, such as cordage, but does not indicate anxieties about wood.

38. C. H. Firth and R. S. Rait, eds., "June 1657: An Act for the Mitigation of the Rigor of the Forest Laws, within the Forest of Dean, in the County of Glocester, and for the Preservation of Wood and Timber in the Said Forest," in *Acts and Ordinances of the Interregnum, 1642-1660* (London: His Majesty's Stationery Office, 1911), 1114–15, http://www.british-history.ac.uk/no-series/acts-ordinances-interregnum/pp1114-1115.

39. Daniel Furzer to the Naval Officers, 27 November 1660, SP 29/21, f.232; Furzer to the Navy Commissioners, 9 February 1660/1661, SP 29/30, f.121, TNA.

40. John Wade, Account of timber and plank brought out of Dean Forest, 28 March 1659; Daniel Furzer to the Navy Commissioners, 4 April 1659; Furzer to the Navy Commissioners, 25 May 1657, TNA.

41. Everett, *The Woods of Ireland*, 131–34.

42. Boate died in 1650, prior to the publication of *Irelands Naturall History*. Boate's brother and the natural philosopher Samuel Hartlib had worked to complete it after Gerard's death. See Patricia Coughlan, "Natural History and Historical Nature: The Project for a Natural History of Ireland," in *Samuel Hartlib and Universal Reformation: Studies in Intellectual Communication*, ed. Mark Greengrass, Michael Leslie, and Timothy Raylor (New York: Cambridge University

Press, 1994), 299–300. For further discussion of Boate and Hartlib on Irish woods, see Everett, *The Woods of Ireland*, 143–45.

43. Gerard Boate, *Irelands Naturall History* (1657), 120–24.

44. Everett, *The Woods of Ireland*, 131–52.

45. Boate, *Irelands Naturall History*, 119–21.

46. Ibid., 123–24.

47. Ibid.

48. "Note on the destruction of woods due to the late rebellion for Fermanagh and Tyrone," HAM, Box 76, folder 13, Huntington Library, San Marino, CA; "Reasons why the Right Honorable the Countess of Huntingdon should let her land to farm in Ireland and Why Not," HAM, Box 79, folder 16. I am grateful to Bríd McGrath for pointing me toward this source and for dating the manuscript. On the 1654 memorandum, see Everett, *The Woods of Ireland*, 146–48.

49. Boate, *Irelands Naturall History*, 122.

50. Deposition of Percy Smith, 4 July 1642, MS 820, fols. 116r–116v, Trinity College Dublin (hereafter TCD). On the 1641 Depositions and the digitization project that has made them widely available, see Eamon Darcy, Annaleigh Margey, and Elaine Murphy, "Introduction," in *The 1641 Depositions and the Irish Rebellion*, ed. Eamon Darcy, Annaleigh Margey, and Elaine Murphy (New York: Routledge, 2012), 21–29. Here and throughout, I have accessed the 1641 Depositions via Trinity College Dublin's 1641 Depositions Project (1641.tcd.ie).

51. See, for example, Deposition of Robert Darling, 17 February 1642/1643, MS 823, fols. 096r–096v, TCD.

52. Deposition of Edmund Bloud, 9 March 1641/1642, MS 816, fols. 153r–153v; Deposition of Richard Stevens, 9 November 1642, MS 829, fols. 199r–199v, TCD.

53. Other reports from the early 1640s suggest a similar focus on landscapes associated with English settlement, particularly woods used for elite sport, see Everett, *The Woods of Ireland*, 135–37.

54. Deposition of John and James Redferne, 7 November 1642, MS 839, fols. 100r–101v, TCD.

55. John Brereton, 9 January 1642/1643 [Date given as 1645 in database entry], MS 815, fols. 370r–370v, TCD.

56. From Phillip Bysse [Bisse] to his brother, 16 February 1641/1642, MS 840, fols. 007r–010v, TCD.

57. Eileen McCracken, "Charcoal-Burning Ironworks," 129; for a list of ironworks operating in the seventeenth and eighteenth centuries, see 126–35. For a list of mainly eighteenth-century ironworks, see McCracken, "Supplementary List of Irish Charcoal-Burning Ironworks," *Ulster Journal of Archaeology* 28 (1965): 132–36.

58. Toby Christopher Barnard, "Sir William Petty as Kerry Ironmaster," *Proceedings of the Royal Irish Academy. Section C: Archaeology, Celtic Studies, History, Linguistics, Literature* 82C (1982): 1–32; T. C. Barnard, "An Anglo-Irish Industrial Enterprise: Iron-Making at Enniscorthy, Co. Wexford, 1657–92," *Proceedings of the Royal Irish Academy. Section C: Archaeology, Celtic Studies, History, Linguistics, Literature* 85C (January 1985): 101–44. Everett's account aligns with this view, noting that coppices used for Cromwellian-era ironworks survived into the nineteenth century; Everett, *The Woods of Ireland*, 150–52.

59. Barnard, "Sir William Petty as Kerry Ironmaster," 18–21; Barnard, "An Anglo-Irish Industrial Enterprise," 126–28, 112.

60. Samuel Hartlib, *The Reformed Virginia Silk-Worm* (London, 1655), 9, 12. A nearly identical text was printed in 1652 under the title *A rare and new discovery of a speedy way and easie*

means, found out by a young lady in England, she having made full proofe thereof in May, anno 1652. For the feeding of silk-worms in the woods; Hartlib Papers 39/2/12A–13B. Hartlib's proposal echoed many of the themes from Bonoeil's earlier writing, and, in practice, continued difficulties with expertise and skill to produce at a commercially viable scale remained. See Stanwood, *The Global Refuge*, 78–80.

61. Hartlib, *The Reformed Virginia Silk-Worm*, 13–14.

62. John Beale, *Herefordshire Orchards, a Pattern for All England* (London, 1657), 38. Part of John Beale to Hartlib, 9 April 1657, *Hartlib Papers*, 52/11A–12B; Beale to Hartlib, 19 March 1658/1659, *Hartlib Papers*, 51/93A–96B; Beale to Hartlib Regarding His Commentary on Standish, 22 March 1659, *Hartlib Papers*, 51/99A–101B.

63. John Beale to Hartlib 7 December 1658, *Hartlib Papers*, 51/39A–40B; Beale to Hartlib, 14 December 1658, *Hartlib Papers* 51/43A–B.

64. Beale to Hartlib, 22 March 1658/1659, *Hartlib Papers*, 51/99A–101B; Joan Thirsk, *The Rural Economy of England: Collected Essays* (London: Hambledon Press, 1984); see Essay 15, "New Crops and Their Diffusion: Tobacco-Growing in Seventeenth-Century England."

65. Extracts of Letters from Hartlib to Evelyn, September–November 1659, Evelyn Papers, Add. MSS 15948, fols. 71A–75B, BL; Michael Leslie, "'Bringing Ingenuity into Fashion': The 'Elysium Britannicum' and the Reformation of Husbandry," in *John Evelyn's "Elysium Britannicum" and European Gardening*, ed. Therese O'Malley and Joachim Wolschke-Bulmahn (Washington, DC: Dumbarton Oaks Research Library and Collection, 1998), 131–52; for Beale's commentary to Evelyn about open letters and his critique of Evelyn's work, see 136–37.

66. Warren M. Billings, "Sir William Berkeley and the Diversification of the Virginia Economy," *Virginia Magazine of History and Biography* 104, no. 4 (1996): 433–54; Billings, *Sir William Berkeley and the Forging of Colonial Virginia*; for Berkeley's move to Virginia, see 50–60; for his agricultural innovations, see 81–95; on policy, see 163–82.

67. Billings, *Sir William Berkeley and the Forging of Colonial Virginia*, 81–95; William Berkeley, *The Papers of Sir William Berkeley, 1605–1677*, ed. Warren M. Billings (Richmond: Library of Virginia, 2007), 192–93. Berkeley's efforts to produce potash represented a clever attempt to produce a largely wood-derived commodity produced mainly in the Baltic and the sourcing for which created continual anxiety in England. See Paul Warde, "Trees, Trade and Textiles: Potash Imports and Ecological Dependency in British Industry, c. 1550–1770," *Past & Present* 240, no. 1 (August 2018): 47–82.

68. Berkeley, *The Papers of Sir William Berkeley*, 192–93; "Petition of Sir William Berkeley, His Majesty's Governor of Virginia, to Lords of the Council for Foreign Plantation," July 1662, CO 1/16, No. 78, fol. 183, TNA.

69. Billings, *Sir William Berkeley and the Forging of Colonial Virginia*, 165–68.

70. Berkeley, *The Papers of Sir William Berkeley*, 1–2, 5. In arguing for diversified commodities, including those from woods, Berkeley was following a pattern that had been used in proposals for the newly captured colony in Jamaica in the 1650s. See Pestana, *The English Conquest of Jamaica*, 139–56.

71. William Berkeley, Sir, *A Discourse and View of Virginia*, 1663, 5–7, 9.

72. Berkeley, *The Papers of Sir William Berkeley*, 33, 179–80.

73. Billings, *Sir William Berkeley and the Forging of Colonial Virginia*, 168–76, 196–220; Berkeley, *The Papers of Sir William Berkeley*, 395.

74. On Virginia's trade with Barbados, including in wood products, see April Lee Hatfield, *Atlantic Virginia: Intercolonial Relations in the Seventeenth Century* (Philadelphia: University of Pennsylvania Press, 2004), 52–54.

75. Evelyn, *Sylva*, 114.

76. For references to voyages to procure New England masts or New England masts at shipyards, see James Marsh, Survey of New England Masts, 3 January 1650/1651, SP 18/17, fol. 1; Francis Willoughby to Robert Blackborne, 15 November 1653, SP 18/41, fol. 301; Thomas Smith and Edward Hopkins to the Navy Commissioners, 3 January 1652/1653, SP 18/45, fol. 20; David Yale to the Commissioners of the Navy, n.d. [c. 1653], SP 18/61, fol. 161; George Monck to the Commissioners of the Navy, December 1653, SP 18/62, fol. 269; To the commissioners of the Navy from John Disbrowe, George Monck, and [R?] Clarke, 11 January 1653/1654, SP 18/78, fol. 121; Thomas Smith and 2 others to the Commissioners of the Navy, 13 October 1654, SP 18/89, fol. 77; Robert Clarke to the Navy Commissioners, 27 December 1654), SP 18/91, fol. 250; R. Clarke to the Navy Commissioners, 9 January 1654/1655, SP 18/103, fol. 59; Captain John Taylor to the Navy Commissioners, 18 May 1655), SP 18/109, fol. 67; SP 18/137, fols. 146 ([C?] Thorowgood to the Navy Commissioners, 26 March 1656), 260 (John Parker to the Navy Commissioners, 31 March 1656), 262 (Thorowgood to the Navy Commissioners, 1656); J. Parker to the Navy Commissioners, 18 April 1656, SP 18/138, fol. 254; John Taylor to the Navy Commissioners, 24 May 1656, SP 18/140, fol. 119; Several documents relating to masts, pipestaves, and other goods in New England, July 1656, SP 18/146, fols. 165-67; Order by the Navy Commissioners, 18 November 1656, SP 18/148, fol. 54, TNA.

77. For early attempts to establish trade in timber and naval stores between New England and England, see Carroll, *The Timber Economy of Puritan New England*, 85–86.

78. David Yale to the Commissioners of the Navy, n.d. [c.1653], SP 18/61, fol. 161; T. Smith and others to the Navy Commissioners, October 1654, SP 18/89, fol. 77, TNA.

79. Thomas Smith and Edward Hopkins to the Navy Commissioners, 3 January 1652/1653, SP 18/45, fol. 20; George Monck to the Commisioners of the Navy, December 1653, SP 18/62, fol. 269, TNA.

80. Francis Willoughby to Commissioners of the Navy, 28 August 1654, SP 18/87, fol. 159; F. Willoughby to the Commissioners of the Navy, 16 December 1654, SP 18/91, fol. 140, TNA.

81. Willoughby to the Navy Commissioners, with attachments, 16 February 1656, SP 18/134, fols. 118-20, TNA.

82. John Taylor to the Navy Commissioners, 21 May 1655, SP 18/109, fol. 67; J. Taylor to the Navy Commissioners, 24 May 1656, SP 18/140, fol. 119; J. Taylor to the Navy Commissioners, 4 July 1656, SP 18/142, fol. 32, TNA.

83. Several documents relating to masts, pipe staves, and other goods in New England, July 1656, SP 18/146 fols. 165-67; the letter from Gookin, Norton, and Broughton is on fol. 166.

84. Peter Pett to the Navy Commisioners, 29 December 1656, SP 18/150, fol. 133; P. Pett to the Navy Commissioners, 9 April 1658, SP 18/190, fol. 35, TNA.

85. Commissioners of Customs to Sir Philip Warwick, 12 February 1660/1661, CO 1/15, No. 16, fol. 34. On New England's Atlantic and Caribbean timber trade, see Carroll, *The Timber Economy of Puritan New England*, 77–86; Roberts, *Colonial Ecology, Atlantic Economy*, 5–7, 76–78, 130–32.

86. Evelyn, *Sylva*, 114; Waterhouse, *A Declaration of the State of the Colony*, 3–5. This line is repeated in a manuscript description of Virginia that copied much of Waterhouse's work, CO 1/4, fols. 130r-131r, TNA.

87. David Pulsifer, *Records of the Colony of New Plymouth in New England: Laws 1623-1682* (Boston: William White, 1861), 3–4, 14, 119; John Noble, ed., *Records of the Court of Assistants of the Colony of the Massachusetts Bay, 1630-1692* (Boston: County of Suffolk, 1901), 2:17, 28, 31.

88. William Bradford, *Bradford's History "Of Plimoth Plantation"* (Boston: Wright & Potter, 1901), 95. As Strother Roberts points out, historians have too often accepted claims like

Evelyn's and poetic denunciations of "wilderness" but have not attended to the myriad actions taken to preserve and regulate woods. See Roberts, *Colonial Ecology, Atlantic Economy*, 15, 17–18, 108–20, 133–34.

89. Nathaniel Bradstreet Shurtleff, ed., *Records of the Governor and Company of the Massachusetts Bay in New England* (Boston: William White, 1853), 2:126; Pulsifer, *Laws 1623-1682*, 119; Trumbull, *The Public Records of the Colony of Connecticut*, 1:214, 243.

90. Nathaniel Bradstreet Shurtleff, ed., *Records of the Colony of New Plymouth in New England* (Boston: William White, 1855), 1:133–34, 169.

91. Shurtleff, *Records of the Colony of New Plymouth in New England*, 2:120; 174.

92. *Winthrop Papers* (Massachusetts Historical Society, 1944), 4:304–5, 311–12; Shurtleff, *Records of the Colony of New Plymouth*, 2:58. Efforts to plan New England settlements around English precedents and to closely manage resources, including woods, were common. See Brian Donahue, *The Great Meadow: Farmers and the Land in Colonial Concord* (New Haven, CT: Yale University Press, 2004), 79, 113–14.

93. David Pulsifer, ed., *Records of the Colony of New Plymouth in New England: Acts of the Commissioners of the United Colonies of New England* (Boston: William White, 1859), 10:266. On the importance of maritime places for the Pequots and their use of timber for shipbuilding, see Andrew Lipman, *The Saltwater Frontier: Indians and the Contest for the American Coast* (New Haven, CT: Yale University Press, 2015), 22–35, 66–72.

94. Shurtleff, *Records of the Colony of New Plymouth*, 2:58, 3:218, 4:8, 64. Christine DeLucia has analyzed how English efforts to define resources were part of a broader colonial strategy to control territory and redefine landscapes, as well as Wampanoag resistance to colonialism. See Christine DeLucia, "Terrapolitics in the Dawnland: Relationality, Resistance, and Indigenous Futures in the Native and Colonial Northeast," *New England Quarterly* 92, no. 4 (November 2019): 548–83. On 8sâmeeqan's legacy, colonial and Native memory, and the proliferation of *Massasoit* statues in the United States, see Lisa Blee and Jean M. O'Brien, *Monumental Mobility: The Memory Work of Massasoit* (Chapel Hill: University of North Carolina Press, 2019).

95. Pulsifer, *Laws 1623-1682*, 183; Trumbull, *The Public Records of the Colony of Connecticut*, 1:214.

96. Virginia DeJohn Anderson, "King Philip's Herds: Indians, Colonists, and the Problem of Livestock in Early New England," *William and Mary Quarterly*, 3rd ser., 51, no. 4 (October 1994): 601–24. Anderson mentions Metacom's complaint about timber cutting on p. 619. She has pointed out the importance of woods as sites for animal husbandry elsewhere. See Anderson, "Animals into the Wilderness: The Development of Livestock Husbandry in the Seventeenth-Century Chesapeake," *William and Mary Quarterly*, 3rd ser., 59, no. 2 (April 2002): 377–408.

97. Cronon, *Changes in the Land*, 108–26; Allan Greer, "Commons and Enclosure in the Colonization of North America," *American Historical Review* 117, no. 2 (1 April 2012): 365–86. Greer has argued that commons, not Lockean private property, were crucial to European expansion in the Americas.

98. Hartley, *Ironworks on the Saugus*. Hartley provided a detailed chronicle of the commercial networks and experience that led to the New England ironworks's creation, but he nonetheless persisted in attributing the enterprise's success to English wood scarcity. See pp. 79-80.

99. Hartley, *Ironworks on the Saugus*, 65–68; *Winthrop Papers*, 4:363–65, 379.

100. *Winthrop Papers*, 4:425–26.

101. Shurtleff, *Records of the Governor and Company of the Massachusetts Bay*, 2:81–82, 126; 3:91.

102. Hartley, *Ironworks on the Saugus*, 259–71.

103. Evelyn, *Sylva*, 114.

104. Cronon, *Changes in the Land*, 110–11.

105. Joseph J. Malone, *Pine Trees and Politics: The Naval Stores and Forest Policy in Colonial New England, 1691–1775* (Seattle: University of Washington Press, 1965), 2–7, 12–13, 17–19, 82–123 (on resistance to efforts at increased royal regulations); Roberts, *Colonial Ecology, Atlantic Economy*, 127–41 (on shipbuilding and the timber trade), 141–54 (on resistance to the White Pine Acts).

106. Lefroy, *Memorials*, 2:6, 51.

107. Ibid., 2:101.

108. Hallett, *Bermuda Under the Sommer Islands Company*, 3:93–94.

109. Ibid., 3:86–91, 96–97, 100–101.

110. Ibid., 3:93.

111. Ibid., 3:158.

112. Lefroy, *Memorials*, 2:111, 123, 126, 130.

113. Ibid., 2:130–31.

114. Ibid., 2:131.

115. Hallett, *Bermuda Under the Sommer Islands Company*, 1:522.

116. Jarvis, *In the Eye of All Trade*. Bermuda's maritime transition had already begun to occur by the time Sayle had become governor and he supported the shift, ignoring illicit or unpermitted intercolonial trade; see pp. 47–50, 55. It was only in the 1680s that the tobacco trade fully disappeared from the islands; see pp. 64–65.

117. Jarvis, *In the Eye of All Trade*, 89–91.

118. Lefroy, *Memorials*, 2:108. On Bermudians' role in timbering expeditions to the Bahamas; Campeche, Honduras; and other sites around the Greater Caribbean, see Jarvis, *In the Eye of All Trade*, 218–33. On the importance of brazilwood in sixteenth-century France and in the iconography of sixteenth-century maps, see Surekha Davies, *Renaissance Ethnography and the Invention of the Human: New Worlds, Maps and Monsters*, Cambridge Social and Cultural Histories (New York: Cambridge University Press, 2017), 111, 117.

119. Colonists in Surinam, for example, pursued specklewood, which was used in furniture making. See Alison Games, "Cohabitation, Suriname-Style: English Inhabitants in Dutch Suriname After 1667," *William and Mary Quarterly* 72, no. 2 (2015): 204. On Surinam as a colony of Barbados, see Justin Roberts, "Surrendering Surinam: The Barbadian Diaspora and the Expansion of the English Sugar Frontier, 1650–75," *William and Mary Quarterly* 73, no. 2 (2016): 225. On local conservation measures and the New England trade, see Chapter 5.

120. Roberts, "Surrendering Surinam," 225–26; Roberts argues that we might use the term "greater Barbados" to describe the "Barbadian-centered colonial models of development," 232 (quotation), 232–34 (on timber shipments). Draper, "Timbering and Turtling," 774–85 (on St. Lucia timbering); Draper argues that "maritime hinterlands" played an important role in the primary industries for Caribbean colonies, see p. 774.

INDEX

1641 Rebellion, 92, 212–13, 229

abolition of all royal forests (proposed), 33
abundance, commercial vs. biological, 108, 115, 117, 126–27, 129, 135; definitions of, 7. *See also* scarcity
Acosta, José de, 144
adventurers, 112–13, 116–17, 120, 122, 129–33, 140–42, 145–48, 157, 159, 161–66, 178, 220, 229–31, 233, 235, 237, 229
agriculture, woods as impediment to, 136
Anthropocene, 168
Apsley, Sir Allen, 99, 112
availability of wood, comparative, 17. *See also* scarcity

Ball, Thomas, 92, 94–95, 101, 121
Baltic, 216
ban on timber exports, 82
Barbados, 10–12, 167–92; as intercolonial market, 221; colonial project of, 236–37
bark. *See* tanning
barrels. *See* pipe staves
Beale, John, 216–18
beauty, 29–31, 33, 47, 51, 184, 186–87, 189, 191
Becher, Henry, 90, 97
Bell, Philip, 147–49, 158
Berkeley, Henry, Lord Berkeley, 25–27
Berkeley, John, 119–20, 123
Berkeley, William, 215, 219–21
Berkeley Hundred, 120–22
Bermuda, 10–12, 125, 131–66; ecology of, 133–34
Bermuda cedars, 132
bibby, 147–51, 159
birds, 139–40
Blacknall, Nicholas, 90, 95, 99
Blacknall, Richard 82, 100–101
Blount, Charles, Baron Mountjoy, 75

Bluett, Benjamin, 117–19, 121
Boate, Gerard 210–13
Bonoeil, John, 115–17
boundaries, 71–72. *See also* maps; surveys; titles; water
boundary trees, 183. *See also* windbreaks
Boyle, Richard, Earl of Cork, 60, 74, 77–80, 82, 84–87, 90–99, 101–3, 117, 121, 142, 211, 214
brewers, 17
Brooke, Sir Basil, 20, 44–45
Broughton, John, 43–44
Broughton, Thomas, 224–25
Browne, Sir Valentine 63–64, 66
building materials, 21, 39, 74, 87, 92, 95–96, 138, 205–7, 213
Butler, Nathaniel, 136, 145, 156, 235

Catholicism, as political threat, 105, 115, 132, 199, 205–6
cattle, 29–30, 47, 55, 69–70, 88, 93–94, 97, 125, 185–86. *See also* pasturing
Cecil, Robert, 76
Cecil, William, 21–23, 28, 66
cedars, as commodity, 134, 136–37, 140–42, 166; preservation in Bermuda, 232–34
Challoner, Richard, 44–45, 120–21
charcoal, 2, 18, 23, 35, 38–39, 46, 94, 110, 120, 125, 211. *See also* fuel
Charles I, 15, 18, 40–51, 82, 126–28, 199–200, 208, 220
Charles II, 196, 198–99, 219–21, 237
Chichester, Arthur, 59–60, 76–81, 84–86, 93–94, 97, 104–6
Civil War, English, 198–200, 209
climate, 54, 108–9, 111, 114, 161–62, 168, 185, 195
coal, 6, 19, 35, 38. *See also* fuel
Colt, Henry, 167–68, 184

Colthurst, Christopher, 98
commercial networks, 11–12, 90, 102, 104, 109,
   113, 121, 214–15, 221, 231–32. *See also* trade
common rights, 3, 6, 8, 14–15, 18, 21, 23–28,
   31, 36–43, 48–50, 64, 66–67, 96, 199–205,
   226–28. *See also* custom
commonwealth, 15, 202–3
Condon, Patrick, 75, 84
Connecticut, 180–81, 226, 228
conversion to Christianity, forced, 118, 122;
   voluntary, 189
coppicing, 20, 22, 87, 89, 92, 94, 102, 138, 211
corn, 155, 157–58
costs of labor and transportation, 195
Cottingham, Philip, 76–78
cotton, 169, 178, 180–81
Council of the Royal Society, 193
Cromwell, Oliver, 201, 206
Cromwellian Protectorate, 198
custom, 23–25, 34–39, 41, 43, 94, 96, 142, 164,
   169, 171. *See also* common rights
Customs, 83, 225

deeds, as historical sources, 168, 171–76, 178;
   limiting land use, 178–79, 181, 181, 183
deforestation, as a marker of progress, 53;
   as goal, 125, 185; in Barbados, 167, 169; in
   England, causes of, 198; rates of, 171–76
Desmond Rebellion, 52, 84
destroyed woods, 7, 211–14
disafforestation, 18, 82, 128, 199–200, 206
disobedience of laws, regulations, terms, 97,
   204, 209. *See also* disorder; exemptions;
   social control
disorder, 148, 166–67, 204, 206
diverse forests, 21, 91
diversification of Bermuda economy, 161; of
   Virginia economy, 113, 120–22, 127–28, 218,
   220; of Virginia economy, disparaged, 125
Dorrell, Henry, 87–88
Drax, Henry, 182–84, 188
drunkenness, 147, 152
Durham, Thomas, 141, 159–60, 163
Dutch merchants, 77, 78, 84, 90, 95, 101,
   104, 124
dyewoods, 171, 179, 236. *See also* luxury goods
D'Acosta, Juan, 195

East India Company, 3, 10, 57, 80–81, 100,
   104, 111–12, 117, 121, 129, 214
Edward VI, 19

efficiency, 29, 35; incentives and responsibility for, 99. *See also* waste
Elizabeth I, 16, 18–19, 21, 24–27, 29, 35, 37,
   49–53, 56, 66, 69, 199
enclosure, 26, 36, 138, 205–6; proposal for
   widespread, 34. *See also* ownership
English trade, 54
erosion, 167
erosion, 44, 125, 184
estates, royal and noble, 15
Europe, Eastern, 216
European merchants, 78. *See also* Dutch
   merchants
Evelyn, John, 8, 193–94, 196–99, 207, 209–10,
   215, 217–18, 221–22, 225–26, 231–32, 237
exemptions, 64, 81–84, 94, 178, 197, 225, 233
expertise, 115–16, 119, 129, 154–57, 219;
   African and Native, 146, 155, 188. *See also*
   knowledge

Falling Creek, 120, 122–24, 128–29; raid on,
   122–23
famine, 61, 144, 154–55
Fenton, Geoffrey, 63–64, 76–77, 79
Ferrar, Nicholas, 114–15
Ferrar, William, 114
Ferrar family, 124, 148
fig trees, 157–59
Finch, Sir John, 44–45
firewood, 21, 25, 41
fish, 125–26, 159, 225
FitzGerald, Thomas, 93–94
Fitz-John Gerald, Thomas, 92
Forest Laws, 7–8, 8, 16, 23–24, 37, 41–42, 44,
   200, 205; revival of, 16, 49–50, 85, 199
Forest of Dean, 100, 119–21, 193, 199–205,
   208–9, 214, 229
forest officers, 8, 21, 28, 24, 26, 28, 40, 42, 44,
   201–8, 237
forestry reform, 33–37, 43
Forster, Josias, 151, 232–234
France, colonies of, 53; experts from, 155. *See
   also* vignerons
fuel, 2, 5, 6, 15–22, 37–39, 42, 45, 50, 74, 87,
   91–93, 98, 100–104, 179–80, 182–83, 202,
   206–7, 213–14, 234, 236; for sugar production, 182–83

glassmaking, 2, 17, 35, 112
Gookin, Daniel, 224, 227
Gray, Robert, 55, 56

grazing, 26, 29, 43
Greatrakes, William, 92, 95

Hakluyt, Richard, 53–56
Hall, Benedict, 42–43, 46
Hamburg, sawyers from, 114
Harriot, Thomas, 55–56, 70, 72–73, 186
Hartlib, Samuel 207, 215–18
Harvey, John, 126, 128
Harwood, Richard, 182–83
Hastings, Lucy, 212–213
hedges, 2, 16, 37, 157
Henry VIII, 16, 18, 23, 33, 35, 37, 40, 246
Herbert, William, Earl of Pembroke, 39, 44, 46, 120
hunting, 15, 24, 27, 33, 51, 139, 202. *See also* parks and recreation
Huntingdon, Earl of, 30, 41
hunting, royal, 29–30

importation of iron and glass, 2; of trees, 162. *See also* trade
introduced species, 134, 153–57, 166
investment, 124
investors. *See* adventurers
Ireland, 10, 12, 18, 39, 52–53, 59–107; civilizing of, 81, 86, 104–5; competition with English, 120; competition with Virginia, 105–6, 112, 118, 121–24; English attempts to understand, 210–211; in Evelyn, 194; pastoralism in, 62; reports on forests, 59–60; stereotypes of, 94. *See also* iron production; pipe staves
Irish people allied with Afro-Bermudians, 152
Irish Privy Council, 94
iron production, 2–3, 8, 17–19, 35, 39–40, 42, 44–46, 50, 56, 195, 201–2, 204, 208, 211, 215; in Ireland, 80–82, 90–94, 101–4, 214; in North America, 55, 109, 111–12, 117, 119, 122–23, 125–27, 130, 196, 217, 220, 229–230; sustainably fueled, 197; taxation of, 79

Jamaica, 184
James I, 1–2, 14–15, 18, 24, 27, 29–30, 34–35, 39–40, 44–45, 49–51, 56, 74, 76, 81, 104–5, 111, 114, 120, 122, 124
Jephson, Sir John, 79–80, 98
Jourdain, Sylvester (and anonymous additor), 135, 137, 144, 154
juniper, 134–35, 163–64

knowledge, 5, 36; English, 190; government, 61; local and governmental, 25, 41, 70, 72, 231; natural, 186–87, 189; of enslaved people, 190–91. *See also* maps; surveys

labor, 135, 141. *See also* slavery
Lea, Philip, 173, 175
leases, as historical sources, 168; terms of, 33–36, 42, 46, 74, 87–92, 95, 95–99, 101–3, 142, 162–65, 178–79, 181–82, 212, 233
legal cases, 23–24, 26–27, 35, 42, 44–46, 75, 83, 138, 157
Ligon, Richard, 169, 171–73, 184–91, 195
Lisfinny, 72, 87–88, 95–96, 102–3
local uses for woods, 176, 178–80, 235. *See also* knowledge; markets; regulation
London, 19, 41. *See also* fuel
Londonderry plantation, 81
luxury goods, 132, 134, 166, 173, 236

management, conflict over, 15, 17, 40; private, 17; royal, 14–17, 28–29, 40
Mandeville, Edward Montagu, Viscount, 163, 165
Manwood, John, 6–7, 16
maps, 64, 67–73, 89, 171–72, 177, 190. *See also* surveys
markets, for Irish wood, 60; local and transatlantic, 179; international, 90, 96. *See also* trade
Massachusetts Bay colony, 226
masts, European sources of, 216; New England, 222–25
Middleton, David, 117–19, 121
Middleton, Thomas, 176–77
miners, customary rights of, 39
mines, iron, 100
mining, 38–39
mobbie, 176
model settlements, 64–66
Mogeely, 72, 75, 91, 93–94, 102
mulberry, 145–46, 154, 157, 161
Munster Plantation, 61–64, 66, 78, 89–90; early records, 74; end of, 75

Native Americans, 109–12, 227–28; armed resistance of, 122; diplomatic relations with, 226, 228; knowledge and practices of, 110
New England, 10, 183, 222; in Evelyn, 195–97, 221; trade with Barbados, 180

Newfoundland, 12, 54
Nine Years' War, 75, 99
Norden, John, 24–25, 28, 30–33, 33–37, 43
Norris, Thomas, 88–91
North America, 18, 53–54
Norwood, Richard, 139, 144, 155

oil trees, 162
olives, 145–46, 154, 156–57, 235
orchards, 132, 154, 156–57, 163–65, 207–8, 218
ownership, 78, 84, 106, 112, 171, 176
ownership, private, 60
Oxenbridge, John, 233–34
O'Callaghan, Conogher, 88–91, 98
O'Callaghan, Terlagh, 91, 98

palmetto, as source of alcohol, 147; locally
    useful (but commercially worthless),
    143–46, 149, 153, 166, 175, 178
pannage, 23, 47, 206
Parliament, 16, 201
pastoralism, 89, 94
pasture rights, 8, 26, 46, 49, 205–6
pasturing, 6–8, 27, 39, 88–89, 125, 176, 206,
    226–28, 231. See also cattle; commons;
    leases; pannage
Pembroke. See Herbert, William
Perceval, Sir Philip , 98, 103
Pett, Peter, 193, 225
Pett, Phineas, 46, 48
pipe staves, 50, 211, 225, 227; from Ireland,
    75, 77–79, 82–84, 87, 93–96, 98–99, 102–4;
    from Virginia, 221; taxation of, 79
pitch, 113, 128–30, 195; European sources of,
    216
plantains, 155–56, 163, 188
plantations, in Ireland, 60–62, 67, 70 (see also
    Munster and Ulster); local control of, 67;
    measures of success, 70
planting, 194. See also replanting
pleasure, 184. See also beauty; hunting
Plymouth colony, 226, 228
poaching, 202
Poland, experts from, 113, 129
pollarding, 21
pomegranate trees, 158
poor, 31, 45–47, 49. See also common rights;
    custom
population, 14, 55–56
Pory, John, 113–15
posterity, 25, 31, 44–45

potatoes, 155
preservation, 133, 139, 179. See also replanting
privatization, 34, 50. See also disafforestation;
    ownership
Privy Council, 46–47, 59–60, 75–83, 94, 104,
    106, 117, 124, 219–20
Privy Council of Ireland, 81, 99
profit, 35–36, 38, 42–43, 48, 51, 86, 110–11; and
    revenue for the Commonwealth, 202; vs.
    sustainability, 86
protection. See regulation
Protestantism, 63
protests, 39, 43
Pyne, Charles, 103
Pyne, Henry, 72, 75, 77–78, 84, 90, 92–94

R. C., 35–38, 49
race, 149, 151–53, 188–90
Ralegh, Sir Walter, 67, 70, 72, 74, 75 86–88,
    90–92
rats, 145, 154–55, 157
recreation, 87, 98; royal, 6–7. See also
    hunting
reforestation, 234
regeneration, 90, 102, 104, 142. See also
    replanting
regulation (of woods) as means of social
    control, 132, 143, 147–53, 158–59, 201; pre-
    serving timber, 137–38, 142–43; preserving
    windbreaks, 141–43, 147; protecting local
    uses, 178–80, 182, 191, 226–27; protecting
    rights of landowners, 183; protecting trees
    as luxury goods, 173
rent. See leases
replanting, 40, 92, 138–39, 183
resistance, woods as site for, 124–25, 191. See
    also woodkern
Rich, Robert, 136, 138, 144, 146, 154–57
Rich, Sir Nathaniel, 136, 138, 141–42, 146,
    155–56, 159, 159–60, 163–64
Robins, Arthur, 67–70, 72
royal forests, 15–16. See also disafforestation;
    ownership
royal grant or sale, language of, 45. See also
    deeds; titles
royal revenue, 44

Sandys, Edwin, 114–15, 117–18, 122, 124, 148,
    219
Sandys, George, 116, 126
Sayle, William, 152, 234–35

Scotland, 88, 196
seasonality, 8
Second Desmond Rebellion, 61
self-sufficiency, colonial, 5, 12, 87, 170, 180, 221, 235–36
Seville, 90
shipbuilding timber, 3–4, 7–8, 15–16, 19–22, 30, 37, 41, 46–48, 50, 52, 54, 127, 198, 201, 208; European sources of, 216; Irish sources, 76–81, 87, 105–6. *See also* masts
shipping infrastructure and security, 223
Shipward, John, 90, 97
silk, 111, 114–17, 121, 125–26, 129, 132, 156, 161–62, 215, 218–19, 221
slavery, 133, 146, 151–52, 159, 188–91. *See also* knowledge
Slingsby, Sir Henry, 34–36, 43
sloth, under guise of preservation, 157
Smith, John, 56–57, 111, 114, 139–40
soil exhaustion, 160–61
Sommer Islands Company, 132–33, 137–40, 153, 157, 161, 165
Spain, colonies of, 53
Spanish Armada, 17, 52, 56
Spenser, Edmund, 53, 61
sport. *See* hunting; recreation
St. Lucia, 236–237
Standish, Arthur, 1–3, 6, 14, 16, 194, 216–17, 234
Stokes, Thomas, 142, 147, 157
Strachey, William, 111–12, 131, 137, 143–44, 154
Strafford, Thomas Wentworth, Earl of, 83–86, 102–4, 106
sugar production, 155, 161, 168–70, 179–82, 184, 187, 191, 236
Surinam, 236–37
surveys, 14, 16–21, 23–25, 27, 30–32, 126–27, 173, 177; fairness of, 28; of Ireland, 61–62, 67, 70, 72–75, 79, 82. *See also* knowledge; maps
sustainability, 33, 187–88
Sweden, 124, 225

tanning, 80, 87, 94, 136, 207, 213
tar, 113, 128, 130, 195–96; European sources of, 216
Taverner, John, 19, 21–22, 25, 28, 33, 46
Taverner, Roger, 19–20, 23, 25
taxation, 64, 70, 72, 79, 157

timber. *See* shipbuilding timber
titles. *See* deeds; leases; ownership
tobacco, 113, 124–25, 132, 140–41, 145–46, 154–62, 164–66, 169, 185, 217, 219, 233
trade, free, 220; between New England and Barbados, 181, 236; intercolonial, 181, 215 221, 225, 231–32, 235; transatlantic, 10, 235; with Baltic, 124
transformation, 189
transportation, 8, 27, 46, 48, 77, 209; costs of, 114, 128, 154. *See also* water
Tucker, Daniel, 136–38, 146
turf, 97–98, 101–2, 104, 206, 210
turtles, 139

Ulster Plantation, 78–83
uncertainties, 10. *See also* knowledge

valuation, 32–33, 70, 72, 74, 168; in Ireland, 63–64. *See also* knowledge; surveys
variety of forest condition, 32
vignerons, 115–16. *See also* experts; wine
violence, 97, 99, 122, 188, 210; against Powhatans, 125; over forest use, 26
Virginia, 3, 10, 12, 55, 57, 108–31, 215; as competition for Ireland, 105–6, 112, 118, 121–24; as source of naval stores, 219
Virginia Company, 2–3, 10, 55–56, 106, 108, 110, 112, 123–24, 131; leadership, 113
Virginia, Council for, 2–3, 56, 105, 119
Virginia, in English imagination, 218; in Evelyn, 194. *See also* iron production; pipe staves; trade

Warwick, Earl of, 27, 159–60, 163–65, 233
water, as barrier, 72; as boundaries, 71; as mill power, 66, 72, 88; as power source, 100, 120, 123; for transportation, 9, 16, 18, 41, 46, 48, 64, 80, 99, 193, 205, 214, 227. *See also* shipbuilding timber
waste, in Irish woods, 76; of timber, 7, 69, 93, 136–37, 141, 200–201, 206; perceived, 74
Waterhouse, Edward, 56–57, 225; necessary for sugar cultivation, 155
weapons production, 18
weeds, 186
Willoughby, Sir Francis, 121, 123
Willoughby, William, 47–48, 223–24, 237
wind, as hazard to tobacco, 160
windbreaks, 139–41, 145–46, 166, 182, 235
windfalls, 96

wine, 115–16, 125–26
"winning of the Forest," 125, 128. *See also*
    Native Americans; resistance; violence
Winstanley, Gerrard, 202–3
Winthrop, John, 180, 195, 227
Winthrop, John, Jr., 229–30
Wintour, Sir Edward, 119
Wintour, Sir John, 42–43, 45–46, 200, 203,
    205, 208

Wood, Roger, 135–36, 162
Woodhouse, Henry, 148, 158, 161, 164–65
woodkern, 62, 82, 167, 210
Wright, Henry, 82, 93, 101
Wyatt, Francis, 125–26, 218

Yeardley, George, 114, 119

Zouche, Sir John, 128–29

ACKNOWLEDGMENTS

No book is a purely individual enterprise. I have been thinking about the issues in *No Wood, No Kingdom* for more than a decade and the comments, conversations, support, and encouragement I benefited from over that time period constitute an unpayable debt. To those named below and those I may have omitted, I offer my heartfelt thanks for your time and energy.

I began research on early modern landscapes and English colonial expansion as an undergraduate at the University of Delaware under the supervision of John Montaño and am grateful for the time and financial support that the Undergraduate Research Program offered. Their support set me on the path to becoming a historian. John has remained a friend and mentor. He read my first fledgling thoughts on early modern Irish landscapes and commented on the entire manuscript for this book.

At the University of Southern California, I benefited from the fantastic mentorship of Peter Mancall and Cynthia Herrup. Peter pushed me to explore the wide ranges of the Atlantic World and held adviser meetings in surf sessions at Venice Beach, while Cynthia kept me grounded in the rigorous archival methodologies of British social history. Over years of drafts in multiple formats, they nurtured my early thinking and helped hone the final edits of this book. Words cannot express my gratitude. In addition, I was lucky to have supportive colleagues and mentors in USC's diverse community of early modernists and those outside the field willing to indulge lengthy discussions of early modern agriculture and forestry: Karin Amundsen, Heather Ashby, Judith Bennett, Lisa Bitel, Daniela Bleichmar, Amy Braden, Justin Clark, Justin Colvin, Christina Copland, Bill Deverell, Ellen Dooley, Kristen Geaman, Josh Goldstein, Karin Huebner, Nadia Kanagawa, Vera Keller, Nick Gliserman, Rebecca Lemon, Alex Marr, Brendan McMahon, Sean Nelson, Lindsay O'Neill, Monica Pelayo-Lock, Nick Radburn, Nathan Perl-Rosenthal, Sean Roberts, Stefan Smith, Max Felker-Kantor, and Patrick Wyman. I am particularly grateful to Amy Braden, Karin Amundsen, Nick Gliserman, and Pat Wyman for continued conversations, willingness to read, and the opportunity to publicly discuss the ideas in this book, and to Nathan Perl-Rosenthal for essential and timely assistance sketching the path forward from my dissertation to this book.

Much of the new research and many of the revisions that made this book took place while I was Howard E. and Susanne C. Jessen Postdoctoral Instructor in the Humanities at the California Institute of Technology. I am grateful to the Jessens for their financial support and their active enthusiasm for the environmental humanities. My Caltech colleagues—Kim Border, Warren Brown, Damian Clavel, Tracy Dennison, Maura Dykstra, Frederick Eberhardt, Mordechai Feingold, Kevin Gilmartin, Dehn Gilmore, Kristine Haugen, Chris Hitchcock, Phil Hoffman, Jocelyn Holland, Jen Jahner, Cathy Jurca, Bettina Koch, Leah Klement, Gideon Manning, Jean-Laurent Rosenthal, Ben Saltzman, Chip Sebens, Noel Swerdlow, Cindy Weinstein, and Nicolás Wey Gómez—provided a wonderful, supportive environment. The opportunities to communicate the significance of my work to an interdisciplinary audience and the comments and recommendations from their varied perspectives helped transform this work. I am grateful particularly to Ben for reading multiple chapter drafts and providing keen comments between sets at El Porto and to Jean-Laurent for reading and commenting on the complete manuscript.

Throughout my time at USC and Caltech, the USC-Huntington Early Modern Studies Institute (EMSI) and the Huntington Library provided generous financial support, unparalleled scholarly community, repeated opportunities to present work in progress, and an idyllic setting to research and write. Research directors Roy Ritchie and Steve Hindle graciously welcomed me to the community of scholars, made constant introductions, and have both read and supported my work over many years. I have had too many meaningful conversations at the Huntington to recount entirely, but I am grateful to Eric Ash, Ali Cathcart, Will Cavert, David Cressy, Brendan Kane, Maryanne Kowaleski, Dan Lewis, Ann Little, Ted McCormick, Bríd McGrath, Chris Parsons, Tawny Paul, Casey Schmitt, Margo Todd, Molly Warsh, Jennifer Wells, Vanessa Wilkie, Nat Zappiah, and Anya Zilberstein for their willingness to read my work and for years of sustained, insightful commentary in Pasadena and beyond.

I completed revisions while beginning as an assistant professor at Illinois State University. My colleagues there have been incredibly warm and welcoming and provided essential insights in the final stages of revision. Thanks in particular go to Saskia Beranek, Kyle Ciani, Linda Clemmons, Tony Crubaugh, Mike Dougherty, Andrew Hartman, Matt Himley, Ron Gifford, Eric Godoy, Richard Hughes, Katie Jasper, Ross Kennedy, Larissa Kennedy, John

Kostelnick, Melissa Oresky, John Reda, Touré Reed, William Reger, Christine Varga-Harris, Stewart Winger, and Amy Wood for conversations and commentary on the final stages of revision and for the opportunities to present work. Alec Foster, in addition to providing a geographer's perspective on my use of political ecology, made the map in Chapter 5. The Summer Writing Camp at ISU provided necessary space, time, and a convivial atmosphere to complete a round of revisions. I am grateful to the New Faculty Initiative Grant, the History Department, and the College of Arts and Sciences for financial support for the final stages of research and for a subvention to defer publication costs.

I have benefited immensely from opportunities to present versions of the work in this book and am grateful to audiences and organizers, particularly those at the North American Conference on British Studies for years of support. In addition to being a long-time friend, reader, and interlocutor, Lindsay O'Neill (along with co-organizer Vanessa Wilkie) invited me to present portions of Chapter 2 as part of the EMSI-Huntington Early Modern British History Seminar. Carole Shammas, who has provided critical advice on my work since I began graduate school, invited me to participate in the EMSI American Origins Dissertation Workshop. There Carla Pestana provided the necessary push to focus on trees as I launched the book project. Carla also provided the opportunity to work on the material that has become Chapter 4 as part of the Global Early Modern Caribbean workshop at the Huntington where I benefited from the Caribbean expertise of Jesse Cromwell, Kelsey Flynn, Melissa Morris, Jennifer Mylander, Gabriel Rocha, Jessica Roitman, Susanah Shaw Romney, Linda Rupert, Winter Schneider, Erin Stone, and Jennifer Wells. Tiffany Werth and John Craig invited me to Simon Fraser University to teach a graduate course on Edmund Spenser and to present portions of Chapter 1 as part of the Oecologies research cluster. I am grateful to the audience at that talk, particularly Vin Nardizzi for comments on the chapter. Steve Pincus and Peter Mancall invited me to present a draft of Chapter 5 as part of the Yale-EMSI Summer Atlantic History Workshop. I am grateful to the entire working group, particularly Alejandra Dubcovsky for extensive written comments on the draft and its revision. Amy Coombs invited me to present portions of Chapters 2 and 3 as part of the University of Chicago's Environmental Studies Workshop. The audience provided rich and extensive feedback, particularly Justin Niermeirer-Dohoney, who gave formal comments on the work.

In addition to those thanked above, I am grateful to Warren Billings for reading and commenting on drafts of Chapter 3 and portions of Chapter 6 and to Nick Popper for reading and commenting on the full manuscript. James Rice reviewed portions of Chapters 2 and 3 when previously published in another format and continued to provide feedback, encouragement, and good company as I incorporated that material into this book. In London, Catherine Chou, Mara Caden, and Asheesh Siddique were wonderful companions during tea breaks at the British Library. Tom Farnsworth provided me with lodging, delicious food, punishing but necessary jogs, and fantastic company in London. Breige Flynn and Eoghan Falvey put me up in Clare and Manchester, provided great company in London, and politely indulged my soliloquies on the woods of County Cork. From our high school in New Jersey to Los Angeles, Mike Atkins has been a constant friend and eager listener, willing to entertain long conversations about my research but also able to divert me and keep me grounded. Joan Redmond has been a friend, reader, and sounding board in Dublin, Cambridge, and Pasadena. Hayley Negrin has been a friend, a generous reader, and a kind host as we both relocated to Illinois. Bob Morrissey and Keith Woodhouse have likewise helped welcome me to the Midwest. I thank Fredrik Albritton Jonsson and Karl Appuhn for their encouragement and willingness to entertain deep discussions of their work at key points in my revision and Fredrik for welcoming me to Chicago's communities of environmental humanists, early modernists, and British historians. I am grateful to the Virginia Historical Society for a Mellon Research Fellowship to conduct research that has become parts of Chapters 3 and 6. Andrew Perchard was a fellow at the same time and our conversations then and since have been immensely beneficial. Annaleigh Margey generously provided me with a high-resolution image for the map in Figure 6, which shutdowns due to the COVID-19 pandemic would have otherwise prevented me from publishing. The staffs at the Huntington Library, British Library, Chatsworth House Archives, Lambeth Palace Library, Bodleian Library, Virginia Historical Society, National Archives (UK), National Maritime Museum (UK), National Library of Ireland, Gloucestershire Archives, and Barbados National Archives were indispensable in the research for this book.

This book would not have been possible without the support and guidance of Bob Lockhart at the University of Pennsylvania Press. Bob began providing feedback and saw the promise in this project as I first began contemplating the path forward from my original manuscript. His willingness to read and reread drafts and his keen sense for what makes a good book have been essential to the shape this work has taken. The anonymous readers for Penn provided essential and insightful feedback at the proposal stage and on the completed manuscript.

Portions of Chapters 2 and 3 are adapted from "Atlantic Iron: Wood Scarcity and the Political Ecology of Early English Expansion," *William and Mary*

Quarterly 73, no. 3 (July 2016): 389–426. I am grateful to editor Josh Piker and the Omohundro Institute for permission to reproduce and to James Rice and the other anonymous readers for their critiques of that piece. I have adapted portions of "Environmental Knowledge, Expertise, and the Development of Slavery in Bermuda," in *Atlantic Environments and the American South*, ed. Thomas Blake Earle and D. Andrew Johnson (Athens: University of Georgia Press, 2020), 176–94, in Chapter 4. I am grateful to the editors and the anonymous reviewers for their comments on that piece and to the University of Georgia Press for permission to adapt it here. Chapter 1 concludes with ideas I first began to develop in "Taming the Wilderness in Sixteenth- and Seventeenth-Century Ireland and Virginia," *Environmental History* 16, no. 4 (1 October 2011): 610–32, but is not drawn directly from it. I draw on a discussion of a case involving wood destruction and landscape change in Ireland previously published in "Cow Trials, Climate Change, and the Causes of Violence," *Environmental History* 25, no. 2 (1 April 2020): 287–309, in Chapter 2. I am grateful to *Environmental History* and Oxford University Press for permission to adapt that material here.

Finally, I am grateful to friends and family for support and encouragement. From the moment I announced that I wanted to be a historian, without really knowing what it entailed, my parents and brother have always believed I could do it. I am particularly grateful to my dad, who read my completed manuscript and called to provide his thoughts on every chapter. Finally, Kristen has known me since before I began thinking about early modern environments and has supported me through all the steps that led to this book. She has been a willing reader and kept an open ear for conversations about my research or thinking but has also known how to crack a riotous joke when I needed one. She has always made sure that I never went too far adrift into the worlds of the past. For her love and so much more, I give thanks.